The Complete
MUHAMMAD ALI

"You Have No Partners
in Pain."
                    Willie Pep

The Complete
MUHAMMAD ALI

Ishmael Reed

Baraka
Books

Montréal

The cover photo was taken by the late photographer, Jose Fuentes, who often traveled with the champion. Unlike photos that are used as covers for the more than one hundred books on Muhammad Ali, some of them showing the champion in a playful pose, or brimming with confidence, this photo is different. Here is the champion at the end of his career. He has been humiliated by a fighter just out of the amateurs. He is about to take on his young conquerer in a return match. The outcome is uncertain. His handlers thought that it would be an easy fight. He has debts. And marital problems. In his next fight he meets Larry Holmes and receives one of the most brutal defeats in boxing history. He fights this and his last fight, while a debilitating brain disease is beginning to form. Here Ali is shown facing tragedy, majestically.

ISBN 978-1-77186-040-6 pbk; 978-1-77186-047-5 epub; 978-1-77186-048-2 pdf; 978-1-77186-049-9 mobi/kindle

Cover photo by Jose Fuentes
Cover by Folio infographie
Book design by Folio infographie

Legal Deposit, 3rd quarter 2015

Bibliothèque et Archives nationales du Québec
Library and Archives Canada

Published by Baraka Books of Montreal
6977, rue Lacroix
Montréal, Québec H4E 2V4
Telephone: 514 808-8504
info@barakabooks.com
www.barakabooks.com

Printed and bound in Quebec
Trade Distribution & Returns
Canada and the United States
Independent Publishers Group
1-800-888-4741 (IPG1);
orders@ipgbook.com

DEDICATION

This book is dedicated to: the great photographer, Jose Fuentes; Barbara Lowenstein, my agent; Shaye Arehart, and to Sam Greenlee Billy Bang, Jack Newfield, Reginald Major, Ed Hughes, Fred Ho, Clayton Riley, Emanuel Steward, Amiri Baraka, Oscar Hijuelos, Sam Greenlee, and photographer Charles Robinson whom I interviewed, but who didn't live to see the publication of this book.

INTRODUCTION

The Curious History of an Icon

I call this book *The Complete Muhammad Ali* because most of the one hundred books about the champion, the majority of which are worshipful, are either too adoring or make excessively negative assertions, like Jack Cashill's blaming Ali and Gerald Ford for the loss of Vietnam. For Mark Kram, Ali is a malicious buffoon. For Thomas Hauser, he's a saint, though Hauser's opinion has changed. White sports writers have been generally hostile to black athletes, yet they monopolize the coverage of athletes and always seem to be searching for a white hope who would best the reigning black champion.

In contrast to some of their copy, Jack London, who allegedly created the term "white hope," was very respectful of heavyweight champion Jack Johnson. Authors of the two bestsellers, one of which was overseen by Yolanda Ali, and the other written by an Ali fan, disregard any information that would interfere with their reference for "The King of the World." Others are those whom I call The Ali Scribes, liberal writers located in the Northeast, who base their admiration of Ali upon his refusal to fight in an unpopular war without noting that he was following the example of his mentor, Elijah Muhammad, who refused to fight in a "popular war." World War II was seen as a war of "The Greatest Generation," against the forces of fascism, while this coveted generation practiced their fascism against black soldiers, who had to fight both the "enemy" and white officers and GIs. Just as George Washington treated English mercenaries better than his slaves, "enemy" prisoners were treated better in the south than black soldiers.

When speaking of the white volunteers who came south to assist in registering of black voters, while in the media version blacks stood by passively like the characters in the film "Django Unchained," Askia Touré could have been speaking of The Ali Scribes. Ali made the sacrifice, while they held meetings in a downtown pub deliberating about his choices.

Askia Touré was one of those responsible for purging northern liberals from SNCC (The Student Non-Violent Coordinating Committee). He said it was done because while blacks were taking the risks, the liberals were calling their friends located in cities all over the North and giving the blacks directions from their tables in coffee shops, or in the immortal words of David Hilliard, a member of the Black Panther Party and one of the guardians of its legacy: "They needed a nigger to pull the trigger." This could be true of The Ali Scribes; they celebrated Ali's defiance of the draft, a sacrifice that they would not make themselves.

The Ali Scribes' genuflection before the champion was a factor in Ali believing in his invincibility—a belief that led to serious injuries in the ring, injuries incurred as a result of his staying in the game long after the powers that were responsible for his ascendancy had been shot. Sports commentator Bill Clayton even provided some punch stats to compute the number of punches Ali received with the decline of his ring abilities. According to Clayton's calibrations, in the first Liston fight, Ali was hit with less than a dozen punches per round. In Ali-Liston II, Liston landed only two. Cleveland Williams hit him with only three punches during their bout. However, Joe Frazier hit him with four hundred forty punches at the "Thrilla in Manila," Leon Spinks hit him with four hundred eighty-two punches in their first fight, and Larry Holmes connected with three hundred and twenty punches (Hauser, 2005).

Ali's legend hangs upon the act of defying the Selective Service, which still brings him either praise or condemnation from his supporters and enemies. His response to the press when asked whether he would serve in Vietnam ("No Vietnamese ever called me a Nigger") was framed by a Nation of Islam (NOI) member Sam X, or Abdul Rahman. Though the Scribes give others credit for introducing Ali to the Nation of Islam, Ali has agreed with Sam X that it was him.

My interview with playwright Marvin X shows that Elijah Muhammad controlled Ali's life to such an extent that he told him when to speak and when not to speak, and Ali's ex-wife, the late Sonji Clay, said that Ali divorced her because Elijah Muhammad ordered him to do so. And so, is Ali being praised for following orders? And what are we to make of his confession, made in confidence to the late Jack Newfield, that he didn't become "a devout, true believer in Allah" until the mid-1980s, "'when my career was over, and miniskirts went out of style'" (Newfield, *The Nation*). Does this mean that his seeking conscientious objector status on the grounds of being a Muslim minister, the move that brought him fame, was disingenuous?

Ali's is also a story of an innocent and wide-eyed youngster who became corrupted by unsavory and sinister members of his entourage, associates who sought to gain financially from his generosity. Mark Kram reports that when Ali traveled to Manila, he was picking up the bills for over thirty members of his entourage. Among these hangers-on were those who encouraged him to fight far beyond his best years so much so that the once magnificent athlete—a man who for some resembled one of the mythic gods of ancient lore—had been, by the time of his return to Louisville, Kentucky, for the opening of the Ali Center, reduced to a stumbling, easily fatigued, and mumbling person. He had become someone who was hooked to a device that could turn him on and off like a radio. For allowing this man to fight while showing signs of Parkinson's disease and kidney damage, these hangers-on should be charged with conspiracy to commit murder. Though many saw Ali's lighting of the Olympic torch as heroic, the image of a physically challenged Joe Louis being wheeled around as a greeter at a Las Vegas casino came to the minds of some of the African Americans and hip whites whom I interviewed. Cus D'Amato, Floyd Patterson's manager, and before him playwright Ntozake Shange's father, a fight doctor, warned, early in his career, of Ali taking too many blows during sparring sessions and *predicting* such punishment would injure his health.

Only in boxing would a man be praised for recovering from devastating knockdowns such as those Ali received from Sonny Banks in 1962, Henry Cooper in 1963, Joe Frazier in 1971, and Chuck Wepner in 1975. When he was sixteen, he was knocked out by a fighter named Willy Moran. Ali had the habit of inviting the hardest blows from his sparring partners, thinking that such a regimen would enhance his tolerance for pain. His final condition was predictable. "Ali stood trembling with Parkinson's, once again showing the world the courage and dignity of a champion for all times," wrote John Stravinsky, author of *Muhammad Ali* (Stravinsky, 1997).

While some blacks and many whites were moved by what was considered a heroic feat, namely his lighting the Olympic torch, some whites were glad to see him in this condition of physical deterioration. His wife Lonnie says he doesn't want to be pitied, yet he is pitiable for someone like me who saw him when he was at the beginning of his career in Greenwich Village and Harlem, while walking with my friend, Malcolm X, in the 1960s, and later in New Orleans.

The blacks whom I interviewed viewed the scene taking place at the Olympics as one in which someone who was regarded as a sassy Bad Nigger was being humbled to the delight of the millions who had hated him when he was a defiant loudmouth, who questioned their values often in cruel and sarcastic tones. Ray Robinson, Jr., son of the great fighter, told me that they love him now because "The Lion has been tamed." The late novelist Sam Greenlee, who paid a higher price than Ali for his defiance, said to me that they love him because he is old and senile. Journalist and novelist Jill Nelson agreed with other blacks whom I interviewed, blacks whose points of views are usually omitted from the tributes to Ali in books by The Ali Scribes, who interview each other, or express admiration for each other's work (and even clothing apparel!).

Just as they can't understand why well-educated young men from comfortable backgrounds engage in terrorism against the United States, they cannot comprehend why many intelligent, young, black men, including Muhammad Ali, and some of those I interviewed for this book, and thousands of other young men whose entry into the middle class was launched by the Nation of Islam, or the Black Panther Party, were attracted to these movements. Despite their well-documented flaws, carried in one-sided commentary, these institutions not only taught them discipline but also introduced them to an intellectual life.

I met Donald R. White at a fundraising party for former Oakland mayor, Ron Dellums, when Dellums was a candidate for that office. At that time, White was treasurer for the County of Alameda. He told me that he learned how to read because he wanted to read Eldridge Cleaver's *Soul On Ice*. After that accomplishment, he went on to college. (Black males will read books that have something to do with their experience!) The difference between the Black Panther Party and the NOI was that one was guided by a left wing philosophy, while the NOI emphasized personal responsibility. (As evidence of J. Edgar Hoover's paranoia about blacks, he investigated a group of blacks whose ideas were similar to his, especially the anti-miscegenation parts, which the Ku Klux Klan would also endorse, and Jonah Goldberg of the Irish-American *National Review* criticized a man whose conservative philosophy would certainly jibe with his, if he were to pay close attention. Toni Morrison spoke of a Southern white-lady novelist, a Grande Dame, whose black characters were always attired in primary colors. That's how factions of the white intelligentsia, punditry, and wonks view blacks. That's the way The Ali Scribes have viewed Ali.) But there exist episodes in the ex-champion's life that are not so "great." Nothing about the Champion's flaws, however, which are covered in this book, will taint the reputation of Muhammad Ali.

None of the champions—Joe Louis, Sonny Liston, Mike Tyson, Jack Johnson, and Floyd Patterson—have reached the legendary status of Muhammad Ali, who is considered the GOAT: the Greatest of All Time. As a sign of his almost mythic status, when you say you're writing a book about Ali, the anecdotes begin to flow about this ring artist, whom writer Clayton Riley compared with the musician John

Coltrane. Like Ali, the tenor saxophonist John Coltrane put his own unique mark on modern jazz so that the chord progressions that he used in tunes such as "Giant Steps" are called Coltrane changes.

Like Coltrane, Ali's father, Cassius Marcellus Clay (nicknamed Cash), was also an artist. A muralist, his scenes of Christian lore can be found throughout Louisville. His son would be the subject of painters from Leroy Neiman to Andy Warhol. (When Ali posed for Warhol, Warhol requested that he stop talking; he complied). Which scenes would Cash have included, had he been commissioned to create a mural about his son's career? The infant Ali, loosening his mother's teeth with a straight right? The white-only water fountain in Louisville where Ali suffered an early brush with racism? The stolen 1954 red-and-white Schwinn bicycle that Cash and his mother Odessa bought for sixty dollars? His intention of finding the thief led to his being instructed in the sweet science by policeman Joe Martin. Included in Cash's imaginary mural would be Corky Baker from whose bullying Cassius Clay freed his neighborhood. Corky was a street fighter and considered the boxing ring a place for "sissies." He finally agreed to face young Cassius in the ring. This part of the panel would show Corky jumping out of the ring and fleeing, after receiving a beating from Cassius. The neighborhood kids would be shown cheering. (In later life, Ali and Corky would become friends. He was killed in a shoot-out with the police.)

There would be a scene of Ali standing and receiving the gold medal at the Olympics, flanked by Zbigniew Pietrzykowski, Giulio Saraudi, and Tony Madigan; Ali receiving a hero's welcome from Louisville's Columbia high school students upon his return to Louisville; a scene of Ali throwing the medal into the Ohio River after being refused service at a Louisville restaurant would be included; Ali, standing triumphant over a prostrate Sonny Liston; reproduction of this photo hung in the office of Senator Barack Obama; Ali, wearing a fez and addressing a crowd, while a bemused Elijah Muhammad sits in the background.

Still others would include Ali addressing a bank of reporters as he explains his reasons for seeking conscientious objector status; Ali at the end of Joe Frazier's Philadelphia left hook in a heavyweight championship fight held at Madison Square Garden (Jim Brown blames the defeat on Ali not getting enough sleep the night before. As for Frazier, he spent six weeks in the hospital and almost died.); Ali knocking out George Foreman in the Congo; Ali defeating Joe Frazier in the "Thrilla in Manila"; Ali defeating Leon Spinks in New Orleans; Ali lighting the Olympic torch.

In Cash's imaginary mural, the scene of Ali refusing to step forward to be inducted into the U.S. Army on April 28, 1967, would be placed at the center. This would become for some his greatest moment, even for those who don't follow boxing. He would also refuse to renounce his religion before the first Liston fight, despite the pressure from the Louisville Group of white investors, who backed the fighter. (Ironically, some of the members of the Louisville group would be there at the end, among those who helped raise funds for the seventy-million-dollar Ali Center.)

Like Heavyweight Champion Jack Johnson before, both blacks and whites would chastise Ali, who inspired many but infuriated millions. Jack Johnson was railroaded and set up for his lack of servility, while Ali was stripped of his prime fighting years. Ali was vindicated in his lifetime; they're still debating whether Jack Johnson should be pardoned for violating the Mann Act, one that was especially tailored to fit him, by white men who resented his companionship with white women, yet helped themselves to women of a variety backgrounds. This is a hypocrisy that persists to this day and the reason why millions of African Americans, Asian Americans, and Native Americans are part white, even some of the most fervent haters of whites, and that includes members of the 1930s NOI. Senator McCain is one of those who have petitioned for the champion's pardon. So far President Obama has refused.

The Complete Muhammad Ali includes more points of view about the champion than the over one hundred books about Muhammad Ali, which duplicate one another. Most of them are scissors-and-paste jobs repeating claims by the same sports writers, camp followers, and insiders. They also lack diversity. This book includes women and the points of view of other minority members whose views have been neglected. The book avoids the same blow-by-blow narrations of his fights, which one can purchase for about five dollars or less on DVD. The other books include the same photographs; the photographs in this book are published here for the first time. The book includes photos of Muhammad Ali, Mike Tyson, Joe Louis, and others. Some were held by Jane Fuentes, the widow of the great Puerto Rican photographer, Jose Fuentes. Jose Fuentes was a confidant of the champion, and Jane has awarded me exclusive use of these photos.

I treat Muhammad Ali not only as a boxer but as a phenomenon, a human mirror for the sixties, as a cautionary tale for the seventies. The book also covers his resurgence, which occurred as a result of a controlled biography and his lighting of the Olympic torch. The political and cultural trends of his time are examined.

In addition to sports writers and insiders, I have interviewed poets, painters, musicians, playwrights, and members of both Orthodox Muslim groups and of Minister Elijah Muhammad's Nation of Islam (NOI), of which Ali was a member until converting to the Sunni faith.

Members of the Nation of Islam, who have been caricatured in other books as thugs and lunatics, speak for themselves here, presenting their sides of the story about the relationship between the Nation and the champion. We've all heard about the criminal elements in the Nation, and I talk about those, but other Ali books have ignored the scientists, scholars, journalists, and a Pulitzer Prize winner who were also members or relatives of Elijah Muhammad. The individual who managed the NOI farms was a graduate of Harvard. Dr. Khalil Gibran Muhammad, the great grandson of Elijah Muhammad, who was dismissed as a "cult racketeer" by one Ali biographer and promoted as a buffoon by the FBI, directs the Schomburg Center for Research in Black Culture.

I have interviewed Ali family members and those who have been left out of the standard biographies, yet have compelling information about "The GOAT." For example, few have noticed the international political implications of "Thrilla in Manila," as they have for Joe

Louis-Max Schmeling fights I and II, during which Louis challenged the myth of Aryan superiority. Emil Guillermo, a Filipino-American writer and journalist, comments about how the Ali-Frazier fight in Manila brought that country into the modern period. Similarly, famed South African trumpeter Hugh Masekela discusses how the "Rumble in the Jungle" buttressed the reputation of the late Congolese dictator, Mobutu Sese Seko. Of all of the books about the champion, this is the only one with a multicultural approach.

I also explore Ali's fronting for criminal operations in Philadelphia while living in a mansion lent to him by Major Coxson, "The East Coast King of Heroin." So protective and in awe of the champion are the writers for the two Ali bestsellers, they fail to even mention Coxson's name.

Though his present wife, Lonnie Ali, is rejecting interviews unless she can control them, I was able to interview Ali's second wife, Khalilah (Belinda), and his brother, Rahaman Ali. Agieb Bilal, former Secretary to both Elijah's Nation of Islam and Wallace's World Community of Al Islam in the West (WCIW), put me in touch with a number of Muslim personalities. I found that there's truth in what Sam X, whom I interviewed, said: "Without Elijah Muhammad, nobody would ever have heard of Muhammad Ali."

As Hugh Masekela said, "We were unreasonable about Ali." Ali's legacy is still being discussed. Writing in *The New York Times* on June 21, 2013, William C. Rhoden commemorates Ali's refusal to be inducted into the armed forces without mentioning his affiliation with the Nation of Islam, and Elijah Muhammad's influence upon his decision. Rhoden calls Ali "a great man."

Is he?

Muhammad Ali and I have some things in common. We were both born in the South, he in Kentucky, and I in Tennessee; we both had middle-class, Christian parents who became alarmed when we rejected their faith; we both could spout; we were both organizers; we both visited Europe during our teens and were influenced by what we observed there; we both knew Malcolm X; we both participated in the rebirth of African-American culture and politics of the 1960s, sometimes referred to as The Second Renaissance; we both experienced exile, he from boxing, and I from my eastern roots; we both suffer from chronic diseases.

Ali and I both are considered innovators. We both received wins, losses, and a draw in New York City, and though I get pegged as pugnacious, I'm capable of penning tender ballads as well. Muhammad Ali could dance, and was admired for his "lyricism" as one writer put it, but he could also slug it out, as he did in his third bout with Ken Norton.

Mel Watkins, then a book editor at *The New York Times*, was the first to notice a similarity in my writing style to that of Ali's boxing style (but when I found myself, in 1979, living in the kind of neighborhood that I grew up in and watching the neglect of hard-working citizens by public and private institutions, critic Jerry Ward began to compare my writing style with that of Mike Tyson. Other critics cited Sonny Liston and Roy Jones, Jr.).

During three important phases of our lives, our paths crossed: first when he and I were young; next when he staged his final comeback; and finally more recently, when Ali is supposedly in physical decline, though he gives no sign of abandoning a vigorous travel schedule, and has outlived some of those whom I interviewed for this book, individuals who were concerned about his health. He outlived Joe Frazier who, in an uncharacteristic moment, mocked the champion's Parkinson's disease, though some would disagree with this diagnosis, attributing it instead to the numerous blows to the head delivered when he was no longer able to dance away from punches. He outlived opponents, among them Archie Moore, Jerry Quarry, Kenny Norton, Sonny Liston, Jimmy Ellis, Ernie Terrell and Floyd Paterson.

I'm considered to be in physical decline as well, having survived a major cancer operation and, according to my diabetes counselor, having beaten the odds in struggling with type 2 diabetes, with which I was diagnosed in 1999.

As black men, both Ali and I are lucky. Most of us don't live past sixty-five. I'm seventy-seven; Muhammad Ali turned seventy-three in January 2015. We both were declared done before we reached our

prime, Ali after his fight with George Foreman, and I in 1983 by
The Nation magazine, and by 1973, according to those who compile
The Norton Anthology of African American Literature. Yet, the FBI
continued to keep up with my work, beyond the seventies. According
to William Maxwell's book *F.B.Eyes*, I'm among the black writers who
would be placed under "Custodial Detention," in case of a National
Emergency. While the white left wing was engaged in hand-wringing
about the National Security State and whether bin Laden's chauffeur
was comfortable, very little attention was paid to the shocking revela-
tions that the FBI has been spying on black writers and considering
them for internment since the Harlem Renaissance.

Of the over one hundred books written about Muhammad Ali,
I believe this one is unique. Voices missing from the others can be
found here; rhythms and music of speech that have influenced everything from the "Toasts" to Hip Hop are presented without being
abridged or cleaned up. Their Africanisms haven't been deleted. The
late, great boxing trainer, Emanuel Steward, discusses Ali's final bout
with Trevor Berbick for the first time. When I interviewed him in
his Las Vegas hotel room, he said, "I'm telling you things that I have
never before said."

In these pages, Louisville friends of the champion talk about Ali,
his father Cassius Clay, Sr., and other members of the family for the
first time.

While the champion's and my paths were similar but often diver-
gent, in 2003, we met on paper when the great editor, Shaye Arehart,
who worked with Jacqueline Kennedy, asked my agent, Barbara
Lowenstein, whether I was interested in writing a biography about
the champion. We were working well and harmoniously until she left
the company, leaving the project as an orphan.

With this assignment, I was launched on a trip that had me col-
lecting voices—voices and points of view rarely recorded in the one
hundred or so books about the champion—and took me everywhere
from McDonald's in Louisville, Kentucky, to some of the plush rooms
of the New York literary establishment. It has gone from the room
of the late, esteemed boxing trainer and commentator, Emanuel

Steward, located in THEHotel at the Mandalay Bay, to one of my Oakland haunts, The Dejena, an Eritrean café located on Martin Luther King, Jr. and 40th Streets around the corner from the famed Marcus Book Store, where some of the research for this book was purchased. I even stopped by Paul's Shoe Repair Service in Berkeley to get the views of two old-timers.

Many of these interviews shed fresh insight upon the career of the champion and his rise and fall as a boxer, and on his comeback, which began with an autobiography managed by Lonnie Ali, and an NBC-designed event which had Ali lighting the Olympic torch to open the 1996 Summer Games. These interviews include those of insiders like Gene Kilroy, Reggie Barrett, and the champion's brother, Rahaman; writers Marvin X, Amiri Baraka, Haki Madhubuti, Sam Greenlee, Nathan Hare, Akbar Muhammad, Bennett Johnson, and the champion's second wife, Khalilah, comment on the champion's relationship to the Black Power movement, the Nation of Islam, and Black Nationalism. Musician Hugh Masekela and poet Quincy Troupe give accounts of behind-the-scenes activities in Zaïre, where Muhammad Ali scored his defeat of George Foreman. Also included are statements from journalists Earl Caldwell and Martin Wyatt, an Emmy Award winner who defies the stereotypes promoted by Ali hagiographers that all members of the Nation of Islam were menacing thugs.

In Louisville, I interviewed hometown friends of the Ali family Edward Hughes, Omar Rose, and Waajid Sabre. These contacts were made through Janene and Atar Shakir, who, like Ali, were followers of the late Imam Wallace Deen Muhammad, Elijah Muhammad's son and successor. They and a guest, who didn't want to be identified because he was still employed by the Ali Center, filled us in on some of the tensions between Muslim converts and immigrant Muslims, and some of the politics behind the creation of the Ali Center. Writers Russell Banks, Darius James, Walter Mosley, Elizabeth Nunez, Barry Beckham, Jill Nelson, Pulitzer Prize winner Oscar Hijuelos, and editor Dan Halpern discuss the impact of Ali on their lives. Sports writers Jack Newfield and Clayton Riley assess the boxer's skills;

so does former boxer and novelist Floyd Salas. Also interviewed are celebrities like Harry Belafonte, Melvin Van Peebles, and Rev. Jesse Jackson. Reggie Barrett talks about Ali's comeback from the' inside. Ray Robinson, Jr. gives an account of the sometimes stormy relationship between the champion and his father, the boxer whom Ali at one time idolized. Folk hero Howard Moore, Jr. comments about Ali's relationship to Harold Smith, who pulled off the largest embezzlement scheme in the history of Wells Fargo.

Among the fights, which have been explored exhaustively elsewhere, I emphasize those that are responsible for Ali's boxing fame. These include his defeats of Sonny Liston, his comeback fight with George Foreman, and his fight with Joe Frazier in Manila, described by Martin Wyatt, one of those black sportscasters whose career was made as a result of the NOI's policy of insisting that black reporters be given access to behind-the-scenes goings-on at Ali's fights.

After working on a biography about the boxer for eleven years, I have concluded that Muhammad Ali's mentor and father figure, Elijah Muhammad, is more complex than his student; indeed, Ali, when a member of the NOI, could have been considered an extension of the minister. Ali was known to repeat Elijah Muhammad's words verbatim, and when asked his greatest accomplishment, Ali didn't mention his glory as a boxer, but "joining Islam."

CHAPTER 1

Though slight in size, one might consider Elijah Muhammad to be one bad black man. We used to call such men "Bad Niggers." We usually think of the Bad Nigger as a sort of illiterate brute whose archetype can be found in the works of Charles Chesnutt, Richard Wright, and Chester Himes, and books on the list of Holloway House authors. Fearless and unable to be disciplined by "Nigger Breakers," whose tasks are described in *The Life and Times of Frederick Douglass*, he's the character in the movie "Mandingo" who, when captured, says to his tormentors who have placed the noose around his neck, "After you hang my ass, you can kiss it." The black cowboy, Cherokee Bill, when asked to say his last words before being hanged, said, "I didn't come here to make a speech, I came here to die." It could be Sojourner Truth who, when heckled by some racist suffragettes, said, "Ain't I a woman!" It could be Shirley Chisholm, who had the audacity to run for president. But there is another type of Bad Nigger: the black person who asks too many questions. The man whose birth name was Elijah Poole was such a person.

Every black person who is endowed with an exceptional curiosity conducts an internal dialectic, which in some cases can lead to early death, depression, ostracism, or even murder. Black women intellectuals get lupus, breast cancer, and ovarian cancer, and the males get diabetes, hypertension, and other stress-related diseases. Irate and often angry about the effects of white supremacy, from the daily annoying examples (micro-aggressions) to lynching and massacres, they find themselves either speaking out no matter the consequences, or they bear it, keeping such rage in storage.

Malcolm X is one of those who was not comfortable with the status quo. Poet and publisher Haki Madhubuti is correct to say that Malcolm X could have waited out Elijah Muhammad, his mentor, had he kept his criticisms to himself, retreated from the public arena, and become an Imam of an Orthodox Mosque. Martin Luther King, Jr. could have become a big shot in the National Baptist hierarchy, spending as much time at a Lexus dealer's showroom as preparing sermons. He'd have gained a large belly from too many fried chicken dinners. However, as with Ali, Malcolm X, Elijah Muhammad, Jackie Robinson, and others, his internal dialectic probably began at an early age. He looked around at the society in which he had been by chance deposited and saw things that puzzled him.

For Muhammad Ali and me, the defining moment was when we were told that we that we couldn't drink from a "white only" water fountain. Ali was six years old. The water fountain incident for me was my "Baltimore moment," based upon a poem written by Countee Cullen; all that Cullen could remember from his trip to Baltimore was being called a "nigger." I recall my mother dragging me away from the fountain before the water reached my lips. She was an attractive young woman with many well-bred suitors; she was a high school graduate. She was always clean and well-dressed in public, yet there were unkempt whites that day on Lookout Mountain in Chattanooga; they could drink from the water fountain and my mother couldn't. This puzzled me.

The water fountain incident wasn't the only puzzling aspect of America for Cassius Clay, the youngster. When he was five years old he questioned his father. He asked, "Daddy, I go to the grocery and the grocery man is white. I go to the drugstore and the drugstore man is white. The bus driver's white. What do colored people do?"

Elijah Muhammad's questioning led him to break with the Christianity that some would say had been whipped into the newly arrived Africans, some of whom were worshippers of Allah and some of whom were forced to denounce their African spirits.

Elijah Muhammad was also devoted to an unpopular, misunderstood religion. The Detroit police, like many of the nation's police departments, assigned themselves to this day to monitor cultural and political trends among blacks and Muslims. They wrongly called the Nation of Islam a "voodoo cult," which as a result of distortions by Hollywood and popular culture is people sticking pins in dolls, drinking blood, frenetic free-form dancing to the accompaniment of mad drumming and the rest. The kind of culture depicted in such films as "I Walked With a Zombie," "The Skeleton Key," and "Ritual," three movies which confuse African religion with Western witchcraft. In 2013, a television series called "Grimm" continued this stereotype. Such ignorance of the faiths of others is not surprising in a country where the Christian majority doesn't have information about that religion quite nailed; a country where one in four Americans think that the sun goes around the Earth according to a report carried by National Public Radio on February 14, 2014.

During the 1930s court appearances held in Detroit, male members of the Nation got into scuffles with the police, whom they accused of disrespecting their women. All of these images—images based upon superstition—arose in the public's mind when Ali announced that he had joined the Nation of Islam.

Yet when the issue of *Muhammad Speaks* (the official journal of the Nation of Islam) appeared after the assassination of JFK, carrying the headline "We Mourn Our Leader," some black intellectuals dismissed Elijah Muhammad as a "pork chop," with all of the connotations that this food would carry in black folklore. The FBI had succeeded in sowing tension between the minister and Malcolm X just as they promoted conflict between Maulana Karenga's "Us" organization and the Black Panther Party. The late Joe Walker, with whom I used to write for a Buffalo newspaper, and who followed Malcolm X to New York from Buffalo to work for *Muhammad Speaks*, told me before his death that he got into trouble with the Chicago followers of Elijah Muhammad because he was deemed too partial to Malcolm X.

All that some of the younger people whom I interviewed knew about Elijah Muhammad was that he was a charlatan and an adulterer. This was a man who not only refused to obey the Selective Service laws of the 1940s, but called for the victory of the country's enemy. While Ali escaped long-term imprisonment, Elijah Muhammad, who is depicted in Hollywood movies as a buffoon, went to prison for five years.

> In 1943, I was sent to the Federal Penitentiary in Milan, Michigan, for nothing other than to be kept out of the public and from teaching my people the truth during the war between America, Germany, and Japan. (*Message to the Blackman in America*, E. Muhammad, 1965)

Did Elijah Muhammad incite an uprising against "the white devils," under whose charge he existed during this time?

"No," he writes. "In August, 1946, I was released on what the institution called 'good time' for being a model prisoner who was obedient to the prison rules and laws" (Muhammad, 1965).

He emerged with an interest in agricultural business (Jesus Muhammad, 2002) and built nationwide businesses whose development were sometimes thwarted by whites both in and out of government, from the right and the left. They were further affected by government infiltrators who sought to sabotage the Nation's business enterprises and by petty criminals from within, those who, unlike Elijah Muhammad, lacked a long-term vision.

The NOI exposed the hypocrisy of a system which criticizes blacks for their dependency yet attempts to frustrate their efforts to acquire assets. Capitalism has been hostile to blacks since Reconstruction when the newly-emancipated slaves were encouraged to place their assets, which totaled a billion dollars, in a Freedman's Savings Bank; the bank failed because it was operated by missionaries who had little knowledge of banking. The government was supposed to guarantee the savings but reneged on the promise. Last year, two banks, Wells Fargo and Bank of America, were penalized for steering subprime loans to blacks and browns. Some loan officers were said to have called blacks "mud people," and loans aimed at them "ghetto loans." The attitude toward blacks held by the capitalist system hasn't changed in over one hundred years, and because of racism blacks have been deprived of entitlements such as the GI Bill.

The biographers of Ali have every right to point out the flaws and the racism of the Nation of Islam (even though the sports writers among them work for newspapers with segregated newsrooms which, in their coverage, segregate blacks to the crime pages or the why-can't-they-get-it-together pages). However, wouldn't a true conservative condemn the government's wiretapping and surveillance of a group that posed no threat to National Security?

And so while Elijah Muhammad has been cast as a hater, arguments that present blacks as subhuman have gained respectability in *The New Republic* and *Commentary* magazines, the voices of Neo-Con America, which find themselves in the company of the Pioneer Fund—a foundation with a history of sympathizing with Nazism—in their agreement about the intellectual inferiority of blacks. The Pioneer Fund was founded by Wickliffe P. Draper, a Nazi sympathizer.

According to Wikipedia, "In August 1935, Draper traveled to Berlin to attend the International Congress for the Scientific Investigation of Population Problems. Presiding over the conference was Wilhelm Frick, the German Minister of the Interior. At the conference, Draper's travel companion, Dr. Clarence Campbell, delivered an oration that concluded with the words: 'The difference between the Jew and the Aryan is as insurmountable [*sic*] as that between black and white... Germany has set a pattern which other nations must follow... To that great leader, Adolf Hitler!'"

Statements that smack of "scientific racism" have become so normal that very few of the chattering and intellectual classes make an attempt to oppose them. *The Bell Curve* (1994) holds that blacks are inferior, intellectually, to whites. Written by Scots-Irish-American Charles Murray, it received high praise from the media. It argued that blacks, as a rule, had lower IQs than whites. Unlike Yacubism, which depicted whites as evil and was adopted, but eventually abandoned by Elijah Muhammad, Murray's "research" influenced public policy and powerful politicians.

During the week of March 13, 2014, Paul Ryan, a possible presidential candidate, announced his conversion to the philosophy of Charles Murray's hypothesis that blacks are inferior, intellectually, to whites. He used Murray's discredited ideas to explain what he referred to as a culture of laziness in the Inner City. The Southern Poverty Law Center reported, "Moreover, there is a disturbing dynamic at play. At the same time that the number of extremist groups is dropping, there is more mainstream acceptance of radical-right ideas."

Many liberals and progressives failed to see that Republicans made gains in 2014 because of resentment against a black president held by older white voters, who have shown again that they are willing to make any sacrifice in order to uphold white supremacy, even if it means voting for those who would reduce their Social Security payments. Ryan's possible rival for the Republican nomination is Rand Paul, who, according to *The Times*, hangs out with people who regard Lincoln assassin John Wilkes Booth as a hero. He hired a man who called himself "The Southern Avenger"; when he was exposed, Rand at first defended him, but after pressure had him fired. In 2014, he wrote the introduction to a book authored by a Confederate sympathizer. So while white right wing ideas can enter the mainstream, those of blacks have a marginal effect. Are racists confined to "Jack Daniels racists" like those who place themselves before cameras at Tea Party rallies? For Accuracy In Reporting claims that scientific racist thought can be found in *The New York Times*.[1]

The Yacub myth was circulated by the Nation of Islam, which was headquartered in Chicago, as if to compete with white racists over which group was the most superior:

> Before the making of the white race, we never had their type of evil people. The Black Man was never under an evil rule. Evil rule was never practiced among the Black People before the making of an evil world by

---

1. Steve Rendall, "Highly Placed Media Racists," FAIR Blog, July 2, 2014. (Consulted Jan. 7, 2015)

Yakub. We never saw or experienced a civilization like the white man's civilization. We never had an unalike people among us before the white race was made. We were all alike especially in color.

The new man, the white man, came from us, but he is different from us. After Yakub grated his man (white man) from us, his man became a new man to us. We are not a part of the white man. The white man just looks like a human being, and he is a human being, but he is not kin to us at all. You say, 'I cannot understand how that is, Mr. Muhammad.' This is true. After the white man was grafted completely out of the germ of the Black Man, the White man was made into a new man different from the Black Man, from whom he was grafted. The white man became a new person altogether and his very nature is new to us. They do not have the same nature as we have. The white man is different by nature than the Black Man and the white man has made many things new. (E. Muhammad, 2002).

In the NOI's mythology, Yacub was a black scientist who launched evil upon the world by inventing white people. Though Ali's biographers assert that the NOI had not abandoned the doctrine of Yacubism, the theory that whites were created by a black scientist to do evil in the world was abandoned in 1974, when Elijah Muhammad told *Final Call* editor Askia Muhammad not to refer to whites as devils anymore. He did not believe in causing trouble for whites and even his enemies agree that he delivered thousands of blacks from lives of prostitution, criminality, and substance abuse. Yet while Martin Luther King, Jr. has a holiday named for him, Elijah Muhammad is still denounced by Ali biographers, writers who never bothered to explore the reasons for his appeal. So what is the difference between the attitudes of millions of whites (the mainstream) about blacks, and those of Elijah Muhammad about whites prior to the 1970s?

Even when it comes to racism, just as there is a double standard to which blacks and whites are held in other areas of society, there is a double standard that applies to white racists and black racists, a double standard that I wrote about in Salon.com (January 23, 1999).

When asked about why whites were more successful, materially, than blacks, a writer for the Irish American *National Review*, who had just recently been naturalized at the time of his C-SPAN appearance, said that maybe "the answer would be found soon in genetics and biology."

History has shown that most whites, by action and deeds, are separatists and, unlike the black separatists, have the arms and political power to enforce their separatism. Evidence supplied by books like *Sundown Towns* by James Loewen, about the many cities and towns in the United States where it was and still is a bad idea for blacks and sometimes Chinese and Jews to be seen after dark, shows that whites are the most persistent of American separatists, even when quoting Martin Luther King to criticize black separatism. Another book that indicts the decades-long effort of many whites to prevent blacks from moving into their neighborhoods is *As Long As They Don't Move Next Door* by Stephen Grant Meyer. While black separatists are criticized by Ali's white biographers, white separatists get to make it to key positions in the country's political, social, and cultural life.

So studied is white separatism that some whites are able to practice white separatism in predominately black neighborhoods. At one time, most of the whites entering my neighborhood came to buy drugs. The criminals did sales in broad daylight and attracted whites from the suburbs who either walked or drove up to their drug house. Beginning in the late 2000s, most of the whites were renters, refugees from San Francisco who had been priced out of that city. Industries that once occupied the neighborhood now house condos. The Wonder Bread factory has been replaced by a condo dwelling called Bakery Lofts.

This neighborhood was once black until the banks decided to issue subprime loans to those who were eligible for conventional loans, typical of the kind of predatory relationship the American financial system has had with blacks since Reconstruction. Taught to fear blacks by the media and their education, the new white arrivals patrol the remaining blacks with a kind of citizens' patrol. The most popular protection devices are pit bulls, which have become known as "fuzzy guns" or "four-legged Zimmermans," which is how Tennessee Reed refers to them in a poem.

Though the newly arrived Latinos, Asian Americans, and some African-born residents get along, most of the white regentrifiers do not mingle with the black neighbors and avoid eye contact with them.

So as a racist before the 1970s and a separatist, why wasn't Elijah Muhammad considered a part of the American mainstream, or are they saying that only whites can be racists and separatists? That's why the persecution of the NOI by the FBI was truly bewildering. Beginning in the 1930s, FBI agents hounded the NOI. Some even resorted to applying blackface in an attempt to infiltrate NOI meetings, but the Muslims were not deceived.

Elijah Muhammad was devoted to American values and next to him, Martin Luther King, Jr. was a flaming radical. Elijah Muhammad believed in non-confrontation while MLK, with whom he disagreed, confronted the most diehard of racists and was murdered as a result of a conspiracy launched by racists. He brought about a revolution that benefitted the black middle class.

CHAPTER 2

The one possibility that Ali biographers overlook is that Elijah Muhammad, a home-schooled, self-made individual, and his wife Clara, who might be considered the grandmother of Black Studies, built a business that was competitive with that of whites, the kind of effort that got some of Ida B. Wells' friends, followers of Booker T. Washington, lynched in Memphis, Tennessee. In a word, they were uppity. They were bad. Not in terms of physical strength, but in terms of what in basketball is known as "mental toughness." They challenged the promise offered to blacks that if they participated in the system, worked hard, and played by the rules, they'd get ahead (while whites were and are the most subsidized group in American history, both by public and private sectors. As a case in point, we can begin with the hundred million acres stolen from Native Americans.)

The Black Panther Party and the Nation of Islam, institutions about which I have made critical comments, showed what blacks could do when organized and disciplined. There was another sixties group that was also influential. Unlike the NOI, the Black Panther Party attracted white allies (although when I appeared with Huey Newton on a panel organized by ABC television a year before he died, he was preaching black superiority). They supported the post-NOI Malcolm X, which brought them into conflict with members of the NOI. When I interviewed Bobby Seale, co-founder of the Black Panther Party, he said that things became so heated between him and members of the NOI that he armed himself. Another difference between the two: the Black Panthers engaged in electoral politics;

local Oakland politicians as well as people elected to Congress have attributed their success to the Black Panther Party. I thought that the NOI was against electoral politics until I interviewed Bennett Johnson, who said that Elijah Muhammad supported electoral politics on the side. The Black Panthers brought political power to the black people of Oakland. They helped put the spotlight on a city that before their emergence was a feudal backwater. As for the criminals and crazies attracted to the organizations, they wouldn't be the first to be corrupted by individuals with bad motives, and to add to their problems they were infiltrated by government agents.

Moreover, it would take the NOI a couple of thousand years to attract the kind of con men, killers, criminals, and crazies that have been attracted to Christianity, which in the United States has become the state religion with theocrats, whose assertions have been far more outrageous than Elijah Muhammad's. They boast about their direct line to former president George W. Bush, who said that his foreign policy was shaped by his conversations with Jesus of Nazareth, a man who has been dead for two thousand years. Kevin Phillips said of George Bush that he was not only the leader of Christian fundamentalism, but also its president.

If conservatives like William Kristol and John Q. Wilson use the metaphor of mugging when discussing why some liberals became right wing, and on the basis of some blacks, a tiny fraction of the black population, mugging people, why can't Elijah Muhammad's critics understand why some blacks would be attracted to a movement that demonized whites? There are whites who, in the history of the United States, have done more than mug blacks and Native Americans, especially in the South. In the South, whites engaged in such macabre, grisly practices as creating postcards of themselves posing next to victims of lynching.

◆

Elijah Muhammad was born in the South in October 1897, during the height of white terrorism in the region. He was the son of William and Mariah Poole, who were Georgia sharecroppers. As a teenager, he raised questions about the teachings of the scriptures and became engaged in theological duels with his father, a "jackleg" preacher. It was his grandfather who called him "the prophet"; he is the man who suggested to him that slave masters, to indoctrinate their captives to accept their lowly status, used the Bible. He also heard of lynching and actually saw the corpse of one of his friends dangling from a tree. Elijah and his wife, Clara, fled the southern hell to Detroit, Michigan, in 1923.

There he became acquainted with the teachings of the controversial Mr. W. D. Fard. Of the meeting Elijah Muhammad said:

> When I first heard of Islam it was in Detroit, back in the early fall of 1931, and I heard that there was a man teaching Islam by the name of W. D. Fard… When I met Him, I looked at Him and it just came to me, that he is the Son of Man that the Bible prophesied would come in the last days of the world. (Muhammad, 1994)

His belief that Wallace D. Fard was Allah and he, Elijah Muhammad, was his messenger, is at the core of what separates Elijah Muhammad's interpretation of Islam from the more Orthodox kind. (However, Sufism is also considered by some to be an aberration of Orthodox Islam, Lutheranism is considered heretical by Orthodox Catholics, and Christian fundamentalists do not accept Mormonism as a Christian religion, etc.) Through the ages, since many religious doctrines depend upon the suspension of disbelief, who is to say whose version of texts, which are often loaded with cloudy language, miracles, and supernatural events, is correct? While Elijah Muhammad's group is still regarded by U.S. journalists as "black Muslims" and given to bizarre doctrines, during the week of October 2005, some of these same journalists reported, without ridicule, that the former Pope Benedict had endorsed schools devoted to exorcising victims of diabolical possession. In addition, *Time* magazine paid tribute to the Mormon Church, whose elders practiced the polygamy of which Hon. Elijah Muhammad was accused. It was even reported on November 13, 2014, by *The Guardian*:

What we do know, and what the LDS [Latter Day Saints] church recently acknowledged after nearly two centuries, is that, by the time he was assassinated in a Carthage, Illinois, jailhouse in June 1844, Joseph Smith had married an unknown (and maybe unknowable) number of women – possibly 40, and quite possibly more.

Some Christians believe that the Mormon religion is a cult, yet millions of Christians voted for a Mormon presidential candidate in 2012 and millions voted for a black president, while millions of others held that he was a Muslim. In the United States, it's always "go figure."

One doesn't have to put Ali on the couch in order to deduce that his father Marcellus Clay's painting of a white Jesus might have influenced Ali's religious philosophy. He said: "We live in a world where black is usually played down; it's not your fault. They made Jesus Christ like you, a white man, they made the Lord something like you, they made all the angels in Heaven like you, Miss America, Tarzan-king of the jungle is white, they made angel food white." The battle over images and symbols rages on. In February 2006, talk show host Chris Matthews compared the cartoons about the prophet Muhammad that outraged millions of Muslims with *The Rolling Stone's* cover photo of Kanye West as Jesus of Nazareth. However, Jesus of Nazareth probably bore more of a resemblance to West than to the numerous Anglo actors who have portrayed Jesus. Given the questions about race that had hounded Ali during his youth, and his satisfaction that the NOI had answered his questions, it was not surprising that Ali would side with the Vietnamese, his Asiatic black brothers, over his fellow white Americans.

For his position on the war, Ali was criticized by some black athletes and counseled by others, who included Jim Brown, Bill Russell, Kareem Abdul-Jabbar, Willie Davis, and John Wooten, but even under their counseling, he possessed such a golden tongue—proof of his Irish heritage, some say—that he nearly converted some of those present to the NOI. Ali was booed and threatened after assuming his new identity when he was introduced at the second Liston fight. The security was tight that night after the authorities perceived threats from the followers of Malcolm X. There were also perceived threats from organized crime, which had, up to that time, controlled boxing.

Yet Liston's grandson, Lynel Gardner, asserts that Ali and Liston were friends despite the carrying-on that preceded the fight and that a threat from the NOI would be farfetched. In the imagination of the public framed by sports writers, possibly the most racist of the Jim Crow fraternity of American news writers, not only were the NOI racists, but also anti-Semites.

Is the animosity aimed at Elijah Muhammad by Ali's biographers a result of his alleged Anti-Semitism?

In March 2005, a CNN reporter introduced Minister Louis Farrakhan, leader of the Nation of Islam, as someone whose views about Jews have been "controversial." No one prefaces an introduction of Christian televangelist Reverend Billy Graham with a comment about his "controversial" views about Jews. Little has changed. Ed Koch overheard former U.S. Secretary of State James Baker saying, "Fuck the Jews," which is probably more abusive than Jesse Jackson's 1984 reference to "Hymietown." Yet when a position on the Supreme Court was open, Baker was on the short list.

Billy Graham conducted his last "Crusade" in the summer of 2005, and the media did everything but wash his feet. Jon Meacham, *Newsweek*'s managing editor, after an interview with the evangelist, said that being in the presence of Graham was what it must be like to be in the presence of God. To his anti Semitic buddy Richard Nixon, Graham said that the Jews were Satanic and owned the media, yet the March 25, 2006 edition of *The New York Times* described Billy Graham as "a role model." Graham apologized when his remarks were revealed by the release of some Watergate tapes, but the media never forgave Louis Farrakhan for remarks that he says were misinterpreted, even after he practiced a Mendelssohn violin concerto for three hours per day for five years "to say in music what I could not say in words." (His performance, under the direction of Oakland Maestro Michael Morgan, is available on YouTube.)

Then, remarkably, on February 26, 2006, Louis Farrakhan appeared on C-SPAN as part of a panel assembled by talk show host Tavis Smiley to discuss "The State of the Black Union," and announced, "There are some good white people." When I interviewed the editor of *The Final Call*, Askia Muhammad, in Washington D.C., he said that upon hearing on his car radio that the great violinist Jascha Heifetz had died, Louis Farrakhan pulled to the side of the road and said a prayer. Besides, some of Elijah Muhammad's statements seem to separate Jews from Gentiles. And what of all the mean things Louis Farrakhan said about people when he was under the sway of Elijah Muhammad (a pragmatist, who, unlike some of his followers and the black writers who made a living from hating white people, was very cordial to Jews and whites in private)? He said:

The Jewish people have a greater sense of justice and humanness than their white gentile brothers [and] have developed a higher sense of ethics, less tainted with the crimes of colonialism, white supremacy and prejudice characterizing Christians.

CHAPTER 3

In 2006, the day after arriving in Washington, D.C., I awaited Askia Muhammad's arrival. Askia Muhammad is an editor at *Muhammad Speaks* and at *The Final Call* and a commentator on NPR. When Muhammad arrived, he was all bundled up and wore headgear. He'd bicycled over to the DoubleTree hotel where my wife Carla, daughter Tennessee, and I had checked in on February 8.

I asked him about the children that Ali had with women other than his wives. He answered, "How many baby mama dramas did he have? He has children other than the children by his wives Belinda [Khalilah] and Veronica. It was a surprise to me because it was quietly kept."

Ishmael Reed: Out-of–wedlock?
Askia Muhammad: He has eleven children out-of-wedlock, I am told.

IR: What about Lonnie, do you know her?
AM: No. Whoever is around Ali is going to do well. It is unfortunate that sometimes the people around him don't have his best interests at heart. You know, I had a conversation with someone while we watched Coretta Scott King's funeral and I remarked on how great Oprah looked. Someone said, "All Oprah needs is a man that puts her on a pedestal and doesn't try to compete." So, in a sense, that is a component. Everybody doesn't have to be a Coretta King or Ali, just be a good person, keep your interest at heart, and just pray that you get a reward for living this pious life as well as the benefit by doing

so. Ain't nobody gonna serve Ali no pig, ain't nobody gonna chump him, or say to him something anti-Islamic.

IR: He hasn't taken a position on the Iraq war and she does all of the talking for him.
AM: God bless her, but then let me say this. Whatever he tells her to say is going to be sharp.

IR: [I asked him when he joined the Nation of Islam.]
AM: I joined the NOI when I was attending San Jose State University. That was in 1968. I was in the Navy Reserve and I was going to Officers' Candidate school. This was the year King was assassinated. I quit the officer program. This meant that deferments were going to end. Stokely Carmichael came to San Jose State and spoke. This had to be November.

I had gotten involved with him through this ninety-year-old white woman who collected all these scrapbooks about him and had given them to the Stanford Library, and so it's like I knew him. She had two or three dozen scrapbooks of him from the 1960s. I had written about her in a local paper called *The Jabberwock* at San Jose State. He came and he spoke. He gave me two hundred dollars to come to a conference at Howard University and that next weekend I went to the conference and missed my reserve duty. That, for the Navy, was the last straw. Their attitude was, "Your ass is going on active duty." What Stokely said had deeper meaning for me. He said, "If you're used by the man you are useless to your people." I thought, "What am I going to do? If I am used, I am useless. I gotta find a way out. I don't want to go to Canada and I don't want to go to jail. What am I going to do?"

The Ali case was bubbling and boiling and I said, "I'm going to go with Ali. He's my age. He's facing it."

So I applied for conscientious objector status and fought for honorable discharge. But I said, "I'm a Muslim," and that worked in 1969. That was the basis of the claim. I had an interview with a psychiatrist. A brother Benjamin in San Jose told me that if I want to make all these religious claims, I'd have to join something. The only community was the Nation. I started attending meetings and taking notes so that I could understand the religion; I threw myself into it.

We'd attend the mosque on Wednesday, Friday, and Sunday in San Francisco. On Tuesday and Thursday we would be in San Jose. I was with them every day. So I was invited to Brother Benjamin's house and I thought, "This is it. This is when we're going to make bombs!" When I arrived, he was making ice cream!

IR: Do you believe that Yacub created white people?
AM: I believe with *Newsweek* that the black man is the original man. If "Eve" was a black woman then that means that the original man was black.

IR: What about the Mother Ship?
AM: What's not to believe? I don't know what's out there.

IR: What about Ali's tithing? (Giving one tenth of one's income to charity).
AM: He gave what he could give. He was a generous giver. I was taught that charity was second only to prayer. That is among the five pillars of Islam. Prayer, charity, fasting, and the Hajj. Charity is second only to prayer. Rev. Ike used to say, "Get some money so that you can give me some money. If you don't have none, you can't give me none."

IR: What about Ali's condition being a curse put upon Ali by Elijah Muhammad from beyond the grave?
AM: I think that Elijah Muhammad loved Muhammad Ali. Everything I saw made me think this way. On one occasion, this was in 1974, December 1974, he told us not to use "devil" when we referred to white people. When he spoke that year he did not use the word "devil." I was editor of *Muhammad Speaks*, and was told not to use the word "devil."
IR: Were there threats made against journalists who were critical of the NOI?

AM: In December of 1973, Paul Delaney [*The New York Times*' reporter], wrote an article and said that he was frail and about to die; there was outrage in the Nation. They started beating up on Paul Delaney, intellectually. This happened for two or three weeks. Elijah Muhammad stopped the retaliation against Delaney.

IR: What was the reason for Ali's suspension from the NOI?

AM: In December of that year, Michael Manley was Prime Minister of Jamaica. He wanted Muhammad Ali and Minister Farrakhan to preach and rally the people. He really wanted Ali to go, and Ali said, "If I go I have to have my Muslim people with me. I can't go speak on behalf of being a Muslim."

So Farrakhan went. The head of the delegation was John Muhammad, Mr. Muhammad's brother. Ali was the big draw. I was part of the group that went to Jamaica. The trip lasted a month, during the time Ali was suspended, but there was an issue of *Muhammad Speaks* published with photos of Ali and Muhammad face to face. "Two champions of the world. The spiritual champion and the physical champion." The article was about Ali, dictated by Elijah Muhammad, which said that Ali had won the championship in the ring and how unjust it was for Ali to be banned from the ring. Unjustified for him to lose except in the ring.

Alex Haley told me that he believed Malcolm X wanted to return to the Nation at the time he was assassinated, but he didn't know how to get back. The people in the Nation who surrounded Elijah Muhammad would not have him back. The politics that were going on at that time was about jealousy of Malcolm.

IR: What about Muhammad's adultery?

AM: Elijah had wives. He had more than one wife. He took wives, and for each one of them he explained what he was doing. Clara Muhammad didn't approve. What wife could?

IR: You spent a lot of time with Elijah. What kind of person was he? Did he have hobbies, did he read books, go to movies?

AM: He read a lot and studied a lot. The time I spent with him was at dinner. During this time, he would teach and have long conversations. The dinners would go on two to three hours, during which he would talk about the Nation's business. I never heard him discuss movies.

IR: Did he like music?

AM: The only music experience I saw him [listening to] was when Mister Farrakhan came and played the violin for him. He didn't go to plays. He just stayed within his home. When he had his driver's license renewed, they did it in his home. So he held court a lot.

IR: What kind of food would be served?

AM: Nation of Islam cuisine. Bean soup. Members of the family dressed at dinner. Business people and others were invited. He was courteous and respectful. He had white and Jewish people for dinner.

IR: What about Farrakhan?

AM: You know all of his stuff went bad for him after he had dinner at Mike Wallace's home with Jewish people. In the 1990s. These were prominent Jewish leaders. The head of Seagrams, for example. Widely regarded Jewish leaders in New York and Chicago, but then the Khalid Muhammad thing happened. But Farrakhan does not back down. He meets with Jewish people regularly. [Author's note: Khalid Abdul Muhammad was a spokesperson for The New Black Panther Party, not the group founded by Bobby Seale and Huey Newton. He made speeches in which he described whites as "devils" and Jews as "blood suckers." He died of natural causes in 2012.]

IR: What about the "gutter religion" remark?

AM: It was "dirty religion." His point was that people use religion to cover their dirty deeds. It was an allegory. People used their daily religion to shield wickedness. You're using Jesus the prophet to hide behind those things that are dirty. He didn't call Judaism a gutter religion. That's that point. He's not a race hater. He doesn't teach hatred of Jews. He doesn't hate white people, he doesn't hate Jews.

There are other Jewish people who can't afford to admit that they meet with him. He meets with them once every three or four months.

IR: Why does he have the reputation of being an Anti-Semite?
AM: He says things that are controversial and that upset people.

IR: What about Farrakhan's group being broke?
AM: I don't know.

IR: How many mosques does he have?
AM: I don't know, but let me finish about this Jewish thing. Since 1984 I have heard this. I knew that Jesse said "Hymietown." I knew that when Jesse Jackson said he didn't say it, he was lying, and Farrakhan came to his defense because he didn't know it was a lie.

In a private conversation I had with him, he said that when he heard the news that Jascha Heifitz [the violinist] had died, he pulled over and stopped and said a prayer. He's a violinist. I don't believe that's a person who hates people just because they are Jewish.

IR: What did you think of Ali lighting the torch?
AM: Ali is Ali forever. Like John Carlos who went to San Jose State and is an exemplary human being—when the time came he made a stand. That's like Ali.

IR: What about Ali's treatment of Sonji and Belinda [Khalilah]? [Ali's first and second wives]
AM: I met Sonji a year before she died and she was living a Muslim life. She was at Minister Farrakhan's house for dinner. She was just talking about herself being a Muslim. Farrakhan was helping her. He helps a lot of people. Dorothy LaVelle, who runs a newspaper on 63rd and Martin Luther King Avenue in Chicago, she said that Herbert Muhammad introduced Sonji to Ali and that Sonji was from the street life.

IR: What about his beating Sonji and Belinda?

AM: I don't believe it. People get physical. That doesn't seem to be part of Ali's persona.

IR: Would you comment about the split between Wallace and Farrakhan?

AM: Not one drop of blood has been shed. So that shows we are nonviolent and won't even jaywalk, but we believe in the principles of self-defense. If you mess with us, we'll fight back. And I don't believe that integration will work because if we live with them they have to be on top.

IR: What about Wallace Fard, the man who introduced Yacubism to Elijah Muhammad? He had a white mother. Does that make him or his mother a devil?

AM: His mother was a Muslim. He came from the Caucasus Mountains and I saw Muslims from Russia and Siberia who were white-skinned with Oriental features. They can recite the Koran.

IR: Was Ali's decision to defy the draft a result of NOI's teachings?

AM: Yes, we who declare ourselves to be righteous Muslims do not believe that we should be participating in wars. It was announced on the back page of the paper [*Muhammad Speaks*] under "What the Muslims Want," every week. In fact, Elijah Muhammad went to jail, as well as his son, during World War II. Why should we fight for the white man? What has the white man done for you? Those were the questions we raised.

IR: So if the Japanese were in alliance with Germany, did supporting Japan mean that you supported the Nazis?

AM: No! Oh no! We believed that we had nothing to fight for. If America were to divide the country and give us something, we might have something to fight for.

IR: So Ali was submitting to Muslim policy. Was Abdul Rahman the man who gave Ali the line, "No Vietnamese ever called me a nigger"?
AM: Yes. He was called Sam X. He became a minister.

IR: Did the NOI ever assault anybody?
AM: You know there's a culture there—a lot of cats that did things. There was an event where some brothers from Vallejo had gone on a shooting rampage and were eventually killed in Baton Rouge, Louisiana. 1970 or 71, somewhere in there. This is not what we teach. But we understand the rage that might be in some people. Mr. Muhammad was speaking in Detroit and a confrontation arose when the police said, "We're coming in," and he said, "You can't come in here with a gun." They said, "No, we're coming in." He said, "This is a private meeting," and they said, "We are coming in." We cancelled the meeting. Elijah Muhammad was against confrontation.

IR: Was this the basis of the dispute between Ali and Elijah Muhammad that he thought Ali to be too confrontational?
AM: Ali was a fighter, a champion. He was making money and became a Muslim at the age when this hormonal thing is going on and you are like a stud. The teachings make you feel superior, and you say, "Damn, I already think I'm bad and now I got this message that makes me feel superior and if I hold onto this God will protect me," so that's what he falls into.

IR: What about liquor sponsorship at the Ali Center opening? I thought that there was a Muslim prohibition against liquor.
AM: There is. But come on, Malcolm X's belongings and handwritten letters were sold in an auction. So I'm just saying that the blind man stands on the corner begging for money; when someone drops something into the cup he says, "Thank you." He's begging for money. Ali wants to build a center. What is he going to do, take it out of his pocket, take it from his kids, his grandkids?

IR: You don't have an opinion on it?

AM: I wouldn't.

IR: What about the late Yusef Bey's sons in Oakland, who allegedly entered some Yemini-owned stores and proceeded to destroy the liquor cabinets?

AM: In Chicago or D.C., Arabs would own little liquor and pig selling stores, but then they were replaced by Haitians and Africans, and then Vietnamese and Latinos. We're suckers.

IR: What did you think about the Bey brothers' actions? Like Carrie Nation. You know.

AM: Vigilantism is not done. I was in a situation that could have become physical, but I shouldn't have been there.

IR: You mean that the organization that ridiculed Martin Luther King, Jr. for his actions was non-violent?

AM: I wouldn't say adopted non-violence, because the Nation was already supporting non-violence. That was the difference. Their policy was not to engage in civil disobedience. So Mister Muhammad said, "Don't break the law. Don't even jaywalk. Don't give the police an excuse to enforce the law on you and if you resist, then the power of the state is against you because you jaywalked and you shouldn't have jaywalked and now people have to defend you for jaywalking."

IR: Ali just got an award in Germany for his work in Civil Rights, after all he said about Martin Luther King, Jr. Do you think he's being repackaged? It seemed to me that the whites controlled his image at the Ali Center.

AM: Well, the Nation freed him from being a product; it gave him a status. He could be Sugar Ray Leonard, successful, the same road, had a package, had an ownership group when he came after the Olympics and did okay. But what made Ali special was this association with guys like Malcolm X and Sam X and the Honorable Elijah Muhammad and the causes and the issues that they were dealing with at that time. So when Ali said "No" when they drafted him, they gave him every inducement. They offered him bribes and then threatened him and he still said no. He could have said, "I'm going to lose millions" and he could have taken a deal, and we would have still loved him.

IR: Stanley Crouch, Jack Cashill, and others say that he was afraid of the NOI.

AM: I mean, come on. If the Fruit of Islam has access to you, it's because you choose to be among them, not because they can pierce whatever shield is around you. They're not a bunch of thugs as they have been depicted. They are black men who came out of the ghetto. And they couldn't talk. Some of them came out of jail, and it's like, "I'm getting this strong philosophy and this moral teaching in a military-type fashion."

IR: Has Ali repudiated Farrakhan? How is their relationship?

AM: It's good. You know, what's not to love? I mean for Farrakhan it doesn't mean as much because he is older. Ali lives in the world and the world owns him.

CHAPTER 4

After Fard disappeared (the followers of Wallace D. Muhammad claim that he became an Imam in Hayward, California, and died a few years ago), Elijah Muhammad continued drawing converts after he was released from prison, where he'd been convicted of draft dodging some years earlier. However, Elijah Muhammad had been under the watch of federal authorities long before that. In the 1940s, he went around making pro-Japanese speeches. Not only had he embraced a religion that had been misunderstood in the West since the 1100s, but chose to follow the interpretation of a man considered by some to be a con-artist masquerading as Allah. This would put the NOI at odds with orthodox Islam, which has its own divisions.

His followers at the time numbered four hundred. He had jettisoned some of the mysticism of the past and, taking a leaf from the much maligned Booker T. Washington, he emphasized self-reliance, which some argue was the result of his spending his years as an inmate at a self-sufficient agricultural farm. When he appeared on the show "Black Journal" in the late 1960s, he said, speaking of economic opportunities, "It's out there, go get it," and said that when he visited Washington, he was treated like a "prince." The once-hated NOI would survive to see some of their projects funded by the government. The influence of Washingtonian thought can be heard in Malcolm X's most famous speech, "The Ballot or the Bullet" (1964). In it he emphasizes self-reliance and black business development.

Sometimes those opposed to the economic progress of the NOI did it through violence, and other times through chicanery. Blacks lose hundreds of billions of dollars per year through banks charging them higher interest rates than whites, and these are not the only institutions in which one finds racial disparities. The NOI's experience in black capitalism shows that while white capitalists have an open route to acquiring capital, even to the point of being subsidized by the government and having property belonging to others seized and turned over to them, black capitalists meet roadblocks every day.

Reginald Lewis's experience testifies to that. As president of Beatrice International, a billion-dollar corporation, Lewis was constantly hounded by economic hit men posing as business journalists even as he was dying. While pursuing the American Dream of ownership, Elijah Muhammad and his followers were the subject of excessive scrutiny, the lengths of which are detailed in an excellent biography of Malcolm X by Kofi Natambu:

> At the Savior's Day convention on February 26, 1958, FBI agents and local police surreptitiously conducted what they called a 'fisur.'
>
> Agents and police roamed the parking lots, noted the license plate numbers of every car, took photographs of anyone who might be a dignitary, and monitored eavesdropping equipment that recorded the speeches.

The attitude toward Islam during the period from 1100 to 1140 was one which, in the words of R. W. Southern, "gave free rein to 'the ignorance of triumphant imagination.' Muhammad became a sorcerer whose magic and deceit destroyed the Church of Africa and the East" (Southern, 1978).

> By going on to sanction sexual promiscuity, his success was assured. Legends growing out of popular folklore, classical literature, Byzantine texts on Islam, and viciously distorted tales from Muslim sources embellished this image. Southern points out that Guibert of Nogent (d. ca. 1124-30) admitted that since he had not relied on written sources, he had no way of separating fact from fiction and had only presented the *plebia opinio*, or popular opinion. Innocently revealing the basis of all ideological criticism, he concluded that "it is safe to speak evil of one whose malignity exceeds whatever ill can be spoken." (Rodinson, 1987)

The only difference between the attitudes toward Islam of the eleventh century and that of today's columnists and television analysts is that in the eleventh century the public demanded information about the religion. On July 30, 2006, during a broadcast of *Meet the Press*, the late Tim Russert said that his guest, Thomas Friedman, whose comments about Islam and Arabs have been haughty and laced with ridicule, was a person "who knows the Arab mind and soul."

Before I began writing this book, I had little knowledge of the Muslims who had wound up in the Atlantic slave trade. I wasn't aware of Lamine Kebe. "There are good men in America, but all are very ignorant of Africa," said African-born Kebe in 1835. Kebe, who had spent forty years of American slavery in three Southern states, complained about the dearth of information about African Muslims enslaved in the America.

> Despite the efforts of its followers, African Islam did not survive in the Americas in its orthodox form. Yet its mark can be found in certain religions, traditions and artistic creations of the peoples of African descent. But for all their accomplishments and contributions to the cultures of the African Diaspora, the Muslims largely have been ignored. They have received scant attention at best, despite a wealth of material: from autobiographies and biographies to letters, newspaper articles, mentions in travelers' chronicles, and notices in plantation records and colonial correspondence. (Diouf, 2013)

Diouf also criticized those who drew a misleading portrait of Muslims in popular culture. Steven Spielberg was the producer and director of three films that were insulting of blacks. Sylviane A. Diouf writes:

> Stephen Spielberg's *Amistad* (1997) features a few Muslims; however, this poorly researched movie, which is particularly offensive to Africans, shows them only for a split second, praying on the ship deck. Strangely, most of the men and girls in *Amistad* wear turbans, which are a Muslim trademark and are never worn by non-Muslims or by Muslim young men who have not gained the right to do so. In addition, at no point in Spielberg's movie is there any mention of religion or any display of religious behavior or attitudes among the prisoners, except rendition of Africans, the Muslims again are poorly served.

Muslims indeed were on the *Amistad,* as has been documented by Richard Madden, who testified on behalf of the Africans in Connecticut on November 11, 1839.

One thing I did know about Islam was the connection of some members of the faith to the slave trade. We are all familiar with the Atlantic slave trade cycle. However, very little is said about the slave trade that went the other way: the Trans-Sahara slave trade. While many lives were lost during the Atlantic crossing, the transportation of black slaves across the Sahara to Muslim countries was also hazardous.

Also, while many books have been written about slave revolts in the Americas, little has been discussed about black slaves revolting against their Muslim masters. The most important of these revolts was the Zanj Rebellion, which was carried out by black slaves from East Africa. It began in 869 A.D. in Basra and was led by Ali ibn Muhammad. He organized an army of fifteen thousand, which captured a number of Iraqi cities. In 883 A.D., the rebellion was crushed and its leader beheaded. Despite its failure, the use of large numbers of black slaves in plantation agriculture declined. It was considered too dangerous. It is estimated that fourteen million slaves were sold during the Muslim slave trade (Segal, 2001).

In some Muslim countries, the enslavement of human beings is still practiced. When many African Americans think of Islam, they think of the slave trade. Members of the NOI haven't forgotten this history, either. In fact, *The New York Times* reported that when Muammar Gaddafi of Libya refused to grant the NOI additional money to start some businesses, members of the NOI called the late Libyan leader "a slave trader." Just as the southern plantation gave rise to bi-racial individuals, which prompted Chester Himes to refer to black Americans as a new race, a team of geneticists used the genome to find segments of African origin in the genomes of southern Mediterranean and Middle Eastern people between A.D. 650 and 1900. This correlates with the advent of the Arab slave trade of the seventh century (Quenqua, *The New York Times*, February 18, 2014).

Moreover, I have found the NOI's association with Nazis to be strange, given the attitudes of the Nazis toward Jews, blacks, and other groups the Nazis regarded as, in the words of the late George Lincoln Rockwell, "scum." Among those sent to Nazi concentration camps were black Americans and Africans. When John A. Williams approached New York publishers with his book, *Clifford's Blues*, about a black American musician interned in one of those camps, the editors didn't believe him:

> Black prisoners of war faced illegal incarceration and mistreatment at the hands of the Nazis, who did not uphold the regulations imposed by the Geneva Convention (international agreement on the conduct of war and the treatment of wounded and captured soldiers). Lieutenant Darwin Nichols, an African American pilot, was incarcerated in a Gestapo prison in Butzbach. Black soldiers of the American, French, and British armies were worked to death on construction projects or died as a result of mistreatment in concentration or prisoner-of-war camps. Others were never even incarcerated, but were instead immediately killed by the SS or Gestapo.
>
> Some African American members of the US armed forces were liberators and witnesses to Nazi atrocities. The 761st Tank Battalion (an all-African American tank unit), attached to the 71st Infantry Division, US Third Army, under the command of General George Patton, participated in the liberation of Gunskirchen, a subcamp of the Mauthausen concentration camp, in May 1945. (http://www.ushmm.org/wlc/en/article.php?ModuleId=10005479)

In 1962, Elijah Muhammad invited the late George Rockwell, former American Nazi party leader, to a NOI convention. But in an angry exchange of letters with J. B. Stoner, a Ku Klux Klan leader, Elijah Muhammad treated the far right as the enemy. Also, in a post-Mecca letter to George Lincoln Rockwell, Malcolm X threatened retaliation against the Klan were harm to come to blacks as a result of their actions. But while Malcolm X drew attention to the NOI, which, before Malcolm X, was regarded as a "cult," Muhammad Ali's conversion to the religion put it on the map.

Ali was the wild card, the Joker, the warrior in a time when the black male ego needed some buffeting.

Black women being disrespected by the white police was an issue that writer Herb Boyd says ignited the race riots of the 1960s. This lack of respect for black women echoed the situation in early 1900s New York when white police officers harassed even church-going black women as prostitutes. One of those who agitated against this practice was Booker T. Washington's right hand man, Thomas Fortune, editor of *The New York Age* at the time. Furthermore, though reviled by some northern intellectuals, Black Nationalist pioneer Marcus Garvey provided the self-help model for Elijah Muhammad who was, to some, Ali's surrogate father. Ali's joining the black separatist NOI made him a hero among black nationalists. He was an example for a black nation hungry for heroes. He defied the resentment, even hatred, of millions of white Americans who couldn't understand why their sons had to go to war while Ali didn't. Some forget that at first Ali received a lower classification that made him ineligible for the draft; in his reclassification, the Selective Service Board yielded to mob sentiment. While any number of Christian sects have been granted religious status, the white men who make the determination of what a religion is couldn't bring themselves to view the NOI as such.

The idea that the Nation of Islam was a religion was laughable to many whites. In fact it still is, with white sports writers, the predominately white jury that every black athlete must face, leading the sneers. Not only was Ali ridiculed for adopting the teachings of his mentor, Elijah Muhammad, but Elijah Muhammad's form of Islam was mocked and scorned. However, the NOI's idea of a spaceship, sent to deliver an oppressed people, is no more fantastic than the Red Sea parting for Moses and his people, or Ezekiel's wheel, or the Rapture, a fantasy that has influenced United States' foreign policy. Their idea of a scientist, Yacub, creating a Caucasian devil race, was no more fantastic than the origin of blacks stemming from Ham being cursed for happening upon his nude father, Noah. When I asked Marvin X whether he believed in the story of Yacub and the Mother Ship, he said he did in the same manner as one would believe in Greek mythology.

CHAPTER 5

Though the Muslims were bold in their opposition to white supremacy, a stance that was reflected in their challenge to the police who
invaded their sacred spaces, some, like Jackie Robinson, regarded
their threats as amounting to woof tickets, empty, as when they
backed down when the Los Angeles police killed Ronald Stokes and
when they mourned JFK after calling him a devil. Others charge
that they are more prone to making violent confrontations against
black people than white. The same might be said of their sometime
rivals, the Black Panthers. Huey Newton assaulted, allegedly, a tailor
who referred to him as "baby." Ike and Tina Turner were roughed up
because of a dispute over payment after they performed at a Black
Panther-sponsored event. I remember walking down a Harlem street
in the early 1960s. It was shortly after I had arrived in New York. As I
approached a corner, I noticed a confrontation between a well-dressed
salesman who was hawking copies of *Muhammad Speaks* and some
elderly black men. He was trying to sell them copies of the paper. One
of the men said, "Fuck Elijah Muhammad!" The young man put some
karate moves on the group of old men, leaving them sprawled on the
pavement. A neighborhood friend of mine speaks of his encounter
with the Fruit of Islam. When he was seen as being disrespectful of
Elijah Muhammad, he received a beating.

During a Harlem speech, I saw a grinning Malcolm X encourage
the assault upon a black reporter, followed by members of the NOI
chasing the man down. After the assassination of Malcolm X, some

of this violence was directed inward. Some even suggest that Ali was forced into accepting the policies of the NOI.

Jack Cashill quotes Sugar Ray Robinson, who says that Muhammad Ali was Elijah Muhammad's marionette because he feared harm from the NOI members of his entourage. However, Bennett Johnson, Elijah Muhammad's liaison with the Civil Rights Movement, denies he was being coerced. As someone who viewed Elijah Muhammad as the strong patriarch, who was different from his father depicted by The Ali Scribes as a domestic violence perpetrator, loser, and a wannabe player (while heaping praise and affection upon Ali's mother), one could understand why Ali would take to Elijah Muhammad in a worshipful manner.

When I told Askia Muhammad about Ali's confession to Jack Newfield that he only began to believe in Allah in 1984 when mini-skirts went out of style, Askia Muhammad, editor of Minister Farrakhan's newspaper, *The Final Call*, said that it was because before that, Ali believed that Elijah Muhammad was a deity.

But thuggery and strong-arm tactics among some of the NOI members have been documented. Often it was intimidation that frightened those who were considered "Uncle Toms," or infidels. Authors who have written about the NOI in a critical manner claim that they have been threatened. Agieb Bilal also says that those who strayed from the asceticism established by the NOI were subjected to corporal punishment.

How much of this violence was directed by Elijah Muhammad is unknown. Agieb Bilal says that Elijah Muhammad never directed harm to be meted out to a person, but knew that those around him were capable of it. However, the Muslim history cannot be examined without a mention of the government spying on the NOI, even though the Nation presented less of a threat to white supremacy than Martin Luther King, Jr.'s drive. This spying led to the Supreme Court's vindication of Muhammad Ali. Though Ali biographers blame the NOI for Malcolm X's assassination, the secret government's role in executing those considered its foes has been documented in such books as John Perkins' *Confessions of an Economic Hitman* and

Chuck Barris's *Confessions of a Dangerous Mind,* as well as the findings of the 1970s Church Committee. The government's role in the assassinations of Martin Luther King, Jr. and Malcolm X cannot be ruled out. Moreover, since the government infiltrated both the Black Panthers and the Nation of Islam, one can never know how much of the organization's bad press stemmed from the actions of *agents provocateurs.*

During my interview with the great boxing trainer, Emanuel Steward, he said that Sonny Liston took a fall in the second fight with Ali because he feared Muslim violence. There was also a rumor that the mob threatened Liston's child if he didn't lose.

Stanley Crouch and others have suggested that refusing to fight in the Vietnam War, the act that still draws admiration for the fighter among those attending the Black Nationalist book fair, was not so much an act of free will, but his submitting to the policies of Elijah Muhammad and intimidation by the NOI. That might explain why he kept Jeremiah Shabazz, an enforcer, in his entourage even after street talk had him ordering the execution of a Hanafi Muslim's family. This ignores the government's offer that Ali should follow the route chosen by Joe Louis, that of serving his military obligations by performing in exhibitions.

Herbert Muhammad, Ali's manager, communicated this offer to him. Whether Elijah Muhammad gave his approval to the deal is a question. Moreover, as Crouch says, the Muslim bodyguards—the feared Fruit of Islam—were there to ensure that Ali would abide by Minister Elijah Muhammad's wishes.

One of those who felt threatened by the Muslim enforcers, so much so that he armed himself, was Black Panther leader Bobby Seale. I Interviewed Bobby Seale in his Oakland home, the scene of many Panther strategy meetings in the 60s and 70s.

Alice Walker proposed that men of the Black Panthers organized that group in order to have dates with each other (she called them "punks" in a *New York Times* Op-Ed, when it was their persecutor, J. Edgar Hoover, who had a bent toward the homoerotic). Later, when I interviewed Melvin Van Peebles, he claimed that during this period, there were two thousand "black cats in Paris getting a piece of ass" on the basis of posing as fugitive Black Panthers. One indisputable fact is that the Black Panthers ushered in an era of black power in Oakland and their influence is still felt. Seale says that his disagreements with the Nation were based upon scientific proof, as opposed to their reliance upon information that was unverifiable.

CHAPTER 6

During the Memorial Day weekend of 2005, I ran into Bobby Seale, co-founder of the Black Panthers, at the Berkeley YMCA where I swim three times a week. I told him that I wanted to interview him about Muhammad Ali. He invited me to come to his home on 57th Street for a Memorial Day party. By the time I got there at about 5:30 in the afternoon, people had already left. And so my holiday treat was a take-out dish of potato salad, macaroni and cheese, and barbecued ribs and chicken prepared by Seale, who is the author of a cookbook—one of the perks I get for having chosen writing as a profession.

The next day, when I showed up for the interview, he was watching the funeral of a high-ranking Nazi official on the History Channel. American television was broadcasting the funeral of Ronald Reagan, who used fear of the Panthers and his role as a fink for the FBI to climb to higher office, where his skills as an actor were exploited by his wealthy backers. In case the public didn't get where he was coming from, he began his first campaign in Philadelphia, Mississippi, where three civil rights workers were murdered. He was being buried with all of the panoply befitting a king. Bobby Seale hasn't changed in his appearance that much since the 1960s, other than his waistline having expanded.

Bobby Seale: First of all, when me and Huey Newton created the Black Panther party, one thing [was that] no religious doctrine would be at the helm of what we were talking about in terms of liberation. We would use good, proven, scientific, evidentiary fact as the basis. We evolved and learned to use and apply some dialectics. But we never did it in a doctrinal manner. It didn't have to do with Marxism. It had to do with the study and research of African and African American history—W. E. B. DuBois' *Black Reconstruction*, the books and works of Marcus Garvey, John Hope Franklin's historical works, and others.

You have to understand I had digested two hundred and fifty slave reports by Dr. Herbert F. Aptheker and all of the wars we had been in. This is my own research. In 1962 I was [on] a quest. At first I was an engineer. I had a full-time job at Kaiser Aerospace and Electronics in San Leandro. I was doing non-destruct testing on all of the engine frames for the Gemini missile program. This is what I was about in 1962-1963. I did not quit that job after Kennedy was assassinated and Malcolm X left the Nation of Islam. I quit the job after two and a half years on the job. I went to Merritt College. I was married a year later. At age thirty I had a kid.

Members of the NOI told us that the Honorable Elijah Muhammad teaches us that all knowledge is based on a complete circle of 360 degrees. You see good science is good enough for me. I'm an engineer. I said, "Brother, you always come up in here talking all of that stuff." I said, "That's a flat terminology. What are you talking about, brother? That cannot represent a concept of all knowledge."

They'd say, "My brother, you see the problem here is that you are here with the white man's education." I said, "Uh-uh. I would take you back to good old Egyptian geometry and give you some structural examples to show that you need a spherical concept of analogy. You cannot use a flat plane of analogy of 360 degrees drawn on a flat piece of paper and say this represents all knowledge as though it's connected. What about the whole sphere of the concept of knowledge?"

So this is where I was coming from in my first intellectual battles with them. I never had much time even in the world of my mother's Christianity. I mean, I love my mother. I probably got my fair shares equality principles mostly from my mother. I got my right to self-defense principles from my father. Both my mother and father were born in Jasper, Texas. My father bought me my first 30/30 Winchester high power rifle when I was twelve years of age. I became a hunter and a fisherman before I was ten and at eleven, we would go hunting with these guys for big game. I couldn't have a high-powered rifle, because I was twelve, so they gave us a twenty-two. We would shoot squirrels and bring them into the camp. We would stay out hunting three or four days around Mount Shasta and other Northern California areas. So guns were our tools and we used them at a particular time and a particular situation mainly for hunting. Guns were always in our house; you see what I mean? We would hunt rabbit, pheasant, deer, duck, bear. You name it, we did that.

It was after the end of World War II that we moved here to the San Francisco Bay Area. By September 1945, the whole family was here. My father sent for us. We came from San Antonio. Some of my family on my father's side moved to Beaumont. My father built our first home in Port Arthur, Texas, just at the beginning of the war. Then in the first two-year process of that home, he got a job in San Antonio because of the wartime jobs. He had a deferment because one leg was one inch shorter than the other. But he was skilled as a carpenter, so he fabricated the framing structures out of hardwood for the fighter aircraft, World War II stuff. So then they transferred his job all the way out here to the Oakland Army base.

Ishmael Reed: When did you first encounter members of the NOI?
Bobby Seale: The NOI would come right around here at Merritt College. There would always be some brothers from the local mosque. Huey and I were going to do some sociological research on local churches. So as part of our research we visited the Nation of Islam mosque here in West Oakland. I happened to look at one of the women and one of the brothers said, "What are you looking at?" I wasn't impressed with them at all.

I liked Malcolm. When I met him at McClymonds High School, he was still with the Nation of Islam. He made a speech. Well, I thought it was great. A lot of the other little doctrinaires and the Nation of Islam people were around. When Malcolm was supposedly expelled all of them boys started talking that talk, like, "They need to kill that nigger." They hung around Merritt.

I said, "You all better keep your ass out of my way. I like Malcolm. You motherfuckers are wrong." I had pawned my pistol and had to get another one, which my brother bought for me. It was a nine millimeter nine shot. When Malcolm got killed, I said, "You gotta get me a gun." I said, "Go down and get it in your name," 'cause the FBI was already watching because I was a member of RAM [The Revolutionary Action Movement], too. The FBI would come here and knock on the door and I would slam the door. I had to get out of RAM, the day that Malcolm was killed. I cut them loose totally. Armchair revolutionaries; they wouldn't do nothing. I had been running with them for a year. I said, "We're talking revolution. You guys don't know how to shoot." They'd say, "Yeah, but that's not important." I said, "I don't want to hear that shit."

I said to my brother, John, "If they come, I'm going to pop those motherfuckers in the ass. I'm going to try not to kill them." There were three or four of the NOI around there talking shit. They had been talking shit for a whole year since Malcolm had resigned, but when he got killed the word was out. If one of them boys had fucked with me I would have killed them. I would have been in prison. First of all, the Nation of Islam structure-wise was a mono-leadership organization. The Black Panther Party was multi-leadership and I kept it that way. The very fact that Elijah Muhammad was a mono-leader was antithetical to my very sense of what democracy and fairness and what human liberation had to be about in a high tech social order. I didn't deal in these polemics of "the white man is a devil." They might have talked about us in an article or two, but normally they didn't deal with us.

IR: When did you first hear of Muhammad Ali?

BS: I heard about him as Cassius Clay on the radio and saw clips and films and stuff. I really liked the guy. I really loved his art. When Muhammad Ali said, "My name is not Cassius Clay, it's Muhammad Ali," I accepted that, because he had a right to do that. It's not about whether or not I would join the Nation of Islam because I knew I would never join the Nation of Islam. It was his right, and when people in the country were downing him for doing so, I saw a certain unfairness, a certain behind-the-scene racist unfairness going on. They were wrong, so I had a tendency to automatically support him, and then of course Malcolm X was suspended from the Nation of Islam after his remarks about the death of John F. Kennedy. Then I thought maybe I should go. Then he created what he called the OAU [Organization of Afro-American Unity], and pronounced that this was a secular kind of organization. I said, "Hey, maybe I'll go join this because this is outside of that religious stuff." I was happy that Malcolm X left the Nation of Islam. And of course during that interim he sort of defined civil rights in terms of human rights.

IR: When did you meet Muhammad Ali?

BS: There was an anti-war rally going on. Twenty thousand people were there. It was during those three years that Muhammad Ali couldn't fight. I shook his hand. I said, "Hey Muhammad, man, how you doing brother?" He said, "Hey, Brother Bobby, doin' all right." He knew me. That was the first time I met him. He had two people with him. I had two people with me. We were armed. I guess his people were armed, too. It was before I went to jail, 1968 or early 1969.

IR: His legacy?

BS: Well, he was opposed to the war; he was opposed to the racist discrimination in the United States of America. In effect, he came out as an example for me as a person who stood basically on his principles. Now they may not be the principles of some doctrinaire Socialists, but I don't care for doctrinaire Socialists. Muhammad Ali was a right-on guy as far as I am concerned.

CHAPTER 7

Did the Secret Government Fear a U.S. Muslim/Overseas Muslim Alliance?

Sam Hamod, PhD, was Director of the Islamic Center of Washington, D.C.; taught at Princeton, Michigan, Wisconsin, Howard, and Iowa; is a poet who was nominated for the Pulitzer Prize and has published ten books of poems; and has been a leading spokesman for Islam during his lifetime, in America and overseas. He was also fortunate to have been a witness and a participant in some of the important events in American Muslim history, not to mention witnessing the discovery of Michael Jackson and The Jackson Five.

Sam Hamod offers a theory that the United States government feared an alliance between the Muslims led by Elijah Muhammad and the international orthodox Islamic community.

Sam Hamod: The Muhammad Ali the media historians don't want to talk about is how much he protested against the war and the damage that was done to his life and his reputation because of his anti-war and civil rights protests. When they talk about Civil Rights, others are listed, but he is not; they always keep that part of Muhammad Ali's life covered up. In fact, he was a very visible protestor on behalf of civil rights in his era; he also influenced many other African American youth to protest not only the Vietnam War, but also to engage in protest against other policies they felt were wrong at the time. Muhammad Ali was then a symbol of an awakening that shot through the black community like a bolt of lightning; to even sacrifice a lucrative financial career for principle and religion, especially the religion of Islam, that had been vilified in the American media.

Ali said, "I'm not going to fight those people because they're not my enemy." Media people and most black leaders never talk about his draft resistance and the part it played in Civil Rights. Part of this is jealousy on the part of other black leaders, and on the part of media; it is both a cover-up and a lack of knowledge of what went on when he came out as a Muslim and when he stood against the Vietnam War. In truth, he was not just a man to be loved but a man to be admired. For his integrity and for his religion, he paid a heavy price.

His cultural significance is two-fold: first, he declared himself a Muslim at a time when it wasn't a popular thing to do. One has but to remember the continuous vitriolic attacks by white commentators who continued to call him "Cassius Clay," or, as he calls him, "Muhammad Aleee." One of the most famous of these was a man who later came to admire him, Howard Cosell. But Muhammad Ali never wavered, and over the years, he has stood by his religion, surviving the media and personal attacks. Through it all, he has kept his dignity. As time has gone on, he is now loved and revered by the whole world, not just by Americans. Now, he is loved and respected throughout the world; thus, his significance continues.

In addition to his standing in the world as a Muslim and as a great fighter, he is also the symbol of the fight against Parkinson's disease. He continues to raise funds against this disease and continues his life, like the courageous fighter he always was.

Many are aware that he was close to Malcolm X (Malik Al Shabazz), but they became distant when Malcolm broke with the Honorable Elijah Muhammad over some political and private matters. Muhammad Ali stood with Elijah Muhammad for some time, but before Malcolm's untimely death, Muhammad Ali and Malcolm had resolved their differences and were bigger men for it. Both men saw that Islam was a universal religion, not one of color or a religion that was meant to separate men or races.

During this time, there was a major media campaign against what were called 'The Black Muslims,' namely, the followers of the Honorable Elijah Muhammad. Some of the media people in Chicago,

New York, and Washington, D.C. tried to enlist the aid of the leaders of orthodox Islam in this attack on Elijah Muhammad and his "Nation of Islam."

There were some among the orthodox Muslims who shunned the Nation group; others were more willing to reach out to them because of their sympathy for what Elijah Muhammad was trying to do in his work to stop the Black Man from using dope, alcohol, pimping, and other things that were destroying their lives and their communities.

Finally, there was a major meeting called at the home of Sam Hamod, Sr., my father, in Gary, Indiana. My father was one of the major Muslim leaders, and a man who had a long relationship with Elijah Muhammad. This meeting took place in the early 1950s. I was a teenager, but was allowed to listen. At the meeting there was Dr. Mahmoud Hoballah, the Vice Rector of Al-Azhar University (the leading Islamic university in the world) and Director of The Islamic Center in Washington, D.C.; Imam Mohammad Jawad Chirri; my father, and I. Before the meeting, Dr. Hoballah had also consulted with Dr. Mahmoud Youssef Shawarabi, who had also been the Director of The Islamic Center in Washington, D.C. before the tenure of Dr. Hoballah.

Imam Chirri was of the opinion that the Nation of Islam should be shunned and condemned for teaching a wrongful Islam. But Dr. Hoballah, counseled that it would be better to be friendly with the Nation and with Elijah Muhammad, so that eventually he could be brought and educated in the true ways of Islam, not the ways he was teaching it at the time. He and my father both also felt that Elijah was doing good work by helping to improve the black community, and that fit also with Islamic teaching against dope, drink, and prostitution. They felt that Elijah had brought people part way to Islam and that eventually, because of his teachings, many would come to orthodox Islam. My father felt, through his friendship with Elijah Muhammad, that he was a man whose intentions were good and that he was the leader of a great revolution in the African-American community and should be respected for this. After much thought and discussion, they all agreed: they should be friendly to the Nation and continue to improve relationships with Elijah Muhammad and his people.

At about this time, another man came upon the scene in Chicago, a Dr. Jamil Diab. He had made friends with many people in the Nation and had begun giving classes in Arabic and also on Islam. He and Elijah Muhammad got along so well that Elijah allowed his sons, Akbar and Warith-a-Deen (now known as Wallace Muhammad), to study with Dr. Diab. This later led to Akbar's studying at Al-Azhar University through the good offices of Dr. Hoballah and Dr. Shawaraby. These men also had communications with Malcolm X, with Muhammad Ali, and also with Minister Farrakhan. All of them were on the same page about the religion becoming one, under the true Islam, though Farrakhan balked at the time, and only recently has come to terms with true Islam, but maintains his respect for the work that was done by the Hon. Elijah Muhammad and the Nation.

Thereafter, my father took me with him when he visited Elijah in Chicago. Elijah Muhammad was a quiet man, his voice was gentle and he spoke with a high-pitched voice. He was a man who knew how to listen and learn. He listened a lot and if he wanted to learn something, he'd ask a question. I remember one day we arrived on a prayer day. Elijah was going to lead the prayer in the wrong way. My father never hesitated; he said out loud, "No, that is not the way. Let me show you how you do it." Rather than raising a protest, Elijah Muhammad let my father lead the prayer and thereafter asked my father to come to teach him the proper way to do and to lead the prayer. My father and I were both light-skinned people of Arab extraction, not dark like the Saudis or Yemenis, and Elijah had a golden-colored skin—but the color of our skin never made a difference when we went to the temple of Elijah in Chicago—though I do remember one time hearing Minister Farrakhan's "A White Man's Heaven is a Black Man's Hell" being played and I wondered where that put me and others of light skin.

Later, in 1967, when more and more of Elijah's people had come to true Islam, the relationship with Elijah stayed strong. At this point,

Elijah was being hounded by the federal government for tax evasion and other alleged offenses. My father then was killed in October 1967, just about the time that the solidity between the Nation and orthodox Islam was coming to full fruition. My father had built a mosque in Gary, Indiana, Mosque Al-Ameen, and hundreds of former Nation members would come by bus, under the aegis of Dr. Jamil Diab, to pray at the mosque on Sundays. Dr. Diab was also a big real estate magnate in Chicago at the time, and had many friends in the Nation, as well as having Elijah's two sons as students in Arabic and Islamic studies. From what my father's cousin, who was a major homicide detective from Detroit, said, my father was most likely killed by a government operative because the government did not want the Nation and orthodox Islam to come together. It was also strange because at about that same time, Dr. Diab left his lucrative real estate business in Chicago, gave up his leadership in the Muslim community, and suddenly moved to Phoenix, Arizona. Later, when I saw him in Phoenix, I asked him why he moved so soon after my father's assassination. He simply said he could not speak about it, but that it had been best for him to move out of Chicago.

As time has gone on, it has become apparent that some in the U.S. government have planned to make Islam the enemy for some time. In that era, Islam was under attack, both the 'Black Muslims' and those who consorted with them in the orthodox community. Also, many of the Christian black leaders were enlisted to speak against the Nation and Islam; unfortunately, the same thing is true today.

The government was afraid of an alliance between international Muslims and African Americans in the U.S. who were organized, disciplined, and financially settled, and with increasing converts. They realized that this could be a huge powerhouse movement. At the same time, the Zionists of Israel were against Elijah Muhammad; they saw him as an enemy, and Muhammad Ali as well, because they both spoke out for Palestinian rights and against Israeli aggression in Palestine.

Muhammad Ali respected what Elijah had done for the black community. He also saw that Elijah had created a vertically integrated

business plan, from having farms in the South, to trucks to haul produce to Chicago, to bakeries, stores, and apartments where consumers
could consume the goods raised and baked by the Nation's people.
Elijah was leading black people out of slavery and out of oppression
long before Martin Luther King, Jr. came on the scene, but as we all
know, he is overlooked, just as Muhammad Ali's social and political
stands are erased from history books and never mentioned in the
media when discussing his life.

Going back to Elijah, he claimed he had been taught by Fard
Muhammad, a Muslim of Middle Eastern descent. The Fard
Muhammad that went into prison did not look like the same man
who came out, years later. Thus, it is difficult to say what happened to
the real Fard Muhammad or if he'd changed that much. In any case,
Elijah said that Fard told him that the races should be in conflict,
and that the "white man was the devil." By this, Elijah meant the
Europeans. So, it is possible that Fard had developed such a hatred
for the power people, who were European, that he helped lead Elijah
to this position as well. But, in his personal life, Elijah distinguished
between "white" as European, and all others were "people of color,
or black." He even carried this into his newspapers. Gamal Abdel
Nasser, whose skin was a dark gold color, appeared to be black in
Elijah's newspapers—another example of his relationship and vision
of all others than Europeans being "black."

Some of this went into Malcolm and then Muhammad Ali, but
as they both grew, they knew this was not Islam and this did not
make sense; that people were people, and all colors had some good
people and some bad people, and that one had to judge each person
by his behavior.

I met Muhammad Ali at a banquet after my father was killed. I
had spoken about Islam and the mosque my father built. A friend
asked me if I'd ever met Muhammad Ali. I said, "No." He said that
Muhammad Ali wanted to meet me because he'd heard about my
father and me. We met and he asked me where I was going after the
banquet. I said I was going home. He said, "No, come with me, I'm
going to see Oscar Brown, Jr., over at the Memorial Auditorium. He

wants to meet you as well and wants me to hear some young kids sing, he says they are really good."

So we took off for Memorial Auditorium, Muhammad walking fast, and me having to run to keep up with his pace. When we got to the auditorium, Oscar said, "You've got to hear these five brothers sing, they blew the competition away." Muhammad Ali and I listened; they were good. I asked, "Who are they?" Oscar said, "They call themselves The Jackson Five, and they are gonna make it big someday!"

CHAPTER 8

While Elijah Muhammad is the most complex figure who has participated in the Ali story, the most controversial figure in my book is Yolanda Ali, Ali's fourth and present wife, and the most misunderstood is Sonny Liston. For some she is an opportunist, a manipulator, and someone who has put an ailing ex-champion up for sale in order to aggrandize herself and to make money. To others, she saved Ali's life. His oldest friend, Ed Hughes, complained to me that she had not only kept Ali away from his friends but at one point kept him away from his son.

When I interviewed his brother, Rahaman, he praised her, but in his private conversation with Ed Hughes on the way to my interview with him, I overheard that there were tensions between Rahaman and Yolanda. His criticism of Yolanda Ali was made public in 2013. He accused his sister-in-law of elder abuse of the champion but a day later denied the story that was carried by London's *Daily Mail*. According to a site called *Wave News*, "Unfortunately, Rahaman Ali was led astray in his interviews with less than reputable publications," said Bob Gunnell, the Ali family spokesman. "The Ali family is disappointed in the sensational journalism that printed these false stories. Rest assured that Muhammad is doing great." Dr. Abraham Lieberman, physician of Ali for twenty-five years, sees him professionally every other week. "If I had Parkinson's, I would wish I was cared for as well as Muhammad," said Lieberman. "I believe he gets excellent care."

Dr. Mahlon Delong, professor of neurology at Emory University Medical Center, said, "We have been treating Muhammad since 1994 and there is no basis to these allegations."

Though the Ali spokespersons were successful in squelching Rahaman's outburst, the grievances of Muhammad Ali's son, Muhammad Ali, Jr., were not as easily silenced. Ed Hughes had told me in 2006 that Yolanda refused to take Muhammad Ali, Jr.'s phone calls.

On January 26, 2014, the son's problems with Yolanda went viral. Muhammad Ali, Jr. was quoted as saying:

"It's like I'm cursed. My life is cursed. I thought about even changing my name to Malik Islam and running away and starting a new life again. But my children stopped me. I want to teach them and give them the discipline I never got."

While Ali was champion of the world at age 22 and amassed a fortune of well over $100 million, his son is living off food stamps. Driving with a reporter to his local cafe for breakfast, he points excitedly at a charity shelter and says it's his savior.

"I go there when I ain't got no food in the crib or the kids need shoes and clothes," he says.

"My life now is crap. I live in a s–t area, a house I don't own. I survive off handouts and food stamps. I've tried for a job, but there's no hiring. I go on the Internet, but I've never been taught how to use it, so it always messes up. I'm stuck. If my father was still around and was coherent, he'd help me. But that's not the case, is it?

"Now when you see him, his hands shake and his face is cold. His expressions are numb. It isn't him. He had always been talkative, joking around, the soul of the party. Now he doesn't do any of that. It's like night and day right now," Muhammad Jr. says. "Sometimes, you look at things and ask: 'Did it really happen? Did he box like that? Did he talk like that?'"

Ali Jr. blames the breakdown in their relationship on Lonnie, his father's fourth wife. This isn't the first time Lonnie, whom Ali married in 1986, has been accused of tearing the family apart. Ali Sr.'s brother, Rahman, spoke out last year about not being able to see his brother and the treatment his sibling was receiving.

Muhammad Jr. says: "He slipped out my life the moment he got married to Lonnie. The trips to see me stopped immediately. She once said that they couldn't afford to come and see me. How can a man who's well respected in the world, bigger than Elvis, with all the money he's made, not afford to travel?"

Lonnie, who has power of attorney, has made it clear Ali Jr. is not welcome, he says. When he phoned his father on Ali Sr.'s birthday, Jan. 17, no one answered. ("Muhammad Ali's son shut off from dad, living in poverty," *New York Post*, January 26, 2014)

Lonnie launched her rescue mission even before Ali and his third wife, Veronica, were divorced. Veronica, according to her critics, didn't seem to be devoted to the welfare of her husband. To some, she was a showpiece and the woman about whom his second wife, Khalilah, still carries a grudge. After all, the ex-champion's carrying-on with Veronica, while still married to Khalilah, subjected her to international humiliation. For Khalilah, whom I interviewed on a cold day in Chicago, Veronica was little more than a call girl, who cared little about the champion. Veronica was one of those who received a letter from Ali's doctor, Ferdie Pacheco, warning about Ali's deteriorating health. She expressed no concern and was among those who encouraged him to fight on even after he fought his last two fights suffering from brain damage, according to his late trainer, Angelo Dundee.

Before leaving for Chicago, I received a call from Khalilah Muhammad, whom I had been seeking for some time, in connection with the book. She was living in Chicago and was available for an interview. This was a further inducement for me to attend the reunion of MacArthur Fellows and an opportunity to observe a Midwest fall, having lived for many years in California where, as the nineteenth-century poet Robert Burgess put it, "seasons unseen pass."

Unlike Khalilah, who tolerated Ali's promiscuity because she was so devoted to him, Sonji, Ali's first wife, defied the restrictive rules placed on women by men in the NOI's hierarchy. A NOI insider told me that originally the NOI had assigned Sonji to keep an eye on Ali, and when she revealed this plan to him, her days as his wife were numbered. Elijah Muhammad called her a disgrace to Muslims all over the world. The next day I took time out from the proceedings to drive into Chicago to interview Mrs. Ali. It was twenty-one degrees Fahrenheit.

My driver was a young man named Lukas who lives in Chicago when he's not at home in Poland. (Those who believe that we now live in a "post-ethnic" America, where all groups except blacks swim comfortably in "the Anglo Saxon" mainstream, should come to Chicago, where one motors through a series of ethnic neighborhoods.) We began a conversation, and when I told him the purpose of my trip, such is the ex-champ's fame that he became excited at the prospect of meeting Ali's former wife. I introduced him to her after Mrs. Ali and I had chicken soup at a Guatemalan restaurant.

She didn't look much different from her 1960s photos. Tall and with a queenly stride, she walked across the parking lot at McDonald's to greet me. She was wearing a grey trench coat over a dress that she had made herself. She said that the champ still hits on her whenever they meet.

I had promised her a sum of money for the interview. She said right off, "I want to get the money out of the way. I'm doing you a favor." She said that she usually charges more for interviews.

Ishmael Reed: [I asked Khalilah when she joined the Nation.]
Khalilah Ali: I didn't join the Nation; I was born into it. My father was Elijah Muhammad's right-hand man, Lt. Raymond.

IR: When was the last time you saw Muhammad?
KA: I last saw Muhammad in July, when he visited his children.

IR: [She shared some strong opinions about the movie *Ali*.]
KA: I disapproved of the movie *Ali* and I sued them too. First of all they didn't get my permission and second they didn't include everything that they should have included. He didn't spurn Malcolm like they had in the movie. They had a good relationship. I can't say what happened in that scene where Ali ridicules Malcolm, but every time

I saw them together they had a good relationship. I knew Malcolm before Ali came around. I was a young girl when I first met Malcolm. I was part of Elijah Muhammad's security. One of his bodyguards. I used to teach our sisters self-defense.

IR: Why did Bingham and the rest of the entourage allow Ali to fight those last two fights? Ferdie Pacheco said that he sent out letters to those in his camp and his then-wife, Veronica, warning of the health consequences of Ali's continuing to fight.

KA: They were out for the money. They didn't care. Veronica was a call girl. She was with Ali in Zaïre.

IR: Was the original purpose for her trip to service Foreman?

KA: I helped to get everybody to Zaïre. I got their passports. Even Ali's women. His girlfriends. I helped them to get there. I predicted that he would win. I had a dream and in the dream Ali won. I told him that if he lost, I would kick his ass myself, right there on "Wide Wide World of Sports." He didn't like that. I'm a karate champion and I can hurt him. I hurt him once. As long as he's outside the ring I can get him.

IR: [I asked her the details of the fight where she hurt him. She said that was for her book and that she was keeping it to herself.]

KA: That one I can't tell. But it was a humdinger. I told him that a karate champion can beat a boxer but he didn't believe me. So he went to Japan and suffered blood clots in his leg after fighting this wrestler [Antonio Inoki]. He wasn't even a karate fighter.

IR: [I asked her about Ali's father, Cash.]

KA: He was the sweetest guy. A comical guy. He could draw art. He did murals of Jesus in the church. This guy was talented. He supported his family. He was sharp as a tack, 24/7. He was fly. He attracted women and he could sing, "I Did It My Way."

IR: Hauser said that he beat up Odessa.

KA: He'd get to drinking [and then] he'd do some crazy stuff. He pulled a gun on Ali one time. They had an argument about Muhammad being Muslim. For Cash, it was Muslim this and Muslim that. He accused the Muslims of taking Ali's money. He took the gun, and told Ali, "I'll take you out of here" and the gun fell apart. [Laughter] Ali told his father, "You crazy."

IR: Her defenders say that his present wife, Lonnie, has been good for Ali.

KA: Lonnie is not a nice person. I didn't like what I saw last time I saw him. He was doing fine. He was talking and he was laughing. He's always in good spirits when he's around me. Lonnie said, "Okay, time for his medicine!" And after she gave him the medicine, he started shaking. I asked her what she gave him.

Lonnie is out to get what Lonnie wants. She's not a Muslim, either. I'm the only Muslim woman that Ali ever married. All of those other women he married—none of them was a Muslim.

They all pretended to be Muslims as part of a hoax to get Ali. A pretend thing. Lonnie is a Christian. She celebrates Christmas every year. The fact of it is—she ain't no Muslim. She used to take care of her father, so she knows about medicine. I think that she is drugging Ali in a way so that he cannot function. Because when he is not drugged, Ali will tell you what to do. He's smart. When she gives him the drugs, it tones him down so that he does what she wants him to do. It scared me once. It was in the 1980s when my daughter graduated from college. I said, "Look May May, [speaking here about Ali's oldest child, his daughter Maryam by his wife Belinda, using her nickname], Lonnie is giving Ali drugs." I said it because I wanted it to get back to Lonnie. She told May May that I shouldn't say that because if I continued she would get a lawyer to sue me. I told May May to tell her to come on and let's do it. I'd go over there, stick a needle into Ali's arm, draw some blood and verify it. I didn't hear no more from her. I heard no more mouth from her. I know what I'm talking about because I know Ali. Ali was my soul mate. I feel everything that he feels. And I know what she's doing to him. I can put my life on it. That's the truth. And I dare her to challenge me on it.

IR: [I asked Khalilah whether there was tension between Laila and Lonnie. (Laila is Ali's daughter from his third wife, Veronica Porsche.) Laila said his condition was bad and Lonnie rebuked her in the press.]
KA: I was married to him when Laila was born. He had children by other women when he was still married to me.

IR: What about the rumor spread by those whom I call The Ali Scribes that the Nation took all of his money?
KA: You believe that? Elijah Muhammad gave him money so that he could continue. I supported him with my college money for three years. When I married him he didn't have any money. My father gave him some money. My father was against my marrying him.

IR: Is there a feud between Ali and Farrakhan?
KA: Farrakhan is like Father Divine. He's in it for the money. That's all there is to it. I ain't going to be lying to you. That's the way it is. 'Cause he's not teaching Islam; he's teaching economics and that's good. I know him like an uncle. And I love him.

IR: What about the charge that Wallace seized control of the Nation?
KA: He was scheduled to take over and that's it. He didn't have to grab it. Allah gave it to him. "A son will come and teach you the right way" was one of Elijah Muhammad's last statements. He was talking about Wallace. It was understood.

IR: One of the old-timers who was with Elijah said that Ali is suffering from a curse delivered to him by Elijah from beyond the grave for his not giving up the name "Muhammad Ali" after Elijah had suspended him.
KA: The curse that was put on Muhammad Ali was for what he did to us. God don't like ugly. As much as I did for him and he turned his back on me and started acting crazy. He put it on himself. It didn't

have anything to do with Elijah Muhammad. Women destroyed his career.

None of the Parkinson's came from boxing. Katherine Hepburn had Parkinson's and she wasn't a boxer. He turned his back on the people who loved him. His family. One day, he's not going to be able to talk or walk. I was with him once when he was talking to Joe Louis and Joe Louis was kind of old and couldn't think and Ali started laughing at him; that's when I knew this would happen to him. It was in Las Vegas and I told him that "Joe Louis opened the door for people like you."

IR: What's your theory of why Sonny Liston was murdered?

KA: Sonny Liston was murdered because he was hired to knock out Ali and he couldn't. In order to knock something out you have to have something to hit. Ali trained running backwards and that's why he could fight moving backwards.

IR: What are your thoughts about Sonji Clay?

KA: She was set up by Elijah Muhammad to keep Ali from running in the streets. They paid Sonji to do that. She was good at what she did; she was a professional. She told me that's what she did.

She was a sweet, clean, and nice woman. She said that she really didn't want to marry Ali, but the Nation gave her the money. I called her the black Elizabeth Taylor. She did her eyebrows like Elizabeth Taylor. She had to do what she had to do. She told him that she wasn't going to put on no long dress and she told him that before he objected to her wearing short dresses. She told Ali that she'd continue to be what she wanted to be and see whom she wanted to see.

IR: How is Ali as a parent?

KA: He's always been a good father. He loves kids.

IR: What happened in Manila?

KA: He introduced Veronica as his wife in Manila. I don't know what he was smoking because he told me to come down there. Told me to bring the family. That hurt me bad. Veronica was a call girl. She didn't care anything about him. He was getting his ass kicked in one fight and she was somewhere getting her hair done. She had an affair with John Travolta. She took my house here in Chicago, the house he bought me. It was located on Woodlawn. It had thirty-two rooms. I designed the rooms to represent different cultures, including Asian and Greek. He begged me to stay. Every once in a while he asks me to come back, and I say I can't do that.

Ali is easily manipulated. He promised that he wasn't going to marry Lonnie. She drags him all over the world for her sake. She wants to have her legacy. When I was at my mother's house in July, two years ago, he came in dressed in a one-hundred-percent woolen suit that I had made for him. I told him that he couldn't come over because he was married. He said, [imitating his voice] "I came over to see whether we can get back together."

He has to sneak to find me. During this year's Ramadan [2006] at The Muslim Cultural Center, he came over looking for me. Kept asking, "Is Khalilah here, is Khalilah here?" He was told that I had been there but I had left.

If he stopped taking that medicine he'd be able to talk and his mind would be straightened out. I was in California three years ago doing something for AT&T where I work. I got a call from a white guy who told me that Ali was in the Sportsman's bar selling shorts with his name on them. I told him to go to the Sportsman's bar, and have Ali call me on his cell phone. He called me on the phone and asked where I was. He said, "Come to me."

I said, "Okay I'm coming over there right now." So I went on over there and he was so excited. He saw me and I started whispering and talking to him; he started doing magic tricks. The white guy said, "Would you accompany us on the tour please, because he ain't acted like this since the tour began. Please, I'll pay you." I said, "This guy is a married man, I can't do that." The white guy kept saying, "Damn, I wish you could go. Damn, I wish you could go." He said, "We have to make another stop in California. Can you just go there with us?" I said, "Okay. I'll go there." Ali started laughing. He came out of his condition like it was nothing and it shocked me. He says, "You know I fucked up. You know I messed up."

I said, "Everybody makes mistakes."

He said, "We can get back together."

I said, "We can't do that." [laughter] She's trying to kill him so that she can take over everything.

IR: [I asked why he turned so right wing, supporting Ronald Reagan and Orrin Hatch.]

KA: That's her, not him.

IR: I was told that there were thirteen out-of-wedlock children by Ali.

KA: There are three. They were born when I was still married to him.

IR: [I asked about the family sojourn in Cherry Hill, New Jersey.]

KA: We were given a house by Major Coxson, a Philadelphia gangster. It was because of me that he gave the house for nothing. He had a beautiful wife and was friends with Cash. I told Major Coxson that we'd pay him back when the champ fought again.

[The house was up for sale in 2006; the real estate company advertised it as follows:

Consisting of "10,000-square-foot-luxury, the asking price, 1.4 million dollar home, a gated home situated on two acres of wooded land" and was described by the realtor as "including a swimming pool and two tennis courts. On one level all the marble floors are heated for those chilly Northern mornings. The master bedroom is an elegant space accented by mirrors that tile the ceiling and add to the openness of the room. This knockout property has a total of four bedrooms."

Muhammad and Khalilah and their children lived here for three years.]

KA: I dreamed about Coxson's murder before it happened. I don't consider myself a psychic; I'm just blessed with God's intuition. I'd been with his family. We went shopping together. I was with them all the time. One Wednesday I dreamed of a circus and there was a man in a blue suit, one of two men on a seesaw.

One man went up, and when the man in the blue suit came down he hit and broke his back and, on the ground, firecrackers went off. After the dream, I went straight over to Major Coxson's house and asked had anything happened and I told his wife about my dream. I asked them what they would do were an intruder to burst into the house. His wife said she'd hide under the bed. I told her that this was wrong and that she should go outside and remain there. Then the conversation got around to eating pork. He was killed that Friday. Shot five times in the head. He was wearing blue pajamas. That shocked me.

IR: What were the circumstances surrounding Elijah Muhammad's suspension of Ali?

KA: Elijah Muhammad suspended Ali because Ali said he was fighting for money. And Muslims are proud people and we don't do sports for money. And if you embarrass Muslims in the press we will put you out.

CHAPTER 9

The Break Between the Prophet and his Disciple

At first, believing that Liston would defeat Ali, Elijah Muhammad was reluctant to give Ali the NOI imprimatur, but after the upset, which ranks with Max Schmeling's upset of Joe Louis, Elijah Muhammad embraced the boxer and assigned Herbert Muhammad to protect him. When Ali returned to the ring, however, Elijah Muhammad gave his reasons for barring Ali from the Nation in *Muhammad Speaks* newspaper in April 1969:

> Mr. Muhammad Ali (Cassius Clay) decided to go with the white man as soon as he found that they had deferred him from going to the Army. This act only shows that the world of sport and play was in the heart of Mr. Muhammad Ali (Cassius Clay) all the time and that he wanted to make money real fast. Holy Quran Chapter 29:64.
>
> Ever since he was a little boy, he had enjoyed fighting his Black brother and sometimes white people, in the ring for the joy of the white man. He knew that they were gambling on his skill as a fighter.
>
> Mr. Muhammad Ali (Cassius Clay), when he crossed over the rope to fight his opponent, knew that he had many people sitting down on the sidelines and all over the country and the world, betting on him to whip his opponent.
>
> An accidental blow could be fatal to his opponent. People are being killed in the ring. How would Mr. Muhammad Ali (Cassius Clay) feel, if he should kill his own brother, for the sake of a "leetle money."
>
> He is asking them to let him come back for the sake of a "leetle money"... going, as though to say that "I was over here and could not get a 'leetle money,' so let me come over there." He was trying to make

the teachings a lie, when Allah (God) cannot lie. He has the power to make that which He says come to pass.

Mr. Muhammad Ali (Cassius Clay) did such a foolish thing, by going back into the ring and wants me to keep him in the pulpit too. Bible Luke: 9:62 tells us that no man who deserts the pulpit for the sake of the world is fit for the kingdom of God. Bible Matthew: 6:24 means that he wants to serve Allah (God) says in His Holy Quran that you cannot serve two gods and be honest with both for you do not have two hearts. Since you have only one heart, then you can only serve one God.

I gave him the Muslim name Muhammad Ali and removed the slave name, Cassius Clay. This made him famous all over the world. In Asia, the Muslim world recognized him to the highest, but no more when they find that he is still Cassius Clay, everywhere. (Muhammad, Elijah, "Clarification of Action Taken Against Muhammad Ali's Action," *Muhammad Speaks Newspaper, April 11, 1969*)

When Wallace Muhammad became leader of the NOI, he gave amnesty to those who had been cast out of the organization. That included Muhammad Ali. Herbert Muhammad however, continued to manage Ali, and though some consider Herbert Muhammad to have been Ali's chief "blood sucker," others say that Herbert Muhammad did not share his father's opinion of whites.

After describing his relationship with Herbert Muhammad as "courteous," Ferdie Pacheco, Ali's former doctor, wrote that toward the end, "Herbert was being pulled in many directions by different men," and felt that "Herbert would be very happy if I disappeared."

Agieb Bilal says that Pacheco was asked to leave for making remarks about Ali's sexual habits. Pacheco called Ali a "pelvic missionary."

Khalilah gives herself credit for bringing Ali back:

When Malcolm commented on the death of Kennedy, he was suspended. We don't praise the death of people, and when you do, we have to put you out. When they put him out they put me out too, because I was married to him. That hurt. That story is in my book. Elijah Muhammad brought Ali back in because of me. I brought him back in.

Did Elijah Muhammad exploit Ali financially, a claim made by some of Ali's biographers? Pacheco agrees with Khalilah. He wrote, "No; I don't think Ali was taken advantage of. Herbert earned his money. He made it the hard way... Ali always presented major problems, on a daily basis, and Herbert was always there to help solve them."

Following our interview, Khalilah had to get back to work. I took some photos of her and a passerby took photos of the two of us.

I introduced her to Lukas, the young Polish cab driver. He was so excited that he could hardly speak. "Nobody in Poland, or my Chicago friends, will believe that I met Muhammad's former wife," Lukas said, and sure enough his phone rang and he told one of his friends about the encounter and the friend didn't believe him.

The June 2014 issue of *Modern Maturity*, a magazine published by the AARP (American Association of Retired People), offered a different picture of Yolanda Ali than the one offered by his second wife, Khalilah Muhammad. The story, written by Jon Saraceno, was based upon his visit to Ali's home in Paradise Valley, Arizona. It was the kind of positive portrait of which Yolanda would approve. Saraceno wrote, "The Ali caregiving story is about love, companionship and devotion."

Lonnie was described as "a smart, tough, resilient woman serving as the voice, guiding light and conscience for an all-but-silenced superstar athlete and civil rights activist." Nothing was mentioned about her treatment of Muhammad Ali, Jr.

As for his perceived role as a civil rights activist, Muhammad Ali endorsed Ronald Reagan for president and accepted a medal from George Bush. Many would say that both presidents are responsible for rolling back decades of civil rights progress. The article did reveal, however, the condition of Ali's health. He needs a breathing machine, occasionally. There was an operation for spinal stenosis in 2005. In 2013, there was an operation on Ali's vocal cords, "which had become thin and brittle."

Writer Stanley Crouch doesn't hold the ex-Champion in very high esteem. He has written book after book about blacks complaining about their victimization. I would later interview Crouch, a street fighter himself, who, a few months after the interview, made the news for slapping critic Dave Peck at the Tartine, a restaurant in Greenwich Village.

I thought of Crouch's description of the three phases of Ali's career: The Wild Bear, the Circus Bear, and the Teddy Bear. At the high school in Houston, Ali was the Teddy Bear. The Teddy Bear image was one that journalist Jack Newfield would support. Newfield agreed with Ashley Shacklett and Sergio Morales that Ali's wife, Lonnie, was doing all of his talking. He said that Ali had become little more than a commodity manipulated by his wife and agent, and that she was refusing support for Ali's brother, Rahaman, who he said was homeless.

Mark Kram described Lonnie's treatment of a daughter by one of Ali's "wives." He gave the child, whose mother and the daughter he had left in poverty, a championship belt. Lonnie followed the child to the hotel lobby and asked for the belt to be returned so that she could send it to the Smithsonian.

Others whom I interviewed dismissed these rumors, saying that his wife, Lonnie, was devoted to him and had stuck with him through his failing health. David Kindred, writing for *Sporting News*, said that without Lonnie's intervention, Ali might be dead or penniless. She, according to this version, expelled the hangers-on from the Ali camp and is credited with removing Ali from the clutches of Herbert Muhammad. As for Rahaman, he showed up on June 11, 2005 at a Laila Ali fight wearing a splendid white suit, but when I posed for a photo with him at the Ali Gala in Louisville, I detected some decline in his cognitive ability as well. Later, when I interviewed him in Louisville, he told me that he had suffered a slight stroke. Cash Clay, his father, told Ed Hughes, shortly before he died, "Both my boys are sick." In 2013, Rahaman was reported to be living on welfare and handouts.

Whatever can be said about Yolanda Ali, the champion outlived some of her critics. Indeed, so far he has outlived some of those whom I interviewed for this book, including individuals who were concerned about his health. Joe Frazier said of Ali's condition: "Clay always mocked me—like I was the dummy. Gettin' hit in the head.

Now look at him: He can hardly talk and he's still out there trying to make noise." Muhammad Ali attended the ex-champion's funeral.

Considering the shape that the champion was in when Yolanda sought to rescue him, with the permission of his then-wife Veronica, the heavy-handed methods that Yolanda has used might be justified. At the time that Yolanda launched her rescue mission, Ali's legs had gone, the reflexes had gone, and the friends, an entourage of over thirty, had left. Some, like Bundini Brown, who had (according to some) a bad influence on the champion, and might have introduced him to drugs, had died. His spiritual advisor, Luis Serra, was dead. His cook, Lana Shabbaz, was dead. His first wife, Sonji, was dead. Praised by The Ali Scribes, who were brought up as Christians, cast aside because she wouldn't conform to what Muslim doctrine required of women, she had become a follower of Minister Louis Farrakhan before she died. Jimmy Young, who (according to some) beat him, had died.

The man whom he regarded as a deity, Elijah Muhammad, had died, and his former mentor, the man whom he had betrayed, Malcolm X, had been assassinated years before. Others had left after the champ's funds had run out. His third wife, Veronica, a showpiece, had gone, giving him only twenty-four hours to move his things out of their Los Angeles mansion. She got fed up with his many affairs, but according to his second wife, Khalilah, she had affairs herself. His manager, Herbert Muhammad, had been cast aside by Yolanda Ali, his fourth and present wife. Some say that Herbert Muhammad exploited the champion. Herbert Muhammad could have asked the champion to listen to Teddy Brenner, who booked fights at Madison Square Garden. He refused to book any more of Ali's fights after watching him take some hard blows from Ernie Shavers and witnessing his slurring of speech in a September 1977 fight, which Ali would win. Instead, Herbert booked Ali to fight Olympian Leon Spinks. Herbert thought that this would be an easy fight. Others told me a different story. Herbert Muhammad turned down an interview with me on the grounds that he was writing his own book. He died about a year after our phone conversation.

His trainer, Angelo Dundee, also died. The Ali Scribes complain about how Dundee was held under suspicion by members of Ali's entourage who belonged to the Nation of Islam. Perhaps their suspicions were warranted. On February 1, 2013, he was exposed as an FBI informant whose assignment was to keep tabs on those members who belonged to the Nation of Islam ("Ali's Trainer Told FBI Of Boxer's Islam Tie; Angelo Dundee met with agents before 1964 title bout," *The Smoking Gun,* February 1, 2013).

This kind of spying on members of the Islamic faith continued in the 2000s under the administration of New York Mayor Michael Bloomberg, considered by some progressives to be a moderate. During his reign and that of his predecessor, Mayor Rudy Giuliani, hundreds of thousands of black and Hispanic men were stopped and frisked. It was reported in the May 11, 2014 edition of *The New York Times* that the "New York Police Recruit Muslims to be Informers: Antiterror Unit Urges People to Eavesdrop at Their Mosques." Muslims complained about being asked by the NYPD to spy on other Muslims.

Perhaps, regardless of his bad health, it is no surprise that Ali endured as long as he had. Every time his critics thought that Muhammad Ali was down for the count, they had underestimated him. The critics who thought that he had no chance against Sonny Liston and George Foreman forgot that every time Ali got knocked down by Chuck Wepner, Henry Cooper, and Joe Frazier, he got back up. By the summer of 2005, Ali, the amateur magician, had managed to pull the rabbit out of the hat again. He had lost his body but his mind and soul were intact.

As a result of Yolanda Ali's intervention, Ali had become one of the most adored persons on the planet. When the Discovery channel polled its viewers for the greatest American, Ronald Reagan came in first, and Abraham Lincoln was second. Oprah Winfrey placed ninth. Muhammad Ali placed twenty-first, outpolling former presidents, scientists, inventors, artists, and astronauts.

ESPN voted Muhammad Ali the second greatest athlete of the twentieth century. Former HBO boxing commentator Larry Merchant, whose comments about black boxers were among the most belittling and who seemed to believe that boxing should be a sport along the lines of wrestling, one without artistry or skills—he would have not found Jack Johnson good HBO material because the champion had a habit of clinching—remembers Ali fondly as someone whose trash-talking was delivered with a smile and not like the hip hop generation's boxer, Floyd Mayweather, who flashes ice, drives a Bentley, and likes strip clubs. Like many white men of his class, Merchant couldn't bring himself to believe that the police often told lies about Sonny Liston.

After defeating Victor Cruz in September of 2011, Mayweather had had enough of Larry Merchant needling him about ducking tough opponents. Mayweather had at the time fought some future boxing Hall of Famers, and said to Merchant on live television, "You ain't shit." Of course, the Jim Crow boxing fraternity took Merchant's side. Contrast Larry Merchant's often mean-spirited comments about black boxers like Roy Jones, Jr. and Mayweather with those made by Jack London about Jack Johnson:

> There is nothing beary or primitive about this man Johnson. He is alive and quivering, every nerve fiber in his body, and brain. Withal that is hidden so artfully or naturally under that poise of facetious calm of his. He is a marvel of sensitiveness, sensibility, and perceptiveness. He has the perfect mechanism of mind and body. His mind works like chain lightning and his body obeys with equal swiftness.

CHAPTER 10

During this feel-good era about the champion, one almost forgets the vicious remarks from sports writers like Jimmy Cannon when Ali announced that he'd become a Muslim. Or Jimmy Breslin, who called him a "Muslim and a bedbug." Ali was forgotten and forgiven during the summer of Ali's resurrection.

He was sent to Tokyo to seek support for New York to be the location of the 2012 Olympics. London was chosen. But the next day, after the bombs were detonated at three London subway stops and on a double-decker bus, the "civilized" world was outraged by this "savagery," and white men and women were rushed on television to explain the Muslim mind. Those who took responsibility for the attacks said that they did it because the British were carrying on a war in Afghanistan and Iraq.

Christiane Amanpour assured the CNN audience that Muslims around the world were outraged by the attacks, but Christians around the world were not called upon to condemn the killing of hundreds of thousands of citizens, killed and wounded as a result of United States' unprovoked assault on Afghanistan and Iraq, when most of the hijackers came from Saudi Arabia. All of this was dismissed as "collateral damage." The American invasion of Fallujah left the city nearly destroyed and hundreds of Iraqis dead. They were searching for "insurgents" but the "insurgents" had left town when tipped off that the Americans were about to arrive.

Rather than attempting to sort out the causes of such terror attacks, the perpetrators were called "savages," presumably because they hadn't learned the "civilized" way of delivering bombs, napalm, or drones. Like the "insurgents" who were dismissed as lunatics and radicals by the media, none of the sports writers took the time to comprehend why Nation of Islam leader Elijah Muhammad, an autodidactic intellectual, whose "formal" education ended at the fourth grade, was able to attract college students, professional people, and athletes like Muhammad Ali to his organization. If they had, they would have discovered that Elijah Muhammad's teachings were in the American grain, even the racism, and after years of persecution by the government, which hounded both him and Muhammad Ali, he was able to announce on an edition of the television show, *The Black Journal*, that when he went to Washington he was "treated like a prince." President Richard Nixon even offered the NOI a deal, which was refused.

And now, his once-protégé, Ali, could say the same thing. In June 2005, Muhammad Ali, a man who was bitterly condemned for avoiding military service, was presented with the Medal of Freedom from then-President George W. Bush, the man who played golf while New Orleans drowned, to the horror of many of Ali's admirers. The man who ordered the attack on a Muslim country, even though the 9/11 hi-jackers were Saudi. Some have regarded this act as the greatest foreign policy error in American history and one for which American taxpayers continue to pay for in blood and treasure. George Bush's support among black voters was two percent. This was a president who, according to Jesse Jackson, was pushing back the gains made during the Civil Rights revolution. By refusing this honor, some say, Ali could have made a heroic gesture, equal to that of his defying the Selective Service. Instead of following Eartha Kitt's example, using the occasion to chastise a president for the mounting civilian and army casualties precipitated in a questionable war, he chose to engage in playful teddy bear-type antics with the president. His wife, Lonnie, wearing street clothes instead of the customary Muslim garb, might also have offended Muslims, but Jeanne Shakir, a Louisville activist to whom Ali once proposed marriage, said that her style of clothing was Koranic.

Andy Warhol's unique color Polaroid print of Muhammad Ali, that was taken in 1977 and signed on the front in red ink by Muhammad Ali, sold for twice as much as requested from Christie's Rockefeller Center June 2006 auction. And finally, Ali, the man who criticized other celebrities and athletes for taking "white money," took fifty million dollars of "white money" in exchange for eighty percent of his image. Furthermore, the person who condemned whiskey had lent his name to the Ali Center, whose board of directors' head was a whiskey heiress.

So many idolizing words have been written about Ali, not only by his admirers but also his detractors, though none have answered the question: how did a man so seriously flawed become, in the words of *Oakland Tribune* sports writer Monte Poole, the most adored figure on the planet? (At that moment, it was the Philadelphia Eagles' Terrell Owens, who was the most despised.) Ali was a man who mistreated and battered women, was a sexual hypocrite, criticized entertainers and fellow athletes for engaging in interracial relationships while conducting at least one himself; a man who justified the assault by members of the Nation of Islam on fellow Muslims and entertained dictators—Mobutu and Marcos—who were guilty of inflicting heinous crimes upon citizens of their nations; a man who was a pimp wannabe and a bad father to some of the children whom he sired with unmarried women.

However, boxers mistreating women is nothing new. Both Sugars (Sugar Ray Robinson and Sugar Ray Leonard), beat their wives. So did Mike Tyson. Rocky Marciano, considered a saint by sports writers who have a grudge against black boxers, "was not a 'family man' where his wife and daughter were concerned. As a fighter, he was away from home more often than his profession demanded of him. Subsequent to his leaving the ring, he and [his wife] Barbara moved to Florida, but he was rarely there. The marriage had become an empty shell" (Thomas Hauser, 2011). He told his daughter that she would inherit a lot of money, but in 1969, he died in a plane crash before revealing the money's whereabouts. Left broke, his wife "Mary Ann Marciano was slinging hamburgers at Burger King, and got so hooked on drugs, she was implicated in an armed robbery" (Brady, 2002). His daughter, Mary Anne, was arrested in 1992 for selling cocaine (Larry Keller, *Sun Sentinel*, February 15, 1992).

CHAPTER 11

Though Sonny Liston was said to have been manipulated by members of organized crime, Ali fronted for some unsavory characters during his sojourn in Cherry Hill, New Jersey. Like other bloodsuckers and boxing leeches (for some, Herbert Muhammad and Don King were the head leeches) who took advantage of the champion, they used his good will to assist them in fronting criminal operations. Some of these characters played a role in the massacre of a Washington, D.C. sect to which basketball star Kareem Abdul Jabbar was connected. Others say that the Muslims took advantage of Ali, that they supplied him with a wife, Sonji, who would be their plant. However, when she revealed their sinister methods to Ali, they made him get rid of her. Agieb Bilal, one time a NOI insider, says that she wasn't a party girl or a whore as she has been depicted, and that they made him choose between them and her.

Bilal, who followed Wallace Muhammad after Elijah Muhammad's death, arrived in Chicago an idealist, but then discovered that some of the brothers—even those who were in charge of Elijah Muhammad's security—were engaging in acts that were forbidden by Islam. Others say that Ali's defiance of the draft, the act that endeared him to northeastern liberal writers, who, one could argue, contributed to the myth of Ali's invincibility, was not a matter of free will. They held that he was commanded to do so by his mentor, Elijah Muhammad, whose orders were enforced by the feared Fruit of Islam, young men skilled in the martial arts and described by Truman Gibson of the International Boxing Club as "a rough bunch." Jack Cashill, author of

Sucker Punch, quotes Sugar Ray Robinson, who said that Muhammad Ali was afraid of the NOI enforcers, the Fruit of Islam. This is why he was forced into positions that alienated All American types like Robinson.

Moreover, some say that since he followed Wallace D. Muhammad from the Nation and adopted the Sunni philosophy, the militancy that made him famous had vanished, and that he had become a conservative. (However, given his remarks about the Civil Rights Movement, one could say that, with the exception of his stand on the draft, he was always a conservative.) Not only did he accept a medal from a president who was despised by millions of black Americans, but people point to his support of Ronald Reagan and other right-wingers reported in *The New York Times*, October 26, 1984:

> Since early October, billboards in New York, New Jersey, Pennsylvania, Ohio and Michigan have shown President Reagan throwing a playful punch at the jaw of Muhammad Ali while Joe Frazier and Floyd Patterson look on. The words "We're voting for the man" accompany the scene. The three former heavyweight champions have all endorsed the Republican Presidential ticket and the Reagan-Bush '84 committee is taking advantage of their support.

This was the fighter who, in criticizing popular black entertainers and athletes for their lack of militancy, advocated their joining the Black Panthers if they found the Nation of Islam unacceptable.

This was the fighter that Joe Walker, a former writer for *Muhammad Speaks*, remembered as having aligned himself with a number of radical causes; a fighter who supported the Cuban revolution and met with Castro as late as September 1998.

Their admirers often give some slack to black athletes who make questionable political moves for commercial reasons and sometimes out of ignorance. After all, the Cuban dictator, Fulgencio Batista, entertained Joe Louis. Willie Mays and Bill Russell lent their names to Coors beer, a company owned by Joseph Coors, who has financed the right-wing American Enterprise Institute and, according to Richard Reeves, the Contras. During May 2014, two star basketball players,

Blake Griffin and Chris Paul of the Los Angeles Clippers, gave muted responses when confronted with a racist phone call made by their team owner, Don Sterling. Unlike athletes of the past like Joe Louis, Jackie Robinson, and Juan Carlos, who spoke out against racism, they were the beneficiaries of lucrative commercial deals with State Farm Insurance Company and the auto company, Kia.

Thomas Hauser, the lead Ali Scribe, whose admiration for Ali had become a form of worship, shows his disillusionment with his hero in his book, *The Lost Legacy of Muhammad Ali*. He criticizes the Ali who was resurrected with the lighting of the Olympic torch. Ali, for him, became commercial, became a commodity. For him, the creation of this Ali was done by his spouse, Yolanda, the M.B.A. He writes, "No event crystallized the commercialization of Ali more clearly than his appearance at the New York Stock Exchange on December 31, 1999. The Ali who won hearts in the 1960s could have been expected to celebrate the occasion at a soup kitchen or homeless shelter to draw attention to the plight of the disadvantaged." No longer would Ali be available to lend his name to the causes of the oppressed for whom, in the 1960s, he was, in Hauser's words, "a beacon of hope." Signs of this distance appeared in the mid-2000s when a plea for the champion to refuse the symbolic throwing out of the first baseball at the All-Star Game was ignored.

In July 2004, I spoke to Olawale Olanrewaju, a spokesperson for those who were attempting to contact Ali about boycotting a request that he throw out the first baseball of the season in Houston, a town that played a part in the legend of the GOAT (Greatest Of All Time). He said that he had attempted to contact Ali, but wasn't having success. He'd sent me a press release:

July 13, 2004

PEOPLE FOR JUSTICE CALLS ON MUHAMMAD ALI TO TURN DOWN FIRST PITCH SELECTION FOR THE MAJOR LEAGUE BASEBALL ALL-STAR GAME
 The group known as People for Justice has also asked that Mr. Ali meet with leaders of the group, so that he might become familiar

with the concerns of the community. Mr. Ali has a long history with Houston, Texas having fought and trained here, and being convicted of draft evasion. On June 20, 1967, a jury for the U.S. District Court for the Southern District of Texas, Houston Division, returned a verdict of guilty against Muhammad Ali on the charge of violating the Universal Military Training and Service Act because of his refusal to be inducted. Judge Joe Ingraham sentenced him to a term of 5 years imprisonment and a fine of $10,000.

The community has concerns about our Brother throwing out the first pitch in this game in a city where the team has no Black players and the city's leadership has no respect or concern for the needs of Black or poor people. Minister Robert Muhammad expressed, "Minorities and the poor supported the building of new sports facilities while our people cannot enjoy them and while their concerns on issues that affect them are trivialized by the Mayor and others with the power to make a difference. How can Houston claim that it's an international city and disrespect a large segment of its community?"

But what was Ali's position on the boycott? He threw out the first baseball and sports news carried a photo of the ex-champion in a now familiar pose: trembling while throwing fake punches.

The champion, who made his mark by refusing to comply with orders that he join the war effort in Vietnam, even though he'd been promised a soft assignment, refused to take sides in the war on Iraq, a war that was being waged against his fellow Muslims. Under the headline "Champ won't take sides in war with Iraq," Chris Kenning (*Courier-Journal.com*, March 26, 2003) reported Ali's appearance before a high school audience as part of a program that urges tolerance of other cultures and religions. During this appearance, Lonnie Ali, his wife, reported her husband's position on the war. Lonnie Ali said her husband was "opposed to conflict," but declined to comment on the Iraq conflict, saying war "may or may not be the answer."

Despite his high-profile opposition to the Vietnam War, Muhammad Ali declined yesterday to take sides about the war in Iraq. Lonnie Ali spoke for her husband, who has Parkinson's disease and limited his remarks to a brief joke when he was presented with a flower ("Is this all

I get?" he asked). There was no mention of the war in their comments to students—surprising and disappointing those who wanted to hear from their idol.

"I think he should've said something," said Ashley Shacklett, a 16 year-old Western sophomore.

Sergio Morales, 16, said he agreed: "I don't think there should be a war. I wish (Ali) would've said something, tried to stop it."

Some, including Khalilah, were saying that his wife, Lonnie, and his then-agent, Bernie Yuman, who was referred to as "serious sleaze" by one of those whom I interviewed, were leading him into an even more conservative direction. In June 2002, in an interview with David Frost on HBO's "Real Sports," when asked about Al-Qaeda he said, "I dodge those questions. I've opened up businesses across the country, selling products, and I don't want to say nothing and, not knowing what I'm doing, not being qualified, say the wrong thing and hurt my businesses and things I'm doing."

CHAPTER 12

The GOAT (Greatest Of All Time): Ali or Louis?

Recently there has been a discussion in boxing circles, including Maxboxing.com, whether Muhammad Ali being the greatest fighter of all time is hype and merely the creation of wide-eyed worshipful white and black biographers, who cavalierly ignore black personalities who had much to do with the image for which Ali is admired as well as some of the seamier aspects of the ex-champion's career. The consensus was forming around Joe Louis being the harder puncher.

The opinion seems to be divided about Louis and Ali, not only in the sports newsrooms but also among the public. On January 26, 2006, I went to pick up some shoes prepared for me by a black shoemaker. He was talking to another elderly black person. I asked them who was the greatest Heavyweight Champion. Paul, the shoemaker, said Joe Louis because he was a boxer puncher. His customer said Ali because he was fast.

On November 24, 2005, about a week after I'd run into the critic, the late Bert Sugar, at the Ali gala, he appeared on ESPN in a six-hour review of the ten greatest heavyweight fighters of all time, where he got into a debate with co-hosts Larry Holmes and George Chuvalo. Bert Sugar listed Joe Louis as the greatest, while Holmes and Chuvalo elected Ali. The boxers claimed that Louis would have had trouble finding Ali, so fast was Ali, and that Louis had success only with boxers who stood there and traded punches with him. Sugar countered that once Louis found a fighter, he'd knock him out. Ali and Louis had the same debate with each other. Muhammad Ali called Louis a "slow-moving shuffling" fighter who would have difficulty with his speed. On another occasion, he referred to Joe Louis as a fighter who fought like "a mummy." Louis criticized Ali for lacking courage, ridiculed his punching power, and said that Ali would have been beaten by a lot of fighters who were around when he, Louis, fought. Louis, however, has been criticized for ducking the best black heavyweight fighters of his time, while Ali faced the best of his.

The great boxing trainer, Emanuel Steward, says that Ali would have beaten Louis. *Who was greater? Ali or Louis?*

Emanuel Steward: The greatest heavyweight champion as champion was Joe Louis. He transcended sports. The fight he had with Schmeling. There was never an event in history where the whole world stood still. He knocked him out during the Hitler movement. Two men, half-naked in a ring, with their two fists predicted the course of history. Joe Louis knocked this man out and this was more than a victory for black people; it was a victory for the whole world. He did more for race relations than anyone else; everyone forgot about black and white. He followed Jack Johnson, who did more damage to race relations than any man could dream of. Jack Johnson was totally wrapped up in himself, and he did everything he could to humiliate and embarrass the white male race. Forget about everything else; that was his obsession in life. Don't list him as a black hero. And some of the things that he did got black people lynched—he didn't care. To come behind Johnson took an unusual man; Joe Louis did that. He was like a computer printout from God. He was part white himself, light complexioned, which made him acceptable to white people. The Jewish people really helped him with his career. He was never seen with white women. It took that kind of black person to become acceptable to the public again. He did so much and he had twenty-five defenses of the title and eleven years as champion. It was just phenomenal.

I think Ali would have beaten Louis. But they were two of the world's greatest heavyweight champions in different ways. Ali would have beaten him in a fight. But no man ever carried the image of champion as well as Louis did. That era is over. Today, I think the boxers' minds are too much into business for them to be fighters. They want to be their own managers. It's all about negotiating. They want to buy their own record companies, etc. Roy Jones is an example. Instead of trying to become the best fighter, their minds are too diversified. They want to be into getting into rights and advertising, etc. There are too many distractions. Their mental and spiritual energy are too spread out.

Heavyweight champion Hasim Rahman seemed to agree with Steward. When he lost to Oleg Maskaev, he said, "I think (American heavyweights) are a little spoiled. They make too much money too quick. They lose sight of the grand prize." Those who question who would beat whom in a contest between Joe Louis and Muhammad Ali ignore Louis's choice for the greatest heavyweight in history: he said Sonny Liston.

The Mob Put Sonny Liston Down For The Count. (Ishmael Reed, 2015)

CHAPTER 13

The Nation of Islam, the Mob, Showdowns in Canada and Sonny Liston

Boxers have had to contend with members of organized crime since the early period of the sport until now when, during August 2014, Teddy Atlas, the commentator on ESPN's Friday Night Fights, just about accused Golden Boy Promotions and Bob Arum's Top Rank of contriving to tilt decisions in fights in favor of their fighters. He was speaking about a fight between Erislandy Lara and Saul "Canelo" Alvarez, which took place at Las Vegas' MGM Grand on July 7, 2014, a fight that Teddy Atlas said Lara clearly won. I agree. However, the judges gave the title to Alvarez.

Another outrage occurred in September of the same year when Jose Benavidez was awarded a decision over Mauricio Herrera. Benavidez was Bob Arum's boxer. It's obvious that boxers need a union to protect them from the likes of Top Rank and Golden Boy.

The television sports commentators cooperate with the promoters in an effort to promote stars and draw pay-per-view customers. Becoming a boxing analyst doesn't seem to require much talent. During the commentary of the Canelo-Lara fight, Paul Malignaggi, someone who earned his credentials in the ring, had to explain to his fellow commentators what "ring generalship" meant. George Foreman quit as an announcer because he complained that his fellow commentators lacked knowledge of the sport. He might have had Larry Merchant in mind.

Just as baseball promotes home runs, basketball pursues slam dunks and three-pointers. In tennis, it's an ace. Merchant seems to prefer boxing in which the contestants stand toe to toe and slug it out, one lacking artistry. It was inevitable that something called Big Knockout Boxing would debut on August 16, 2014, which promises "a smaller fighting space, shorter rounds, and more knockouts." While the contemporary promoters put their stars in soft and there seem to be a growing number of fights in which their opponents only have a short time to train or are out at the last minute or are last minute substitutes.

At least in the old days, when gangsters ran boxing, a fighter had to fight tough opponents from time to time.

Showdowns in Canada

Of the three outstanding Canadian Champions, one, Tommy Burns, won the heavyweight championship. Yvon Durelle came close to dethroning two of the great American fighters, Archie Moore and Floyd Patterson, while George Chuvalo claims that were it not for the mob, he would have been declared champion over the mob's champion, Ernie Terrell. The George Chuvalo-Ernie Terrell fight was also the stage for a showdown between Organized Crime and Main Bout, a franchise of the Nation of Islam. These crucial showdowns between American and Canadian fighters, with two groups competing for control of boxing, and the attempt on the part of Canadian boxers to wrest championships from American boxers, occurred in that country across from my hometown of Buffalo, New York. A place to where fugitive slaves fled and where each summer, we'd visit Crystal Beach, an amusement park that we traveled to by boat across Lake Erie. Once when my friend Carman Nelson and I missed one of the boats that would return us to Buffalo, because we were having so much fun, his mother, who was assigned to retrieve us, said, here we are stuck all the way out of the country. We caught the next boat.

We imagined Canadians to be as well kept as the beautifully clipped lawns that we saw at the botanical gardens at Niagara Park in Ontario. Unlike these racist suckers we had to deal with on a daily basis, Canadians were good, decent people who kept their doors open in case a stranger wandered by. They'd offer the stranger soup.

The Archie Moore-Yvon Durelle fight on December 10, 1958, in
Montreal, is considered one of the greatest fights in the history
of boxing. Moore won by knockout in the eleventh round.

Our colonial education made no room for the truth about Canada,
or even our own country. Though fugitive slaves were welcomed many
experienced discrimination after they arrived, Native Americans were
dealt with harshly. We didn't know that Canada had been invaded from
Buffalo and that the invasions had been repelled. We didn't know that
there was a French Canada and that many Canadians like Durelle were
bilingual. He writes, "I never run into any French-English trouble
myself. I think that if any guy mentioned that to me I would have
hit him, give him a hell of a beating. I don't care about race... I had
a colored guy for a manager once in Halifax, and I lived with the
blacks down there. They're very nice people." Such a willingness of
Burns, Chuvalo and Durelle to take on all comers was Burns' undo-
ing. By accepting a challenge from Jack Johnson, he defied the racist
conventions of the time. Jim Jeffries appointed fighter Marvin Hart as
his successor. Hart defeated Jack Johnson on March 28, 1905. Hart was

dethroned by Burns on February 23, 1906. (Johnson was knocked out in three rounds by a Jewish fighter named Joe Choynski, February 25, 1901. Choynski also beat Jim Jefferies). He fought Jack Johnson on December 26, 1908, at South Wales, Australia, and received such a beating from Johnson that the police stopped the fight in the fourteenth round. Johnson outweighed Burns by twenty-four pounds. Burns was the smallest of the heavyweight champions. Jack London later apologized to Burns for "taking liberties with the truth."

London wrote of Burns' performance in the *New York Herald*. "The fight? There was no fight. No Armenian massacre could compare with the hopeless slaughter that took place today. The fight, if fight it could be called, was like that between a pygmy and a colossus... But one thing now remains. Jim Jeffries must emerge from his alfalfa farm and remove the golden smile from Jack Johnson's face. Jeff, it's up to you! The White Man must be rescued." As one-sided as the fight was, Johnson didn't escape the bout without injury. He had to go to the hospital with broken ribs. Burns's defenders say that Burns was willing to continue and the police should not have stopped the fight. Even though he remains the only heavyweight champion to win eight successive defense titles by knockouts, Burns was disgraced in the eyes of racists of the time, especially American sports writers, who resented both a Canadian holding a belt and a black champion succeeding him. Even though he would win the British Heavyweight Championship, the loss to a black fighter would haunt him for the rest of his life.

Burns had said, "I draw no colour line, nor bar any man in the world." This was a fighter who fought six black boxers and a Native American fighter before fighting Johnson. He was briefly married to a black woman. Was he Branch Rickey, the man who gets credit for integrating baseball? No. Burns was a racist, who assaulted Johnson with racist epithets when they met before the fight to choose a referee, and they exchanged racist insults during the fight. "Come, and get it, little Tommy, come and get it! Who told you I was yellow? You're white, dead scared white-white as the flag of surrender," taunted Johnson. Burns replied: "Come on and fight, nigger! Fight like a white man." But Burns could have continued ducking Jack Johnson. Johnson gave him credit for accepting his challenge. Ironically, both Johnson and Joe Louis were accused of avoiding the best black heavyweights of their times. So was Floyd Patterson.

Jim Jeffries said:

> Burns has sold his pride, the pride of the Caucasian race... The Canadian never will be forgiven by the public for allowing the title of the best physical man in the world to be wrested from his keeping by a member of the African race... I refused time and again to meet Johnson while I was holding the title, even though I knew I could beat him. I would never allow a negro a chance to fight for the world's championship, and I advise all other champions to follow the same course... All night long I was besieged with telegrams asking me to re-enter the ring. I answer them now as I have answered them hundreds of times: "I have fought my last fight".

Jeffries finally came out of retirement and fought Johnson in 1911. Johnson won and the rest is history. Burns spent the rest of his life training boxers and operating successful businesses. In 1996, he was elected to the International Boxing Hall of Fame

Durelle and Chuvalo exhibited the same grit. These were Canadians who could hit as hard as a "mule's kick," which is how Archie Moore described being hit by Yvon Durelle. Unlike the tolerant, clean Canadians that we imagined, Durelle's idea of a practical joke was to defecate in a colleague's gym bag. These were white fighters whose biographies read more like those of Sonny Liston and Joe Frazier than Muhammad Ali's. Ali grew up in a middle-class household.

By contrast, Durelle says that his mother beat him every day and his father would stage fights between his children, both girls and boys and in the first to draw blood would receive a penny. But his mother was in some ways "the man of the house." Durelle remembers his mother, who weighed two hundred pounds, grabbing his father by the throat, lifting him off his feet, and holding him against the wall with one hand and hitting him with the other. He said of his sisters that they could knock out a man anytime they wanted to, and his older brother could tear the door off a car. But sometimes their fighting zeal got out of hand, as when Durelle beat up his sixty-five-year-old school teacher, one off the two teachers who were on the receiving end of his rage.

Though everybody was poor in his Acadian hometown of Baie Ste-Anne, the Durelle family, though poor, always had enough to eat. So did George Chuvalo's family. This was because his mother had a job as a chicken plucker at Royce Poultry Packers on Dupont Street in Toronto, which was owned by Irving Ungerman, the man who would become his manager. She had to pluck four hundred chickens to earn two dollars. His father was a cattle skinner in the days when knives were used. He never took a vacation and for forty years did the work of two people. He fed his family by rescuing tendons, beef tripe, cow brains, kidneys, and other organ meats that were destined for the garbage cans at work.

Both Chuvalo and Durelle had trouble in school. Durelle had to drop out and help support his family when his father became ill. Chuvalo's own role as a father reminds one of the line in Albert King's song, "Born Under A Bad Sign": "If it wasn't for bad luck, I wouldn't have had any luck at all." Like the drug-addicted wife and daughter of Rocky Marciano, Chuvalo lost three sons and a wife to drugs and suicide (Chuvalo, 2013). And so both chose a sport that didn't care where you came from as long as you entertained fans by trying to knock somebody unconscious. Nobody cared whether you were an ex-felon or even a murderer like Don King. Floyd Patterson, Archie Moore, Sonny Liston, Henry Armstrong, Mike Tyson, and George Foreman all had run-ins with the law. Muhammad Ali must have also thought that Canadians were soft. Couldn't fight.

Muhammad Ali underestimated George Chuvalo, referring to him as a "washerwoman," yet it was Ali who went to the hospital following that fight. Ali was urinating blood. Archie Moore was also dismissive of Yvon Durelle, who had him down and almost out in the first round of their fight at the Montreal Forum, called by some one of the greatest if not the greatest fight in history. It was Moore's class and skills that won the day instead of his opponent, who was seeking a knockout from round one after surprising Moore by leading with his right.

It was Archie Moore's class that I had in mind when I met Moore at Norman Mailer's house on March 30, 1965. The party was held to celebrate Jose Torre's winning the light heavyweight championship after knocking out Willie Pastrano in Madison Square Garden. The newly crowned champion danced with my then girlfriend throughout the evening; "If it's o.k. with you," he would ask, and of course I gave him permission. I called Moore, another guest, "the poet of the ring," not only because of his eloquence but because of the grace he exhibited as he met the barrage of a fighter who, ironically, would have been successful had Moore been his trainer. Though Moore was about forty-four at the time and Durelle twenty-nine, the younger fighter was exhausted after having punched himself out in the first round. His trainers were incompetent. If Ali, the brash youngster who left Moore's training camp because he felt that the menial tasks to which he had been assigned were demeaning, had listened to Moore, perhaps he would have learned defense. When his legs were done, he would not have been so vulnerable to being hit. Unlike Moore, whose diet and discipline enabled him to exhaust a twenty-nine-year-old Yvon Durelle, George Foreman's lack of stamina contributed to his being knocked out by Ali, Ali's greatest ring victory. Ironic, because Foreman was trained for the fight by Moore.

When Foreman came out of retirement to win the championship for the second time, he was using Moore's "crab-like shell" defense. When asked about this defense, Durelle the "Fighting Fisherman" quipped, "Being a fisherman I know quite a bit about handling shellfish." The fight showed the Marciano bull-like toughness of Durelle, who was the underdog. This wasn't the only brutal fight in which Durelle was a participant. He later met George Chuvalo and was subjected to what could be called a ring massacre. As a result of the Moore-Durelle fight, which lengthened Moore's career, Moore convinced doubters that he wasn't washed up, having participated in a great fight. Moore and Durelle developed a respectful relationship. And if Moore hadn't called on him at a boxing dinner, nobody would have recognized him.

Some boxing analysts agree that Chuvalo was robbed of the heavyweight championship by the mob. Was Chuvalo behaving merely as a poor loser or was he on to something?

The Bad Luck of Sonny Liston

Mob control of boxers dates back to as early as 1892: John L. Sullivan was sponsored by a Chicago crime boss. Gangsters like Owney Madden, Meyer Lansky, Bugsy Siegel, Blinky Palermo, and "Fat" Tony Salerno have at one time or another owned pieces of the sport. Henry Armstrong was controlled by George Raft. Some boxers, like Sugar Ray Robinson, could not be intimidated.

His son, Ray Robinson, Jr., told me that Frank Sinatra approached Sugar Ray Robinson and requested that Robinson meet some friends of his. I asked him, "Why couldn't the mob control your Dad?" He replied:

> When we lived in Venice, a postal worker asked whether I was Sugar Ray's son; I said yes. He went to the back and brought out a photo of his uncle, Mr. Gambino, and my dad together. Mr. Gambino said that Dad was not to be bought and that he was crazy. Dad kept putting famous people out of the training camp, like Frank Sinatra. This was at Camp Greenwood Lake. Sinatra asked whether my dad could do a little something for some friends of his. My dad said no. He was also approached by Frankie Carbo. In those days, they wanted you to extend the fight a little bit, not to take a dive.

Muhammad Ali has been associated with criminals in and outside of the ring. However, before he was managed by Don King, he was under the control of Herbert Muhammad and the NOI, which presented the mob with a competitor. King took the fifth when asked whether he knew John Gotti. At one point, King, slow in returning payments for a loan to mob figures, had to beg that a contract on his life be removed. *The New York Times* revealed on April 7, 2014, that Reverend Al Sharpton played down his involvement with Mafia figures, although "[Sharpton] worked with the FBI in the 1980s in an investigation of the boxing promoter Don King. His spying on King for the FBI was part of a deal that kept him out of prison as a result of a drug sting."

The NOI threatened the Gambino crime family after Muhammad Ali's name came up during an FBI wiretap of a meeting that included members of organized crime. Learning of this, members of the NOI threatened that if any harm came to Ali, they would go to the Waldorf Astoria and throw Frank Sinatra out of the window. This contradicts the image of black characters who appeared on the popular series "The Sopranos," where they were shown as inept and stupid, or the attitude of some Ali biographers that the Muslims were cowards. (Emboldened by their making organized crime back down, some rogue members of the NOI took the Philadelphia heroin trade from organized crime.)

The NOI's attempt to enter the boxing business was blasted by sports writers, some of whom tolerated the exploitation of boxers by organized crime. According to Michael Ezra in his book, *Muhammad Ali: The Making of an Icon*, "when the leaders of Main Bout, Inc., which had NOI backing, complained that their efforts were being undermined by the mob, the sports writers dismissed these complaints." Furthermore:

> Clearly these sports writers weren't reporting the whole story, because the Federal Bureau of Investigation (FBI) launched an inquiry into the failed promotion of a bout between Ali and Ernie Terrell that was supposed to occur in Toronto and be sponsored by Main Bout, Inc. It suspected that Terrell withdrew not only because of financial concerns—they couldn't guarantee the two hundred fifty thousand dollar purse that they'd promised—but also because of death threats to him and Bernie Glickman by Chicago Mafia figures, which would no longer profit if the bout were moved to Canada. Investigators were unable to link the boycott to the mob, and no further federal examination of the fight took place.

The Pittsburgh Courier sighed, "as usual, the casting of light on supported underworld control of boxing still remains unfulfilled." Robert Lipsyte wrote, "To the underworld, the new organization meant only that a 'rival gang' had moved in and was in a position to 'ace them out' by not dealing with 'trusted' closed-circuit television operators or exhibitors as well as the other businessmen who normally get pay days from a title fight." A UPI writer added, "New York Mafia interests were enraged at the attempt of the Muslims to take over closed boxing through Main Bout, Inc."

George Chuvalo told a different story about the competition between the NOI and organized crime. He said that Glickman, a representative of Tony Arcado, the mob boss of Chicago who had links to Frankie Carbo, told Ali's manager that if Ali beat Terrell, he'd end up in a cement box. The Fruit of Islam (the paramilitary arm of the NOI) paid a visit to Glickman and rendered a beating from which he never recovered. He died in a mental institution. Terrell "complained about training expenses or some baloney like that," said Chuvalo. He continued:

> What happened was Bernie Glickman was in the hospital at that time in Chicago beaten within an inch of his life. Why was he beaten within an inch of his life? He went from there to a mental institution where he lost his life. He never saw the light of day again. He was questioned by the police but never said who beat him up. Let me try to figure this out for myself; he must have gone to see Herbert Muhammad (Ali's manager) and threatened Herbert Muhammad much the same way that he threatened Irving Ungerman. If Ali wins he ends up in Lake Michigan. All Herbert Muhammad had to do was snap his fingers, and all his Islamic guys are right there and bing-bam-boom that's it. And that's why I got the fight with Ali.

Former ABC reporter Martin Wyatt told me, "Elijah Muhammad really wasn't all that hot on Ali's fighting, but he wanted to make certain that he wouldn't be ripped off and that's why he chose Herbert Muhammad to manage Ali. To protect the boxers from people like the interests that Bernie Glickman represented. Gangsters and crooks, who surrounded the boxing game." Liston's being tied to the mob, specifically to Frankie Carbo, was used to thwart his boxing career, yet some of his accusers were also tied to the mob. Cus D'Amato used Liston's mob connections to deny Liston a championship bout with Floyd Patterson. Though Floyd Patterson's manager, Cus D'Amato, was squeaky clean (his brother was cited by the Kefauver Committee as having ties to organized crime), the first fight between Patterson and Ingemar Johansson was promoted by an organization of which mob figure Fat Tony Salernor was a partner.

According to a *New York Times* article, "In 1959, when he was already well known to the Manhattan District Attorney as a 'gambler, bookmaker and policy operator', an investigation into the Mafia's involvement in promoting boxing found that Mr. Salerno had secretly helped finance a heavyweight title fight at Yankee Stadium between Ingemar Johansson and Floyd Patterson. Mr. Salerno was not charged in the case" (*The New York Times*, July 29, 1992). Anthony (Fat Tony) Salerno died in prison at the age of eighty.

Was Liston the only boxer who had connections to Frankie Carbo, described as "the underworld czar of boxing?"

Frankie Carbo owned other boxers as well, along with sports writers and the managers of boxers. He owned Rocky Marciano's manager, Al Weill. Teddy Brenner, who worked for Al Weill in the late 1940s and subsequently became president of Madison Square Garden Boxing, later acknowledged, "Carbo had his fingers on the throat of boxing. If he did not own a certain fighter, he owned the manager. Weill was a boxing politician who held hands with the mob. When Weill was Marciano's manager, he was controlled by Carbo."

Gangsters like Frankie Carbo and Blinky Palermo ran boxing until 1960. In an earlier time, the notorious mobster, Legs Diamond, was involved in fixing fights. Some give credit to Herbert (named for Herbert Hoover) Muhammad for ending mob control of boxing, but others contend that organized crime maintained partial control by using a black promoter as a front. He was identified as Don King to me in 1978 by Bob Arum.

It becomes obvious that Liston became bogey-manned by boxing promoters and sports writers because he was not pretty and telegenic like Ali, Sugar Ray Leonard, and the current box office attraction, Alvarez. He was also big and black. As Nick Tosches, author of *Night Train: The Sonny Liston Story*, reminds us, "In those days, bad niggers were not the darling middle-class iconic commodities and consumers of white-ruled conglomerate culture. In those days bad niggers were bad news." So why were Sonny Liston's gang ties singled out and those of others ignored? On the day that Sonny Liston was found dead, a Canadian promoter announced that Liston had agreed to fight Chuvalo.

◆

If animals and insects had an advocacy group in charge of challenging their defamation, they'd have a lot to complain about. When we want to describe a contemptible person, we might call him or her a weasel, a snake, a spider, or a rat. Since apes are cousins of humans, a relationship to which, in view of human history, the apes might object, those who are considered sub-human are often associated with apes, chimpanzees, and baboons, though none of these animals are aiding in their extinction. Humans are doing that for them, and for themselves.

Conducting interviews for *The Complete Muhammad Ali*, I found that while a number of my contacts are still angry with the champion for his referring to Joe Frazier as an ape or a gorilla, only one man, the late Emanuel Steward, the great boxing trainer who presided over the Kronk gym, would defend Sonny Liston. Liston had to fight his way up, taking on all comers, knocking out a bunch, only to be avoided by Floyd Patterson, then champion. Patterson's manager, Cus D'Amato, had put Patterson in against soft opposition and was biased against black fighters, who could have given Floyd, a true light heavyweight, problems. When they finally met, Liston knocked Patterson out and, in their rematch, knocked him out again. This is not to diminish Floyd Patterson's achievement as a heavyweight. As a middleweight, he was as fast as Muhammad Ali. When he fought Oscar Bonavena in 1972, he still had some speed and pop. His problem was a weak chin.

Sports writers, who have a history of issuing venomous copy against black athletes, over-did their hatred when it came to Liston. They called him "a hoodlum... dumb... lazy... A person possessed with animal cunning." The former president of the United States, John F. Kennedy, felt that Liston was not suitable for wearing the belt of the heavyweight champion and Kennedy appointed Patterson as the "white hope" who would end Liston's drive toward the championship. Kennedy, who had his own mob connections, was upset over Liston's even though Frankie

Carbo, the mobster who controlled boxing at the time, was out of the picture when Liston fought Patterson. Senator Kefauver, who headed a committee investigating organized crimes connection to boxing, gave Liston a crime-free bill of health and said that he saw no reason for Patterson to deny him a fight.

The sports writers who considered Liston to be an ape didn't buy Liston's excuse that a shoulder injury led to his quitting on his stool during the first fight with Ali. It turns out that he did suffer from a shoulder injury, bursitis, which was verified by medical inquiries. The Miami Boxing Commission knew about the injury before the fight but refused to postpone it, which nowadays is routine. Furthermore, Liston didn't stop the first fight. His manager did.

Not only did the sports writers, politicians, and celebrities disdain Liston, but the public also saw Liston (in the words of Geraldine Liston) as the champion that no one wanted. Such rejection sometimes brought Liston to tears. When he appeared on the cover of Esquire as Santa Claus, some members of the public lost it totally. Esquire lost seven hundred thousand dollars in advertising revenue. After the second fight, when Liston went down from what was considered a soft blow from Ali, Liston's remaining reputation was shredded. The photo of Liston lying prostrate graced the wall of Senator Obama's office, but Ali is standing above Liston because former heavyweight champion of the world Joe Walcott didn't direct Ali to a neutral corner. Walcott later apologized for his role in botching the fight and permitting a sports writer, Nat Fleischer, to call the fight instead of a ring official. There have been many accounts of why Liston remained down. He said that he didn't get up because he thought that Ali was crazy. Others say that he was threatened by the mob and by members of the Nation of Islam, Malcolm X's followers who were upset with Ali because he had betrayed his former mentor. If they were bent upon shooting Ali, Liston felt that he might have been shot as an innocent bystander.

If you watch the film carefully, you'll see Liston's head snap as he comes into contact with Ali's anchor punch. Given his actions when knocked down, it appears that the punch upset Liston's equilibrium. He didn't remain on the canvas, which the famous photo might lead one to believe. He rose and continued to fight, until the hapless referee Jersey Joe Walcott stopped the fight on the instructions of the sports writer.

Nat Fleischer had a problem with Sonny Liston and didn't include him among the top heavyweight fighters of all time. Though the Ali biographers tend to breeze by Liston's 1960 fight with Eddie Machen, Machen's strategy provided the blueprint for Ali. Machen ran, ducked, and fought in flurries. He showed that Liston was vulnerable to an overhand right, as evidenced by the egg-like swelling over Liston's left eye.

Liston wasn't able to knock out Machen as he had done with other contenders and became so frustrated that he delivered three low blows. I gave the final round to Machen.

After the fights with Ali, Liston was never again given the opportunity to fight for the championship, but continued to bust up some contenders. His reputation was destroyed by sports writers and commentators who, then as now, believe that they know more about boxing than the fighters. This includes those who broadcast Floyd Mayweather's second fight with Marcos Maidana; they said that Mayweather had been helped in his defeat of Maidana with the aid of the referee. They also disputed Mayweather's claim that he'd been bitten by Maidana. "How," they asked, "could he have been bitten when he was wearing gloves?" Paulie Malignaggi had to explain to them that he'd been bitten by a boxer while wearing gloves and it hurt. Similarly, while sportswriters who have never entered the ring (like jazz critics who fake it) accused Liston of being in on a fix, three champions, Rocky Marciano, Jose Torres, and James Braddock ("The Cinderella Man") said that it was a legitimate punch that knocked Liston down.

They say that for an aging champion—and Liston might have been forty when he fought Ali—power is the last asset to go. So it was with Liston. His last fight was with Chuck Wepner, whose knockdown of Ali was the basis for the Rocky films. Liston beat him so badly that Wepner was to say that "every time he hit me in the face, he broke something." Liston received thirteen thousand dollars for that fight. He was supposed to have received fifteen thousand.

So was Liston an animal? Liston had a dry wit, and a shrewd intelligence. He loved children, and there is an account that the mob frightened Liston, threatening to kidnap one of his children if he didn't take a dive. He gave money to charity and was known to do good works. Most of those who knew him vouch for his good character and his intelligence. A few mention his witty repartees to Ali's clever verbal jabs, in the hundred or so worshipful books about Muhammad Ali. They feature his clever goading of Liston, which got Liston so angry that he fought a clumsy first fight with Ali.

His spouse, Geraldine, said that Liston was a good husband. Like many, however, he could be a mean drunk, and there are a couple of accusations of rape. Liston continued to have bad luck. He was often harassed by the police. Two of these jokers thought that it was funny to give him a traffic ticket every day for a hundred days. He was once given a traffic ticket when he wasn't even driving the car. After that he busted up a drunken cop who called him a "black ass nigger." During a second incident involving the police, he deposited a cop into a trash can. He was persecuted by the police in Philadelphia, St. Louis, and Denver. He was arrested, capriciously, by both the Philadelphia and Denver police.

Certainly, he got into trouble with the law during his youth, but so did Patterson and other fighters like George Foreman and trainer Emanuel Steward, who trained for their careers by participating in street fights. A judge sent Floyd Patterson to the Wiltwyck School for Boys, a school for black juvenile delinquents.

When Liston's body was found upon his death, it was surrounded by drug paraphernalia. His friends, however, said that he didn't touch drugs. Geraldine Liston said that he was afraid of needles. Moreover, wouldn't his drug use have been detected when he was examined for the Wepner fight, three months before his death? Emanuel Steward and Khalilah (Belinda) Muhammad told me that he was probably murdered.

At any rate, thousands left their gambling tables and scoreboards to witness the Liston funeral procession pass through the Las Vegas strip. Among the celebrities were Ed Sullivan, Doris Day, Ella

Fitzgerald, Jack E. Leonard, Jerry Vale, and Rosey Grier. Many were in tears, because deep down they probably knew that Sonny Liston, born into poverty and without schooling, called by Joe Louis "The Greatest Heavyweight Champion," had been dealt a bad hand. He said that he was treated like a "sewer rat," but while Ali was hailed as a hero for the middle class for his stand against an unpopular war, Liston represented the underclass that President Obama and the Harvard circle disdained. He was one of twenty-four children and was born into a condition of "slavery without the name." His father beat him. He traveled to St. Louis to be with his mother who, instead of giving him an affectionate greeting, wanted to know why he showed up. Having no education, he, like other members of his class, committed petty, high-risk crimes. An armed robbery landed him in prison. He got into trouble with the law and sports writers like Larry Merchant after he defended himself against a drunken armed cop who lied about the incident, as some cops regularly do. His wife, Geraldine, was correct when she called him the champ that nobody wanted.

CHAPTER 14

Questions have been raised about some of Ali's fights: did an illegal rabbit punch assist in Ali knocking Foreman senseless? Did Foreman get up at the count of nine; was he drugged? Was Muhammad Ali the recipient of gift decisions in bouts that his opponents actually won?

Furthermore, did Doug Jones actually win the fight that put Ali in line to fight the heavyweight champion, Sonny Liston? What about Ali vs. Norton III? Norton won the first fight, breaking Ali's jaw while beating him. George Foreman said that Norton won the second fight, trainer Eddie Futch said that Norton won the third, and there are some boxing commentators who believe that Norton won all three. Some say that Ali lost the first fight due to his having sex with five women a few nights before as part of a bet (Kram, 2001); Emanuel Steward, perhaps the greatest of contemporary fight trainers, maintains that while Ali received the decision, Jimmy Young won the fight.

One of those who have witnessed the physical and political changes of Muhammad Ali was the late writer, Jack Newfield. In April 2003, Newfield called me to talk about his receiving the 2003 American Book Award for his book, *The Full Rudy*, a book about former New York Mayor Rudolph Giuliani, who, because of serendipity, became a hero to millions of white Americans while alienating some black and Hispanic citizens. This was a result of his stop-and-frisk measures and his insensitivity towards victims of police brutality, and even the smearing of black men who were shot by the police under controversial circumstances. Newfield's book, questioning the over-the-top praise for this political figure, departed from the mainstream media's excessive affection for a political figure whose approval ratings were about forty percent before the attack on the Twin Towers and what was considered his heroic response. I told Newfield that I was writing a book about Ali and he volunteered that when Ali was about to travel to the Congo for his fight with Foreman, he asked Angelo Dundee how he should fight the champion; Dundee instructed him to back him up, advice that Ali didn't follow.

In those days, George Foreman was considered a bully whose role model was Sonny Liston, not the smiling sports announcer he became, a jolly brown giant and hawker of cooking equipment. (In one commercial, he was even shown sharing a table with a white family.) He had transformed himself from a scowling menace into what one might call a teddy bear, as well as a manufacturer of cooking equipment. Salton Appliances had paid Foreman a reported one hundred thirty million dollars to advertise their merchandise. He also owed his status to having contributed to the making of the near mythic Ali.

However, while Foreman was contemplating a comeback at the age of fifty-five (he eventually decided against it), Ali's condition was worsening as he fought off the deteriorating effects of Parkinson's disease. Or perhaps it was *dementia pugilistica*, brain injuries from taking too many blows after staying in the ring long after his skills had waned. New research with football players suggests that Ali might be suffering from chronic traumatic encephalopathy (CTE), a progressive disease diagnosed post-mortem in individuals with a history of multiple concussions. Ali might have suffered his first concussion as early as sixteen, when he was knocked out by Willy Moran. Or perhaps, as some of Elijah Muhammad's followers would say, it was a curse delivered by Elijah from beyond the grave, who requested that Ali give up the name he'd given him after he joined the Nation. Since then, Ali suffered thousands of hard blows to the head.

In an interview after Ali was suspended from the movement, Elijah Muhammad referred to his former protégé as Cassius Clay. Ali would get no sympathy from Joe Frazier, either. However, in an appearance on ESPN in April 2006, Frazier seemed to bury the hatchet, expressing no malice toward the man whom he had fought three times.

The program included footage of Frazier performing before a large audience in New Zealand. Backed up by some shimmying women, he belted out "Mustang Sally" to the appreciation of his fans. He seemed to be enjoying himself. In a later interview conducted during the same year, he wished Ali well. He then gave the television audience his version of "I Did It My Way."

Meanwhile, Ali was bravely keeping up public appearances, being trotted around like a show horse. One week at the Kentucky Derby, another week abroad. Was this the black, heavyweight champion's affliction, to end his career broke, or in bad health? After Evander Holyfield took a beating from a passive aggressive boxer like Larry Donaldson, boxing authorities were deciding whether the former heavyweight champion would meet the medical standards required to engage in future fights. (His defeat of a retired insurance "salesman" in August of 2006 perhaps, tragically, only whetted his appetite for more punishment.) Many of his fans were concerned about his health; but like Holyfield and Holmes and the others who followed Ali, he had another problem. They all had to try to fill the shoes of the man who referred to himself as the King of the World.

Some would find it laughable to call Mike Tyson an intellectual, but he is. He was supposed to have read over one hundred books while incarcerated for rape in a trial in which the prosecutor, Greg Garrison, chose the judge, and some jury members said they would have voted for acquittal had they known that the plaintiff and her attorney were after money. (This same prosecutor was ignored when he said that the murders of Nicole Simpson and Ron Goldman looked like a mob execution.) Tyson had an opportunity to become even greater than Ali, and in one of the sad images from this brutal sport, posed with Ali, both of them with glazed, sedated-looking expressions, in his dressing room, before Tyson entered the Washington, D.C. arena for his career-ending fight with Kevin McBride, a journeyman palooka who won by leaning his pounds on his smaller opponent.

As Emanuel Steward told me later during an interview conducted at the Hotel at Mandalay Bay, Tyson always had trouble with big men.

CHAPTER 15

The Taunts: Marketing or Racism?

Another reason for the Ali legend was Ali's brilliant taunting of his opponents, a strategy that fattened the gates of his contests even when his opponents were black. His poetry, his pre-fight tussles which approached hysteria before his first fight with Sonny Liston, and his predicting the round in which his antagonist would fall, endeared him to fans and star-struck northeastern writers. He successfully predicted the round in which he would defeat Sonny Banks, George Logan, Will Besmanoff, Alejandro Lavorante, Charles Powell, Henry Cooper, and Archie Moore. And like the traditional badman of folklore and rap, he bragged and indulged in narcissistic posturing. He even provided his opponents with nicknames: Liston was The Bear; Patterson was The Rabbit; George Chuvalo was The Washerwoman; Ernie Terrell was The Octopus; George Foreman was The Mummy; Joe Frazier was The Gorilla; and Ernie Shavers was The Acorn.

Though white wrestler Gorgeous George has been cited as the inspiration for such PR antics, credit might also go to Archie Moore, the "old mongoose," who saw the advantages of advertising and psychological warfare when facing down an opponent. When Moore was trying to entice then-heavyweight champion Rocky Marciano into a fight with him, Moore issued a wanted poster with Marciano's picture on it. To fill seats for a fight in Las Vegas, Moore donned a cowboy suit.

Jack Johnson also used a marketing strategy in which he chose the role of the villain or "the heavy" in order to attract customers who, in Jim Carey's words speaking about Ali at the Gala, wanted "to see somebody kick his ass."

Like Ali, Johnson ridiculed the talents of his opponents. After defeating Tommy Burns, he bragged that his defeat of Burns was "even easier" than he expected. He said of his fight with Jeffries, "My younger brother, Charley, is studying to be an undertaker, and he graduates July 1. I will give him his first customer. I will start a job and brother Charley will finish it."

Leon Pryor of the *Denver Statesman* said, "Jack is a little smarter than people give him credit for being. He knows just how to get plenty of free advertising and notoriety" (M. E. Sharpe, 2002).

However, as Jose Torres observed, Ali's rapping and trash-talking, a gift for gab that he inherited from his father, was more effective when psyching his black opponents than his white ones. When I asked Ed Hughes, an old friend of the Ali family, how Ali was able to get away with his trash-talking in Louisville in the 1950s, in a South where many black men were lynched for being smart, Hughes said that while he might have boasted to black people, he was deferential to whites.

Ali was a fighter who entertained inside the ring as well as outside. Some, however, contend that his ribbing of opponents went over the line and even smacked of racism. Though racism is seen as a phenomenon that exists between races, much has been written about the racial tensions among people of the same race, light-skinned versus brown-skinned, a division captured in the verse, "If you're white, you're all right; if you're brown, stick around; if you're black, stay back." Moreover, when some are making generalizations about blacks, they ignore the wide genetic variation among them. When Joe Frazier called Muhammad Ali "a half-breed," he was referring to a division between those with "pure" black ancestry and those who have whites among their ancestors. Since looks are deceiving, Joe Frazier, a dark-skinned black American, might also have white ancestry. Brent Staples, a dark-skinned *New York Times* writer, had a sample of his DNA examined and found his ancestry to be mixed black, white, and Asian. He was surprised by his Asian ancestry, but shouldn't have been. Because of what American historians call "The Indian Wars," the Native American male population declined, forcing Native American women to choose black partners. My grandmother, Odessa LeNoir, was a Cherokee woman who married Rufus LeNoir, who was part Cherokee. They met in Indian school.

Jonathan Smith, whom I met at the Ali Center gala, also said that the white colonialists thought that breeding blacks with Indians would make it easier to convert Indians into slaves, similar to a plan after World War II to interbreed the Japanese with Pacific Islanders so that they would become "docile." Ali's white ancestry has also been documented.

When Ali called himself "pretty," was he referring to his "half–breed" looks as opposed to the more "black" looks of Frazier, whom he referred to as a "gorilla?" No white fighter would have gotten away with calling Frazier a gorilla. During one incident when Ali referred to Joe Frazier as a gorilla, someone threw a toy monkey into the ring. Of all of the racist appellations, many blacks find being compared to monkeys, gorillas, and apes to be the worst. A Bryant Gumbel "Real Sports" episode dealt with the racist remarks issued by white fans, some of whom flew Nazi flags, against black soccer fans. They made sounds associated with apes and threw bananas onto the field.

Movies like "Gorillas in the Mist," whose title members of the LAPD joked about on their way to beating Rodney King, and movies like "King Kong," make many African Americans uneasy, because they are alert to the sub-discussion, or signifying being offered by such films. What are we to make of the San Francisco Zoo's owning an Ape named O.J., and Wal-Mart recommending a film about Martin Luther King, Jr. to potential buyers of a "Planet of the Apes" DVD (*San Francisco Chronicle*, January 7, 2006)? Wal-Mart blamed it on employee error.

When Ali compared Frazier to a gorilla, or called Liston "ugly" and himself "pretty," was he speaking from the point of view of an honorary European or someone who had adopted European standards of aesthetics? Was this what happened when he referred to African women as ugly and joked about Africans as cannibals? In a letter to

Elijah Muhammad, J. B. Stoner of the Christian Knights of the Ku Klux Klan agreed with Ali's remarks about African women being ugly, which Ali had made while traveling in Africa, criticizing the "ugliness "of the African women. He made fun of their features and their hair, and suggested they needed "white blood" to give them beauty. The men, he said, needed a good shower. He said that he was glad that his ancestors got on the ships.

Elijah Muhammad replied:

> We see you day and night after the so-called Negro women whistling and winking your eyes and blowing your car horns at them; making advances to every Negro woman that walks, rides, flies or works for you in your homes, offices and factories. Not in America alone but all over the earth wherever you go among the black, brown, yellow and red people, we see that you are after our women, whom you say to be 'ugly.'

Do some whites connect with Ali because they view him as one of their own? It seems that at least one writer feels that way. The author of *The Rough Guide to Muhammad Ali*, commenting on Ali's Irish heritage, says, "This heritage bore one precious gift for young Cassius: his genetics. By lineage, by birth, by fluke, he had been touched by the gods. He was handsome, strong, and athletic, sublimely talented. Cassius Clay was one in four billion." The implication here is that one who does not possess "European genes" lacks these qualities.

Ali's ribbing of his opponents was often done in good nature and to sweeten the box office, but some of it could be vindictive and vicious, like those barbs issued against Joe Frazier, verbal scaldings that were hurtful both to the champion and his family. Ali might have been intimidated by Frazier being "a pure Negro" (Kram, 2001), someone who didn't have to make a big show about being black. However, one of the moments during which he ridiculed George Foreman came close to making him appear as the malicious buffoon that Kram observed; before their fight in Zaïre, Ali confronted Foreman at the annual Boxing Writers' Dinner, and screamed at Foreman, "I'm gonna beat your Christian ass, you white, flag-waving bitch, you" (Stravinsky, 1997).

By the time Ali fought Larry Holmes, gone were the rhymes and jingles and playing the dozens that characterized his trash-talking of former years. Facing the power punches that would be delivered by Holmes, Ali vilified his opponent with a language that was bereft of the cleverness, humor, and poetry used when hyping the gate for his previous fights. He said to Holmes: "You dumb motherfucker… asshole… fuckhead. You ain't shit as fighter… never were."

What impresses some of the Ali groupies was that he could back up his boasting in the ring. Dr. Nathan Hare, who, unlike some sports writers and Ali biographers, actually spent some time in the ring, commented about some of the rules that Ali broke in the ring, like leaning back to avoid a punch—a no-no, and one that Teddy Atlas warns about every week on ESPN's "Friday Night Fights." Ali added flair to the promotion of his fights. He not only invented nicknames for his opponents, but nicknamed his technical moves as well: The Ali Shuffle, the Linger Punch, the Anchor Punch, and the Ghetto Whopper (Kellerman, 1998). Though some still maintain that the first Ali-Liston fight was faked, it ended because of Liston's shoulder injury—or as Joe Louis put it in his commentary during the fight: Liston's shoulder had been thrown out of its socket which resulted from his attempt to connect with Ali's elusive chin—Floyd Patterson also suffered a shoulder injury while attempting to connect with Ali's jaw as he leaned away from coming into contact with Patterson's fists, but nobody accused promoters of fixing that fight. As an example of the rust that had set in after his problems with the draft, Ali was unable to evade Joe Frazier's "Philadelphia Left Hook" in their first meeting. In his book *Box Like The Pros*, written with William Dettloff, Frazier says it was a long left hook that floored Ali.

◆

My high school history teacher, Mr. Simon, always told me in class, "Reed, you concentrate on the minutiae of history instead of memorizing names and dates. You fail to capture the big picture." That was after I answered a question about Napoleon by pointing out that Napoleon held his hand inside his vest because he suffered from stomach cancer. I'd read this somewhere. Isn't history's big picture composed of minutiae, just as the body is composed of atoms? What, for example, would have happened to the history of boxing if Schwinn hadn't manufactured that red-and-white Schwinn bicycle Ali rode at age twelve? Where would the history of boxing be, without the angry, three-hundred-pound pig that chased Joe Frazier, causing him to fall and injure his left arm? His not being able to straighten his left arm was the reason that his left hook became one of the most lethal weapons in boxing. What would have happened had Sonny Liston believed an informant who told him that Ali's rib had been bruised in a sparring session with Ron Lyle? What would have happened if close decisions with Ken Norton and Shavers had gone the other way? The crowd booed the decision going to Ali in the final bout between him and Norton. After his retirement, George Foreman said that he received a message from Ali asking Foreman to fight Norton because he, Ali, couldn't beat him.

After getting a bad decision in Norton-Ali III, Norton wept. What would have happened if Angelo Dundee had acceded to Ali's request that the fight with Liston be halted, or if Joe Frazier's corner had heard that Ali wanted to quit after the thirteenth round of the "Thrilla in Manila." I wanted to ask Ali these questions and others.

I had been trying to contact Ali's office for an interview, only to get a runaround when a Muslim living in my neighborhood provided me with the number. He is a repairman now, but was formerly a well-known rhythm and blues guitarist who was friends with the great Ike Turner and Charles Brown. He speaks of his former incarnation with contempt, as though he were another person; and so Muhammad Ali and Cassius Clay became two different people, so profound was the influence of Elijah Muhammad's Nation on the boxer.

CHAPTER 16

To be frank, many African Americans lionized Joe Louis, Jack Johnson, and Sugar Ray Robinson because they beat the living daylights out of white people, even though Sugar Ray's son, Ray Robinson, Jr., claims that Sugar viewed himself not as a black but as an American. It was as though their fists made up for all of the hate, spite, and insults suffered by blacks at the hands of whites in everyday life.

Ali received cheers from blacks and whites for defeating those who found themselves on the lower rungs of the United States' color caste. Mark Kram has pointed out the intra-racial nature of the feud between Joe Frazier and Ali. In order for American whites, who are not considered as such in some parts of Europe—the Klan considers anybody to the south of France and Naples to be black—the myth of uninterrupted African ancestry of blacks has to be maintained. Otherwise, the unspeakable crimes of white men against African captive women would be exposed.

Millions of African Americans have European ancestry, and the European ancestor is most likely to be Irish or Scots Irish. Like Ali, Willie McCovey, a dark-skinned baseball player, also met his Irish ancestors when he traveled to Ireland. On other occasions, though, the wealthy Southern planters blamed the growing numbers of bi-racial people appearing around them on the Irish when it was they, the planters, who were the culprits. When Duc de la Rochefoucauld-Liancourt visited Monticello in 1796, he was told by Ellen Randolph Coolidge, Thomas Jefferson's granddaughter, that the bi-racial children on the plantation were the result of "Irish workmen." Georgia University Press released a study headlined: "Skin tone more important than educational background for African Americans seeking jobs" on August 15, 2006. It states:

> Athens, Ga. – Everyone knows about the insidious effects of racism in American society. But when it comes to the workplace, African Americans may face a more complex situation—the effects of their own skin tone. For the first time, a study indicates that dark-skinned African Americans face a distinct disadvantage when applying for jobs, even if they have résumés superior to lighter-skinned black applicants. Matthew Harrison, a doctoral student at the University of Georgia, presented his research today at the 66th annual meeting of the Academy of Management in Atlanta. Along with his faculty supervisor, Kecia Thomas, a professor of applied psychology and acting director of UGA's Institute for African American Studies, Harrison undertook the first significant study of "colorism" in the American workplace.

So was Ali's taunting of his black opponents racist, or an attempt to hype the box office? The evidence is inconclusive. In one piece of film footage, Ali is signifying on Sonny Liston. Liston refuses to be baited. Ali then says, "Come on Sonny, let's make some money."

Those who maintain that Ali's baiting of his opponents had no malicious intent have support in an encounter that the late Floyd Patterson had with the champion. He talks of running into the champion after their fight:

> He gave me a big bear hug when I walked to the door, and there was real warmth there... then he said that he would like to go on a boxing tour with Liston and myself to make some extra money. He was very polite and gentle throughout the evening, and when he said good-bye I called him Cassius—I never called him by his Muslim name, Muhammad Ali—and then I added, "It's all right if I call you Cassius, isn't it?" He smiled and said, "Anytime, Floyd." (Floyd Patterson with Gay Talese, "In Defense of Cassius Clay," *Esquire*, August 1966)

After defeating Sonny Liston, Muhammad Ali declared himself the "King of the World." In some societies, the health of the king mirrors the health of the state. At the height of his powers, deserving or undeserving of the title, he was one of the leaders of a modern slave revolt, a slave revolt that was necessary because for one hundred years the promises that resulted from the Union victory and a temporary populist alliance between black and white farmers were destroyed by demagogues who instilled in whites the fear of black domination. This strategy is still being used. Just as they warned the Oklahoma Indians that if they aligned themselves with blacks they'd be treated the way blacks were treated, white farmers feared that a continuing alliance with black farmers would mean that they'd be disenfranchised the way blacks were. (Few textbooks have recorded that in 1892, Tom Watson, a white populist, was able to draw one thousand white farmers to a town where they halted the lynching of a black populist.) The promise of a New South that could have emerged after the Civil War was shattered and the old feudal order was restored through terrorism. A character in Charles Chesnutt's 1905 novel, *The Colonel's Dream*, comments that slavery still exists after observing the convict labor system in which black men were arrested on trumped up charges like vagrancy in order to supply cheap labor to white businesses, a belle, who has fallen on bad times, agrees.

In the 1960s, using both non-violent strategies and militant self-defense, Black America fought back, and a newly found feeling of pride swept the ghettos. Martin Luther King, Jr. put his life on the line each day in order to bring the continued system of oppression to the nation's attention. Malcolm X, who received worldwide attention before being murdered, had threatened to bring the issues of black oppression to the United Nations. While Martin Luther King, Jr. and the Black Panthers marched, African-American artists also stepped up. Nina Simone recorded "Mississippi Goddam" in 1958 and Sonny Rollins' unadorned, chord-savvy horn protested racial injustice with "Freedom Suite," which one writer has called "Jazz music's first explicit extended instrumental protest piece." In 1960 Max Roach recorded "Freedom Now Suite," and Curtis Mayfield joined in with "People Get Ready." Martha and the Vandellas prophesized the coming riots with "Dancing in the Streets." Painter Joe Overstreet took Aunt Jemima out of the kitchen, where she stood making pancakes since 1889, and armed her with a machine gun. For Betye Saar, watermelon became a food for sacrament.

Black poets were spreading fight-back poetry through the publication of chapbooks, which were disseminated through bars, beauty parlors, and churches. They took to television, a show called "Soul," where their verses reached thousands of people. Melvin Van Peebles' hero in "Sweet Sweetback's Baddass Song" (1971) was a poet too, but his verse was limited to movement. A deadpan expression that his character carried throughout the movie. It was cathartic for those blacks who'd had unpleasant and sometimes lethal encounters with the police: the majority of black American men. Van Peeble's character was a modern fugitive slave who, like some fugitive slaves, fled to Mexico (others traveled to Canada), and as some fugitive slaves did, murdered the dogs who were sent after him. Sam Greenlee took Peebles' revolt a step further. While Peebles's film was a scathing indictment of law enforcement, Greenlee's book and film "The Spook Who Sat by the Door" ends with black guerilla warfare against the United States.

There was a time in the 1960s that looked as though black Americans would, in Martin Luther King, Jr.'s words, "reach the promised land." However, it all changed, so that now after the triple plagues of crack, AIDS, and a powerful far-right attack machine that holds African-American values, not racism, accountable for the social problems that have debilitated Black America, their champion, their King, Muhammad Ali, was battling an opponent that didn't win by a knockout, but incrementally, on points. The King of the World's health was the health of the black nation in the 2000s, and even though some who get paid to write about this nation from Cambridge and Greenwich Village assert that the condition is self-inflicted—the "tough love" millionaires—the racism that robbed Ali of his best boxing years was still in effect.

Although the election of Barack Obama, a black president, was supposed to have made up for all of the hurt inflicted upon the black population for centuries, his election only revealed the psychosis of racism. A serious secessionist movement was begun. His every move was blocked and filibustered. Obama and his family are subjected to ugly comments that bordered on the deranged. Nazism, no longer a fringe movement, entered the mainstream. One of Rupert Murdoch's newspapers, *The New York Post*, printed a cartoon of the president as a chimpanzee, a depiction that gave the president less humanity than Hitler gave to blacks. He said that blacks were only "half-ape."

CHAPTER 17

Author Marvin X attributed Ali's conservatism to his having joined the late Wallace D. Muhammad's group, which publishes a newspaper whose front page is emblazoned with the American flag, like Fox News.

However, his shift to the right didn't seem to put a dent in the respect and affection for the champion held by those whom I interviewed; and the problems that Omowale Olanrewaju's group addressed weren't peculiar to Houston. They were happening throughout the nation. Harlem, where the unemployment rate among black men is fifty percent and where, as a result of gentrification and, as Charles Blow of *The New York Times* points out, police harassment, blacks were having to move to places like Pocono, New Jersey. This was also evident in the African-American exodus from San Francisco. *Street Spirit*, a publication of the American Friends Service Committee, carried the headlines, "Relentless gentrification and soaring housing prices in San Francisco trigger an exodus of African-Americans, families with children, poor and working-class people."

During a visit to Buffalo, New York, I heard about the same problems that were confronting San Francisco, Houston, New York's Harlem, Oakland, and many other cities with large black populations. Recently, over a two-month period, two former black women inmates have testified before a panel called "Prison Health" carried on C-SPAN, reporting that the medical complaints of black women inmates are ignored or even ridiculed, resulting in needless deaths. Other problems facing urban black populations include payday loans, meted out by fly-by-night operations that are financed by big banks that charge borrowers up to three hundred-fifty-percent interest. Banks like Bank of America and Wells Fargo made subprime loans to blacks and Hispanics, sixty percent of whom were eligible for conventional loans. In addition, white restaurant workers revealed that blacks receive service that is inferior to that of whites. Racism against blacks abounds in Silicon Valley due to the Intel having been invented by William Shockley, a race science quack. Furthermore, on September 8, 2014, it was reported on KPFA radio that blacks are prescribed more psychotropic drugs than whites. The speakers reported that Big Pharma uses blacks and even black children as guinea pigs for testing their experimental drugs, an issue that I tackle in my play, "Body Parts." Thousands of black students are suspended, disproportionately, and because of police presence in schools are arrested for talking back to the teacher or wearing the wrong school colors. A six-year-old was handcuffed for "throwing a tantrum."

◆

Yes, Ali could be gentle, as Stanley Crouch portrayed him as a Teddy Bear, but he could also be vindictive and mean. The vindictiveness came across in his taunting of Floyd Patterson, Ernie Terrell, and others who had ridiculed his conversion to Islam. Nonetheless, he never beat a man within an inch of his life as Jack Johnson did, who beat Tommy Burns so badly that the police stopped the fight, or Floyd Patterson, when as a light heavyweight champion he beat one of his former stable mates so badly that the man wasn't any good after that.

It was Patterson, however, who had made the 1965 fight a holy war between Christianity and Islam. At the end of the fight, it was Ali who made cruel remarks about his former mentor, Malcolm X. He confided to Jim Brown that he was breaking with Malcolm X even while enjoying his hospitality, after defeating Sonny Liston. Ali was the one who launched into an Anti-Semitic tirade after beating Leon Spinks (yet contributed one hundred thousand dollars to prevent a Jewish nursing home from closing, and shared his steaks with rabbis while residing at a Florida hotel). Bob Arum, who told me about this incident, blamed it on the entourage who, in his words, got Ali all worked up. In 2012, while attending the funeral services for Joe Frazier, Ali stopped off to witness the Bar Mitzvah of his grandson, Jacob Wertheimer, at Rodeph Shalom on North Broad Street in Philadelphia. Khalilah Ali-Wertheimer, Jacob's mother, told Ali biographer Thomas Hauser that though her father raised his children Muslim, he was "supportive in every way. He followed everything and looked at the Torah very closely." Ali had come along from his Yakub period when he described bi-racial children as "Little pale half-white green-eyed blond-headed Negroes."

I wasn't the only one upset with Ali long after Malcolm's assassination. My encounters with Malcolm X were key moments in my intellectual development. After Ali defeated George Foreman in the Congo, for me and for many of us, he could do no wrong. Even a congenital skeptic like me would fall under his magic. We even looked the other way when, after defeating Joe Frazier in Manila, he bussed the notorious dictator, Marcos. And according to Reggie Barrett gave Ms. Marcos and his daughters more than a bus. Maybe he should have ended his career with the "Thrilla In Manila," because after the two fights with Spinks he faced Larry Holmes. I sat there at the old Academy of Arts on 14th Street and watched the great champion receive a humiliating defeat from Larry Holmes, a former sparring partner.

However, aren't these the demands that we make upon our athletes, especially those whose job it is to give their opponents a concussion? We call it a knockout, and Ali wouldn't be the first or the last that would suffer from repeated poundings in the ring and during sparring sessions.

Finally, a man who ridiculed the Civil Rights Movement, on December 17, 2005, ironically received the Otto Hahn Freedom medal for his work for civil rights. In heaven, Martin and Coretta must be chuckling at that one. In an interview with Thomas Hauser, Ali said:

As far as my outlook is concerned, I'd say that ninety percent of the American public feels just the way I do as far as racial issues are concerned; as far as intermarriage is concerned; forced integration and total integration such as many Negro civil rights groups are trying to accomplish today... But as a whole, the whites believe like we do.

CHAPTER 18

I interviewed the late Jack Newfield at Caffe Mediterraneum in Berkeley. It was Rudy Langlais and Jack Newfield who had persuaded *The Voice* to hire me to cover the second Spinks-Ali fight in 1978. I invited my daughter, Tennessee, to accompany me, because I wanted Newfield to tell her about his experiences accompanying Robert F. Kennedy on the campaign trail. If Robert F. Kennedy had become president, Jack Newfield would have been his press secretary. We had coffee in the upstairs section of the famous Mediterraneum restaurant—called The Med by its denzens—one of the last hangouts for the aging Telegraph Bohemians whose heyday was the counter culture 60s. Newfield was concerned about Ali's health. (In October of the same year in which I conducted the interview (2004), Newfield was diagnosed with kidney cancer and died.)

During our discussion, Jack Newfield told me the following:

> I did a *Village Voice* article on him [Muhammad Ali] in 1962. He was walking down MacDougal Street and was reading his poetry. He said, "I'm going to read you my latest poem, 'Save All Your Money and Don't Bet on Sonny.'"
>
> Sonny Liston was owned by the mob; he couldn't read or write and he was a strikebreaker. He was old. In the second fight, Ali is standing over to him, demanding that he get up, but he was frustrated and he went down from a glancing punch. Film of the fight shows Liston's head snap as a result of what has become known as 'The Phantom Punch.'

I first saw Muhammad Ali in March 1963, when he arrived downtown in Greenwich Village for a poetry reading. He was billed with poet Diane Wakoski at a café called "The Bitter End." I remember a large, youthful man with eyes that expressed curiosity. He was in town to fight Doug Jones. I attended the fight at Madison Square Garden with my friend Harvey Peace, III, whom I met in Buffalo, New York. He was a student then. His book, *The Angry Black South*, about the student sit-ins, was among the first to reveal the growing quest for civil rights in the 1960s south. I remember our running into Jim Brown there and Jackie Robinson receiving cheers as he entered the garden, the spotlight following him. He was on crutches. Though many thought that Jones won the fight, I could understand why the judges would vote that Ali pulled it out in the tenth round. As Emanuel Steward would tell me later, Ali simply threw more punches. I listened to the first Ali-Liston fight in a beat-up hotel called the Midway, which was located on Broadway in the West Nineties. My fellow listener was the late John Black, a union leader for 1199 Hospital Workers. He was a Trotskyite who kept interrupting my hearing of the fight with lectures about how the boxing business exploited the boxers. I didn't pay attention because that night, I was worried for Ali, because I thought that Liston would administer a severe beating to a boxer who had captivated us with his wit, and daring. Of course, my radical friend was correct. Except for some poor Irish American boxers, most of the whites connected with boxing wear suits. They do the commentaries on the fights and write the sports copy.

They also do the brainy parts like write the books while the black, Latino, and poor white fighters get the brain injuries. Mike Buffer, the announcer whose trademark became "Let's Get Ready to Rumble," has earned more from that phrase than Muhammad Ali made risking his life in the ring. When I heard that Buffer had earned over four hundred million from roaring this phrase, which he says was copied from Bundini and Ali's "Rumble, young man, rumble," I thought of Leon Spinks fighting a fight while suffering from brain damage and having to borrow five dollars the next morning to buy breakfast.[1]

---

1. "By trade marking his catchphrase, Buffer has generated over $400 million in revenue, selling the rights to music, video games, merchandise and while making personal appearances. His business venture is so successful, Buffer doesn't even have to say his catchphrase to make money. He makes more from the trademark than he does announcing in the ring." *AtlNightsports.com*, July 5, 2011.

Newfield explained the problem that Ali had in convincing a skeptical public of the rightness of his draft position:

> Your whole career is based on violence and brutality and you tell us not to fight in Vietnam? What's the difference? When he announced that his name was Muhammad Ali and not Cassius Clay, the reporters began harassing him. He said to them, "I don't have to be what you want me to be."

Newfield discussed the atmosphere during the fight in the Congo, then called Zaïre:

> Don King had a gun in the ring in Zaïre. If you look at the footage where Ali knocks out Foreman you can see King, in the ring, hugging Ali with a big gun on his hip. King put the fight together between Ali and Foreman. He had Mobutu give him ten million dollars and he split five with Ali and five with Foreman. Mobutu rebuilt the stadium and a new road to the stadium.

Newfield was the author of an anti-King book that records the familiar charges against him, the murder of two men, as well as the exploitation of boxers like Tim Witherspoon, Mike Tyson, Larry Holmes, and Muhammad Ali. In 2005 and 2006, Zab Judah blamed his loss to an unknown on King for involving him in the promotion of the fight, therefore not leaving him enough time to train. Chris Byrd also complained that King was not doing enough to obtain big fights for him, but others, like Ernie Shavers, cite him as a benefactor. A Friar's Club toast to King held on October 28, 2005, in the New York Hilton presented a complicated picture of the infamous fights promoter:

> King's career as a promoter spans three decades and includes more than 500 world-championship fights, but it began as a humble plea to help save a Cleveland hospital in 1972. Facing a severe shortage of funds, Forest City Hospital was prepared to shut down. King knew the hospital served a vital function to a poor, working-class community. He sought out heavyweight champion Muhammad Ali and asked him to come and support a fundraising benefit to help turn around the hospital. The two men hit it off, and a new era began in boxing.

Don King is a generous philanthropist, he established the Don King Foundation, which has donated millions of dollars to worthy causes and organizations. He is a longtime supporter of the National Organization for the Advancement of Colored People (NAACP), the United Negro College Fund (UNCF), the Martin Luther King Jr. Foundation, the Simon Wiesenthal Center, National Hispanic Scholarship Fund, National Coalition of Title 1/Chapter 1 Parents, Wheelchair Charities, Our Children's Foundation, among other organizations, charities, colleges, and hospitals that has made him one of the world's leading philanthropists.

The NAACP recognized Don with its highest honor, the President's Award, and he received Lifetime Achievement accolades from Grambling State University. Shaw University, the oldest black college in the South, bestowed Don with an honorary doctorate degree and named him to its prestigious Board of Trustees. He also recently received the prestigious "Legacy Award" for Outstanding Community Service from Medgar Evers College in Brooklyn, NY. All three major boxing organizations, the IBF, WBA and WBC, have proclaimed Don King the "Greatest Promoter in History."

In the 2000s, Don King's career was in abeyance, but he made a comeback in April of 2014 when his fighter, Bermane Stiverne, defeated Chris Arreola and became the first Haitian-born heavyweight champion of the world. He was defeated in his first title defense.

While writing the King book, Newfield was introduced to the grimy underbelly of professional boxing:

But one out of a thousand fighters turn out okay. I did a book on Don King and I visited a lot of fighters and a lot of them were in horrible circumstances. I saw Jeff Merritt [a fighter with such a lethal punch that he broke Ernie Shavers' jaw] standing in front of a Las Vegas arena, homeless, on crack, and begging for money. I would say most fighters have sad endings. The three greatest fighters that ever lived were Joe Louis, Sugar Ray Robinson, and Muhammad Ali. They all had sad endings. Robinson had Alzheimer's and diabetes, Louis had dementia, and Ali has Parkinson's. I think there is a big connection between being hit all of the time and the brain.

Senator John McCain can't get a meaningful bill that would protect boxers through the Congress. The Republicans believe in deregulation and he wants regulation. Boxing is the only sport that doesn't have a national commissioner and it is not unionized. Until you get a health plan and a pension plan, they will continue to get cheated and robbed. The fringe promoters are now beginning to realize that working with the unions is their only hope.

All of the negative stuff about Ali is unfair. Some say that the only reason Ali resisted the draft was because of death threats from the NOI. I don't believe that. I think his views were why he resisted the draft. He did it out of bitterness because they drafted him by lowering the qualifying score and [ignoring] the recommendation that his religious background should be cause for resistance. Ramsey Clark, the Attorney General, overruled it, and he was indicted. Ali should not have been indicted. Four years later, the Supreme Court rules eight to nothing, overturning the lower court's decision.

Frazier said that Ali took the first fight because if convicted he'd be sentenced to five years in prison. Ali admitted that he wasn't ready. He said, "I have to fight Frazier now because I'm going to jail in May."

Ali loved rock and roll and rhythm and blues. I said, "You're a great hero. Who are your greatest heroes?" He just named all of these really great singers like Sam Cooke and James Brown.

After one fight, Ali summoned Sam Cooke to join him in the ring, and another fight was co-narrated by Red Foxx and James Brown. James Brown kept saying, "Ali is as serious as cancer."

CHAPTER 19

Boxing and the Brain

In 2005, it was reported that Leon Spinks, former heavyweight champion of the world, was suffering from dementia and working as a janitor in Columbus, Ohio, or as one publication put it cruelly, "cleaning toilets." The last time I saw Spinks was in 1978. He was being chauffeured around in a block-long white Cadillac by Mr. T.

Furthermore, it was announced in January 2006 that Oliver McCall, former heavyweight champion, had been arrested.

The saddest news of all is that on May 11, 2006, Floyd Patterson died after years of suffering from prostate cancer and Alzheimer's disease, the disease that took the life of Sugar Ray Robinson, pound for pound, the greatest fighter of all time.

After a second trip from Louisville, I learned that Mike Quarry, brother of Ali opponent Jerry Quarry, had died in June 2006 as a result of "boxing-induced dementia." Jermain Taylor, whom I saw defeat Bernard Hopkins in Las Vegas in 2005, experienced an episode of brain bleeding after being knocked out by Arthur Abraham. His run-ins with the law since then have been traced to the brain damage suffered by Taylor.

Obviously, Ali was a casualty. Ferdie Pacheco warned those close to Ali of what the consequences would be were Ali to continue taking punishment. After detecting signs of kidney damage (a lab test showed blood in Ali's urine), Pacheco pleaded with Ali to quit. He sent out five letters, certified mail with a return receipt requested, to Herbert Muhammad, Angelo Dundee, Veronica (Ali's wife at the time), Wallace Muhammad, and Ali himself. None answered. By contrast, when boxing expert and trainer Teddy Atlas was asked by Michael Moore, former heavyweight champion of the world, whether he should make a comeback or retire, Atlas, his former trainer, didn't quibble. He said by no means should Moore continue. Moore retired right then and there on ESPN live television.

◆

Judging from their more frequent appearances on television, black sports writers and commentators seem to have more power than before. Traditionally, some sports writers seem more interested in boosting white supremacy than assaying the talents of athletes objectively, regardless of race. Some vestiges of this former history remain. It's obvious to me that during the 2013 NBA championships, the San Antonio Spurs basketball team was treated as "the white hope" against the Miami Heat, whose team had more players of a dark complexion. During the games, there were more promotional efforts on behalf of the Spurs than the Heat, even though the Heat were the defending champions.

Larry Holmes was also the defending champion when he fought Gerry Cooney, yet it was Cooney's face that made the cover of *Time*. Larry Holmes writes bitterly of his treatment when training for the fight in Las Vegas. Tiger Woods, the Williams sisters, Floyd Mayweather, and Kobe Bryant have all been abused by nasty sports copy. Tiger Woods is not held to the same standards as Phil Mickelson.

The treatment of LeBron James became so ugly that Rev. Jesse Jackson spoke out. According to the Associated Press, Rev. Jesse Jackson was upset with an open letter written by Cleveland Cavs owner Dan Gilbert after LeBron James, his star player, decided to move to Miami. According to Jackson, "The bitter comments directed toward the free agent sound like they're directed at a 'runaway slave.'" However, in 2014, Gilbert's attitude changed when LeBron announced that he was returning to the Cleveland Cavaliers. But regardless of how they are treated by the segregated sports fraternity, they are heroes among the black masses. Even though the Joe Louis-Max Schmeling saga is portrayed as Americans rooting for Louis against the Nazi, a number of those in the audience were rooting for the Nazi. One sports writer said that Louis was such an animal that he didn't even have to train. The more scathing the comments about black sports heroes, the more these heroes become admired among blacks. Richard Wright writes about Harlemites and their feelings about Louis after a victory in the ring:

> They shouted, sang, laughed, yelled, blew paper horns, clasped hands, and formed waving snake-lines, whistled, sounded sirens, and honked auto horns. From the windows of the tall, dreary tenements torn scraps of newspaper floated down. With the reiteration that evoked a hypnotic atmosphere, they chanted with eyes half-closed, heads lilting in unison, legs and shoulders moving… "Ain't you glad? Ain't you glad?" (Richard Wright, *New Masses*, July 5, 1938)

In the words of Ron Chernow:

> In the slave-based economy, physicians often attended the auctions, checking the teeth of the human chattel and making them run, leap, and jump to test whatever strength remained after the grueling middle passage. (Alexander Hamilton, 2004)

Measuring the commercial value of African captives might mark the beginning of black sports in the United States. Though the sport of boxing has European roots, the beginning of blacks in boxing might have been the cruel sport which entertained the slave masters, in which a slave from one plantation would be pitted against slaves from another in a fist fight. In his interview with Nathan Hare, published by *Black Scholar* magazine, Muhammad Ali shows his awareness of this history and so did Joe Louis.

In his excellent book, *Forty Million Dollar Slaves*, William C. Rhoden writes:

> But there was a wider range of sporting activities in which African slaves were involved. In plantation South, slaves or rival plantations were used

as oarsmen in high-stakes boat races, as their respective masters steered. Foot racing, an enormously popular sport in the United States during the 1830s, was equally popular on the plantations and provided a convenient backdrop for wagering. Plantation owners exploited the speed of the fastest slaves by entering them into races against neighboring slaves or local challengers in various town races.

Some slaves like Tom Molineaux, an African captive from Virginia, was said to have earned his freedom by boxing rivals from other plantations. He went to England in 1809, and won two bouts. Later, black fighters would work their way out of the ghettos with their fists, just as Molineaux had done to earn his freedom. A number of them became heavyweight champion.

Of these fighters, Joe Louis, Sonny Liston, Mike Tyson, Jack Johnson and Floyd Patterson have reached legendary status, and of this elite, Muhammad Ali is considered the GOAT: the Greatest Of All Time. As a sign of his almost mythic status, when you say you're writing a book about Ali, the anecdotes begin to flow about this ring artist, whom writer Clayton Riley, who died about a year after I interviewed him, compared with the musician John Coltrane.

Like Ali, the tenor saxophonist John Coltrane put his own unique mark on modern jazz so that the chord progressions that he used in tunes such as "Giant Steps" are called Coltrane changes.

CHAPTER 20

Ali's Feet

Chezia Thompson, a poet, invited me to the Maryland Institute of the Arts to do a reading and to look at some poetry written by students. It was also requested that I examine the works of some student artists. One young woman had made a miniature atomic bomb from plastic-looking material and miniature planes of lead. Planes that couldn't fly. I told her about Howard Hughes's Spruce Goose, a plane that flew only a few feet before stopping. She hadn't heard of it. A young African-American woman made a bed that was covered with eggshells, a bed that you couldn't sleep on. Skeptics were saying that such was the state of heavyweight boxing and its different divisions. It was made up of men who wore boxing gloves, but couldn't fight.

On Friday, April 17, 2004, I took US Airways to New York's LaGuardia and caught a cab to The Southgate Tower. Some championship fights were taking place that evening across the street at Madison Square Garden.

After checking in, I took a cab to Clayton Riley's West Village apartment. Riley was a white-skinned man whose texture of hair identifies him as a black man, an identity that he chose for himself. In its obituary of Riley, *The Village Voice*, for which he wrote, summarized his accomplishments:

> Riley's range as an actor, writer, radio host, producer, professor and activist over five decades established him as a city landmark—a unique truth teller and embodiment of African-American outrage.

In addition to writing for the *Voice*, Riley produced work that appeared in *The Times*, the *Amsterdam News, Ebony, Newsweek, Sports Illustrated, Crisis* and the *Liberator*. He collaborated with Rev. Martin Luther King, Sr. on his 1980 autobiography, *Daddy King*, and edited *Black Quarter*, a collection of plays by Ben Caldwell, Ronald Miner, Ed Bullins and Amiri Baraka (then known as LeRoi Jones).

His radio shows on WBAI, WLIB and elsewhere attracted a sizable progressive audience. He taught at Sarah Lawrence, Cornell, Fordham, and the New School, and also served as the master of ceremonies for The Langston Hughes Festival at City College for many years.

His acting credits included *In White America* and *Dutchman*, and he also helped produce *Nothing But a Man*, starring Ivan Dixon and Abbey Lincoln. He was one of the founders of the Frank Silvera Writer's Workshop, which developed the work of black playwrights.

Clayton Riley's apartment is filled with African and Asian art. He answers my first interview question about George Foreman's remarkable comeback:

George Foreman had the ability to reconstitute himself. You look at many fighters who lost the way he lost to Ali; they're ruined physically and psychologically. Foreman did not allow that to happen to him. He didn't allow himself to be discouraged and so many guys can use him as a model. He didn't let [Don] King ruin his life.

Ali's was the fastest jab in any division. What Ali did was time the jab point from the rest point to its fullest extent and his jab was so swift down to the millisecond.

Sports Illustrated reported that "his fist actually covered the distance in four one-hundredths of a second, about the period of a blink of the eye." According to Riley:

He was a self-created genius. There is no previous model for the way he fought. His style is unprecedented, his coordination and his ability to move so quickly. First of all he avoided the punishment that most heavies had to take.

People talk about how he leaned back from punches [which] most people can't do because they can't do it as quickly as he did and they don't have the sense of a punch coming at them. I saw him fight at the

East West Golden Gloves in Madison Square Garden. At that time they followed the regional finals in Chicago and New York. Ali was fighting for the Chicago team. He was a tall, skinny kid, a 178-pound light heavyweight. He was 6'3" and built like a string bean. His opponent was a beefy Marine who was built like a tank.

In the first round, the guy bullies Ali all over the ring. In the second round, Ali starts eluding this guy; the guy couldn't corner him. He couldn't really engage Ali, and Ali was peppering this joker with feathery-type jabs until you began to see this guy's face look like a bag of broken raspberries—he just beat him into bad health or, as one of my relatives would say, beat him like a stolen mule.

He was so much faster than anybody you'd ever seen. He tended to disorder many fighters with his speed. The only one who was not undone was Doug Jones. Doug Jones was a fast fighter; he was also very crafty and very smart.

When Ali fought Zora Foley, who was a well-conditioned fighter, and very smart, he used all of the techniques that people were familiar with, only up-tempo. It's like what John Coltrane brought to music, not only a different style but also a different tonality. Even more so than Charlie Parker.

Sonny Stitt said, "I was playing that way before I ever heard of Bird." Ali brought a style that was more like the style of welterweights and middleweights. It was something that people had never seen before. The corner would tell their fighters to "go out there and knock the Ali out" and the fighters would say, "I'll do that if I can find him."

Very few trainers knew how to defend against Ali's style. He was so smart in the ring. When I interviewed Angelo Dundee, I asked him to tell me about the Rope-a-Dope. He said, "Clayton, we didn't know anything about this." And you hear in the film of the fight, shouting, "Get off the ropes. Get off the ropes!" Especially like Foreman, who could break your arms if you lay off the ropes. More than anything else, Ali knew that Foreman would tire. The way that he was built around the chest—solid and muscular—he had problems in later rounds when constriction occurred; so if you look at the film, you can see that Foreman goes down more as a result of exhaustion.

Ali was the best fighter of his time. He had an effect not only on black men, but the way black men were perceived. He *was* the assertion of what black men could be, as opposed to what people said we were, and as opposed to how so many of us came to see ourselves. He had the grace that so many would associate with dancers and the power that many could associate with John Henry, driving those stakes into the railroad tracks.

He brought many aesthetic things as well. The speaking style of the street corner, the pools halls, the cadences of church worship the song form. All these things come together in what people would call his doggerel.

Floyd Salas, president of PEN Oakland, called by *The New York Times* "The Blue Collar PEN," admired Ali's boxing abilities. Unlike many commentators about Ali's skills, Salas has actually stepped into the ring.

Like Nathan Hare, Hispanic novelist Floyd Salas had to choose between boxing and an intellectual profession. His book, *Tattoo the Wicked Cross*, published by Grove Press, was the literary projectile that established his fame. Born in Oakland, California, Salas was also the writer for NBC's gangster series "Kingpin." A writing workhorse, his first book of poems was over a thousand pages. Salas had about fifty gym wars and was assistant boxing coach at UC Berkeley for fifteen years. He was offered the job as head coach but turned it down.

He lives in an apartment that is stuffed with African sculpture. While illustrating his points, he engaged in some shadow boxing:

Muhammad Ali is one of the truly greatest champions of all time. I heard about him when he turned pro. I thought that he was fantastic. He was really pretty, light on his feet. Fast hands. He moved around all the time like a small fighter. There are boxers and there are punchers, and he was a boxer. Personally, I like boxer punchers like Sugar Ray Robinson. He was a boxer puncher. Nobody could box better than he could. He could knock you out in one punch, too, you know? But Ali didn't have power like that, okay? I thought he was actually beautiful. A couple of my friends were amateur fighters and when they fought in The Golden Gloves finals they said that Ali was voted the outstanding boxer of the finals. I think Stanley Garcia, a middleweight champion, told me how outstanding he was.

I was up in Tahoe in 1972 and a young woman up there didn't like him. She thought that he was a smart aleck. I said show-off, yes, but a charming show-off. I didn't care whether he shot off his mouth. He was entertaining. He was fun to watch. He broke the rules.

You are not supposed to lean back. You are always supposed to lean forward. He was tall so that he could get away with it. See, amateurs lean back to evade a punch and they get knocked out. But Ali would lean back and he'd make his opponents miss. That was unorthodox.

As for the first Frazier-Ali fight, I don't think that Ali was rusty. If you keep fighting regularly, even in the gym, then you stay fit. Your timing is okay. Frazier was just a better fighter that night. I loved Frazier. He was a tough motherfucker, man. He would go get you. When you fought Frazier, you had to fight. He'd make you fight. He was almost like a one hand fighter, a left hooker.

Ishmael Reed: What about Larry Holmes' charge that Ali used the referee? That he clenched and waited for the referee to break it up?
Floyd Salas: Ali's the one who did the clenching usually, but I have seen him with a guy on the ropes—punching him on the ropes. I think it was Ron Lyle. He was punching him, but Ali was not a great puncher. So not all of these punches were getting through, but he couldn't stop Lyle and so Ali calls the referee to stop the fight. In that case, he used the referee.

He didn't look like he had any deterioration until he got heavier and he couldn't dance around. So he used the rope-a-dope until Foreman punched himself out. Ali must have had an iron stomach to take all of those blows from Forman.

IR: How did Ali acquire his iron stomach?
FS: Exercise.

IR: [Salas, who is in his eighties, has a flat iron stomach, which he maintains by working on a slant board every day.]
FS: In the gym there is a medicine ball, which you throw at the boxer's stomach.

IR: What about Joe Louis's suggestion that Liston fought the wrong fight in Ali-Liston I? That he should have concentrated more on Ali's body instead of head hunting. This is the strategy that Louis used in Louis-Conn I. Louis concentrated on Conn's body during the early rounds and so by the time that he got knocked out by Louis, he'd slowed down and was forced to slug it out with Louis.

FS: He's absolutely right. Kill the body and the head will fall. The way to settle a fast boxer is to hit him in the stomach and he slows down. Foreman didn't have the defensive skills in that first fight. But when he returned, he was using the crossed arms defense of Archie Moore.

IR: Foreman was one of the hardest of punchers. Should Ali have quit after that fight?

FS: No. He shouldn't have quit. I disagree with people when they say that. Ali outsmarted Foreman. The fact that Ali could take all of those body punches made him unique. Foreman just got tired of hitting the punching bag, which was Ali's body.

IR: What about protecting boxer's brains with head gear?

FS: The crowd wouldn't go for it.

IR: How did you feel when it was revealed that he'd become a Muslim?

FS: I didn't care about him becoming a Muslim. I remember a peace rally '66 or '67 held at Civic Center in San Francisco. They had Ali on the stage because he opposed the war. He told everyone to join Islam. I booed him. It was about peace, not about Elijah Muhammad. Some colored person told us to stop. I think that Elijah Muhammad was a dictator. Ali stopped talking because we were booing him. But I loved him. That's when he became a liberal. He became an icon for the peace movement. "I have nothing against Viet Cong," he said. He will be remembered as a boxer. He is one of the greatest fighters of all time.

When I returned to the Southgate from interviewing Clayton Riley, the lobby was full of fighters and their attendants. Later, Chris

Byrd and Andrew Golota were headlining a fight card across the street at Madison Square Garden. I was to interview Stanley Crouch of the *Daily News* at two in the afternoon. I came down to the lobby to get some coffee at Starbucks and some Dr. Atkin's sugarless candy. I was diagnosed as a type 2 diabetic in 1999 and my blood sugar has remained normal, but I don't take many chances.

I saw Referee Richard Steele stumbling through the lobby. I was the only person who recognized him. Many fight fans still haven't forgiven him for the notoriously quick stoppage of the fight between Cesar Chavez and Meldrick Taylor with only three seconds left in the twelfth round. If Taylor, ahead on points, had survived that round, he would have been the first fighter to defeat Chavez. Pernell Whitaker was also robbed in a decision that went to Chavez. Pernell turned to cocaine after losing a decision to Oscar De La Hoya in a fight that he won. Meldrick Taylor's career went downhill after that fight. Later, he began exhibiting the symptoms of *dementia pugilistica*.

A tall, black man who wore a white cotton jumpsuit and white beret beckoned me. He introduced himself as Muhammad Ali's pedicurist and showed me photos of him and Ali and of Ali's feet. When I finally contacted Ali's office, I was told that he was not available for an interview. Because of a book being written by one of his daughters, he was under contract not to give any interviews.

Though a few black authors have written books about Ali, it's usually been a white male writers' club. The Ali Scribes have had full access to him, traveled with him, visited his farm. Some members of The Ali Scribes got even closer than that. One even boasts that he slept in the same bed with him. Dave Kindred writes, "I took off my shoes and put myself under the sheets with the once and future heavyweight champion of the world." The passage ends with Kindred commenting on the size of Ali's penis. Another sports writer commented on the size of Sonny Liston's penis and how many hotel owners' wives would miss Sonny after his death.

I called Larry Holmes' office every day for a while, only to get the runaround. In his book *Against the Odds*, Holmes writes about how close Howard Cosell got to him. He says that on two occasions, a drunken Cosell approached him in Las Vegas, rubbed his thighs, and panted about how much he'd like to make love to Holmes. Dammit! Some writers have all of the access.

The closest I got to the champion in connection with the writing of this book was a look at photos of Ali's feet and later, after attending the dedication of the Ali Center, I caught a brief glimpse of the champ as his van rounded the corner on 6th Street in Louisville. I was standing on the corner talking to a photographer from the *Detroit News*.

Heavyweight champion Chris Byrd and his entourage entered the lobby followed by promoter Carl King. The pedicurist approached Byrd, but his efforts to solicit business were blocked by a young woman. They had words. The pedicurist addressed the woman as "Sir." In the United States, the sure way to insult a woman is to give her masculine attributes and the way you insult a man is to call him feminine.

Stanley Crouch arrived to my room. He'd brought a sandwich, some kind of grape drink, and some sugarless cookies. He's also suffering from diabetes.

Ishmael Reed: [I asked him whether Muhammad Ali is a hero because of his stand on the war.]
Stanley Crouch: His anti-war stance was imposed upon him by his body guards, I think, because Elijah Muhammad went to jail during World War II. People have chosen not to remember most of the statements he made during that period. He was against interracial marriage, interracial dating. There's a fantasy element associated with him and most of his fame is based upon fantasy; the idea that this guy is smart, for example. He's the kind of guy who, when a teenager, would throw rhymes and stuff. He's a boxer. Not particularly smart. Funny, maybe. But he had such a naïve vision that there was something that Africans have that we lost—now if Rwanda is an example—I'm glad that we lost that. Yet when he went to Africa he insulted the women over there. He said that they needed to get some white blood so they'd look better.

Now there's no doubt that he was one of the greatest boxers of the twentieth century, but the thing about Ali is that he knew he was an entertainer. He always knew that he was in show business. So the only time he became dull was when he got into the Nation of Islam, because the Nation of Islam doesn't have room for someone who is interesting.

You can be a hysterical fanatic, but you can't be interesting. That's impossible. That was Malcolm X's problem. He was getting too much attention. I went to the Freedom of Information Act to look up Fard Muhammad. Fard Muhammad was a Hawaiian. He was a pimp. He's like the L. Ron Hubbard of Black Nationalism. He turned what was essentially a street hustle into a cult. His idea was, "We're going to make money out of this cult." You had the same thing with Malcolm X. He went to Saudi Arabia and somehow didn't notice that white people could come from there. He didn't notice that until 1964. He was a fraud, too.

Ali's fame is the result of bumper-sticker thinking. Identity based on slogans, not even icons. Usually with an icon there is some lengthy discussion somewhere. But with Ali and others it's like a little box with pictures of a lion and a tiger. It's like animal crackers in which you dip in and there's a piece representing Martin Luther King, Jr., Rosa Parks, Ali, and slogans like, "Off The Pig," "Black Power," "I Have a Dream," and so Ali fits perfectly into that mold.

In the 50s, blacks seemed to have had a set of values, which included both group support as well as being part of the society. Martin Luther King, Jr. made Elijah Muhammad's brand of separatism acceptable, which is kind of strange to me. Like you go to someone's house, the husband is making one hundred thousand a year, the wife is making seventy-five to ninety Ks, and they're celebrating Kwanzaa. Now the holiday is a fraud. A Negro named Ron Karenga made it up. Why are they celebrating? They say black people need some kind of holiday.

The career of Ali is like that of a bear in the woods. A real bear is not a joke. It will tear a horse to pieces and out run a man; a bear with a hat on in a circus is a different bear, one chained to a pole; a bear that becomes a teddy bear is totally distanced from the real thing. Ali's career was like that. When he was a Muslim and hating white people, he was a real bear. Then he came in a little bit and got the Muslims set off to the side. Then he went to the circus and was chained to a pole and he was okay with that.

◆

When I saw Ali being led up to the stage before a ninety-five percent white audience at the thousand-dollar-a-ticket gala, held before the opening of the Ali center in Louisville, I thought of an observation that Geronimo made:

> I have never considered bears very intelligent, except in their wild habits, but I had never before seen a white bear. In one of the shows, a man had a white bear that was as intelligent as a man. He would do whatever he was told—carry a log on his shoulder, just as a man would; then, when he was told, would put it down again. He did many other things, and seemed to know exactly what his keeper said to him. (Geronimo, *The Autobiography of a Great Patriot Warrior*)

At the gala opening of the Ali Center, at the end of performances by the famous, Ali was brought to the stage and following instructions, he struggled bravely to wave a flashlight which was supposed to represent the Olympic torch as the bejeweled and heavily furred, hair sprayed, and sparkling audience waved the ones with which they had been supplied. At that moment, I thought of what writer Stanley Crouch told me. He said that there were three stages in Ali's career: the forest bear, the circus bear and the teddy bear:

SC: He began to call black people "animals," etc. Then after his career ended, he became a teddy bear. And he is about as articulate now as a teddy bear. Now that he can barely talk, you can read anything into him that you want to read into him. When HBO did that thing about him, Frazier apologized for ridiculing his current disabled condition. Frazier's apologizing, I thought, was majestic. As for Foreman, very few people with the exception of Jack Johnson could have gone into Zaïre and won that fight, because Johnson was the only fighter who had the audiences like Foreman.

IR: Black fighters weren't the only ones who had to be protected from hostile crowds. Jack Dempsey had to be secreted out of town after the town lost money because of a foolish promoter named Loy J. Molumby, a cowboy who promised Jack Dempsey three hundred thousand dollars to fight Tommy Gibbons. The Great Western Railroad pulled out of the fight, which made it difficult for fight fans to travel to Shelby, Montana, where the fight was being held. This killed the gate. While Dempsey got out with his hide intact, his manager had to bribe a railroad engineer in order to escape a lynching.

SC: So Johnson was able to go into the ring with a hostile audience and win a fight. The Foreman who beat Moore had more endurance than the Foreman that night in Zaïre.

There's nobody like Foreman in the history of the country, going all the way from being ridiculed as an Uncle Tom to where he is now. He was a country Negro from Texas. So when he came out as just himself people fell in love with him.

All of these guys who fought Ali and had to bear the brunt of his criticism, Frazier's kids having other kids calling their father an Uncle Tom—I wonder how Ali feels when he runs into them.

Now Liston. He didn't train for those fights. He felt that he was just going to go out and knock him out. Ferdie Pacheco said that Ali got hurt in the first fight. He suffered from those body blows. Pacheco said that those blows left their mark.

CHAPTER 21

Mr. Dick

For some athletes, women were places where you had orgasms, like one would fill up a gas tank at a service station. At least Rocky Marciano, who has been treated as a saint by some of the same sports writers who give black sports figures a hard time, felt that way about women. "If Rocky ever went to some place and there was not a girl waiting for him, he'd never come back. He never had an affair. I don't think he had sex with the same girl twice. Any girls he had sex with, you couldn't bring her to dinner no more. That's it. Get rid of her. He never wanted to see her again. Rock was insane about girls, all the time," Richie Paterniti, a friend of Marciano's, remembered: "That's all he wanted to do. Rock had orgies and parties. We had girls every single day and night. I had a suitcase that I took all over, filled with vibrators and electric massagers and all kinds of creams and oils." During the last stages of his boxing career, Sonny Liston's recreation was shooting craps with Joe Louis, eating fast foods, and sex. He had thirty young women at a time.

Of Muhammad Ali's enormous sexual appetites, Larry Holmes writes:

> I know how he lived. I knew what he did. I seen the people come into camp and leaving camp. I know he walked around with a stiff dick every day. I knew that. He would fuck a snake if you hold its head. You don't even have to hold the mutherfucker's head. Just give him the snake.

Of interracial dating and marriage, Ali said in an interview with *The Black Scholar* in 1970, reprinted in Summer 2012.

I hate to see black women and black men—once they get prestige and greatness, where they can go into ghettos and pick up little black babies and make them feel good, and once they big, to go leave and marry somebody else and put the money in that race. That makes me so mad. People like Lou Rawls and Eartha Kitt and Leslie Uggams.

I know those Negroes. Floyd Patterson—and his first wife, Sandra. A pretty black wife and four beautiful children. He quit her and went all the way to Sweden to marry a white woman. (That's why I gave him such a good whuppin'.)

Now the white man's got the heavyweight champion—Joe Frazier's got a white girlfriend. She's in his training camp all the time. When he's singing in those nightclubs. I went up and caught him one night. I'm not condemning white women, white women are beautiful—for white men.

Ali could also be hypocritical. In an interview with Nathan Hare, a scholar and former boxer, printed in the *Black Scholar* magazine, he ridiculed Floyd Patterson, Joe Frazier, and a number of black celebrities for their conducting interracial relationships.

Given some of the comments in this interview, one can understand why Jim Brown would refer to Ali as a "sexual hypocrite." Training for the first fight with Sonny Liston in Miami, Ali told Jim Brown that he'd been celibate for a year. Brown found him three weeks later in a hotel room. "He had just been with three women." Brown also says that after a fight, "Ali would have four, five, seven naked women up in his suite, and he loved it. He might screw five women—move from room to room."

As for his criticism of Patterson and Frazier for consorting with white women, Brown recounts being in London and partying with white women. Ali was present. Brown writes, "I pulled Ali to the side. I said, 'Ali, I thought you didn't fool around with white girls.' Ali answered, 'Well, Him, Elijah, taught us it's only the German white people and the American white people who are bad. These English folks are all right.'"

Joe Louis shared Ali's sentiment about the English, especially their women. He was spending a nice afternoon being serviced by two English girls when his wife, Marva, interrupted the dalliance.

Ali had an affair with an Italian girl, according to Brown. Brown said, "Damn Ali! You're always preaching to your brothers, 'Don't mess with any white girls,' and here you are messing with this girl.' Replied Ali, 'Jim, you know Italians aren't white.'"

I wonder if The Ali Scribes knew about Ali's relationship with white women, would they have been so enchanted by Ali—the Ali who said he wanted nothing to do with white women, and, when tempted by some, refused to succumb to their advances, so the story goes.

Though mainstream punditry might convince the public that Thomas Jefferson and Strom Thurman were the lone perpetrators of sexual relationships with black women, for a few hundred years white men had been "talking white, while sleeping black"; in the 1960s, some black men and black women "talked black while sleeping white," conducting interracial intimacy the way it's been conducted up to now: in the dark. Louisiana Governor Earl Long was committed to an asylum for commenting on the sexual hypocrisy of such white men. Jack Johnson was nearly lynched for refusing to be a sexual hypocrite. It's been revealed recently that race mixing reached all the way to the Confederate White House as the bridal photo of Jefferson Davis and his new wife, Varina Howell, shows.

After Johnson's example, Joe Louis was warned to refrain from such liaisons. He had to sneak around with Sonja Henie and Lana Turner. In his biography, he hints that there were others:

> A big movie star would see me, the Heavyweight Champion of the World, and wonder how I am in bed. I see a big beautiful movie star and wonder how she is in bed. We would find out very easily. These were just one-night stands. But we both knew how to keep it cool. Neither of us could afford to be found out in America in those days. (Louis, 1978)

Like Robinson and Ali in his early years, Joe Louis had a severe Johnson problem. His friend, Leonard Reed recalls, "One, three, four

Bridal photo of Jefferson Davis and his new wife, Varina Howell. Race mixing
appears to have made it even up to the Confederate White House.
(See photo of Varina Howell Davis in the photo section.)

girls he'd have after a fight, each going in [hotels] and staying fifteen
to twenty minutes."

So Ali, who taunted Floyd Patterson while meting out a merciless
beating, deliberately prolonging the ex-champion's suffering, engaged
in the same activities of which he accused Patterson. Also, by sneak-
ing around with white women, while being seen publicly with black
female companions and wives, both Louis and Ali were able to avoid
the condemnation that Johnson received for carrying on with white
women in public. While Louis and Ali achieved the status of Orishas
or deities, among blacks, Johnson paid dearly for carrying on in public
in the manner that both had in private. He was the only ex-champion who wasn't introduced from ringside when Joe Louis met Max
Schmeling for the second time, a deliberate snub. When Malcolm X
confronted Elijah Muhammad about his adultery, Muhammad said
that he was merely trying to be like King David. One of the iconic

figures of Western civilization is King David. David was the symbol that Rev. Jesse Jackson invoked while consoling President Clinton, during the scandal involving his assignations with a White House intern. Later, Rev. Jackson was found to have his own King David problems. Were Ministers Elijah Muhammad, Jackson, and Ali following biblical precedent, or were they, as Agieb Bilal said, following their male ancestors' roles as breeders?

Bryant Gumbel's *Real Sports* carried an episode about a horse that, though not having won many races, sired winners. The horse was very much in demand and received thirty-five thousand dollars for each time he mated with a female horse. In plantation days, black men were the horses. They were the black bulls that sapped the cows. Booker T. Washington said that his mother's master, his father, had as much regard for his mother as one would have for a cow. And so while planters looked on, the black male would mount the black female as one animal would mount another animal for the purpose of turning out new human farm machinery for the proprietor, and people like the warped Thomas Jefferson would gaze at the mating as the whites in Melvin Van Peebles' *Sweetback* watched a round of black lovemaking. How else would Jefferson know that black men were "ardent" with their women or be able to speculate that they were prone to premature ejaculation, or comment on the sexual behavior of Native Americans. He observed them from the point of a zoologist. This founding father was a creep.

In the 1960s, the novelist Robert Gover was using a black prostitute as an informant for a book he was writing. She told him that one of the most popular sexual attractions in Las Vegas involved a white Southern couple swapping with a black couple, and a leader of the Klan was reported to have one of the most extensive libraries involving combo sex in the country.

CHAPTER 22

In his book *Out of Bounds*, Jim Brown talks about Ali's buying prostitutes while "lying to the public and his friends, saying he was pure. Pure? Ali was a superfreak." He also adds some interesting information: "Ali's greatest fascination in life was with gangsters and pimps, and other men who could control women. He always wanted to be known as a Mac Man, a bad brother who could rap to any chick."

If Ali admired pimps, pimps also admired Ali. Pimps on parade with their ladies is one of the sideshows of major boxing events. When I covered the Spinks-Ali Fight, and most recently attended the second Hopkins-Taylor fight, I was impressed by the large contingent of players and their ladies, the people whom Quincy Troupe criticized when they exported that ostentatious style to Zaïre. One of those who attended Marvin X's Liberation book fair was a player and author. A handsome, dark-skinned man, he was attired in black leather. Someone said that he reminded them of Richard Roundtree in *Shaft*. His book is *The American Pimp*, subtitled *The Exploits of Rosebudd the Pimp*. His name is John S. Dickson, aka Rosebudd Bitterdose.

John S. Dickson, aka Rosebudd Bitterdose, "Why do pimps admire Ali?" He replied:

First of all, I'm from the streets. I went to school and graduated from Sonoma State back in 1974. For me and for all black men, Muhammad Ali represented the same thing that the pimp represented. Not that he was that way, but he had the attitude that he did what he wanted to do the way he wanted to do it, and when he wanted to do it, and how he wanted to do it, and you're going to like it. That's the attitude that players have. I was proud of him when he used to predict what he was going to do. Actually, when you think about it, you think it's set up, but it's not, you know what I'm saying? The Liston fight wasn't the only one. He would take the name of Archie Moore and rhyme it with four and actually do that. You'd think that that was set up, but it merely showed how bad he was.

I realized that he may not have grown up in the streets, but when you have a certain confidence about your skills, you can do anything. He had the confidence that he was the baddest on earth. That's why he was so great.

Back in '63, he was one of the first rappers. You got to understand something. You don't want to be a pimp if you don't want to be seen. You don't want to be a pimp if you don't want to make a mark in life. Ali, like each individual pimp, thought he was the baddest, and so when players attended an Ali fight they were paying homage to a comrade. They also wanted to show that they had the money to attend a fight. It's all about networking, you know who's going to be there, where they're staying, what kind of seats they have.

Just because I'm in California doesn't mean that I don't have friends on the other coast, like New York and New Jersey, or the Southwest, like Texas. Before the fight, you'd call all of them to find out who is going to the fight. Like, I went to Leonard-Hearns fight. You have to dress as fly as you can be. You don't know whether you're going to be on TV, but you behave as if all of the cameras are on you. You dress like that. That's why my book is so important, because it's not just about pimps and whores and selling pussy or pimps beating up whores, it's about what is really going on. Like, people say that whores are threatened or insecure, but you be at a place where people have hundreds of dollars, maybe even thousands to give to someone who appeals to them; you can't be insecure in a place like that. The average person thinks that I have to be out there and make these broads trick when actually when the broads are out there on the street, they're only concerned with the trick and the police. If it were against their will, they would stop the cop and ask him to do something about it. These are fallacies that I debate in my book. They want to be whores. I can't talk these women into being whores, I can only ask them to be a whore for me. That's all I can do. If she doesn't want to be a whore, she's gone.

Players go to entertainment events, shows, and things like that. They are going to stay certain places. I've only gone to one, which was Sugar Ray Leonard-[Tommy] Hearns. Boxers, your average male big entertainer—they all want to be pimps. They all emulate pimps in their attitudes.

Ali has a special place for my respect. He's going to attract a lot of women because power is an aphrodisiac, so women are going to gravitate toward a person with power. I attract a lot of women because of the power I have. I don't think that whores are weak or less than the average woman, because I know that they are a woman first and a whore second. Like I'm a man first and a pimp second. In order for me to be a successful pimp I have to know how to handle women. I don't say I have known how to handle whores, I have to know how to handle women, so I have to study women. I remember when I was so mad at a whore I wanted to kick her ass. You know what I said? "You're fired." That broad would do anything I asked her after that.

I think that what Ali did for black men was the same thing that Laurence Fishburne did in [the film] *The Cotton Club*. [Fishburne played "Bumpy" Johnson, a black Harlem racketeer.] Regardless of all of the negative things said about the pimp, in the days of oppression, the pimp did what the fuck he wanted to do, making everybody else think that they could do what they wanted to do if they found a way to do it. Here's this pimp rolling around in this bad car, jeweled up, and got bitches working for him. Ali had the same effect when he went to jail for being a Muslim. He was saying, I don't give a fuck what you think about my being a Muslim, I'm giving a fuck about how I want to be a Muslim and if I have to go to jail for being a Muslim then I'm going to jail. What really made him great was his defiance and not his ability to fight. He defied the people in control of us. They said to him, "You can't do this," and he said to them, "This is what I'm going to do because this is the land of freedom."

CHAPTER 23

The Opening Ceremonies, November 2005

If you're in a flood like Katrina and you don't have a car, you end up in an Astrodome with no food or water. That's one America. If you pay a thousand dollars for a ticket in connection with writing a book, you enter a white world. Those who can't afford the admission stand across the street from the Kentucky Center, craning their necks at the celebrities who are arriving in limousines and walking up the red carpet. A whole forest of animals must have been emptied in order to furnish the women with coats. Angelina Jolie, Brad Pitt, President Clinton, and others arrived. Before I took my red carpet walk, I headed away from the Kentucky building toward the Ali Center located around the corner. I walked across the street to the side where the bleachers were set up and fell in behind about six black teenagers. I asked the kids what they thought of Muhammad Ali. The girls said, "He's pretty." One of the boys said, "Float like a butterfly—" He was unable to supply the rest of the quote, "sting like a bee."

I entered a tent that led to the Ali Center. There were waiters passing out hors d'oeuvres and drinks. I stood in line. Standing in front of me was an elderly white man and his wife. He was a banker. Two of the few black people attending the gala, an assemblyman and his wife, stood behind. We struck up a conversation. I took his card and planned to interview him when I returned to Louisville in June. His office didn't return my calls.

The exhibit consisted of a multimedia presentation of Ali's career, from his beginnings as the "Louisville Lip" to his role as an inspiration to people the world over. After the tour, I headed to the Kentucky Center where tents had been set up for the gala dinner. Afterwards, I felt foolish walking up the red carpet.

As I entered the Kentucky Center I noticed the late Angelo Dundee, Ali's trainer and boxing historian, the late Bert Sugar, and Rahaman Ali, Ali's brother. I took their photos and posed with Sugar and Rahaman. Bert Sugar agreed with Floyd Salas that Joe Louis was the greatest. He criticized Ali for holding his hands low, holding his opponent's head, and says that Ali was not good at inside fighting. For some reason, Don King's name came up. Sugar said that Don King has fucked more blacks than Little Richard.

I entered the tent. My table was #112. This turned out to be fortuitous because I made contact with Reggie Barrett, the man who played an important role in Ali's comeback. Also seated at his table were Jonathan Smith and Barrett's wife. I interviewed Barrett the next day at the Starbucks section of the Marriott. I milled about the tent where the eighty-five percent white gala revelers were dining.

Once in a while there was a commotion as the diners surrounded celebrities. Lennox Lewis, in his familiar dreadlocks, was towering above a group of fans. Evander Holyfield was seated, dining. His ticket and airfare were paid for. Missing were George Foreman, Larry Holmes, Ken Norton, and other opponents. While Lennox Lewis contributed to the building of the Center, donations from other athletes were missing. Holyfield wants another go at the heavyweight title—pathetic. However, some say that given the talent in the heavyweight division, perhaps he has a chance. (Holyfield retired in 2014.)

I approached Lewis for a photo; his bodyguard blocked my passage. "The champ is eating," he said. Some of the people who are members of Louisville society don't even know about boxing. "Who was that fellow?" an elderly, white-haired, coiffed woman asked me. It was Evander Holyfield. However, these people know each other. After dinner, I went into the lobby and stood on the sidelines as some of those who had paid for less pricey tickets awaited a glimpse of those who were exiting the tent. I recognized the late folk singer, Richie Havens, who was sporting a white beard as long as cartoonist Robert Crumb's "Mr. Natural." Musician Herbie Hancock was greeted warmly by the crowd. There was no reaction to ex-boxer Laila Ali, who exited the tent briskly, her entourage in tow.

Later, during an appearance on ESPN, she said that her relationship with her father had been "bumpy." During the opening ceremony the next day, I could detect some tension between Laila and the rest of the family. While Ali's twins made some remarks from the stage the next day, Laila declined. When she issued a report that her father was fading and that he was out of her reach, Lonnie Ali (to some, Ali's dedicated caretaker, to others, a manipulative Lady Macbeth, or a Lady Machiavelli), shrewdly maneuvering the image of Ali for profit, rebuffed her.

Rahaman Ali had accused Lonnie of marrying Ali for fame and for his money. Though ill, his brand name is worth millions and a commercial using his voice was aired during the 2015 Super Bowl. Tim Smith of the *Daily News* writes that after Ali's death, his estate might be worth more than those of "Marilyn Monroe and Elvis Presley." As for Laila's concern about her father, Lonnie Ali wrote, "She doesn't see her dad that often." And in what amounted to a dig, she said, "The only thing I can think of is over a lifetime of when she did see him until now (she noticed this change). Knowing that her schedule is busy, when we're in L.A. is when we're able to connect. It's usually after a long workday where he's been making appearances. She stops by and he's usually very tired. I don't know what she was thinking when she said that."

Having observed Ali over two days, I would come down on the side of Laila. In comparison to the huge, muscular, confident, and articulate man I'd run into as I opened a door at the New Orlean's Fairmount hotel, he was drawn, ashen, stooped over from neck surgery, and after sitting on a stage surrounded by the flags of many nations, he was carted down to a building and taken to the rear of the first floor where he sat down. The press photos of Ali that came out of the event were complimentary; the photo I took of Ali sitting on the cart told the whole story. To add to that, Angelo Dundee told NPR the next day—I heard it on my radio while walking through

O'Hare Airport—that Ali had "fought his last two fights while suffering from Parkinson's disease."

Regarding that fight, there have also been some serious charges against Dr. Charles Williams, Elijah Muhammad's personal physician, and his administering of a controversial and dangerous thyroid drug to Ali before the Holmes fight. Larry Holmes, who had delivered a beating to the former champion, is blameless. After all, the sports writers, who were as enchanted with the Ali myth as The Ali Scribes had made Ali the favorite in that fight. I hadn't, and in my *Village Voice* (October 16, 1978) piece about the second Spinx-Ali fight, I predicted that he would lose if he were to fight Holmes.

As I headed for the Whitney Hall, I noticed promoter Bob Arum entering the tent from where others were exiting. At one time, Arum was Ali's manager, until Don King showed Ali a bag full of cash totaling two hundred twenty-five thousand dollars and told Ali that he could do as much for Ali as "that Jew." But if King exploited Ali, he wasn't the only one. As Ali said when he didn't pass the Selective Service exam, "I said I was the greatest, not the smartest." Near the entrance to the theater, I noticed a crowd gathered about blues singer B. B. King.

We had to wait about twenty minutes before the doors were opened. For the entertainment, held in the Whitney Hall, located inside the Center, I was seated next to a slender blonde woman who introduced herself as Tanya. She said she worked as a volunteer. Though a Cincinnati paper said that the opening was a "yawn," the thousand-dollar tickets were sold out and the seats in Whitney Hall were filled with stars from sports, entertainment, and politics. A man, whose silver hair had been blow-dried to his scalp, passed by us in the row in front of us with a blonde woman in tow. Tanya said it was the governor and his wife. Three people left before the entertainment was over and Tanya said of the two who were married that they had to leave because "they just had twins."

The first act was a bit of shadow theater, which had actors playing Ali and Howard Cosell, engaged in some humorous banter imitating the sort of exchanges that took place between the actual pair. It was pointed out to the audience that Lonnie, Muhammad, and former President Clinton were seated in a box above stage right. The audience began chants of "Ali, Ali, Ali." We were told that representatives from thirty countries and five continents were seated in the audience. Among the performers were Kris Kristofferson, American Idol star Ruben Studdard, Michael Franti, James Taylor, Richie Havens, and Blair Underwood, who read a Martin Luther King, Jr. monologue about his being a drum major while an actual local drum major marched about the stage. Bryant Gumbel, Matt Lauer, and David Frost delivered tributes. Only Gumbel made mention of Ali's problems with Selective Service and Franti, Ali's Muslim affiliation, but there were few Muslims among the one thousand patrons and Lonnie had severed Ali's ties to the Ali Circus, the name given to his entourage

In the ceremony the next day, there were more references to Saint Francis of Assisi and Thomas Merton than to Muslim philosophers. The highlight of the evening's presentation was Attallah Shabazz, Malcolm's daughter. She is the legacy that Malcolm deserved. Tall, beautiful, articulate, gracious—the daughter of "the knight in shining armor" to some—a woman with pedigree. She is very respectful of Ali even though this is the man who played Judas to her father. Another high point was Kathleen Battle's rendition of two spirituals, "Over My Head" and "Hush, Somebody's Calling My Name."

Howard Bingham, who might be one of the world's most fawning sycophants, made a blubbery, tearful tribute to Ali that ended with his pledge to be there for him. One wonders, then, why he stood by and allowed Ali to be nearly killed in the ring. I don't want this kind of person to be there for me. Some of the presentation was visual. By video hookup, former President Carter saluted Ali's role for negotiating the release of prisoners from Iran and Iraq. Carter also recalled Ali's role as an ambassador at large to several African countries. He didn't mention that some of the leaders of those countries considered sending Ali, a boxer, as ambassador, to be an insult. Julius Nyerere refused to receive him. Muhammad was some player on the geopolitical stage. Receiving such a warm reception in England, Ali voiced doubt that England ever engaged in warfare.

Comedian James Carey, another trickster and therefore able to say what others only think, said, "I wanted somebody to kick his ass" when he heard Ali say, "I am the greatest," and "I'm bigger than boxing." A nervous titter came up from the thousand seats. Finally, it was President Clinton, under whose administration more blacks were incarcerated than any time before in history and the iniquitous Welfare Reform bill was signed, which has families eating out of garbage cans. Clinton's role in the repeal of Glass–Steagall Act of 1933 that limited commercial bank securities activities allowed them to speculate. Such speculation led to Hispanics and blacks losing hundreds of billions in equity. Taking the stage with Ali and Lonnie was among the symbolic gestures that Clinton employed to disguise the fact that Clinton was one of the worst presidents for blacks. They all started hugging one another. The following week, the head of the Democratic Leadership Council, appearing on C-SPAN, just about bragged about how Clinton embarrassed Jesse Jackson at a meeting of PUSH when he condemned Sister Souljah for singing anti-white lyrics allegedly. That way, he said, Clinton stood up to special interests that dominated the party. If he thinks that blacks were a special interest group that dominated the Democratic Party, he's delusional.

Given Clinton's successes with the Martha's Vineyard and Lionel Hampton blacks—the name given by whites to those sections of the Hamptons occupied by blacks—while giving the finger to millions of poor blacks, I'm sure that George Bush regrets that he didn't learn to play jazz saxophone.

After more three-hankie praises for the ailing athlete, the evening ended with everybody waving lanterns with which they had been supplied; Ali struggled with his. This was to be like his lighting the Olympic torch. Lonnie announced that she was going to cart him off to Germany the next month.

CHAPTER 24

December 2005, Las Vegas

I had to book an expensive suite at The Hotel at Mandalay Bay. This was because the regular Mandalay Bay was sold out! I'd read that Muhammad Ali was going to launch a Marathon Race, which would begin at 6 a.m. on Sunday, December 4. I wanted to be there. I bought two tickets on Southwest for the hour or so flight from Oakland to Las Vegas, fight city. George Foreman said that, "You gotta be right in Vegas. You gotta be in shape. No one gives you an easy fight there" (Dahlberg, 2004). It is the land of Bugsy Segal and other gangsters, Jewish and Italian, who raised this city from the sand.

Cash would have much to choose from if he were to create a mural of this place: George Foreman, Frank Sinatra, and Sinatra's mom exchanging greetings backstage at Caesars' Palace Pavilion; Muhammad Ali leaping into the ring to needle Sonny Liston at the Las Vegas Convention Center rotunda; George Foreman, kneeling at prayer after knocking out Michael Moorer, November 5, 1994; Lennox Lewis knocking out Hasim Rahman at Mandalay Bay, November 17, 2001 (I won eighty dollars and later met Rahman at the Southgate Tower hotel); Sugar Ray Robinson losing to Fred Hernandez, July 12, 1965; Archie Moore and Nino Valdez dressed in cowboy duds; Ali stopping Floyd Patterson on November 22, 1965.

The Las Vegas Marathon is the reason that the Mandalay Bay is sold out, and so throughout the casinos and restaurants were marathon racers. You could see people of a variety of weights, sizes, and races wearing their marathon sweatshirts, but I didn't see any sign of Ali.

I was beginning to think I was stalking the ex-champion, like one of those "stalkarazzi." Thursday night, we ate at a wonderful restaurant called the Cantina, which is among the restaurants located off the casinos. My wife, Carla, had a chicken dish stewed with figs and potatoes, greens carrots, and onions and I had a lobster dish. As we were returning to the room, who would be walking in our direction but Emanuel Steward: perhaps the greatest contemporary boxing trainer! I could hardly speak as I approached him, but unlike some of the full-of-themselves personalities I'd run into in connection with writing this book, people who gush out their very souls to The Ali Scribes, but won't give me the time of day, Steward is very down to earth and accessible. I told him that I was writing a book about Muhammad Ali and requested an interview; he consented.

When I got to his room, we began by Carla taking a number of photos of Emanuel Steward and some of Steward and me. His room was laid out in the same way as ours: Art Deco mixed with some of the International style.

Steward kept telling me to stop interrupting him and so I was off balance and had to improvise instead of asking the elegant questions I had prepared.

Ishmael Reed: [Like Tyson, Foreman, Liston, and others, Steward began his career as a street thug. I asked him about his trainer, Bill Miller.]

Emanuel Steward: Mr. Miller was one of my trainers. Actually, to be honest with you, I'm a self-trained fighter. I was probably the only one ever. I was born in 1944. I started boxing when I was seven years old in West Virginia, a place near Bluefield. You've probably never heard of it. As a result, I started boxing when I was eight. I had about thirteen illegal-type fights, where they were spending money and we would take our shoes off and jump around. Me and different little boys. It was different from battle royales. We weren't blindfolded. Our fights were boxing matches that were unsanctioned. I had about eleven or thirteen. I never lost one of those, which was amazing. I would get into trouble for street fighting. And I boxed. That's all we did. There wasn't baseball and all of that. There were Cowboys and Indians and boxing.

So when I got to Detroit, I got into street fights. I beat up a guy and I didn't realize he was fifteen years old and he was like a big hero. But that's all I did, boxing and wrestling. My father was a coal miner. My parents divorced and my mother moved to Detroit and got a job at a restaurant as a waitress.

By the time I was fourteen, I had gotten into enough trouble where they wanted to put me away in juvenile detention. I hit a boy in the head and he was in a coma for four days. When he came out of the hospital, one officer made a deal when everyone else wanted to put me away. My mother kept pleading, and he said if I went back to boxing they wouldn't put me away. Instead they would give me six months to see how it would work out. So I went to a center called Brewster Center, the same recreation center that Joe Louis came from and where Ray Robinson studied boxing before he moved to New York. I entered a tournament there. I won the city championship as a junior Olympic boxer. In 1963, I won the National Golden Gloves championship—leading Detroit to its first championship in twenty-four years. So in the twenty months, from the thug that I was in Detroit and being the biggest street fighter, I became the biggest hero to the city when I came home from winning the National Golden Gloves victory. In 1964, when the national championship had moved to the Convention Center here in Las Vegas, I couldn't get the proper person to manage me. So in 1964, I ended up quitting boxing and getting married. I went to work for Detroit Edison as a labor worker in the construction department, and in a year's time I got an electrical apprenticeship, and three years later I was an electrician. And then I became a special projects director, which was like an engineering supervisor. And this all happened by the time I was twenty-six.

I had four hundred ninety-two people working under me, and I didn't have a college education. I had a younger brother, a half-brother, since my father remarried in West Virginia. He was fifteen years old and his name was James Steward. He wanted to box, so he came to live with me. We were about nine years apart. I started teaching him how to box in the evening. He won the Golden Gloves in 1969. I got back into teaching kids how to box, in addition to working my job at Edison. I had seven others and they won the Golden Gloves. It was a record. It was in the papers all over the country, "Young Coach In Detroit Produces Champions Who Won 21 Consecutive Victories Over A Five Year Period." That was in 1970. That began the Kronk Gym legend. Everybody saw this young coach, who had the Midas touch, who could produce nothing but winners. I taught them the basic fundamentals and aggressiveness.

Being a professional fighter myself, I didn't get into boxing because my father was a fan, I got into it because of these small fights, these illegal matches, and then I got into a serious phase because I was a street thug fighting all of the time. Nobody pushed me into it or whatever, so I didn't like boxing really, I liked fighting. I just liked to fight. So anyway, I ended up an amateur because I lost three decisions out of ninety-four fights. All three of those went to the national champions who were older than I. I got a chance to fight in rematches and I knocked them both out.

I don't really recall when I saw a professional fight for the first time. I don't know if it was on TV or if it was in person. The first time I saw a professional fight in person probably would have been in Detroit when I was fourteen years old. It was a small club fight, at a place called the Gray Stone Ballroom. It was a lightweight fight. One of the fighters was my across-the-street neighbor at the time. We couldn't get in so we sneaked through the side door, you know, we got inside, me and a couple of buddies of mine. So that was first time I saw a professional fight in person.

IR: [I asked him who, in his opinion, was the greatest fighter of all time.]
ES: Sugar Ray Robinson was the greatest fighter ever. He could do everything.

IR: Mike Tyson?

ES: Well, it's not that hard to beat Mike Tyson. Lennox Lewis was just physically too big and Mike always had problems with big fighters. I knew Mike Tyson from the amateurs. I have a lot of respect for Mike. Mike's a little old man, though. When big guys who have skills are not afraid of him, he is always going to have problems. I still have much respect for what he has accomplished. As a big man, Lennox was not afraid of him and he was trained to fight like a big guy, to push Mike around, pull him by the head, push him back, pull him and do things to take advantage of him mentally, to break Mike in two. Mike starts crying, because most bullies become very intimidated very easily. You bully a bully. When you fight a guy like Mike you have to be really physical. You have to do things that make him feel your strength.

IR: When did you meet Muhammad Ali?

ES: In 1963, the year I won the National Golden Gloves tournament. They came to Detroit and parked a bus outside that said, "Cassius Clay, the most colorful fighter in the world" all over it. And they actually had people come and pay twenty dollars, which was a lot of money, to see this workout. And the only people who could box and train that day were Emanuel Steward and Cassius Clay, because I was the fighter of Detroit. We trained together the same day and it was jam-packed in that gym, to see us train. The media, press, everybody was there. He'd just won that National Golden Gloves three years before, at the same tournament in which I participated. He was a professional already.

Well, I thought he was a good boxer, but in my mind no one was going to beat Sonny Liston. He was my favorite fighter and I still think he was one of the best heavyweight fighters; he doesn't get enough credit. Because when Sonny Liston ascended to the number one position, he was the only fighter who had beaten every contender in that weight group all the way up, because they didn't give him the opportunity to fight for the title. He knocked out everybody. He fought his way to the top and when he got there he beat everyone.

But I guess age began to factor in. But anyway, he got to the championship, and when he got the title he became relaxed and there was nobody up there for him after he knocked out Floyd Patterson twice and he was forty, his real age, around forty years old. And at the time he started to drink, here in Las Vegas, and golfing and doing everything that was bad for a boxer to do. But he was a middle-aged man now so his lifestyle had changed, and he wanted to golf, drink, and gamble and it was a different world.

IR: Was he murdered?

ES: Yes. At the time, Cassius Clay was still fighting. So then I saw a fight in the early part of 1964 with a guy named Doug Jones. Cassius won the fight because he out-fought him. First of all, it was a ten-round fight, and when you talk so much and you build yourself up so much, and you don't do what you predicted you'd do, the crowd goes against you and you lose. Doug Jones did better than was expected, but he didn't throw enough punches. And then during the last two rounds, Cassius Clay pulled it off. He threw a million punches from all angles and that's what wins fights. That's what helped him. Doug Jones' biggest claim to fame is that he had a close fight with Cassius Clay, but Cassius Clay beat him because he outfought him. He didn't knock him out like he said, but nevertheless, I watched the fight quite a few times, and he beat him. As a result, they announced that the next fight would be between Cassius Clay and Sonny Liston. I witnessed him struggling to get by Doug Jones and thought, "Sonny's going to kill him," because I remember the Sonny who knocked out everybody. And when they fought a tough, competitive fight, Cassius stopped him. Cassius Clay beat Sonny Liston because he had great boxing skills and he had been fighting regularly, while Sonny Liston was drinking and golfing and gambling and that was a difference at the time. The timing was everything.

I was with Cassius about a year later, just before he legally changed his name, and I said, "You know, you really surprised me when you beat Sonny Liston." He said, "Well, let me tell you something, Emanuel. You know when a person's active, doing something on a regular basis, if everything is close, always go with the activity guy because what happens is he does things instinctively. He doesn't even have to think because he's been fighting every month, every two months, and every three months. When I was fighting Sonny, Sonny was drinking, Sonny was golfing. So even though I might even be fighting bums it doesn't mean that I didn't spend eight weeks in the gym preparing, so my mind had been in the boxing world compared to Liston."

At that time, Cassius Clay's whole world was nothing but that of being a boxer. He ate and slept boxing. He was only twenty-one years old at the time. Sonny Liston's world was the golf game and gambling and going out to party. That was a difference between the men at this stage. That was the Cassius Clay in his prime who went on to become Muhammad Ali. In the next fight Sonny was scared and was intimidated by the Black Muslims and so he quit. I don't think that he threw the fight, but like most bullies, he didn't have a very big heart. Later on in Ali's career, in '73 and '74, after he beat Liston, Ali had to have five women every night. Women were all over the place, and he was out partying. He stopped putting in the effort that had made him the champion. The entourage was a big traveling party. Very few people in the training camp really were working employees.

IR: What about his victory over Foreman?
ES: Ali had the advantage over George Foreman psychologically, even though I had picked Foreman to kill him. By the time I met Foreman, I felt the same way about Ali that I felt about Liston because Ali was older at the time.

IR: What about Jim Brown's statement that Ali lost the first Frazier fight because he had stayed up all night?
ES: That could very well have been. At the time, Ali had become so much of a celebrity, more likely the leader of the player's world by that time, so to say, that his entourage, his party life, his abundance of women—there is a good chance of what Jim Brown said is right—and he underestimated Joe Frazier, too. Joe Frazier had a dogged

determination, too, something Ali had not been used to. Ali always had it, but he was not used to an opponent with the same dogged determination—and as a result, Joe surprised him and beat him. Ali showed that he had one of the greatest chins in history after being knocked down in the thirteenth round. I mean his jaw nearly broke and as soon as he hit the floor at the count of three he was coming back at the end of the round. He was throwing a million punches again.

The "Thrilla in Manila" was just a brutal, brutal fight that at the very end, Joe Frazier was getting hit with so many right hands, Eddie Futch, his trainer, said that he didn't want to see Joe continue. Later on we found out that Joe Frazier had problems with his left eye and that's why he never fought in California, because they have strong eye test rules. So therefore, knowing that on top of everything else, his people had to pick certain states where Joe Frazier fought.

I think Ali should have stopped fighting after he beat George Foreman. His style after that was just to take punches and outlast someone. He lost his legs and his hands were damaged. He couldn't punch as hard, so he had to win fights by a million punches, slapping and everything and outlasting people. In his early career. his hands were okay, but in the later part of his career he was getting shots for his hands; every fight became a hard fight. Everybody says that the three-year lay-off affected him. It may or may not have. You never know. Those three years may have made him become bigger as a world figure, but that may have changed him as a boxer. He became like a symbol of the stand-up guy, a person who believes in his principles, a character who was established as something bigger than boxing.

Overall, I don't regret it because it made him become a world leader. It had changed him because otherwise he would have been a boxer, preaching on "Blackism" and civil rights, but his stand made him acceptable to the world, as someone who stood up for his convictions.

So I don't know, those three years might have helped him to come back on top. Right now it is really sad. I have been at some functions with him, too. He is an amazing man and he really cares about people. I have a lot of respect for him. What made Ali special was not so much that he was a good boxer, because at one time, he was a very evil person. That was when the Black Muslims had him brainwashed, so that's why some people still dislike him, hate him. Some people have never forgotten that, and one of them is Joe Frazier. You have to respect and understand Joe a little bit. Everybody is different. Because he was called a "gorilla and this" and "your whole family is this." Joe felt this was so unnecessary, especially when Joe actually gave him money, and helped him on his bills when he wasn't allowed to fight and Joe never said anything to the public about his generosity, and it was Joe who pushed to get him a boxer's license. Joe did that quietly, did everything for him. And Ali's comments weren't necessary in Joe's mind. This doesn't mean that the public should hate Joe and tell him to let it go. They should understand where he is coming from. Joe is a very proud man. And the same stubborn streak in Joe is what made him the fighter he was.

In the late 1960s to '68, he was wrapped up with the Black Muslims and he did a lot of bad things to a lot of people. Ali, at that certain phase, had the Black Muslims create who he was. Everything around him was centered around race consciousness. Herbert was more into business. He was never wrapped into the racist part and that made him easier to work with, and he did a lot with Bob Arum and the white business people. He was a business a man. He was not wrapped up in the race part like his father. They had to use that to bring people in.

IR: So what happens when Ali goes to Mecca and sees white Muslims and he realizes that the Black Muslims he belonged to was a racist organization?

ES: When he came back, his attitude really changed as well as Malcolm X's. He was no longer a Black Muslim. He realized that they were worshipping the head of the organization more than Allah.

So they killed Malcolm because he was causing dissension. When Muhammad Ali went over there, he found out the same thing. Then he came back. Because he was famous, they couldn't kill him. He disassociated himself from the Black Muslims. When Ali came back and realized that the Black Muslims was a racist organization, based on intimidation and fear and not so much on religion, he became a true Muslim. People don't understand this. You never see him with Farrakhan. He became more associated with white people and he changed his whole attitude, became a bigger figure. He would come to small, simple places, like schools.

I told him that my son was having a birthday—this was at a mall, and he was surrounded by people and he was fighting that night at Madison Square Garden. He came to the birthday party at 2 p.m. One day we had a fundraiser for a recreation center and he came for that, crowds of people were waiting outside. All those small things made him popular. After he left the Black Muslims, he blossomed and was open to everybody, and that's why people, black and white, are crazy about him. From 1964 to 1968, they remember his evil side, those who had contact with him. They still have bitter memories and haven't accepted him and they have not let it go.

I hate to see him as he is now. He was in the ring too long. The human body is not made to be beat on that much. His style became that of absorbing blows because he couldn't move anymore.

IR: I asked about his having to fight the last two fights suffering the symptoms of Parkinson's.
ES: It was horrible. Angelo Dundee was one of the few who cared, who didn't want to see him fight.

The Rumble in the Jungle continued

Steward went on to fill in some more details about the "Rumble in the Jungle":

George Foreman gets off the plane in (Kinshasa) Zaïre with his two dogs, these big German shepherd dogs. That was a big, big, big mistake given the history of their use by the police. Then there was eloquent Ali. He made it into a big Black thing. He was Black this and Black that and Ali had the looks, he had the entourage, and whatever. Foreman was mentally in total disarray. He had never been in this type of situation, so emotionally he was just totally beaten up, spiritually and morally. Everywhere Ali went, crowds were screaming and cheering for him, so naturally they started to boo Foreman.

When the actual fight happened, Foreman came out and fought his actual fight. He threw all of the punches and he almost beat Ali. Ali took the punches by leaning against the ropes. When you lean back it takes the power out of the punch. It's not like I'm standing in front of you so that you can hurt me. Foreman kept punching and the ropes loosened from the sweat of the guys. This wasn't done on purpose. Ali just realized in the beginning that Foreman was too strong so he took a gamble to outlast Foreman and it worked. After eight rounds, Foreman was just totally exhausted from wearing himself out. It was not a real knockout; he was totally exhausted. Ali hit him with a short punch and Foreman was so exhausted he couldn't turn around and so Ali hit him again and Foreman fell. Ali, being the sportsman that he is, had time to hit him while he was on his way down, but he didn't. It was exhaustion, and Foreman was about to fall out on his own.

And so Ali just outsmarted him, he made a great adjustment. He came out with one plan, to out-box him, and he just realized that Foreman was too strong and was coming in so fast, so he just changed his plan and just decided to see if he could weather the storm; he gambled and he won.

Foreman then lost to Jimmy Young and I don't think it was because he was carrying him. Foreman had problems with people who threw straight punches. He succeeded with wide punchers, like Joe Frazier; you could see the punches, but if people, for whatever reason, threw simple one-twos, like Ali, that bothered Foreman. So don't forget Jimmy Young had beaten Ali, too. They just gave the fight to Ali. So Jimmy Young was a just a terrible opponent for anyone to fight, a very scary guy who would throw straight punches and hold on quickly.

CHAPTER 25

The Frazier fight, the one that occurred in 1971, while I was working on my third novel, would be the fight that was supposed to be Ali's glorious return to the heavyweight championship. The "people's champ" would become the legitimate champ.

However, if one would contrast Ali's biography with that of Frazier, Frazier had more in common with the people than Ali. If Ali's brother, Rahaman, and his Louisville friends are to be believed, Ali grew up in a middle-class household.

Frazier's parents worked on white men's farms and though they had ten acres, Frazier remembers it being "white dirt"; the land was so bad you couldn't grow peas on it. His mother worked from sunup to sunset "pulling radishes, cutting cabbage, and digging potatoes for a white man named Trask." She was paid fifty cents a day. "The home that he shared with his parents and nine brothers and sisters had six rooms. It was "set on oak blocks and had a wood roof reinforced by tin" (Frazier with Berger, 1996).

Like heavyweight champion Ezzard Charles, who had to follow the international hero, Joe Louis, Joe Frazier saw his career overshadowed by Muhammad Ali's. And so Ali loyalists boycotted the fight that was held to decide who would succeed Muhammad Ali, whose license had been revoked. Frazier dismissed them as "scamboogahs" (scammers or swindlers). It was held on March 4, 1968. Frazier hit his opponent, Buster Mathis, with a right to the chin and a left to the temple, and he toppled over. The referee, Arthur Mercante, stopped the fight and Joe Frazier became heavyweight champion.

We wished fervently for an Ali victory, as though wishing it would make it happen. We couldn't accept the result. For reassurance we clung to William Greaves's film about the fight, *Ali, The Fighter*, which challenged the decision. I accepted this fiction while continuing to work on my own.

Those of us who had questions about Frazier's victory over Ali ignored the fact that a contender has to go the extra mile to take the championship away from the reigning champion. Frazier scoring a knockdown in the thirteenth round was enough to ensure that he won a decision. His chance for regaining the heavyweight championship seemed to be fading, but on January 28, 1974, Ali defeated Joe Frazier in their second fight. With Joe Frazier defeated, the reigning champion became George Foreman. His defeat of Frazier in the second fight led to his meeting with Foreman in the "Rumble in the Jungle."

This is how Gene Kilroy, Ali's former business manager, described Ali's preparation for what some considered his greatest triumph:

> Well, I'll tell you a little story. We were getting ready to leave for Zaïre, Africa, and Ali said, "Let's call Cus d'Amato" [the legendary trainer who handled the careers of Floyd Patterson, Jose Torres, and Mike Tyson] and so we called Cus on the phone and Ali said, "Cus, I'm getting ready to fight George Foreman. What do you think?" Cus said "You must make your first punch devastating. With bad intentions."
>
> "Yeah, Cus. You're right, you're right."
>
> Cus said, "He's a bully."
>
> I said, "Look what he did to Kenny Norton and Joe Frazier."
>
> Cus screamed, "But they're not Ali!"
>
> Ali said, "You're right, you're right, you're right. Cus is right."
>
> Ali challenged Foreman at all the press conferences, degraded him. Talked down to him, you know. I went into George Foreman's room when they were wrapping the hands in preparation for the fight. Archie Moore was walking around saying. "There's death in the air," like there was going to be killing. When I went back to Ali's dressing room, I said, "George said he wants to put your children in an orphanage." Ali said, "I'm gonna get him, I'm gonna get him. Ohhhhh, I can't wait to get him."
>
> So if you watch the first round when Ali came in, he hit George Foreman with that right hand, bang! Foreman's lights went out, and

then *he* was on the defensive. And then Ali humiliated him, the whole fight, and verbally abused him. No one ever talked to George like that. He taunted him throughout the fight: "You're a sissy, you can't hit, show me something, George, is that the best you have? I'm gonna beat your ass, you're in trouble tonight, George."

You know, I used to get the tapes of all the fights that George had and we studied them. And he watched George Foreman fight Joe Frazier and this is the one in New York, and when he knocked Joe Frazier down, he leaned back on the ropes trying to return to the corner, and Ali said, "No stamina, he has no stamina." And during the press conference, Ali told him, "George, round two, round three, round four, round five, you're out of gas." He would tell him in the ring, "You're out of gas. There is no gas station out here."

Getting back to Zaïre, Africa. When we arrived in Zaïre, people were cheering us. We were getting off the airplane and Ali says to me, "Who don't they like over here?"

I said, "White people."

He said, "You can't call George Foreman a white man; we'll get in trouble, and they'll see that I'm with you and Angelo so we can't use that," and we laughed.

I said, "Well, they don't like the Belgians."

So we got off the airplane and the people were yelling, "Ali! Ali!" He couldn't see anybody because it was pitch dark. All of a sudden he raised his hands and shouted, "George Foreman is a Belgian!" and the people shouted, "Ali boma ye!"

So I said to the interpreter, "What does boma ye mean?"

He said, "That means 'kill him.'"

So when George Foreman got off the airplane he had a German Shepherd police dog with him, and that's what the Belgians put on the people of the Belgian Congo. I said, "We're home-free." George didn't know what "boma ye" meant. He thought it meant for him to beat Ali, and when he found out what it meant that shook him up a little bit. Mobutu got scared that Ali would take over the country. Bundini brought a lot of T-shirts of Ali and the government bought them lest they fall in the hands of the people. The Zairians would have followed him. Mobutu didn't even attend the fight.

CHAPTER 26

June 16, 2004

Two of those who played a part in "The Rumble in the Jungle" were trumpeter Hugh Masekela and poet Quincy Troupe. During my interviews with them, they revealed behind-the-scenes accounts of that epic event that have never found their way into print.

My daughter, Tennessee, and I went to San Francisco's Adagio Hotel to interview the famed South African trumpeter, Hugh Masekela. His book, *Still Grazing*, had just been published and he was on tour. The Hotel Adagio is some hip digs. As their promo materials describe it: "The new Hotel Adagio features a fresh design that bridges its Spanish Colonial Revival architectural roots to a clean and contemporary design aesthetic."

Masekela's boyish looks betray his senior citizen status. His has been an exciting life, but one gets the feeling that when he arrived in the United States, with American hosts craving for a connection with "the homeland," that he was spoiled in the form of wine, women, drugs, and access to some of the most stellar names of the African-American literary and entertainment worlds.

Masekela was in charge of organizing the music entertainment for the Ali-Foreman fight. He gave some details about the action that occurred behind the scenes at Zaïre, printed here for the first time:

> I'm sixty-five. One day you wake up and say, "Shit, I'm old." You don't feel it unless you look at the mirror and you say, "Who the hell is that?"

I put together the festival. See, I had lived in the Congo for a year before. In 1972, I went on a pilgrimage to Africa because, although I was from there, I had never traveled around the continent; I had peaked here [in America] and I didn't feel like fighting in the musical turf wars here, you know? I was just not interested in the style of success that was expected of a person in America. All flash, and it's gotten so bad that you don't have to have any meaning for whatever you do. Yeah, I call it stupid money, and if you wear enough rings and "bling bling" then you don't have to talk about anything. You can get down on women and other people.

I traveled to Africa and I followed my favorite African records. I went to the Congo because of my favorite musicians, [Ngungi] Franco [Luambo] and Tabu Ley Rochereau, and then I went to Guinea. The Congo was like everything Brazil would like to be. The people lived just for music. We went to work in Kinshasa. I'd go to work in the morning and return for a siesta and then back to work at seven, refreshed. We went to the dance gardens every night. You could catch each band until seven in the morning, when you had to go to work, and they only looked for us to dance. Mobutu [Mobutu Sese Seko Nkuku Ngbendu wa Za Banga] got in through music. He was popularized through the musicians of the Congo, because before that nobody knew him. Franco Luambo and [Tabu Ley] Rochereau especially took him around the country because everybody knew them but didn't know who Mobuto was. He was a devil but the musicians popularized him. Once he gained power he got rid of them, too. Anyway, when I lived there it was during the time of what we call *authenticité*. What Mobutu did was to lead the people, to get away from being French and to being Congolese.

His name was Desiré, but he changed his name. He had everybody get rid of their Christian names. This was during the time that Zaïre was really booming economically. The copper sales were strong. That's when Don King came in and decided to arrange the Muhammad Ali-Foreman fight, because Ali couldn't fight anywhere else.

Rhythm and Blues singer Lloyd Price was a friend of Don King, so when Don King got the right to do the fight there, they also decided to do a music festival as well. I knew Lloyd Price in the 60s. I met him through singer Johnny Nash, who was a good friend of mine. So I called Lloyd and said, "Lloyd, you don't know the Congo, but I have lived there for a year. I can help you get it together. You can get it through the musicians, because the musicians have Mobutu's ear."

So to cut to the chase, I flew with my producer to New York to meet Don King. I got Don King on the phone and outlined my idea. He said, in a nutshell, "If you can get the money for this, you can give me ten percent; you can shoot everything, you can shoot the fight. We can call it ten days of music and fighting." I had lived in Liberia and knew Steve Talbot, brother of the president. He loved the idea. He put up two million for the festival project, which was a lot of money in 1974. With that we hired a World Airways plane and flew over three hundred artists with twelve crews. We also chose Leon Gast, the filmmaker, who shot *When We Were Kings*.

In the end, the interest in the festival became bigger because the fight was way down the line and Don King got more and more involved. When we got to Zaïre, we had, like, musicians and music in every meaningful corner in the city. So Don King wanted ten percent more of everything, so I said, "Fuck you, Don King." When we came back, he put an injunction on everything. I had a lot of clashes with Don King. For example, Mick Jagger was a friend and he wanted to meet Don King. This was in New York.

In his book, *Still Grazing*, Masekela says that Don King was nude with some nude lady, when he greeted Jagger, which angered Jagger. King responded by reminding Jagger of his own tabloid reputation. We continued our interview:

I met Mobutu. He was an asshole. He was an imperialist. He was very smart and very manipulative. He would raise his hand, if he had enough of you, and you were dismissed.

We had to take charge of everything. We had to take care of everyone's needs. That included drugs.

I had met Ali long before. I met Ali when I was starting out my career. It was 1965. Ali had just refused to fight in the war and so we had happened to be in the same interview. He was talking about the problems in South Africa. He was brilliant. Ali is one of the most articulate, eloquent people that I have ever met. He is very principled and had a very clear vision of what he wanted. At the time, he was wallowing in the pride of having turned down the government's demand that he fight in the Vietnam War.

I was an unreasonable Ali fan. There was major Ali mania at the time and Ali couldn't do any wrong. We were radical, political, and social activists. The fact that he'd been ousted and his title had been taken away from him without his being beaten made him a major hero to us. The fact that he had stood up to the American government by refusing to fight in the Vietnam War made him a hero.

I was part of the anti-Vietnam War [movement] with all of the flower children in Golden Gate Park. I admired Ali for not only his boxing skills, but for his fantastic sense of humor and poetry and mainly for his being able to get rid of an argument in one sentence, not even in a paragraph. He had probably had the smartest answers of everybody I knew for doing retorts. Even Don King was afraid of him. He could talk shit with everybody, but Ali would eat him up.

His Kinshasa suite was next to mine. It was a time of transition because he had taken up with another woman [Veronica Porsche]. I didn't think Ali is the type of person who would beat up a woman, but he handled the drama very well. Unless you knew, you didn't know what was going on. He was very friendly with everybody. If Ali had a beef with somebody, he would never give you a chance to know. If he had a confrontation with somebody, Ali always waited for the right moment to make sure that you would never argue with him again in public.

I saw him a few times and we would talk. We didn't talk about the Vietnam War. I told him that "if you don't whip Foreman, I will whip your ass because we are depending on you." And whenever we met, we would mock spar. He'd say, "Let me show you what I am going to do to him."

I wasn't surprised. I was ready for him to knock everybody out. He was the people's champion. For all of the radicals and revolutionaries, he couldn't make mistakes. When Ali lost we nearly cried. I nearly cried when he first lost to [Ken] Norton. When he fought Larry Holmes, he shouldn't have been fighting anymore, because Holmes was one of his young sparring partners in Zaïre. I spent a lot of time with Larry Holmes and Bundini [Drew "Bundini" Brown]. Bundini was great. Great, rough, and funny. He talked shit all the time.

The movie *Ali* was a joke. I saw it in Durban and nobody was in the theater but my wife and me. Bundini was a clown and he reminded me of a woman in a Pentecostal church in Harlem that I used to go to for the music. She would say, "I am God's clown." She used to make funny moves and we would all laugh. Bundini was no stupid person. But Jamie Fox's portrayal—that wasn't really Bundini. I thought the script was a joke, though Will Smith was focused and centered. It was like he was doing his own movie within a movie. He really got his part right.

Traditionally, the film industry has done its part in poisoning the relations between racial and ethnic groups in the United States. Hugh Masekela wasn't the only person who denounced the movie. The Muslims I talked to were also offended by Michael Mann's *Ali*. In it, Elijah Muhammad was depicted as a buffoon, which is how the FBI depicted him. Their suspicions about the producer's attitudes toward black men would be confirmed with the release of his film *Collateral*, in which Jamie Fox played the kind of role that was once assigned to Willie Best in the old Charlie Chan movies, a groveling hapless surrogate who serves his superior. In one hurtful scene, the Fox character is verbally abused by his mother while she flirts with the Tom Cruise character. Mann's pasting on a heroic ending for Fox didn't offset the demeaning portrait that preceded the end. Masekela continued:

> Michael Mann, the director, knew that I was involved in Zaïre. I couldn't play in the movie because it was over thirty years ago and I am too old to play who I was back then. I also didn't perform in the festival so it was pointless for me to be in the movie. I was busy getting people on and off the stage and fighting all kinds of superego battles. I had to work with three hundred and sixty musicians. Zaïre was something else. Musicians and Don King.
>
> I think the fact that if Africa were united, if the people of African origin decided that they were all one people like the Chinese, pulled together and connected economically, I would think it would really mess up the whole Western industrial complex's plan, because raw materials out of Africa would become more expensive and whatever cheap labor that exists in the non-unionized countries would disappear. You have to understand that African countries and even South Africa are free but the economy is in the hands of the Western companies and white people. That is the invisible battle. So if I came to you and said, "Listen, don't free this country. Free the president, but don't free the country because it will be two billion dollars for you in the Swiss bank if you fuck up the place," you have to have a major conscience to say, "Fuck you, I don't want two billion dollars."

Mobutu was the most highly paid African president in history because Zaïre is a land next to the Sudan in Africa. And it served as a buffer. The West African countries like Nigeria and Ghana and all those countries were well armed and able to threaten South Africa militarily, but they couldn't pass through on land unless they came through Zaïre. He literally closed down the Congo. During his last three or four years, you couldn't travel by land because the roads were closed. You had to travel by river. The place was completely locked and he had gotten rid of all of his enemies.

There are many despots like that in countries where there is wealth. If it is a poor country, they don't give a shit. All the wars in Africa are surrogate wars. There always have been collaborators in the human species and Africans are no different. Our president [in South Africa], Thabo Mbeki, has formed an African parliament and African union and the partnership for the economic advancement in Africa. He has asked the Western countries to be his partner in healing Africa, which has really confused these guys. When he came into office the people thought that he would be anti-Western, but he turned out not to be. South Africa's freedom is an unselfish freedom, because we brokered peace in all of the central and Southern African countries.

Until Africa stops all of its wars, freedom doesn't mean a thing. The people have to have time for recreation and to enjoy their wealth and the continent. Africans do not enjoy their continent because they don't have time. They are always on the run from wars. They are oppressed because of despots, crazy soldiers and dictators. I guess a lot of South America and Asia went through that in the 50s and 60s. If they can get over it so can we.

There is endless negotiating and hustling to convince people that this is not that way. Nelson Mandela is retired from public life. He was a symbol of our freedom. The African National Congress chose him as a symbol of South Africa's freedom. It was Oliver Tambo who kept the African National Congress going, built Mandela's name and his wife, Winnie, built his name and the Congress and people built his name.

When Mandela came into the presidency, people who wanted to protect their properties became his friends, and were prepared to pay anything and romanced him. He was willing to forgive them and that gesture enabled him to open schools and hospitals. Whites still control the economy. There has never been a place where people have said, "Sorry we've oppressed you so long, here's your money back."

I asked him about [Zimbabwean president] Robert Mugabe:

I think that something has happened to him, mentally. We were all with Mugabe when it came to land restitution, but when you do it to the disadvantage of your own people, there is something wrong. He suffers from the trap of not wishing to give up power. But if he gives up power, we will find out all of the dirty things that he did. He would rather die in office. Like there was a clash with Southern Zimbabwe. He put his fifth army brigade in Southern Zimbabwe and they massacred people in the 1980s. It's been a secret; nobody mentions it. That's another reason the mf doesn't want to retire. He's afraid that he might be brought to trial. The greatest atrocities are in the rural areas and nobody knows what's happening.

I asked Masekela about how things have changed in the relationship between African Americans and Africans, since the heady days of the Ali-Foreman fight in Zaïre:

The African Americans in South Africa have become a community unto themselves. They're just there for opportunities and the strength of the dollar. They complain about Africa. I tell them to learn how to speak the fucking languages. I said that the first thing that I did when I came to the States was to learn how black people talked.

They live very well in South Africa. They have wonderful homes and businesses. But the white Americans learn the language, not they. African Americans have a superiority complex. They were taught long ago that they were superior to Africans and that they don't have anything to do with them, because they didn't come from there. They're Americans.

This is another sign that the solidarity between African Americans and Africans, which had been so warm during the sixties when both were drunk on independence, Black Nationalism, liberation, and revolution, was withering. The independence was transparent as Western powers created rump puppet regimes in the Congo and overthrew Prime Minister Patrice Lumumba. Ghanaian President

Kwame Nkrumah was overthrown while he was on a trip to China. Now, according to Masekela, African Americans were introducing their attitudes into South Africa. My Nigerian friend, Maria Epere, told me that when her children attended schools, African-American kids taunted them with racist epithets. These kids were products of an education that not only erased their links to Africa, but to their own African-American history.

Perhaps the Ali-Forman fight constituted the zenith of African/African-American cooperation, even though it was held under the auspices of a man all of us despised. Ali doing a victory lap while being saluted by crowds surrounding his motorcade shouting "Ali boma ye" is an echo of a time long past.

CHAPTER 27

On January 8, 2005, Carla, Tennessee, and I left for New York. I had three assignments. The first was to travel to Englewood, New Jersey, to do another album based upon my writing, part spoken word, and part songs, performed by me and some notable jazz musicians. Second was a book party for the late Amiri Baraka, whose book of drawings I have published, to be held on January 9 at the home of Margaret and Quincy Troupe. And lastly was to interview Troupe, who covered the Ali-Foreman fight in Zaïre; Herb Boyd, a journalist, author of *Pound For Pound*, a biography of Sugar Ray Robinson; and Agieb Bilal, who is a member of Wallace Muhammad's group. Homeland Security subpoenaed Bilal because a school of which he was principal was visited by some of the 9/11 hijackers. He had some information about Ali and Malcolm X that has never been published. I met him some years ago through a friend of mine named Paul Lofty. At that time, he was in charge of placing students from Saudi Arabia in American universities.

Troupe is the editor of *Black Renaissance Noire*, published under the auspices of New York University. He is also Miles Davis's biographer. Margaret Troupe runs an artists' salon in their spacious apartment located in the historic Graham Court. Graham Court is a historic Harlem apartment building. It was commissioned by William Waldorf Astor, designed by the architects Clinton and Russell, and constructed from 1899 to 1901 as part of the great Harlem real estate boom. A writer can sell more books at a Margaret Troupe salon than at the chain bookstores. Their living room is so huge that it can accommodate up to fifty people. Entering each room is like entering a gallery. The walls are decorated with paintings, mostly by well-known contemporary artists. Margaret's sisters have been up all night preparing food for the book party.

I was to meet Bilal in Philadelphia, but he said that he'd be in New York by coincidence, saving me a trip by train to Philadelphia. I told him to meet me at Quincy and Margaret's apartment. I arrived about an hour and a half before the beginning of the party to interview Troupe. On the morning of our flight, Troupe called to ask me whether my plane would be on time. He had heard a report that storm conditions were preventing planes from departing from San Francisco. In the course of our conversation, he mentioned that Jesse Jackson might drop by on the day of Amiri's book party, but before we began the interview, he received a phone call. The phone call was from Jesse Jackson and he planned to arrive at the Troupe's house within the hour.

During our interview, Quincy Troupe said the following:

> At the time, I was dealing with a man named Jay Acton who was working as an editor, and agent. He asked me to write a book around the fight. What I found out was that he was also an agent for Wilfrid Sheed. Because Wilfrid Sheed wasn't going, he was going to use my stuff as a resource for Wilfrid Sheed's book. He was going to feed my stuff to Wilfrid Sheed. When I found that out, I broke up the whole relationship.

Troupe was disappointed. He'd put a lot of work into his Ali book only to find that he was merely a resource for another writer's book about Ali. Black writers complain about this happening to them in Hollywood. They write the scripts; white writers get the screen credits. Many jazz critics would have given their right arms for the opportunity to write Miles Davis's biography. When the late jazz trumpeter chose Quincy Troupe, there was much resentment among establishment jazz critics. He says:

> All of the white writers, jazz writers, didn't want me to write the Miles Davis book, but Miles insisted that it would be me. They were pissed about that and so what they do now is they just rake that book for

all kinds of stuff. They use that as a primary source. So this is what happened.

When I came back from Zaïre, I had all this information. I had written all these pages. Acton takes me to dinner at this really great restaurant downtown in the Village. I can't remember the name. He said, "Get what you want. Anything you want." Then Wilfrid Sheed came in. Sheed asks, "You want some champagne? You want some of this?" I didn't know who Wilfrid Sheed was.

At dinner, Acton made it known that Wilfrid Sheed wanted to write the Ali book and he wanted me to tell him about some stuff that happened over there. I said, "Why should I tell you all about that?" They had a whole contingent of white writers over there. This happened in the film [*When We Were Kings*] too. That's why you see mostly white writers in the film. Leon Gast interviewed everybody but me. This is the way they create false records. When I found out that I was not going to be published in this book, that he was going to use my stuff as a primary source for Wilfrid Sheed, I was left hanging. They gave me some money, yeah, but I was left hanging.

They were going to use me, like I said. Wilfrid Sheed had a huge contract to do a book with pictures, and I threatened them and backed out of the deal. Wilfrid Sheed went on and published a pictorial book. If you look at it, it doesn't have much text, because I was supposed to provide the text, see? So I called Hoyt Fuller, editor of *Black World*, and said, "Listen I got this big, long piece on Muhammad Ali. Would you like to see that?" and he said, "Yeah."

So when I got back, I sent it to him. He published it with photographs by Roy Lewis. It was a long piece talking about the fight in Zaïre. The fight happened in 1974, so the article was published in 1975.

In boxing, with an exception of some poor white people, usually Italian and Irish American fighters, the white men wear the tuxedos while the black men carry the buckets and the towels—a complaint made by Muhammad Ali during a press conference following Ali-Spinks II. The same demarcation exists in the world of writing about boxing. Quincy Troupe began to discuss his trip to the "Rumble in the Jungle":

Muhammad Ali, middle Gene Kilroy, top left Jose Fuentes,
top right Jack Newfield, New Orleans, October 1978

Don King, Kathryn Jackson, and Mike Tyson
(Photo by Ishmael Reed, Las Vegas, 1975)

Ferdie Pacheco and Ishmael Reed
(Photo by Jose Fuentes, New Orleans, October 1978)

Newark's First Lady, Amina Baraka, Amiri Baraka, Tennessee Reed, Marvin X,
Ishmael Reed, Askia Toure, Timothy Reed, San Francisco, April 2001

Ishmael Reed and Rahaman Ali

Reggie Barrett and Bert Sugar
(Photo by Ishmael Reed, Louisville, November 2005)

Bob Arum of Top Rank boxing and Ishmael Reed
(Photo by Jose Fuentes, New Orleans, October 1978)

Angelo Dundee
(Photo by Ishmael Reed,
Louisville, November 2005)

Bert Sugar and Ishmael Reed,
Louisville, November 2005

Ishmael Reed and Hugh Masakela
(Photo by Jose Fuentes, October 1978)

Unidentified man, Joe Louis, and Mary Campbell Simmons,
mother of Al Young, former poet laureate of California.
Joe Louis and Ms. Mary Campbell Simmons were between marriages.

Ishmael Reed and Melvin Van Peebles
(Photo by Linda Gomez)

Ray Robinson, Jr.
(Photo by Ishmael Reed, New York, July 2006)

Ed Hughes
(Photo by Ishmael Reed, Louisville, June 2006)

Waajid Sabree and Omar Rose
(Photo by Ishmael Reed, Louisville, June 2006)

Ishmael Reed and Rahaman Ali
(Photo by Tennessee Reed, June 2006)

The Confederacy's Dark Secret; bigger than Sally Hemmings: Mrs. Jefferson
Davis (née Varina Howell). This photo, taken in Montreal in 1866 by William
Notman, leaves little doubt about Jefferson Davis's wife's mixed-race back-
ground. Montreal's British colonial elite class welcomed the Jefferson Davis
family with open arms when they fled after defeat of the Confederacy.
(© Musée McCord)

Ishmael Reed Interviews Amiri Baraka at the Black Books Fair
on February 7, 2004. (Photo by Tennessee Reed)

Ishmael Reed at Ali's punching bag
(Photo by Tennessee Reed, June 2006)

Janene and Atar Shakir
(Photo by Tennessee Reed, June 2006)

David Hammons, Paul Spooky Miller, and Ishmael Reed, April 2006

Margaret and Quincy Troupe
(Photo by Ishmael Reed, New York, April 2006)

Dan Halpern, Hettie Jones and Russell Banks
(Photo by Ishmael Reed, New York, February 2006)

Haki Madhubuti
(Photo by Ishmael Reed, Chicago, October 2005)

Harry Belafonte
(Photo By Ishmael Reed, Oakland, July 2006)

Rev. Jesse Jackson
(Photo by Ishmael Reed, New York, February 2006)

Front Margaret Troupe, Maria Arias, Billy Bang, Ishmael Reed
(black and white scarf), Earl Caldwell, Lenna Sherrod, Quincy Troupe, Harlem

Bundini Brown and his wife
(Photo by Jose Fuentes, New Orleans, 1978)

Ishmael Reed and Khalilah Ali, Chicago, October 2006

Ishmael Reed, unidentified, Ernie Terrell
(Photo by Jose Fuentes, New Orleans, October 1978)

Muhammad Ali and Dick Gregory
(Photo by Charles Robinson)

Ishmael Reed (far left) and Malcolm X (center) shaking hands with Joe Walker
(Photo by Fred Tabron, *Buffalo Criterion Newspaper*, Buffalo, 1960)

I was on the World Airways flight with all of those people. Man, that flight was one of the funniest flights from start to finish. We went out to I think it was Kennedy or some airport. I forgot where the hangar was, but it was somewhere out near Kennedy because we were all bussed out there from downtown. It was a charter bus. Ali was already in Zaïre. So we had a big party. Lloyd Price, Al Sharpton, James Brown, Don King, all kinds of people there. All the stars were there, like Celia Cruz, Bill Withers, John Pacheco, Felipe Luciano, B.B. King, all the stars that were at that fight were there. Everybody was out there partying.

They had a big party before we went over there. So we all went on this one plane. We didn't know that James Brown was taking all of his equipment over there. They had to take all of the Latin All-Stars equipment off because we needed room for Brown's equipment. We didn't know that, though. So when he got there he was going to do a concert. He said he wanted to take his own sound equipment. So he took all of his sound equipment and kicked everyone else's stuff off. They told us later that our plane barely got off the ground because of all James Brown's equipment. Now, James Brown and his band were all sitting in the front. We were all sitting in the middle rows and the Latin All-Stars were sitting in the back.

Stewart Levine was on the plane. Stewart Levine was one of the organizers of the music festivals. He was Hugh Masekela's partner in the whole thing. He was a big producer. He produced B. B. King and all types of people. We managed to take off. It was uneventful.

Everybody was drinking. I think there were all kinds of drugs. Everybody was happy. People were making love to some of the flight attendants on the plane, all the way to Madrid. It was one of those big planes. These were the Latinos who were doing this. So anyway when we landed in Madrid, we get off the plane and they had a portable stereo that James Brown could put his forty-fives on. So in the middle of the airport he stacked his records and he plays them loud. Everybody was saying, "Wow, this is deep."

Brown was saying all sorts of stuff to Bill Withers and Bill Withers was getting mad. He was getting really mad. So we get back on the plane and everybody dislikes James Brown. Everybody on the plane, including me. The seats in front of the plane were roped off and the stewardess says, "Nobody can sit in these seats because the plane is too heavy and we may crash because there is too much weight."

They were referring to James Brown's stuff. So everyone in the front had to go to the back; it was like poetic justice. But James Brown got on the plane and saw the seats that were roped off and says, "Fuck this. James Brown don't sit in the back of the plane. James Brown sits in the front." So he took the front ropes off and his manager cuts the ropes off with a knife. At this point it was like a circus. Everybody wanted to kill James Brown at this point.

So the plane takes off and goes all the way to Kinshasa. It barely got off the ground. And because he had been saying all this stuff about Bill Withers, Bill Withers is really getting pissed. In Madrid, Withers had bought one of these saber swords as a gift. So James Brown is screaming about Bill Withers who had all of these records. He was saying, "You can't sing, man, you can't sing. This is James Brown. You can't sing with me man. You're just a one hit singer, blah, blah, blah, blah, and that kind of shit."

Everybody is drinking and everybody is high. All of a sudden Bill Withers—I heard him because he was close to me—he said, "Man, I can't take this fucking shit no more." So he jumped out into the aisle and got the sword and was going down front to hit James Brown in the head with the sword.

Stewart Levine jumped up and said, "You can't do that!" and everybody was trying to grab him and make him sit back down.

James Brown was saying, "Let that motherfucker go," you know, this dumb kind of shit. This is a real sword. There was a lot of tension at the point, all the way there. It was palpable.

People were walking around saying that James Brown was all fucked up and was going to kill them. So the plane lands in Kinshasa and it lands at night. There was a lot of tension, but there was also a lot of fun. There was a lot of partying. There was a lot of drinking on that plane. They continued to seduce the stewardesses. It was a once-in-a-lifetime trip because everybody was doing whatever they wanted; they were getting the best food and the best champagne, drugs, everything.

Soon as we got off the plane and we see all these people, bands, and dancers. It was incredible. There was a lot of dancing and singing, the whole thing. It was a big party. And all of a sudden out of nowhere we saw Muhammad Ali. He came out to meet everybody. We went down the stairway. Black Americans were kissing the ground because they had never been to Africa.

I've been there three or four times. The first time was in 1972. I went to Nigeria, Ghana, Ivory Coast, Senegal, Guinea, Tanzania, and Togo. I was teaching at the University of Ghana and Lagos University. So I was used to it.

Ali greeted James Brown and he shook hands with everybody. It was beautiful. It was one of those rare moments. We went inside and they had food. At the airport, they had African cuisine and food from France and Belgium. Prime ribs, snacks, and beer. They had everything at the airport. Mobutu paid for all of this because he was rich. Some of the top politicians were there. Zaïre politicians. Hugh Masekela was already over there. Don King.

The plan was that you come off the plane, you get your bags, you get on a bus, and you're taken to a hotel. It was discovered that James Brown had knocked off the Latino band's equipment. I don't know why they took those Latin All-Stars' bags and stuff. I don't think it was any racism against the Latinos. I just think theirs were the last ones in. I don't know. All of their stuff was gone. All of their clothes, everything was left in New York, but a lot of people brought their equipment on board. I guess everybody got their stuff except for the Latinos.

So we got on a bus and we went to the Holiday Inn where everybody was staying. That's where Ali was staying. That was the first night. It was gorgeous and stuff but still there was a lot of bad feelings about James Brown. It was just multiplying. The Latinos, they wanted to kill him. They were put on the other side of Kinshasa. They weren't at the Holiday Inn, which made it more odd for me. I don't know what the reason was for that. All the Latinos were on the other side of town. Maybe it was because they didn't think they were big enough stars. We were here because Felipe Luciano and Johnny Pacheco and some others were over there. I was going back and forth and that's how I know how mad they were. I went over to see Felipe and, man, they were so pissed at James Brown because their clothes didn't come for about two or three days. So that was a trip for them. They were, like, pissed off at James Brown. That was the big incident.

But then everybody started settling in. At this point in time everybody had a hotel; I was staying with Elombe Brath. He's from here. He's a nationalist. I like him. He's a nice guy. We are friends to this day. We are different in a lot of ways. He was trying to get off on the women over there. We didn't know about AIDS. He didn't drink and he didn't get high, but we did. We all stayed at the same hotel. Everybody was treated like kings. I mean this food; I mean every night there was something. You didn't have to buy nothin'. You could just go downstairs at night from eight o'clock on. I mean every night there was something. I mean they provided us with prime ribs and the best French food. It was incredible. You could get bottles of champagne, whatever you wanted. Mobutu did this for everybody. This is what was happening. You could go to the bar and drink. There was, like, music in the bars.

I asked Quincy about the visitors' attitudes toward Mobutu in light of the fact that he was considered a U.S. puppet and had replaced the democratically elected leader and hero to millions of Africans and African Americans, Patrice Lumumba. He replied:

Nobody said nothin' because Mobutu was cold-blooded. Everybody knew you could disappear because of the famous story of Dick Young. Dick Young was working as a sportswriter for *The Daily News*. He got there before we did. The first week he was sending back daily pieces about Mobutu because for some reason he hated Mobutu. He just hated him. I mean, I did too.

But he was sending these daily pieces on Mobutu to the paper. Mobutu told him if he did that one more time he would be thrown out of the country. So he wrote another. The secret police went and took him out of the hotel, put him on a plane by himself, and sent his ass back to New York. People took notice of that. They said, "Whoa. That was cold."

Then, they told everybody in Kinshasa, "Don't bother the Americans." That warning happened before I got there or maybe it happened while I was there. "Don't mess with them; don't steal nothin' because if you do we're going to kill you. We are going to hang you."

Some young boy around sixteen years old went and pickpocketed somebody. I think it was Don King. They caught the boy and they hanged him in the square. They hanged his ass. They hanged him in front of people. That was it. So everybody was like, "Whoa, this guy [Mobutu] is deep."

We found out that our drivers were the secret police. They knew where you were going and what you did. So one day the guy says, "The president wants to meet you."

I said, "The president wants to meet me? What does he want to meet me for?"

The guy says, "I don't know, but he told me to bring you over to meet him."

So we go over there. His palace was opulent; a beautiful place on the outskirts of town. It was a big place, cars parked, kind of like a European-style palace that was beautiful. So we go in and sit down and after ten minutes of waiting, here comes Mobutu with bodyguards and he's got his hat on and glasses. I never met anybody in my life that tall. He comes in and sits down and we stare at each other. I never felt that cold-blooded of a guy in my life.

So he says, "Mister Troupe? You're a writer. I like writers. What kind of things do you write? What kind of poetry?" I mentioned two Zairian poets. That kind of softened it a little bit. He said, "Are you over here to write poetry?"

"No. I'm a writing a piece."

"What are you writing about?"

"The fight."

"Only the fight?" he said. "Not politics?"

"I'm not interested in the politics. I don't know anything about the politics."

"Oh, good. Okay." He got up, shook my hand and that was it. He wanted to find out what I was going to write.

Cocaine was everywhere. Bundini and I asked this guy, Chim, for some grass. He said, "We have very good grass, very good grass."

So he took us out one day to a bush on the outskirts of Kinshasa. We see these people coming down the hill with these big bags on their head. He comes up to us. So Bundini said, "I don't want no big bag like this. Maybe just a couple of joints." They start talking to the guy. They said that it was a gift. He told them that we were very important. They were insulted. They picked up all the shit and left. That was the end of that. We didn't get it. They went back up in the hills. We laughed about that for a long time. It was incredible.

I went to Ali's camp at Deer Lake before I left. I talked to Ali. He was cool. He called me "the poet." I had given him a book of poems. He was sparring with Holmes and Jimmy Ellis. He was a very open guy. He was friendly so I liked him a lot.

I also met Foreman. Foreman wasn't open like that so I didn't stay over there for very long. Foreman wasn't talking. He was sullen at that point. He was a different kind of guy so I really didn't—I couldn't get close to him because he was hostile to the press. I went to his camp for a couple of days. That was in Texas. Then when we got over to Kinshasa, I saw Foreman again. He was in a sparring [session]. I had a couple of conversations with him.

He had these two big, beautiful German Shepherds. He'd go downtown to throw a stick for them to fetch it and people would scatter. People told me about this. I went to his camp; he was still sullen. I said, "A lot of people downtown are getting upset with you because you are going downtown and throwing the stick and the dogs are running out there and the Belgians used to have German Shepherds down here on these people. They are getting a little upset with you."

And he said that he didn't give a damn whether they were upset. They were his dogs. I said to myself right then, this guy is in danger of losing the support of his people. The hostility got worse. He just didn't talk to nobody, while Ali was talking to the crowds and going downtown. I remember one time when we went downtown and nobody knew Ali was coming. He got out of the car in the middle of the square and within minutes fifty thousand people came from everywhere. They were shouting at him. "Ali boma ye!" When I saw that, I was thinking, this is some heavy stuff, this is some heavy, heavy stuff against Foreman.

Foreman got an injury and they had to postpone the fight. That meant I had to stay there about a month. The concerts went on. That was the funny thing about the order of the concerts, which turned out to be another case of poetic justice. Unfavorable to James Brown.

James Brown decided he had to play the opening night. The day before James Brown was going to play, Mobutu had a rally in the stadium. Seventy thousand people came. I don't know if he ordered people to come or whether they chose to come. Everybody was there and they were hollering, "Mobutu! Mobutu!" and this helicopter came and circled twice or three times getting lower over the stadium and it landed on the outside of the stadium. He came into the stadium with this entourage. He was wearing glasses, a cap, and used his famous walking stick to walk around the track. People went nuts. I ain't never seen nothin' like this. He got up on the stage, said some words, and left. That's all he did. I said, "Damn, this man's got a lot of power."

The next day was the opening of the whole thing. James Brown wanted to play on the first night. What he didn't understand was that the first night was just for the dignitaries who paid a thousand dollars a seat. Everybody was laughing; Hugh Masekela and all of them were snickering, because the place was empty. James Brown had said, "I wanna do this. This is my stuff, I wanna do this. The first night." I was in the audience when he came out. He came onstage and said, "Where the people at?"

They said, "This is it. This is the dignitaries' night, all of the rich white folks and the ambassadors."

He says, "What about me?"

And they said, "Tomorrow's the night when everybody is going to come." He was mad as hell, because the next day there were a hundred seventy thousand people in that stadium. It was rockin'.

Everybody played the next day: The Latin All-Stars, Bill Withers, great African bands, B. B. King, Sister Sledge. Brown was so mad so he was trying to get Hugh to change it so he could play the next day. Hugh said, "I can't do that because Mobutu is here and Mobutu came to see you, so you better go on. I don't know if he's coming tomorrow, but he's coming tonight." JB was a pro. He went up there and did it, but he was pissed. He was so pissed he didn't know what to do. That was kind of funny.

[I asked Quincy how he spent his time during the period when the fight was postponed. He answered:]

My routine was to go and eat and watch Foreman and Ali train and go to parties. There was a lot to do. There were parties every night. People opened up their houses to us. I visited people. There was a lot to do.

Everybody thought Ali was going to lose, including me. But he said to me one day, "You think George Foreman is going to beat me? Man! George Foreman is too stupid to beat me. I'm going to play with him and then I'm going to knock him out."

I didn't know what he meant then, but now I understand. Foreman was one-dimensional. It was amazing how prescient Ali was; he could see that and that's how he played with Foreman.

There was an incident. We were sitting around the swimming pool, myself, Fletcher Robinson, a Virgin Island doctor, Archie Moore, and two or three other people. We heard all this screaming and hollering and noise. Then all of a sudden it was quiet. One of the security people went and got Fletcher Robinson. He said, "Can you come with us? Right now. Immediately."

In about forty minutes he comes back and says, "Man, you won't believe what happened."

"What?"

"Ali's wife jumped on him and he had to knock her out."

This was Belinda [Khalilah]. He was with Veronica, and Belinda had caught him with Veronica. I guess he hit her or something.

"You serious?"

"Yeah. Tomorrow, you'll see Belinda with sunglasses."

The next day, she was wearing sunglasses. She had attacked him, and he hit her. (In my interview with Khalilah, she denied that she was knocked unconscious. She said that it was she who bested him, because she was trained in the martial arts. She cited the difficulty that the champion had with a kick boxer named Antonio Inoki in 1976. Though the match was regarded as a joke, Ali's legs were damaged so that there was talk of an amputation as a result of an infection that he suffered. His left leg was badly swollen and blood clots showed up in both legs. For his part, Inoki broke a leg. After fifteen rounds, The fight was declared a draw.)

Another undercurrent was the hostility of the wealthy African Americans over there. These Negroes were walking around the hotel with high-heeled shoes and diamonds, gold, and minks in ninety degrees weather. I told some woman, "Do you know how warm it is outside?"

"Excuse me?" she said.

"It's ninety degrees outside. You can't wear mink over here. Why are you wearing mink? For what?"

"This is my coat," she said.

You had all of that. You had the clashing of values of African Americans and Africans, even the upper-class Africans who knew some things didn't understand. A lot of these people had gone to fights in the United States so they thought it was Madison Square Garden or Atlantic City or Las Vegas.

There was a lot electricity over there. I don't know how to say it. It was just electric, the whole thing. After Ali told me the guy [Foreman] was too stupid for him, I thought he could win, but I also thought Foreman was too strong for him. I thought he was a little crazy when he remained on the ropes. What is he doing? I thought maybe he was trying to see the guy punch himself out.

When Foreman was knocked out, people went nuts. Ali's a hell of a closer. If Foreman had gotten up, he would have just been knocked down again. And if he didn't get knocked down, he was going to be beaten to a pulp. But everybody was so happy. The whole thing was a memorable experience. The fight was anticlimactic.

I got to hear all those Zairian bands. I was listening to such great music. I heard the greatest bands in all of Africa. It was fabulous. I was just going to hear the music. It was wonderful for me. I was twenty-five. I left shortly thereafter because we had to go. They detained Hugh Masekela because they owed a whole lot of money. People ran up big hotel bills. I took his stuff back for him. Everybody was glad to return home. I was partied out. I had such a great trip. Hugh really put it together. I saw a lot of paintings and sculptures, but the music was the most interesting.

After Rev. Jesse Jackson arrived at Quincy's apartment, he and Quincy and his entourage disappeared into Quincy's office. Meanwhile, guests began to arrive for the book party. Margaret changed clothes as her sisters continued to prepare the food.

Herb Boyd was ready to be interviewed. He is a prolific writer as well as former editor and one of the web pioneers with *The Black World Today* online. He not only writes about civil rights, but also is an avid sports writer. When I called to set up our interview, I reached his cell phone. He was at Madison Square Garden receiving an award.

I asked him about the claim that was made that Ali was the heavyweight Sugar Ray Robinson, Robinson having been described as pound for pound the greatest fighter of all time, though Henry Armstrong might disagree. When he fought Robinson, Armstrong complained that Robinson was afraid of him and ran. However, Robinson received the decision.

I next asked him about Sugar's bi-sexuality. He replied:

There is a little about his bisexuality in this book [Edna Mae's biography]. That was coming from Bundini Brown, who apparently walked in on a situation where Sugar Ray Robinson was in bed with another man. This was reported to Edna Mae Robinson [ex-wife of Sugar Ray] and Edna Mae put this in her manuscript. Edna Mae left a three hundred and seventy-five page manuscript. It was never published. She could never get it published, so her son gave it to me. She has things in her autobiography that Sugar does not have in his. Now who in the hell knows what the real deal was? But I said you can take your choice. This is what Sugar Ray had to say and what Edna Mae had to say about it.

In 1981, I was executive producer of a film that Walter Cotton, Steve Cannon, and I produced, called "Personal Problems," which was directed by Bill Gunn. Though it never received wide distribution, it premiered at the Pompidou in Paris, was shown at the Whitney Museum in the 1990s, and in 2010 played at the BAMcinématek. During February 2015, it was part of a series of black independent film called "Tell It Like It Is" sponsored by the The Film Society of Lincoln Center. The stars were Walter Cotton, my friend from Buffalo, and Verta Mae Grosvenor. Playing her father-in-law was the late Jim Wright. Jim Wright played Johnny Dollar in the race movies. He was also a member of the Copasetics. This was an organization of great hoofers, which at one time was headed by Billy Strayhorn, the great composer. It was our luck that Jim Wright invited us to attend the Copasetics' annual party, the party of a lifetime. Legendary Harlem entertainers were present, Johnny Hartman sang, and sitting at the head table was the queen of Harlem, Edna Mae Robinson, Ray Robinson's wife.

CHAPTER 28

Fighters like Ron Lyle and Earnie Shavers penetrated Ali's rope-a-dope defense, landing punches through his guard. Unlike Zaïre, he didn't have ropes that he could lean on. Shavers said that he could have knocked out Ali if Angelo Dundee hadn't undertaken one of his in-between-rounds maneuverings.

As his powers began to fade, Ali became more like Rocky Marciano: taking a lot of punches in order to land power shots against his opponent, Ron Lyle said about Ali's returning to the ring. Lyle added that his opponents started "reaching him. Touching him. Before that, they couldn't put a glove on him."

Foreman contends that he could have knocked out Jimmy Young, but was advised by Don King to carry Young for a few rounds. Jack Newfield continued:

> Frazier still carries a grudge. I spent a lot of time with Frazier and [could] really see his point-of-view. Frazier once said to me, "Look at my skin. I'm darker than he is. I grew up in a ghetto, and he grew up in the suburbs. I grew up in South Carolina working on a plantation. One day the boss man said, 'The mule died last night, and now you're the new mule.' I had a much harder life than he did. He can talk to me and dehumanize me and he made me the White guy."

Newfield discussed Foreman's arrival in Zaïre:

> Foreman came off of the plane with a German Shepherd dog. Ali's people saw the German shepherd and were scared of it.

It took Foreman ten years to get over Ali knocking him out. Foreman lost to Jimmy Young and then he became a preacher for ten years and then he comes back to being champion, but he loves Ali.

It was cruel. He made all of his Black opponents the White guy and he never, to my knowledge, taunted the White opponents.

His Parkinson's is getting worse and worse and he won't take his medication. He's been slipping each time I have seen him for the last five or six years to where it breaks my heart to see him. I avoid going to dinners where he is honored because he is being fed and the food drools from his mouth and this is the greatest of the greatest. I think that Ali is the greatest of all time. He knocked out Liston, Foreman, and stopped Frazier. These were the three other great heavyweights of his era and he beat them. They were very difficult fights.

He was faster than any heavyweight I ever saw. And his defeat of Foreman was his greatest triumph because he wasn't as strong anymore. I watched him train for the Foreman fight in Deer Lake and he had two young sparring partners; he let them hit him while he was laying on the ropes. The two young partners turned out to be Larry Holmes and Tim Witherspoon. They became champions. I asked him why he was letting them punish him like that, and he said, "I'm building up my threshold for pain. That's how I have to beat George."

He should have quit after Manila. He had a big lifestyle supporting various wives and bloodsuckers and he was at first the most famous fighter in the world and then the phone stopped ringing. That's why Michael Jordan came back, and why Sugar Ray Robinson came back.

Newfield also could have mentioned Sugar Ray Leonard, Cesar Chavez, Felix Trinidad and Riddick Bowe, and now, sadly, Tommie Hearns.

CHAPTER 29

Aix-en-Provence

Many writers know the feeling: a subject that one is focused on begins to stalk the writer. I'm in a room located in the Hotel Le Pigonnet in Aix-en-Provence, France. Outside is a sculpture garden. I'm having breakfast with people like Patti Smith. The receptions are great, the food is wonderful, and life is good. They get me to introduce Melvin Van Peebles' "Sweetback's Badass Song" at one of these French art cinemas. I prepare a forty-five minute introduction, but can tell from scanning the faces of the French audience that they haven't the slightest idea of what I'm talking about. We dine at a suburban restaurant within view of Picasso's home. But there's also guilt accompanying this kind of trip. Every time I return to Buffalo, my home town, I hear about one of my friends who lived in the projects where we grew up, either having been killed, being in a mental institution or having disappeared; the success stories are few.

On television there is a broadcast of an interview with George Foreman. He's a different person from the fighter who made excuses for his loss to Muhammad Ali. He had complained that he didn't like Zaïre. He said there was no edible chow, and that when his cook, Tyree Lyons, sought edible chow in Kinshasa, he got a mysterious ailment that swelled his hands and eyes. His first quarters were an old army base guarded by drunken soldiers and infested with rats, lizards, and insects. He blamed his loss on dehydration, the condition of the ropes, a close friend whom he saw at ringside rooting for Ali, the referee, Zack Clayton's, quick count. The most serious claim was that he was drugged by his trainer, Dick Sadler. "I believed that my water may have been mickeyed," he said.

I asked Reggie Barrett about Foreman's complaint that he had been drugged. "Yeah," Barrett said, "drugged by Ali's right fist." By 2004, during an interview on a program called CenterStage, a mellow George Foreman admitted that he had been making excuses when he tried to belittle Ali's victory over him in the ring.

Foreman repeats his theme, "You can dream until you die." Though Foreman had acquitted himself well in the Holyfield and Moore fights, he took a lot of punishment along the way. He succeeded in knocking out Moore, but his face was swollen after an intense and grueling nine rounds. Foreman says on this BBC program that I'm watching in my hotel room that he wants to box somebody in their twenties. He also wants to return the spokesmanship for boxing to boxers instead of having Bob Arum, Don King, and promoters speaking for boxers. Fortunately, he retired before taking a fight with a twenty-year-old and being carried out on a stretcher.

Ali was the favorite even when fighting a patriot like George Foreman, who defied the militant mood of the times by parading around the Olympic ring with an American flag in hand. (Few of Foreman's critics recalled that Ali had also made patriotic statements when receiving the gold Olympic medal. In 1960, he told a Soviet journalist that "The USA is the best country in the world including yours" (Hauser, 2005)). Foreman said that he did it because American society had been good to him. He'd received an education and had advanced. But while Frazier remained bitter by his humiliation by Ali, until both were entering their senior years, Foreman has become mellow. His admiration for Ali is generous and expansive.

Something that I hadn't heard before: that when Foreman became number one again, Ali refused to fight him. He went on to fight Jimmy Young and says that he lost the fight because he was told by Don King to carry the fighter for a few rounds. He was defeated, or as his trainer put it, "robbed." Young had knocked him down, and after that fight, in his dressing room, he experienced a dark night of the soul—a vision of death that led to his becoming a Christian preacher.

In his autobiography, however, so powerful was the Muslim appeal to intellectuals as well as athletes, he admits to at one time considering the Muslim faith. After the Foreman fight, Ali had faced opponents who were either overmatched or those who offered stiff tests like the late Ron Lyle, Joe Frazier, Ken Norton, and Earnie Shavers. (Though the judges gave the second fight to Norton, George Foreman had Norton winning.) His ability to evade punches began to fade, which is what happens to boxers whose main asset is speed. When Roy Jones, Jr. slowed down, his opponents began to knock him out!

◆

His boxing career over, after his defeat by Trever Berbick, Ali tried to become a diplomat. In 1980, President Jimmy Carter asked Ali to undertake a five-nation tour of Africa in order to recruit African countries to support his boycott of the Moscow Olympic Games, in protest against the invasion of Afghanistan. *Time* magazine, on February 18, 1980, called his mission a disaster:

> Arriving in Dar es Salaam, Tanzania, Ali immediately demonstrated that he had not been well briefed for his mission. He was apparently unaware that the Soviet Union had been backing revolutionary liberation movements on the continent. Why, some local reporters also demanded, should Africa boycott the Moscow Olympics when four years ago the U.S. had opposed an African Olympic boycott called to protest New Zealand's sporting links with South Africa? Ali fumbled for an answer and found none. The former champ, who was hurt to discover that Tanzanian President Julius Nyerere would not receive him, threatened to call off his trip. Said he: "If I'm to be looked at as an Uncle Tom or a traitor or someone against my black brothers, I want out 'cause that's not my purpose."

Then he was off to Nairobi, Kenya, where he accused Carter of sending him to Africa to take a "whipping" over U.S. policy toward South Africa.

In 1982, Ali was diagnosed with Parkinson's disease. The great, lightweight boxer Willie Pep, regarded by Carmine Basilio and

Angelo Dundee as the greatest pound for pound boxer, said of a
fading boxer, "First the legs go, then the reflexes, then the friends."

One of my brothers, New York Attorney Kip LeNoir, who saw Ali
at the beginning of his boxing career and at the end, is able to offer
a before-and-after picture of Ali:

> We're talking about 1957 when he came out of the Olympics. Archie
> Moore was a good friend of my father, Henry LeNoir, in Dallas,
> Texas. Ali was in Moore's training camp. I was working at the desk at
> the YMCA in North Dallas. He happened to come through. No one
> paid attention to him. He was solo. We had a conversation while I was
> working at the desk. He showed me a trick where he took a drag on the
> cigarette and put it through the handkerchief where the nicotine and
> tar showed up. [Heavyweight Champion Ezzard Charles also did card
> tricks and played at hypnotizing members of his entourage.]
>
> I invited him to a weekend party at a Catholic church. He had his
> jacket on all the time. I picked him up at the Y and we had a flat tire.
> His poetry was vague at the time. He would talk about girls and some
> of his experiences. I invited him to James Madison High School in
> Dallas. He met the principal and spoke to the children. That was my
> experience with him. It was short, but it was the kind you wouldn't
> forget. He was a youngster from Kentucky who hadn't yet blossomed
> into what he became.
>
> In the 1990s, I was walking through the airport in Chicago and he
> was alone. I walked over to him and introduced myself to him as Kip
> LeNoir, and asked whether he remembered me from Dallas. He said,
> "Brother, if I remembered what happened two weeks ago I would be
> happy."

Ali's fate could have been worse, according to some, if he hadn't
been rescued by his current wife, Lonnie. For some, Lonnie is a
scheming and manipulative opportunist and only in it for the money,
but Dick Gregory told me that she had cleaned him up in more ways
than one. Those who, like his second wife, Khalilah, believe that
Lonnie is exploiting him or using him for her own gain by placing
him in situations injurious to his declining health might find evidence
in Deron Snyder's report of Ali's appearance at the opening of Miami
Marlin's new stadium on April 4, 2012:

The scene didn't fit the rest of the evening, which was joyous, festive and celebratory. Instead, Ali's appearance was sad, awkward and eerie. When the crowd stopped trying to muster up cheers and a half-hearted "Ali! Ali!" chant, it watched in stunned silence. The seventy-year-old former champion, his frail body ravaged by Parkinson's disease, trembled uncontrollably as Marlins owner Jeffrey Loria wrapped an arm around him.

Loria, who isn't very popular among fans, likely would have been booed if Ali weren't next to him. That's one reason the move to include Ali seemed so exploitative—Loria using him as a shield and as an unnecessary, high-profile prop.

I found Lonnie's parading Ali around at the 2012 London Olympics and whispering instructions to him as though he were a creature to be off-putting. However, if Lonnie was using Ali in such a manner, for Michael Ezra, Yolanda "Lonnie" Ali was his savior. Mrs. Ali's childhood crush on the athlete became more than that when they were married on November 19, 1986. She says that she was so disturbed by him stumbling and stuttering and slurring his words during a luncheon engagement that took place in 1982 that she decided upon an intervention. A friend told Mrs. Ali that "if somebody doesn't help him, I think that he's going to die."

Ali's earlier interest in the young woman paid off. Even though he was married to Veronica Porsche, Lonnie, with Veronica's consent, moved to Los Angeles to look after the champion. Ali paid all of her expenses while she did her graduate studies at UCLA. Lonnie and Ali married after the champion and Veronica divorced in 1986. Though Veronica and Ali had a pre-nuptial agreement, Ali had it rescinded so that the bulk of his estate would go to Veronica and their children. One report has it that Ali was given twenty-four hours to retrieve his things from the mansion and when he arrived, Veronica and her relatives had cleaned him out and all that remained was a copy of the Quran. Veronica would go on to marry an actor; he died of leukemia.

It was Lonnie's business acumen that lifted Ali from poverty—it was rumored that he was so broke, he was reduced to earning a thousand dollars to show up at fights. As Ezra put it, "Without her intervention, there's a good chance that Ali would be financially insecure, convalescent, or dead." Her having an MBA provided her with the skills to market the champion, to the chagrin of some who felt that Ali was becoming apolitical and a commodity. Lonnie began her MBA studies at the University of Louisville.

Her efforts at rehabilitating Ali, an effort that some called the Ali Renaissance, culminated in Ali's selling eighty percent of the rights to his name and likeness to CKX, the same outfit that markets Elvis. This move caused dissension among Ali staffers, one of whom resigned. On April 12, 2006, Tim Povtak of *The Orlando Sentinel* explained the deal this way:

> Instead of working for a sports star in a traditional sense, like IMG does with Tiger Woods and Vince Carter, and taking a percentage of their earnings, burgeoning entertainment company CKX paid Ali cash for the exclusive rights to market him and his image. Anything with Ali's name or likeness, whether it's sportswear, boxing gloves, movies, books, museums, will be sold under the CKX umbrella.
>
> "They essentially have bought the rights to sell the rights," said Dan Migala, editor and publisher of *The Migala Report*, a sports marketing trade publication in Chicago. "It's just a new way of looking at things in sports. It has taken an old concept, used in other businesses, and applied it to a new area."
>
> Migala explained it in real estate terms. Instead of an agent getting permission to sell a house and take a small percentage of the sales price, CKX has bought the house outright and now can sell it for whatever price it wants, and pockets the profits.

An example of the marketing of Ali as a commodity occurred when a photograph of him and his grandson appeared in magazines and newspapers in 2012, the purpose of which was to peddle some expensive Louis Vuitton luggage that followers of "The People's Champ" can't afford. His voice was heard in the background of a 2015 Super Bowl commercial.

With Lonnie's cooperation, Thomas Hauser became the official spokesperson for the Ali Renaissance. Ali, a man who'd addressed a Klan meeting and who, though one of the creators of the Black is

Beautiful philosophy, adhered to Western standards of beauty as evidenced in his comments about Joe Frazier's looks and those of African women. A man whose relationship with Philadelphia gangland figures and with a man who might have ordered a massacre of women and children, has been ignored by his admirers, whose books have been rightly called hagiographies. Hauser's book of the Saint Ali was called *Muhammad Ali: His Life and Times*. The manuscript was supervised by Lonnie Ali to fit the vision of Ali that she desired to commercialize.

According to Michael Ezra, author of *Muhammad Ali: The Making of an Icon*, "She wanted a book that would place Muhammad in context, not just as a fighter but also as a social, political, and religious figure." Ezra feels that Hauser was too close to the Ali camp to write a book that would reveal Ali's warts, a criticism echoed by Howard Cosell, who wrote, "My theory is that Hauser has gotten too close to his subject and is too enamored of Ali to write a completely honest and objective book."

In 2003, Thomas Hauser, no longer in contact with the Ali camp, exposed the autocratic side of Mrs. Ali, a woman who, according to some, will cross anybody in order to preserve the legacy of Ali for dollars. His contribution to an extravagant, gross, ugly thing called *GOAT*, a seventy-five-pound, four-thousand-dollar coffee table book made of ceramics, silk, and leather, was rejected. Ezra, however, suggests that Hauser wanted to use Ali as his own prop, as a "conduit between America and the Islamic world."

CHAPTER 30

Ali as a Black Nationalist
San Francisco, January 2004 Black Liberation Book Fair

In January 2004, some of the pioneers of the 1960s black nationalist movement gathered at a book fair organized by Marvin X, a writer who is much venerated in black nationalist circles. Some of those gathered were die-hard Malcolmites who are cool to Ali and attribute his mainstream acceptance to the white public's gloating over the fact that the man once called "The Louisville Lip" has been muzzled by a disability.

Though still regarded with respect, some black nationalists will never forgive Muhammad Ali, their one-time hero, for turning his back on Malcolm X, their idol. Some of those who dismissed Joe Frazier as an Uncle Tom are giving Frazier a second look. He is no longer regarded as the usurper who deprived the exiled champion of his glorious comeback. An example of Joe Frazier's lack of sophistication was his mistaking "Uncle Tom" for "Peeping Tom." In the words of Marvin X, "Malcolm gave me political consciousness. He stood up against America. Ali on the other hand is now speaking on behalf of America."

Marvin X provides further evidence of the influence that the Nation of Islam had on Muhammad Ali's decision to forfeit his duty to serve in the armed forces. He provided a biography, which gives a historical background to the presence of African-American Muslims in this country. According to Marvin X:

I would like to delineate my lineage. As a spiritual descendant of West African Muslims, I begin my literary biography in the Mali Empire, among those scholar/poet/social activists of Timbuktu: Ahmed Baba, Muhammad El-Mrili, Ahmed Ibn Said, Muhammad Al Wangari, and the later Sufi poet/warriors of Senegal and Hausaland, Ahmedu Bamba and Uthman dan Fodio.

In America, this literary tradition continued under the wretched conditions of slavery with the English/Arabic narratives of Ayub Suleimon Diallo, Ibrahima Abdulrahman Jallo, Bilali Mohammad, Salih Bilali, Umar Ibn Said. [Note: There is some suggestion that David Walker, Frederick Douglass, Booker T. Washington, and Benjamin Banneker may have been descendants of Muslims.] In 1913, Noble Drew Ali established his Moorish Science Temple in Newark, New Jersey, later Chicago, and created his Seven Circle Koran, a synthesis of Quranic, Masonic, mystical, and esoteric writings.

And most importantly, Master Fard Muhammad arrived in Detroit, 1930, to deliver his Supreme Wisdom, mythological Sufi teachings, to the Honorable Elijah Muhammad, later summarized in Elijah's primers of mystical Islamic theology and Black Nationalism, *Message to the Black Man* and *The Theology of Time*.

The next major work is Malcolm X's *Autobiography*, with the assistance of Alex Haley. This neo-slave narrative bridged ancient and modern Islamic literature in America. Let us also include Louis Farrakhan's Off-Broadway drama "Organa" and his classic song "A White Man's Heaven is The Black Man's Hell," anthem of the Black revolution of the 60s. Amiri Baraka utilized the Muslim myth of Yacub in his play "A Black Mass," one of his most powerful works, an examination of the cloning of the white man. Askia Muhammad Touré must be credited for his Islamic writings, along with poetess Sonia Sanchez (Laila Mannan) who served a brief tenure in the Nation of Islam. Yusef Rahman and Yusef Iman created powerful Islamic poetry as well.

At the Black Liberation Book Fair on January 31, 2004, Marvin X said:

Well, you know we both had the draft problem as Muslims. Ali followed Elijah Muhammad's directive to go to prison instead of going into exile like I did. I went to Canada. I was there about six months. Well, because I got tired of Canada. There is an expression, "Racism is as Canadian as

Hockey." First I went to Chicago and linked up with the group around *Black World*, which was edited by Hoyt Fuller, Haki Madhubuti, and others. I was in Chicago when Martin Luther King, Jr. was killed. After I left Chicago, I went to Harlem. This is now '68. Then I went to New York to work with the New Lafayette with Ed Bullins and the whole crew at the Lafayette Theater.

I went to Montreal for a visit. I had met a girl from Montreal. At the same time there was a struggle at Sir George Williams University. Bobby Seale was up there and a brother named Dominique, I think it was Dominique, and Rosy Douglas. There was a student struggle going on; I got busted coming back from Montreal, coming across the border without papers. And so I [was] put in jail in Plattsburg, New York, and then released on OR [Own Recognizance] and then they gave me a trial date, a court date in San Francisco, for the draft. I was invited to lecture at Fresno State in the Black Studies Department. Richard Keyes was the chair. So actually I was going to two trials, one with Reagan at Fresno Superior Court and one in San Francisco at the Federal Court.

I met Eldridge Cleaver, who was then working for *Ramparts* magazine. He was supposed to interview Muhammad Ali, but he couldn't go because he was under house arrest and so he arranged for me to do the interview. I went to Chicago to wait around for the interview. Muhammad Ali was in Detroit. He finally came back to Chicago. We were at Elijah Muhammad's house. Well, there were a few people there. I saw Elijah Muhammad's wife, Clara, and Muhammad Ali, but I didn't see Elijah. Before we got ready to do the interview, Elijah Muhammad called him into a room, and when he came out he said, "Elijah Muhammad said not to do the interview." That he had said enough about the draft. This was, like, '68.

Well, we were probably in the house for about an hour. He said that Elijah was "a man I am willing to die for so I do what he says." Well, that's how most Muslims felt. Both Black Panther and NOI attitudes about the draft influenced me. That's why I was in Canada. What I'm saying is that Elijah said, "Resist the draft." The Panthers said, "Resist arrest." So I resisted the draft and I resisted arrest. That's where I was coming from.

Ali asked me if I needed any money, and I said, "Yeah." He gave me a hundred dollars. Why did he? I don't know. I guess maybe it was his personality. I was at Merritt College with Huey [Newton] and Bobby [Seale] from 1962 to '64 and we identified with Malcolm X and so I didn't join the Nation until '67. I think I was looking for something more than what the Panthers were offering, because I could have easily gone to the Panther Party because they were my friends. It was a spiritual dimension that I was looking for. But I also got some Marxist material from the Panthers. But, you know their Ten Point Program was just a rehashing of the Muslim Program and put into some Marxist language.

Malcolm gave me political consciousness. He stood up against America. Ali, on the other hand, is now speaking on behalf of America. That's not really strange for him to do that and I think I say that about him in my review of the movie *Ali* in my book *In The Crazy House Called America*. He became a follower of Wallace Deen and Wallace Deen has an American flag on his newspaper. So Wallace accepted his American identity and I guess his followers follow that.

Wallace left his father before Malcolm. He never came back. Ali said he followed Wallace after Elijah made a transition, because as far as he was concerned, Wallace came with the true Islam, the spiritual Islam, after the Nation had become corrupted. And then Norman Brown told me last night that as far as he was concerned, Wallace just bought into Arab Nationalism and Arab racism and turned Negroes into Arabs.

In his book *In The Crazy House Called America*, Marvin X is far more critical of Ali's move to the right. He blames it on the champion following the teachings of the late Wallace Muhammad. In the book he writes:

We understand that he [Ali] has been requested to make public service announcements supporting America's war on terrorism. Would this be a more dramatic ending: the people's champ who fought against oppression, finally broken down to a servant of the oppressor… the tragic truth is that Ali is a member of Warith Deen Muhammad's sect that was known for flag waving before 9/11. Warith had rejected the teachings of his father, the Honorable Elijah Muhammad, in favor of orthodox Islam, dismissing the Black Nationalism of Elijah for Americanism, so it is not whack for President Bush to call upon Ali to be the "voice of America" to the Muslim world, nor for Ali to accept. If indeed, our hero has been co-opted, let us be mature enough to realize humans are not made of stone and we know in real life people change, not always for the good—thus the danger of hero worship and thus the Islamic dictum: nothing deserves to be worshipped except Allah.

In 1998, I received a three-year grant from the Lila Wallace Foundation, which required me to accompany adults who were learning English at Oakland's Second Start Literacy Program to the theater. In the course of three years, I saw a number of plays and musicals, many of which were overrated, and quite a number of which were insulting to minorities, like "Miss Saigon" and "Rent" and the most reprehensible of all, "Stonewall's House," a play that tried to clean up the Confederate insurgents' reputation and which argued that blacks were better off in slavery, and that because of political correctness, white male playwrights were oppressed. In other words, plays by blacks dominate the Great White Way. The play that I found the most compelling was produced by the Black Repertory Theater in Oakland. It was called "A Day in the Life," and it was written by Marvin X. Like some of the other black revolutionaries of that period, Marvin X turned to drugs after the disillusionment set in, and the revolution was busted, partially due to a sinister COINTELPRO (Counter Intelligence Program) operation. Some of the more vibrant, charismatic, and militant of the activists were permitted to morph into non-threatening positions as college professors, where they still engage in correcting those whom they feel are not revolutionary enough. All one has to do is contrast the swell-headed, boastful play "Big Time Buck White," in which Muhammad Ali starred, with "A Day In The Life" to determine the corrosion of the sixties optimism and the pessimism of the current political climate.

Black nationalists and those on the black left have been among President Obama's harshest critics, while black support for the president has remained in the ninety percent range. Cornel West, whom white progressives were agitating for a run in a primary against the president, referred to the president as "a black mascot for Wall Street," which makes you wonder why Wall Street backed his opponent, Mitt Romney. Marvin X has called the president "a black hangman." The Marvin X play includes a scene with the late Black Panther leader Huey Newton (with whom I appeared on a 1988 ABC TV show, which can be seen on You Tube, the year before his assassination over a drug deal gone wrong. In Marvin X's play, he shares a crack pipe with the man who would later assassinate him.

Inspired by the Harlem Book Fair, Marvin X decided to organize his own. Thus the Black Liberation Book Fair was held in the
Tenderloin district of San Francisco (San Francisco's Skid Row) on
January 31, 2004. This event included a veritable Who's Who of black
nationalist personalities. With the tendency of the segregated media
to tokenize every aspect of African-American life, some of these
people are unknown to the general public, but connoisseurs of black
politics and culture know about them and recognize their important
contribution to the modern slave revolt of the 1960s. If anyone would
give an unsparing portrait of Muhammad Ali, it would be them.
For the 1960s, Muhammad Ali was their leader, but some, like Haki
Madhubuti, still resent the champion's betrayal of Malcolm X, who,
among black nationalists, is regarded as a deity.

The book fair was held in the basement of Saint John's Church.
While the media of the 1960s made a few civil rights and Black Power
personalities famous, some of those who had worked behind the
scenes, those who did the intellectual heavy lifting, were present at
this book fair. That included poet Askia Touré, my 1960s roommate
Nathan Hare, the late Sam Greenlee (whose film version of *The Spook
Who Sat By The Door*, about an armed uprising against the government, drew the attention of the FBI), and the late Reginald Major,
the author of *The Black Panther Is A Black Cat*, which remains one
of the best books on that group's career.

I asked Reginald Major, "What is the significance of Muhammad
Ali?" He responded:

> Just his existence, man. That simple. I saw him on television, fighting
> in the Golden Gloves. I used to travel with my kids Devorah [a former
> poet laureate of the city of San Francisco] and David every summer;
> we'd see him in Englewood, New Jersey, and watch him fight on TV.
>
> I finally met him at San Quentin. It was family day. All of the
> prisoners were ranked by behavior. The most compliant ones were in
> the front, and the terrible ones were in the back. Muhammad Ali went
> straight to the back and talked to the terrible ones; he was sparring with
> them and carrying on—he was, of course, more skillful than the guys
> he was sparring with, but he didn't try to overpower them. Just watch-

ing him do that with no language was an incredible thing. The guards were terrified. This was in 1978, and the guards didn't know what to do. They couldn't push him around, and he stayed in the back until it was time for him to go up the stage. I found him to be a friendly, really nice fellow, that's all. Just watching him with the prisoners, it was an incredible thing. The phase where he said "no Viet Cong ever called me a nigger," made him a major influence on African-Americans—he spearheaded the whole anti-Vietnam thing.

Reginald Major died on June 20, 2011.

Sam Greenlee's *The Spook Who Sat By the Door* remains one of the few uncompromised representations of black armed resistance in the United States. Dewayne Wickham, *USA Today* columnist, provides context in the DVD's introduction to the film: "It was a story of aggressive reaction to white oppression."

On its initial release, the film garnered mixed responses. Whereas, according to Wickham, "There was violent reaction in some parts of white America," for many black viewers, it was a wakeup call. Theaters in Chicago, New York, Los Angeles, and Oakland sold out for the three weeks the film was in release. Greenlee and Dixon contend that the FBI pressured the distributor to pull the film (in keeping with other tactics deployed the Bureau's COINTELPRO).

I asked Sam why the public that despised the champion so during the 1960s was now showing him so much affection. He responded:

> I guess they love him not only because of his skills as a fighter but because of the courage and dignity he demonstrated by refusing to go to war. I think it cost him, mentally and physically. One of the reasons for his current condition is because he had to sit out three years, and when he came back he had lost his speed and as a consequence had to take a whole lot of punishment. But he will be an icon for the rest of his life.
>
> There are some elements in his struggle that are similar to my own, in the way they came down on him because of his courage. He is just one in a long line of black men and women who had to stand up and who were attacked in all kinds of ways, and because he was taking more pressure than I, it took some of the pressure off of me. The affection that he is receiving now is because he is old and senile. When he was

young, proud, defiant, and sexual, they hated him. Now that he is a doddering old man—they like doddering old black men. They love us. When I start walking around with a cane, they'll love me.

Sam Greenlee died in 2014.

Next, I interviewed Amiri Baraka, former Poet Laureate of New Jersey and one of two hundred fifty members of the exclusive American Academy of Arts and Letters.

Amiri Baraka was one of those who picketed the heavyweight championship fight between Joe Frazier and Buster Mathis, his contention being that Ali, who'd been stripped of his license, was the real champion. He said:

> He beat everybody's ass and then refused to go to Vietnam. He said, "No Vietnamese ever called me a nigger." He was a stand-up icon. He made the wrong decision when he supported Elijah Muhammad over Malcolm X. He was a young brother and didn't know what was happening. He thought that Elijah Muhammad was the final imprimatur on the movement. Then, when [Muhammad Ali] abandoned Malcolm X, he made a mistake. I have to look at Muhammad Ali for his particular contribution, which was to defy the U.S. government. Changing his name. Those were the most important things.
>
> I saw him fight Doug Jones in New York. Everybody thought that Jones won the fight. I didn't think that because I didn't want to think that. I also saw him when he was going down in the Village, reciting poetry. I met him, and I thought he was a great man; in fact, he is still a great man. When he went to the 9/11 site they asked him, "How do you feel that a member of your religion was responsible for this?" He said, "How do you feel that Hitler was a member of your religion?"

Amiri Baraka died in 2014.

Nathan Hare and his spouse, Julia, both of whom run the Black Think Tank, were seated at a table on which they were displaying their books. Hare has very sharp features that betray a Native American heritage. Later, I would see Hare in some sports footage in the company of a jubilant Ali. He coined the term "Ethnic Studies," which has become a big academic moneymaker.

Nathan Hare, a scholar and activist is one of those who fought for the inauguration of Ethnic Studies at San Francisco State College (now University). His advocacy for a broadening of the curriculum brought him in contact with President S. I. Hayakawa, who was rewarded with a senate seat by conservatives who admired his handling of the multicultural alliance that Hare, novelist Floyd Salas, poet Askia Toure and others were able to ignite at San Francisco and Bobby Seale at Merritt College. His promotion of progressive causes also made him a target of a then-conservative administration at Howard University. A psychiatrist, Hare continues to be productive as the head of the Black Think Tank. He was a founder of *Black Scholar Magazine*.

Nathan Hare, who was once Ali's jogging partner and stands next to Ali in the film *A.K.A. Cassius Clay*, has followed Ali's career from the beginning: when he won State Golden Gloves titles, two National Golden Gloves titles, and two National Amateur Athletic Union titles; winning the gold medal at the Summer Olympics in Rome, September 5, 1960; when in the Light Heavyweight Division, Ali defeated Zbigniew Pietrzykowski of Poland in a popular, unanimous decision for the light-heavyweight championship. Ali had difficulty with the Pole's southpaw stance, but had figured him out by the third round. He began his professional career in Louisville with a six-round decision over Tunney Hunsacker. In a Miami Beach fight against Lamar Clark on April 19, 1961, he began the practice of predicting the round when he'd KO an opponent:

> He [Ali] represented a new kind of sports personality. When I first saw him, he was seventeen years old and winning the Golden Gloves. I remember running through the house and telling everybody to come watch this great fighter. He was a light heavyweight then. When he became pro, he became a heavyweight. He went through everybody, swimmingly, but he didn't just fight inside the ring; he fought outside the ring. He was political. He was also endowed with social consciousness. He popularized the "Black is Beautiful" concept. He said that he was beautiful. That he was "the greatest." He gave people hope because they could identify with that. At the same time he raised consciousness, he

was part of the Nation of Islam. By that time he had changed his name from Cassius Clay to Muhammad Ali. He came to Howard University to speak in the spring of 1967. He was getting bored in the hotel and so he said, "Let's go out and get the newspapers; see what they are saying."

People came down to the Hilton by the hundreds. They'd formed crowds and, looking through the car windows, would be little kids saying, "Mama, there goes Dassius Day." He insisted that he be called Muhammad Ali and eventually everyone, even the racist whites, would accept him as Muhammad Ali. Another thing I saw in the hotel—in the restaurant, for example, the white waitresses would be trying to get his autograph for their kids. Everyone loved him. He was a force for uplift and consciousness, something that athletes were not known for before.

I was with him by chance at the University of Indiana, I never saw anybody take over a crowd as he did. He addressed a mostly white audience, and he took the roof of off the house. He had these white kids just screaming. He said that although he was barred from the ring, he wasn't barred from talking about the war. He was saying that he was one nigger that the White man was not going to get. White kids went crazy. He kept on saying that. This was Indiana, not the most liberal state there is, it being in the Midwest.

I went to his house. I met him when the Black Power committee and I brought him to speak at Howard University. When the administration at Howard heard that he was coming they put a padlock on the auditorium. They closed it down for the whole semester. James Nabrit was the president then. He'd argued the case that led to the desegregation of the Pullman cars before the Supreme Court.

But by 1967 he was an Ambassador to the United Nations. He didn't want this kind of thing. When Amiri Baraka came down to speak, he had to speak in front of the School of Religion. Ali spoke on the steps of Frederick Douglass Hall; I personally put the microphone up. The Muslims brought him. Four thousand people gathered there on the spur of the moment. A lot of people didn't expect him to come. I interviewed him for *Black Scholar* magazine. Asked him what he felt like being barred from the ring. I met his wife Belinda and stayed around and interviewed him for the weekend. That's the last time I remember seeing him.

I wasn't too fond of his reaction to Malcolm X's death. At that time, he belonged to a very tightly knit organization and he was also amazingly submissive. Some men, no matter how strong, have this longing for the father figure. Ali was uncontrollable, but he had this need for someone to look up to and to obey.

His father figure was Elijah Muhammad. Not only was he barred from the ring by the government, he was also barred from the Mosque for a year to make him not want to sell his body and entertain white people as a fighter. I think it was because Elijah Muhammad was protecting him. Elijah Muhammad didn't fight in WWII and was put in jail because he didn't want to fight a "white man's war." So that was part of the belief system of the group. When Elijah Muhammad suspended Ali, Ali said that he deserved to be banned and I was again struck by how submissive he was. He downed himself in the speech he made in Indiana. But Ali was loved by much more people than he was hated by. He could walk up to any young black woman and get a phone number. He was hated because he did represent a strong black man. But now he has Parkinson's and has become a pathetic relic of himself, but I don't think that should detract from the acceptance he had before this. He talked all the time. He also wrote his own poetry. He could point to the round when he'd knock somebody out and make it rhyme.

Nathan Hare discussed the Ali-Foreman fight, to some, his greatest triumph in the ring:

Foreman was really strong. He was a big hitter. People thought that he was going to lose to Foreman. I went to Dreamland and saw the fight with a friend. After the first round, I said that Foreman was not going to knock him out. After the third round I told the friend that Ali was going to beat him. But I was surprised when it happened. He was doing rope-a-dope, and then boom Foreman was down. With this technique, he changed the strategy of boxing, because you weren't supposed to fight on the ropes, you were supposed to fight in the center of the ring, because it was easier to move around. Part of it was because his legs were gone. And I agree with Cus D'Amato, that he took too many punches in the gym clowning and letting people hit him and even Foreman, he let Foreman hit him.

But then people started to try to dance like Ali. He learned from Sugar Ray and developed that and after Ali, boxers began to speak up a little better and do what they wanted to do a little better.

Another stick-and-move heavyweight champion was Gene Tunney. Hare said:

Before that they were dominated by their trainers, but he did things like expose his chin and pull back, but as he got slower and his powers waned, he wasn't able to get away with that especially from a skillful technician like Larry Holmes. Holmes was very precise. Often these fighters get killed in the ring, and people think that it was caused by the person they were then fighting, when something was wrong all along.

Ali was a symbol of black pride; the man could do what he was going to do better than everybody else. Who could also say he was going to do it name the time and that kind of thing and dance and look pretty as he was doing it. Heavyweights didn't box like that. Power was the whole thing. That's why I don't like to watch many of them; I prefer the smaller weights. But he fought like a welterweight, and was trying to imitate Sugar. I fought as a welterweight, I never stuck with it, I was in and out, but in those days you couldn't be a scholar and a boxer both and so I kept on quitting and my wife got hysterical about my boxing after Benny Kid Paret got killed—and then Davey Moore died, and I didn't go back to the gym.

Bad refereeing might have hastened Paret's death. In a December 9, 1961 fight held at the Las Vegas Convention Center against Gene Fullmer, Fullmer was allowed to trap Paret on the ropes, hold him, head and shoulder butt him until he knocked him out in the tenth round. Though the crowd booed Fullmer's tactics, referee Harold Krause did nothing to warn or penalize Fullmer. According to Hare:

Then I took a fight because a fighter didn't show up and I won easily and was about to knock my opponent out, but at the ringside was the Associate Dean of Liberal Arts and the Dean of Men and his wife, and after the fight I came out of the dressing room and sat with them and apparently for them boxing wasn't becoming of a Howard professor and so I told them that I was there because I was doing research on a book about fighting and they called me in the next day and asked me to choose between teaching and fighting and I started to choose fighting, but my wife wanted me to quit.

CHAPTER 31

A few years ago, I attended a reunion of members of The Abraham Lincoln Brigade. The old timers entered the auditorium on canes, some in wheelchairs and some even wearing berets. Some of those in attendance at this Black Liberation Book Fair were persecuted by COINTELPRO, an operation whose goal was to undermine the Black Revolution. Like The Brigade survivors, who sought to head off fascism before it gained a foothold in Europe, these black nationalist survivors saw their friends murdered, careers ruined, and suicide, mental illness, and drug addiction resulting from a challenge against the most formidable opposition in the history of the world. While some of the white revolutionaries of the 1960s, like Weatherman Mark Rudd, whom I interviewed for C-Span, Rudd described his years underground as "cozy" because he had wealthy progressives who kept him afloat; some black radicals remain in prison. The prosecutor said kind words about Rudd when he turned himself in, even though he'd participated in an armed robbery and a jail break. He took advantage of a racist criminal justice system, which treats whites differently than blacks. Rudd acknowledged to me during my interview of him on C-Span that black revolutionaries fare far worse than the white ones.

Even though the FBI didn't perceive the Nation of Islam as a threat, they were placed under surveillance as though they were a threat to National Security. One of those who came to the government's attention was Minister Louis Farrakhan, who maintained the Nation of Islam after Imam Wallace Muhammad led his father's followers into the direction of Orthodoxy. One of those who followed Imam Wallace Muhammad was Muhammad Ali.

Somebody who is close to Minister Farrakhan is Akbar Muhammad—Lecturer, Historian, World Traveler, Businessman, and Foreign Diplomat (Nation of Islam). Mr. Muhammad was born in Hampton, Virginia, and raised in New York City. He is currently the International Representative for the Nation of Islam with offices and residences in Accra, Ghana, and the United States. According Minister Akbar Muhammad:

> The first thing I think is that Ali, [who] barely made it out of high school, went to the Olympics to defend the American reputation. A man named Samuel X introduced him to the teachings of the Honorable Elijah Muhammad in 1959 and it sent Muhammad Ali in a totally different direction.
>
> It so happens that today, January 31, 2004, they're honoring Abdul Rahman in Atlanta. He's seventy-two years old now. He raised Ali's consciousness. This was during the Vietnam conflict and the controversy centered around Malcolm X being at his training camp and his accepting the name Muhammad Ali. And what ratcheted the controversy up to the highest level was his protesting the war in Vietnam and all of the progressive people could see that he wasn't just becoming a Muslim to pray about going to heaven, but he joined something that would make an impact on the consciousness of black people in America.
>
> I think that's the legacy of Muhammad Ali, and then his ability in the ring made him one of the most known faces and respected sportsmen in America which is part of the whole history, but he wouldn't be known as a controversial fighter or the most well-known fighter if he were just a negro like Sonny Liston, or Joe Louis. It was his level of consciousness that made a difference throughout the world.
>
> His condition is so bad now that people know what he gave and so there's this feeling for him. He's only sixty-one. He doesn't like to be pitied even, but people feel sorry for him in the condition he's in right now.
>
> [Football great] Jim Brown gave the greatest lesson at the height of his career; he stepped away and Jim says that he looked at all of the brothers who stayed too long who were broken up—he says that he has

a problem walking right now. And so he felt that if he stepped out of at the time he did, at least his body would be in shape.

Muhammad stayed in because it was like a drug to him; he just couldn't get enough of the idea that he was good enough to keep coming back, but those fights with Larry Holmes and ones with Joe Frazier—they did tremendous damage to him and there's no doubt that the Parkinson's disease resulted from his taking a lot of blows to the head over that period of time.

They say that the Nation of Islam took advantage of him, especially this last film, the one with Will Smith. But this is the twist that Hollywood does—just like "Malcolm X"—Spike Lee's movie—Malcolm's involvement in Africa was dismissed completely. When they ran out of money they had to run to the whites for funding. And the whites had say so on the final cut, and they spent more time on the dance scene and left black Africa out completely, other than Ali's arriving on a camel in Egypt.

They never say that when Ali was in difficulty it was the Hon. Elijah Muhammad who took care of him and gave him money that sustained him when they took his crown and he could not fight. He had no money, and what he did for the Nation of Islam was small compared to other contributors, people with real money.

CHAPTER 32

October 2005, Chicago

On October 27, 2005, I flew to Chicago to interview poet and publisher Haki Madhubuti, as well as Bennett Johnson. Johnson is Vice President of Madhubuti's Third World Press and a veteran of the Chicago political wars. He was also Elijah Muhammad's liaison to the civil rights movement and arranged the famous meeting between Mr. Muhammad and Martin Luther King, Jr. He gave a more complicated view of the Elijah Muhammad, whom he called a genius and Muhammad Ali's mentor and father figure. His portrait in most of the hundred books about Muhammad Ali is not as flattering. This includes Jack Newfield, who dismissed Elijah Muhammad as a "cult racketeer," the same derision aimed at Noble Ali, a Harlem leader who is considered to be one of the forerunners of Elijah Muhammad. An army of Op-Ed writers criticize African Americans for not participating in "the ownership society"; 2012 presidential candidate, Mitt Romney, accused them of relying upon "free things," and another candidate, Rick Santorum, said that he didn't want to take white people's money and give it to blacks. In light of the policies of criminal banks, it's the other way around. Moreover, blacks have practiced self-reliance and operated businesses since colonial times. Elijah Muhammad and the Nation of Islam demonstrate that even when founding capitalistic enterprises, they are treated with the kind of disrespect accorded welfare mothers.

Bennett Johnson described a Bahamanian fishing deal that could have brought hundreds of millions of dollars to NOI coffers. Not only

did the Cuban's squash the deal, but they also threatened the NOI
with violence were the deal to go through. Here as in enterprises both
legitimate and suspect, Muhammad Ali's name was used to front a
corporation. According to Bennett Johnson:

> C. B. Atkins was a football player. He was married and divorced from
> Sarah Vaughn, and that's how he got up into this whole celebrity thing,
> and that's how he met Richard Durham [Ali's biographer]. Durham and
> he were as thick as thieves. Calvin Lockhart told him that Sir Lynden
> Pindling, prime minister of the Bahamas, had declared Bahamian
> waters off-limits for fishing except for Bahamian nationals. This
> included Florida and Cuban fisherman. He offered a deal to Ali that he
> could set up a fishing fleet. I was asked to put the deal together. John
> Ali, Don King, Durham, Atkins, and myself were to be officers of the
> corporation. Herbert Muhammad calls a meeting where he announces
> that John Ali was the secretary. I was the vice president and he was the
> president. Any questions?
>
> The name of the group was Tribune Fish Company. I can't remem-
> ber the exact corporate name. We bought four fishing vessels that were
> owned by Desco Marine, the largest manufacturer of fishing vessels in
> the world, based in Jacksonville, Florida. They had a monopoly on the
> making of boats. After going back and forth with the Bahamians, we
> decided to have the Bahamians fish for us: red snapper, crawfish, and
> spiny tail lobster. Based on that, we had four vessels retrofitted by the
> Whittaker Corporation. They told us that if we set this thing up right
> they would build a factory in the Bahamas to build seventy-five-foot
> fishing vessels and the Bahamas would have a monopoly on the fishing
> trade in the Gulf. We had started out in Miami. One of the Lockhart
> family members was a boat designer. After about a week, a Cuban guy
> came and said that he'd heard we were making boats for the Bahamas,
> and threatened to "blow up" the place where we were making the boats.
> We decided to move up to Jacksonville.
>
> We went to the National Oceanic Atmospheric Agency. A black guy
> was working there. We filled out the application and nothing happened.
> We asked Andy Young, then a Congressman, what happened, and he
> couldn't find out. Whittaker asked a senator to check it out and found
> that the CIA didn't want this to happen. We got a change of flag and
> went ahead and did it. We moved the boats from Jacksonville to Nassau,

the Bahamas. We really had a great thing going. The Lockhart family had the company and we had the vessels. We were going to lease the vessels to the Lockhart family and they would fish for us. And they would pay us in fish. We were going to sell the fish in the United States. It was lucrative for them because the money would stay in the Bahamas and the money was tax-free. It was an incredibly great deal. Muhammad Ali was the figurehead. I did all of the work.

We had Robert Vesco's apartment. [Robert Vesco was a wealthy fugitive and one of Richard Nixon's big contributors.] We had everything set up. We went to get a license and couldn't get one even though we had a hookup with the Lockhart family, who was related to the Pindling family. The CIA got in somehow. They said they were going to tear this thing down.

Ishmael Reed: What about the farming enterprises?
Bennett Johnson: We attempted to get black farmers to change their crop types, crops that would be more marketable in the inner city. We would have a Black trucking company that was marketed in the inner city. We were going to have a frozen food outfit. The model was Gandhi's book that he wrote in South Africa, talking about that Indians using weaving, something that they had, in order to create an industry.

Gandhi said, "For me, the spinning wheel is not only a symbol of simplicity and economic freedom, but it is also a symbol of peace." Muhammad was saying the same thing, from the beginning.

IR: [I asked Bennett about a NOI idea that has drawn the ridicule of the NOI's detractors: The Mother Plane, which at the right moment would rescue black people.]
BJ: There was also this thing about the Mother Plane. There was a man from Alabama who always wanted to fly. His name was Emmett Stovall. He came to Chicago and set up a shop near Midway Airport. He had Elijah Muhammad's Lockheed Constellation four-turbo-prop plane out at Midway field around '69 or '70. They also had a Lear jet that they used to get around in. He maintained the plane and taught Herbert's son, Sultan, how to fly it.

The Mother Plane was a vision, but it was also real, like Elijah saying that the original man was a black man.

The Orthodox Muslims say he wasn't consistent, but he was. Elijah was a brilliant man; he was a genius. He had to form a message that was compatible for black people: freedom, justice, and equality for the black man. Black Nationalism. He would like to have recruited me but I'm a-religious. I'd heard Herbert [Muhammad] and [biographer Richard] Durham talk about some Ministers being out of line, stealing money, etc. And so I was not motivated to join the NOI. But I was very close to the old man.

IR: What was his relationship to Malcolm X?
BJ: He was like Malcolm's father.

IR: What about his attitude toward electoral politics?
BJ: They say that the man wasn't political. Even though he advised against participating in electoral politics, he supported candidates on the side. We ran a guy named Sammy Rayner. This had to be 1965. They hit it off and Elijah went off on a monologue for hours. I said we had to go to a meeting. He asked one of his people to bring out a cigar box. So when we got into the car, I asked Sammy how much money was in the cigar box. Ten thousand dollars! Sam had asked for three thousand dollars. Sam ran against William Dawson and garnered twenty-five percent of the vote, which was unheard of at the time. Elijah also helped to finance an independent candidate named Charlie Chew, whom we ran in 1963.

IR: What was your role in the Ali camp?
BJ: I didn't like all of the bullshit, so I didn't get into the fight thing. That was C. B. and Durham and them. I just dealt with the old man. After the old man died, I began working with Herbert as his administrative assistant. Elijah Muhammad was among many who did not believe that Ali could beat Liston. Durham came to me and asked whether he thought that Ali could beat Liston. I checked Ali's record and told Durham that he could.

Malcolm did not bring Ali into the Nation. The glue that held Ali to the Nation was his being in Chicago and working with Durham and others at the time.

On some Sundays I would bring people from the outside. I brought Stokely [Carmichael] there and a lot of civil rights folks. The King meeting with Elijah was different. They just sat around together. They were very relaxed and friendly. King raised this thing about white folks and Elijah just said that whites were evil. And he didn't say it in a vitriolic manner. Although he would say he was against white men, he dealt with Jews and with whites. My feeling about the whole thing [was] that it was the development of a line.

IR: To energize the base?

BJ: Right. If you brought a white person before him he wouldn't be disdainful and say "get out of my face," he'd be polite. His attitude toward Ali was a pragmatic one. He was against boxing but he saw value in Ali's being champion and asked Herbert to take care of him. Herbert was the one who drove Ali back to boxing. Members of the Nation assisted Ali during the time when he was banned from boxing.

Johnson's assertion about Ali runs counter to the assertions of The Ali Scribes, authors of adoring, nearly worshipful books about the champion, who accuse the NOI of exploiting Ali financially. One could argue that it's Ali's current handlers who have converted Ali into a money-making product.

IR: [I asked why Ali turned his back on Malcolm after Elijah suspended Malcolm.]

BJ: Two reasons. New York was the black capital of the world and Malcolm X was their guy. The whole underpinning had to do with the tension between New York and Chicago, the second city. Chicago was where the temple was. Muhammad Ali had an affinity for Elijah because not only was Elijah charismatic but a good guy. He had a lot to do with Ali refusing to be inducted and Ali wasn't coerced into doing so, either. Elijah sent Malcolm to New York to recruit followers for the religion. He was pleased with the whole Mike Wallace thing ["The Hate that Hate Produced."] As for Elijah's adultery, Malcolm knew about that from the beginning. Everybody did.

IR: Was Malcolm attempting to assume leadership of the NOI?
BJ: I don't think that he was trying to assume leadership. The only rumor that I heard was that the Socialists were talking to him. The Trotskyites.

IR: What about Malcolm's claim that he didn't know that the Islamic religion included white people?
BJ: I don't know. The old man knew because he spent a lot of time at the Library of Congress. [His mentor, Fard Muhammad, instructed Elijah Muhammad to read one hundred books about Islam at the Library of Congress.] He was not only brilliant but he was learned. So I don't know about Malcolm.

We traveled to Iran and Iraq in '94. A guy named Khair Shahi, who had hooked up with Herbert, invited him for a state visit. You know, Herbert always had these deals going. So this guy approaches me because I would screen people for Herbert. Before we left we were approached by a guy from Kuwait because Saddam [Hussein] had taken a lot of prisoners from Kuwait. He wanted the prisoners back.

So they asked us while we were over [in] Iran to check with the embassy. We talked to the people at the embassy and they said you can go to Baghdad and talk to the folks over there. We'd sit down with the folks in Iran to work out something. Ali was all pumped up about it. We'd meet with government officials. And then we'd have another and yet another meeting. Then came a Mullah who seemed to be running the whole thing.

These religious guys—they had other prerogatives and they wouldn't work with us. But we crafted something. We drove down to Baghdad to meet with the folks down there. All of the top guys in Iran and Iraq were educated in the United States. We met with a guy named Alshaaf and he said he would give us a list of prisoners. So we came back to Tehran and Ali was all excited because we got what we wanted. We're in a hotel and a kid invites us to a ceremony. We go to a Sufi family restaurant and we sit around this room with about one hundred people and the kid, a medical student, takes charge and here come some guys dressed in white and they show us a sword and they take the sword and they run it all through this guy. There was no blood. They did this to [him] several times. They run a saber through another guy. Ali and I are looking at each other and then they bring out a saber and a drop of blood comes out and they say that it's because there's an infidel in the room and they say it's because this white boy is in the room. He is a cameraman from *Newsweek*. I got it all on tape.

IR: What about Ali's refusing to take a stand on the war and supporting Reagan?

BJ: The problem is who is driving Ali now—his wife [Lonnie] blames me for keeping Ali in Iran for three months. She wanted him to return to do some book signing. I haven't had any relationship with him since then.

IR: What about Newfield's claim that Lonnie and the Ali agent were using Ali as a cash cow?

BJ: He sent Lonnie to UCSC to get a master's degree in business. What pissed me off was that she moved Ali to a white management group instead of a black management group and that is a problem.

IR: Do you have any examples of the famous Ali wit?

BJ: The first night in Iraq, Ali wanted dessert in this restaurant. This is during the sanctions, and so the waitress said there was a shortage of sugar. Ali said, "When you fuck with Uncle Sam, you don't get no dessert."

CHAPTER 33

Why Ali remained with Elijah instead of following Malcolm

For some of Ali's biographers, Elijah Muhammad is a "fanatic." For others, he is inserted as a bit of comic relief in the story of the champion. They delight in telling the tale of the FBI finding Elijah Muhammad rolled up in a blanket, hiding under the bed, when they came to arrest him for sedition. Hilarious. But how many of them could have endured what followed? Five years away from their families, and incarceration in a prison system that has been hostile to black men since the days of slavery, places where many innocent black men have perished.

Rarely mentioned in these books are the economic successes of the NOI, a membership that not only included "thugs," the usual description of the NOI membership by The Ali Scribes, but journalists, intellectuals, artists, and scientists. Obviously, the NOI accomplished more than getting blacks to feel good about themselves.

One of those who found a home at the Nation of Islam after abandoning memberships in progressive movements was Agieb Bilal, former Assistant National Secretary from 1972 until Elijah's death, in 1975. He is a lean, wiry man with a voice that becomes high-pitched and glides when he is dwelling upon an irony, and though he was under legal pressure from a regime that plunged the country into a disastrous, costly war, he still had a sense of humor.

When I talked to him again, in July 2005, I asked him to assist me in setting up an interview with Herbert Muhammad, Ali's former agent. He put me in touch with Herbert Muhammad. When I talked to Herbert Muhammad, he declined to be interviewed, saying that other writers were paying him money. "Six figures," according to Agieb Bilal, who asked him to reconsider when both were participating in a Muslim Holy Day.

Bilal gave me his opinions about the split between Malcolm X and Elijah Muhammad, and why Muhammad Ali sided with Elijah Muhammad:

> There are so many lies about Malcolm. He has been idealized, which is not to take anything from him. He's a sacred cow. You can't say nothin' about him. But with the Honorable Elijah Muhammad, you can put all of his business out in the streets. And there's a reason for that. I see it as a very specific reason. For instance, we are supposed to believe that Malcolm, for the first time in his life, in 1964, went to Hajj, went to Mecca, and saw Muslims of all different races. This is the popular belief. Somehow, we are to believe that he had some type of "Road to Damascus" experience. This is an utmost lie. It's designed to do two things. It's designed first of all to deny any knowledge of Islam among indigenous African Americans. Number two is to give the Arabs credit for our Islam, and this is not the case. The reality is this: Wallace Muhammad, Elijah Muhammad's son, was the minister of Temple Number Twelve in Philadelphia in 1959. At that time the people in Philadelphia, members of the Nation of Islam, Orthodox Muslims from all different communities, would come from Boston to Philadelphia to attend his Tuesday night teachings of the Quran and Arabic, even though he was there as a minister under his father.
>
> The Nation of Islam schools were the first to teach Arabic and the Quran concurrently. We were the first independent Black schools, too. People don't want to deal with the realities of this history. This is what is paradoxical: though Mister Muhammad is calling himself the messenger of Allah, he was bringing in Arabs that were teaching the Quran and Arabic. They were coming in saying, "You're not the messenger of Allah," and he said, "I know, keep teaching my children," and he'd give them money.

Agieb Bilal's account squares with that of writer Sam Hamod. Bilal continued:

Mister Muhammad really didn't care so much about what the Muslim world was saying about his teachings, but he had to respond to a challenge to his Islamic credentials, within the black community, and that challenge had come through Imam Talib Dawud, who at the time was married to the singer Dakota Staton. He accused Elijah Muhammad of ruining the teachings of Islam. So Mister Muhammad didn't really have to worry about the Muslim world. He did have to respond to this particular challenge. This is why he sent Malcolm overseas to test the waters. Malcolm went overseas and was accepted as a Muslim like anyone else.

The beginning of Malcolm's disillusionment with the Nation of Islam really consisted of three different things, and then he chose in his own way methodically to make his move. He didn't feel the Nation of Islam was involving itself enough in the struggles of black people on the frontlines. He was looking at the civil rights movement. Even though we disagreed tactically with Dr. King, we felt that Dr. King, though misguided at the time, was concerned about black people.

The other issue was, of course, about an incident that occurred between members of the Nation and the Los Angeles police. In 1962, the police invaded the Mosque in Los Angeles and they killed the Mosque secretary, Ronald Stokes, and they shot some other brothers up. When that happened, Malcolm came back to Harlem and he had to address the issue to the people in Harlem who were used to the Nation of Islam "selling woof tickets."

IR: This was an accusation made by Jackie Robinson.

AB: Now, here was a Muslim killed by the white police and our people were sitting there saying, "What you Muslims gonna do? You call this man the devil and say we should go to war. We should do it."

Malcolm had to swallow the advice that Mister Muhammad had given him, which was that the NOI never told you we weren't going to lose people. This was a long-term struggle and Mister Muhammad said to Malcolm, "I'm not going to let you go out to Los Angeles and get the Nation of Islam involved in a fight with the Los Angeles Police Department," because during that time the Nation operated as a nation. If one thing happened to a Muslim, regardless of where he was in America, it affected all of us. So it would have been the Nation of Islam basically against the Los Angeles Police Department.

One thing that came out of the incident, though, which I think is very significant, was that all the segments of the black community came together and rallied behind the Muslims. Los Angeles was a watershed event. Malcolm had achieved so much power that the mayor of Los Angeles called Mister Muhammad and told Muhammad to bring Malcolm home. Mister Muhammad looked at the situation from the point of view of statesmanship and having the responsibility for all of our lives. He knew that the Nation was going to be in a lose/lose situation.

So Malcolm had to come here to Harlem and tell the people that the Honorable Elijah Muhammad and Allah would take care of this problem. For Malcolm it meant losing a lot of credibility. At the same time when he went to Chicago, he found out that Mister Muhammad had these wives. Malcolm had picked up the rumor from other people and it was Wallace who confirmed it. That is a very important point, because when Malcolm struck out, he struck out against Elijah Muhammad's family, he struck out against Wallace, and he put Wallace in this situation where Wallace was looked upon as being the person behind Malcolm. This was not true. Wallace had his own issues with his father, which he stood up in his father's face and told him. So it's very important to understand that.

The other thing that is important to understand in terms of this whole idea of Orthodox Islam, and this could be verified by Ozzie Muhammad of *The New York Times*—he is a Pulitzer Prize winner in *The New York Times* and one of Muhammad's grandsons—he can bear witness that his Uncle Wallace taught Malcolm how to make prayer, how to recite prayer, what positions to make during prayer, when Malcolm stopped in Philadelphia in 1959 before going overseas Everybody knew that by 1959, when they came to Chicago and wanted to see Elijah Muhammad, that Elijah Muhammad was not available. Everybody had to go see Wallace because he was the assistant to his father, not officially, but unofficially, when it came to the teachings. What the government was good at doing was putting him in jail so they could create a big conflict. That was in 1961 and 1963, to create conflict between Malcolm and Elijah Muhammad.

The break came about as a buildup—it was a buildup of different scenes, and then Malcolm came to the mansion one day to report to Mister Muhammad and found Mister Muhammad slapping a sister, which was totally out of character.

In 1959, the Honorable Elijah Muhammad lived with Clara Muhammad in a monogamous relationship. I heard rumors myself and there hasn't been proof so I'd drop that about the niece in Detroit. Malcolm didn't want to believe it, so he went to Wallace, Wallace confirmed it. And when Wallace told him, he thought Malcolm knew this.

Polygamy is what the Emirs and Princes do. But that's lust. That's not Islam. Islam restored to us respect for family life and the respect for our women. Our family life had been destroyed by slavery.

The Quran says you can have one, two, or four, but one is best, and that you have to treat them equally. Now suppose I was married for thirty-five years and I went to a high school and got me twenty young girls. My children aren't going to see those women as their stepmothers; they're going to see them as daddy's girlfriends. And they're going to have resentment against me because of their mother, even though the Quran says that I can take another wife.

The Quran in Sura 4:3 says:

> And if you be apprehensive that you will not be able to do justice to the orphans, you may marry two or three or four women whom you choose. But if you apprehend that you might not be able to do justice to them, then marry only one wife, or marry those who have fallen in your possession.

AB: Could Muhammad Ali afford those women?

We have to look at genetics. What's the genetic proclivity of an African-American male? It's polygamy. Our slave history has made us breeders and irresponsible providers for our families. All I'm saying is when you got these two issues and then you have to overlay the economic issues of modern day America it's hard enough to keep one woman satisfied.

IR: [I asked Agieb Bilal why Muhammad Ali didn't side with his mentor, Malcolm, after Malcolm's break with Elijah Muhammad.]
AB: What else was he going to do? Malcolm didn't have nothing. What did Malcolm have? He left this temple right here (Mosque #7, located in Harlem) with a handful of brothers and then he got writers and artists like you—don't misinterpret what I'm saying—he got artists and the nationalists. They could not build an organization. He was used to discipline, as the head of the organization. He would say, "Do something." He didn't have to say, "Tomorrow, do so-and-so." He would show up tomorrow at eight o'clock and the task would be done. Malcolm had all these brothers in the OAAU (Organization for African-American Unity) with him and then he went overseas. While there, they were supposed to get him an OAAU charter. They down in the Village with Norman Mailer and white girls and smoking cigarettes while Malcolm is overseas putting his blood out. And when he comes back, he asks what happened with the charter. Nothing.

Mrs. Shabbazz was just like Coretta King. "Lip's" assassination saved his marriage in the eyes of black America and history. Malcolm's assassination had also saved his marriage in the eyes of black America and for history. He had left that woman [Betty Shabazz].

IR: What about the charge that the NOI was responsible for Malcolm's murder?
AB: Five people killed Malcolm and only one was caught. The others were never brought to justice. The two brothers who were picked were goons and so no one had sympathy. And everybody knew that nothing would happen until Mr. Muhammad died.

IR: [I asked him about the rumor that Muhammad Ali had to have bodyguards because Malcolm's followers had threatened to kill him.]
AB: Those are mythologies. No one was concerned about that. We read about the Mafia discussing a hit on a Muslim brother and Ali's name came up. We told the Mafia across the bridge here that if anything happened to Muhammad Ali, they would be caught cold and we would kill Frank Sinatra and we knew where they lived and we

would kill them, their wives, their babies, and wipe out the Gambino family. [This challenges the black characters created by the writers for the show, *The Sopranos*. Black characters on that show were presented as cowardly and stupid. Emboldened by their making organized crime back down, some rogue members of the NOI took the Philadelphia heroin trade from Organized Crime.]

Ray Robinson, Jr. suggested that Frank Sinatra was one of the contacts between organized crime and professional boxers. Was Frank Sinatra's support of Floyd Patterson in the Patterson-Ali fight an effort on the part of the Mafia to return the Heavyweight Championship to Mafia control? Or was Sinatra just a fight fan who found the Muslim Yacubism foreign to his egalitarianism? While he disdained Patterson for his defeat at the hands of Ali, when Ali was defeated by Larry Holmes, Sinatra paused during his Las Vegas performance to pay tribute to Ali. There is also a photo of Sinatra and Ali sharing the pallbearer duties at Joe Louis' funeral, and Ali and Sinatra appeared on a record together aimed at improving the dental hygiene of children (*The Adventures of Ali and His Gang Vs. Mr. Tooth Decay, a Children's Story*).

Agieb Bilal put it this way:

This is what happened. There was a Muslim brother working in Newark, a regular brother, a Nation of Islam guy, and he was working on a construction site. He beat up a Family member with a shovel. Right, okay. They were going to kill him. All of the families had a sit-down and decided that they couldn't mess with these people.

According to *The New York Times'* report of the incident, the Capos decided that the Muslims might not know who they were. Bilal continued:

So as a result we sent a message to them in a way that they understood. We made an offer that they couldn't refuse. I will just leave it at that. Any boxer today should bow down to Muhammad Ali because up until that time the guineas told you who you were gonna box, when you were gonna box, and if you wanna win, what round you would be knocked out at, how much money you were gonna make. They ran all of the venues.

Not only did Malcolm return to the United States to find that he had an undisciplined organization, but he'd discovered that Uncle Sam still ran Africa and that an independent Africa will never be until they leave the dollar, franc and pound zone of capital. He also scared the Palestinians who wanted to be on the side of the United States. After Malcolm saw all these contradictions, he realized that his days within the Nation of Islam would be numbered.

Then the assassination of JFK occurred. We were confronted with the same situation that happened in Los Angeles in 1963. Mister Muhammad knew that when you went into black peoples' homes in 1963, you'd see Kennedy and Jesus on the wall. And they hadn't even gotten to the point of putting Martin Luther King on the wall, because he was still going to jail. So black people worshipped Kennedy. This is why Mr. Muhammad said, "Don't say nothin' about the man."

He knew that there'd be a backlash from our own people as well as one from the government. He was looking out for the Nation. That's why the following week, there was a photo of JFK on the front page of *Muhammad Speaks* with the headline, "We Mourn Our President," when before, we'd been calling the man a devil. Mister Muhammad was supposed to speak across the street from Macy's the week after the assassination. He canceled and Malcolm spoke instead.

That night, Malcolm read from his speech instead of speaking extemporaneously. He gave a brilliant exposition of American foreign policy. He didn't mention Kennedy. Everybody wanted to know his response to the death of JFK. Malcolm used metaphor. He talked about the U.S. killing Lumumba and making his wife a widow. He used a metaphor from the farm. He said, "It is only a question of time for these ills, these sins come back upon the perpetrator" and as a result of his being an old farm boy, he said that "the chickens coming home to roost never made [him] sad." At this time in the United States, the three top speakers were Madame Nhu, Barry Goldwater, and Malcolm. So on the front page of the paper, it said, "Malcolm: JFK Murder Made Me Glad."

Mister Muhammad went ballistic. Mister Muhammad knew that this would get innocent Muslims killed from the backlash and from our people. They loved John F. Kennedy. They loved that devil. They didn't like Martin Luther King or Malcolm. If they tell you that back then they loved Malcolm, they lyin'. He had the media, okay. Mister Muhammad knew what this would do to us. He'd already been through these trials and tribulations with the community, okay? He didn't want this. He wasn't interested in being in the public eye, which he was thrust into by Malcolm after Mike Wallace's "The Hate that Hate Produced."

Mister Muhammad calls Malcolm up and says, "No public speaking," and that means even in the Mosque. The newspapers said, "Malcolm silenced." Ali is training for the Sonny Liston fight and so he scoops up Malcolm and his family because Ali is a young brother, but he is not sensitive to what's going on. He's not really close because he's a boxer. He liked the teachings and the brothers and the food, but Malcolm is just one person while Mister Muhammad is an organization. This is what people didn't understand at the time. You should imagine what people like me thought about this time. At that time, you could count the number of educated black people on one hand. I was already black and politically out there. I knew that God was not white. I was attracted to the Nation because it was an all-black, alternative culture, multi-generational and with institutions. That was what I was looking for. I was in SNCC and the Black Panther Party. I left Berkeley after that shootout [between the Black Panthers and the Oakland Police Department, during which Bobby Hutton was killed]. When the Muslim brothers came to me and said that you couldn't do it with guns, I had no problem with that. I had seen the Black Panther Party blow up overnight. Originally, it was a community organization, and then when Huey went to jail, Eldridge Cleaver took over and they got linked up with the Peace and Freedom Party. It was a mess.

To get back to Ali and Malcolm, Ali sees Malcolm in trouble and so he went with Elijah.

Sonji, his first wife, was given to Ali. They'd [the NOI] find a brother who got something to offer like intelligence, a good business sense, and good leadership, and it's all about power. You've got to understand that. They'd be feeling you out.

I asked him about the report that Ali had beaten his first wife, Sonji, at a party for refusing to obey the dress style required of Muslim women, and when Sugar Ray Robinson tried to intervene, he threatened to beat Sugar Ray's "lightweight ass." He replied:

He didn't abuse his wife. He maybe slapped her once in a while.

Well, you've got to look it at two ways. You're dealing in Ali with a man who is uneducated. He's a performer. His earnings were fifty-eight million and he got forty-two out of it. People say it's exploitative but he was an average donor to the Nation. So I don't know what they are talking about. That's why he stayed with Mister Muhammad.

Now what happened was this. In 1942, all of the male Muslims, regardless of their age, were rounded up and put in prison. [The book *Racial Matters: The FBI's Secret File on Black America, 1960-1972*, by Kenneth O'Reilly, puts the number of Elijah Muhammad's followers who were indicted for sedition at eighty. The grounds were that they had a "pan-colored" identification with the Japanese.] All of the Muslims were rounded up, and those who weren't—once they found out other Muslims, and that Mister Muhammad was in jail, they said, "Send us to jail, too." And that's well-known history and that means that from 1946 to the end of Elijah Muhammad's three-year prison sentence, Sister Clara Muhammad, Elijah Muhammad's wife, ran the Nation of Islam. She was the one who stood in front of the door and told the FBI agents that "over my dead body will I let my child go to your devil school."

Ali knew it wasn't a question of his going to Vietnam. He wasn't going to go because he knew the teachings. That's what the teachings said in the Nation of Islam. So what happened was almost the way it happened the way they showed it in the movie [Ali]. Ali was a folk hero. He had his own way of processing his stuff. He has a brilliant mind. Don't no sleeping man have no brilliant mind. If God takes one thing away from you, He compensates you in another area. Ali didn't know anything about Vietnam. He knew there were poor people and some rice eaters and they were getting killed, bombs being dropped on them. He said he wouldn't go over there, and so he suffered the consequences.

Ali was short of geopolitical facts. He found the English so amiable that he concluded that they'd never been involved in a war. I asked why Elijah Muhammad had suspended Ali. [According to Askia Muhammad, Ali was praised on the cover of *Muhammad Speaks* during the suspension.] Agieb Bilal explained:

He got on a TV show and they asked him something and he said, "Well, I might have to go back and fight again because if they pay me enough money I will go back and fight."

And Mister Muhammad said boxing and sports were entertaining the white man. He had always been against that. He discouraged brothers from doing music and other things like that. They came to Mister Muhammad and told him that he was the heavyweight champion of the world. They said he could deal with millions of money. But the NOI didn't need his money. Mister Muhammad felt Ali was embarrassing himself and the Nation of Islam by depending on the devil for his livelihood. So he said, "The man's talking about boxing. I thought I had gotten him out of that. I made him a minister. I'm taking the name away from him since he says he's going to do that again."

He suspended Ali. Mister Muhammad gave you just what he wanted done and then at the time I think John Woodford was the editor of *Muhammad Speaks*. Mister Muhammad wrote the suspension but Woodford did the editing. Mister Muhammad said, "I gave him a dignified minister name. Then he goes back and entertains the devil."

Though followers of both Wallace and Farrakhan deny the claim by The Ali Scribes that Muhammad Ali contributed more to the Nation of Islam than what was expected of him, Ali's fame was certainly a draw that lured capital to the Nation's coffers. His fame was a factor in Libyan leader Muammar Gaddafi's willingness to make a grant to the Nation.

CHAPTER 34

Eventually, the government realized that the Nation of Islam was devoted to free enterprise, no matter how much their efforts were thwarted by white racism, which is why whites sabotaged their farms. This was not the only enterprise that the NOI launched that was sabotaged by racists. They owned a two-thousand-acre dairy farm, which housed one hundred Holstein cows, a hen house of twenty thousand layers, and ten thousand fryers. The farm produce was picked up by a fleet of eight trucks and delivered to NOI outlets. The livestock in Alabama were often slaughtered.

Though maligned by the press and the FBI, when the man behind these enterprises, Elijah Muhammad, died, he was no longer the hater of whites but had been accepted by the establishment. *Time* magazine noted:

> Throughout his controversial career, Elijah Muhammad was the nation's most potent preacher of black separatism. Yet when he died last week at 77, he was mourned as a statesman. Proclaimed Chicago's Mayor Richard J. Daley: "Under his leadership, the Nation of Islam has been a consistent contributor to the social well-being of our city for more than 40 years." ("Religion: The Messenger Passes," *Time*, March 10, 1975)

A *New York Times* editorial noted his movement's "success in rehabilitating and inspiring thousands of once defeated and despairing men and women." It states:

> Muhammad's recent respectability came not from the creed of his "Black Muslims," as they are known to outsiders, but from his "do for

self" philosophy, which generated black enterprise. As much a captain of industry as Messenger of Allah, Muhammad was the supreme ruler not only over 76 temples and some 50,000 to 100,000 disciples, but also over some 15,000 acres of farmland and a complex of small businesses that range from pin-neat restaurants to stores to a 500,000-circulation newspaper. Some estimate the worth of the Nation of Islam's business empire at $75 million. The businesses all have a long-range object: to prepare for the day when Allah gives the nation its own land, perhaps a sizable chunk of the present U.S., which Muhammad predicted was doomed to collapse before 1984.

◆

Educator and publisher Haki Madhubuti's office is a huge space that is part of a three-storey rectory that was sold to his group by the Catholic Church for two hundred fifty thousand dollars. Each story contains thirteen rooms. Writer Jack Cashill told a Kansas City audience that the black movement went astray when personalities given to self-aggrandizement took over, proving that talking about black issues is a profession that doesn't require a gift for nuance.

Haki Madhubuti has been recognized as one of the stars of the black movement, but one who avoids the spotlight. Since buying a rectory and school from the Catholic Church, Haki and his associates have bought half of the block surrounding the rectory for 1.5 million dollars. He told me, "We sold the church for 350,000 dollars. That's how we got the loan. We have four schools and two are being leased."

His Third World Press published one book per month in 2005 and had upped that to twenty-four books in 2006. The Covenant, a book edited by Tavis Smiley and published by Third World Press in 2006, became the first book published by a black press to reach the number one position on The New York Times bestseller list. Haki Madhubuti has been given credit for Minister Louis Farrakhan's comeback after Elijah Muhammad's death left the Nation in disarray. "I helped him get back up," he said. "I hooked up with him at FESTAC. I told him that I wasn't a leader, but that I could pull leaders together."

Haki Madhubuti was also responsible for the reconciliation between Minister Farrakhan and the late Betty Shabbaz, Malcolm X's widow. According to him:

There was a war over who was going to take Elijah's place. In 1976 and '77 we met in my home. During the first two meetings in my home he didn't have many brothers with him. Two months later, the brothers were coming back. Before we decided to help, we asked him his role in the murder of Malcolm X. He said that he created the climate. He and Jesse [Jackson] are protected, because they get away with stuff.

Haki said that his role with the schools was that of fundraising and "running interference with the board of education," and to provide as much "cultural substance to our schools as possible." He mentioned recent visits to the school from Spike Lee and Danny Glover. While public schools throughout the nation are failing black male students, his schools have had some success. His four schools expose one thousand students to a curriculum which he describes as essentially "African-centric." By that he means that at two-and-a-half years of age, his students are exposed to African and African-American culture in a way that is not "didactic." Furthermore:

We teach both the students and the teachers to learn how to learn and how to love to learn. We have computers. My son is a computer scientist who came through our schools and then went on to Northwestern where he received an undergraduate degree. He's now working on his master's. Three years ago, we graduated five engineers who went on to universities. Three of them were women. We are African-centric, which means that we examine the best of African civilization to see whether it can work for us. It has worked. Our test scores were so successful that the Chicago Board of Education put us in charge of an elementary and a high school.

We have a professional and competent staff. Two of our principals are PhDs. Our curriculum is part of our success but another part of it is that we love our children. We're not afraid of our children. The children are from the community that we live in. We've been doing this for a long time and so we've worked out most of the kinks. In our lives we had to struggle to find basic knowledge; you and I had to read books on our

own. Now, we supply the books. My wife has a PhD from the University
of Chicago. She's brilliant. I give her all the credit in the world.

I asked him, "When did you first hear about Islam?" He replied:

I didn't hear about Islam until Malcolm. I was in the army in 1959 to
1969. I changed my name in 1974. I accepted my new name because of
the fame that Don L. Lee got. You get caught up in people knowing
you, yet not knowing you. I wanted to be authentic. I was with Amiri
Baraka at the time and the Congress of African people. My name, Haki,
means "just," and Madhubuti means "justice, awakening, strong." So I
listened to Malcolm because Elijah Muhammad didn't have the same
kind of appeal or the same kind of draw.

In the army, I trained a boxer from the South. You see, the white
soldiers always wanted to confront us. We said, "Okay, you get your
man and we'll get ours. We'll let them fight it out." Our man was an
amateur boxer. They didn't know that. They got this big farmer and in
three rounds, our man took him apart. We took all of their money. He
was one hundred seventy-five pounds, muscles, tall, black. He played
with the farmer. First round, he let the farmer hit him and knock him
around and so the bets went up four or five to one in favor of the white
farmer. Third round he took him apart.

Because Ali studied boxing, he was very great. If a boxer knows
what he is doing, he won't get hurt. He went on too long. I think that
he should have quit after Frazier III. Ali had enough money at the time.

I also think that we throw the word hero around too loosely. I think
that Cassius Clay, a.k.a. Muhammad Ali, is a hero because of his stance
on the war. For that he is a hero. What he did in terms of the war would
not have been possible, were it not for his being a champion.

But Ali as a man is diminished because of what he said about Frazier.
Frazier was not a [Uncle] Tom; Frazier was a man, and what people do
not realize is that Frazier helped Ali. He helped Ali get back into boxing.
Gave him the fight. So I love Frazier, too.

We give Ali too much credit. And I didn't appreciate his response
to Malcolm X's assassination at all. When Malcolm made his move to
leave the Nation and made his comments about Elijah Muhammad, he
knew he was dead. He was a man of integrity. If he didn't say anything
he would still be alive. Following Wallace Deen Mohammed [Elijah's
son and successor] at that time was the only thing that Ali could do

because Ali was not a man of Islam and what he knew about Islam came from Elijah Muhammad and Malcolm X. But he was not a scholar.

As for George Foreman, he had become duped into the whole American thing and a lot of us who were political were glad to see him defeated. And the way that Ali beat him was tactically superb. Foreman became exhausted and his ego was just torn up.

[John Carlos, who gave the black power salute at the 1968 Summer Olympics in Mexico, disputes the notion of George Foreman as an Uncle Tom. Foreman told Carlos that it was his agent's idea to wave the American flag at the Olympics and that during Carlos' years as an outcast from sports, Foreman came to his aid.]

I don't doubt that Ali is sincere at this point because what else can he do? He is not a threat; that's why they like him. He's safe. He's an icon. I don't doubt his spiritual commitment, I just don't know what kind of health he is in or the influence that his wife, Lonnie, has.

After my interview with Haki Madhubuti, Bennett Johnson drove me through the Chicago South Side, which unlike other cities I visited gathering interviews, hasn't been gentrified. He pointed out some of the landmarks: a club where Muddy Waters held forth during his last year; the church where Jack Johnson's funeral was held; he gave a vivid description of the crime wars that happened when the white ethnics tried to muscle in on the black numbers racket.

The next day, I walked through the downtown area on the way to the Chicago Art Institute. There were few blacks on the street. The Grant Wood that I wanted to see at the Art Institute wasn't there. They had some wonderful Archibald Motleys and a Horace Pippin. I get a wintry chill in my bones when I examine his sharp browns and whites. But Beauford Delaney's sardonic self-portrait, in the image of a clown, I found to be stunning.

CHAPTER 35

February 4, 2006, Oakland, California

In an interview with author Clifton E. Marsh (*The Lost-Found Nation of Islam in America*), Imam Wallace Deen Mohammed provided a brief history of the Nation of Islam, which he described as more a movement of social reform than one devoted to Orthodox Islam. He said that it was feared in the 1930s because it was identified with socialism.

Though he did not mention his name, he designates Fard Muhammad, "a foreigner," as the original leader, who, because of his organizing blacks, was ordered out of Detroit and then Chicago. He said that Fard Muhammad was influenced by black nationalist leader Marcus Garvey, and Noble Ali Drew, who started the Moorish American movement. The idea of whites as devils, the Imam said, was begun by Drew, or more precisely, he didn't exactly say "devil" but described the white man as the pale horse whose rider is death. In the interview, Imam W. Deen Mohammed dismissed Fard Muhammad, a white man who called white people "devils," as a charlatan prone to engaging in "cheap tricks."

Were members of the Nation of Islam the first black American Muslims? Allan D. Austin, author of *African Muslims in Antebellum America*, identifies seventy-five African-born Muslims who were brought to North America between 1730 and 1860. One of those attracted to the Nation of Islam in the twentieth century was Martin Wyatt.

Martin Wyatt was a sports director and the weekday sports anchor on the San Francisco Bay Area's ABC7 News at 6 when I interviewed him. In addition, he hosted *Monday Night Live*, the Monday night football post-game analysis show. From 1980 to 1985, Wyatt was ABC7's weekend sports anchor and hosted the station's weekly sports wrap-up show, *Plays and Players*.

In November 1999, Wyatt was inducted into the California Black Sports Hall of Fame. Also in 1999, he was the recipient of the Humanitarian of the Year Award from Athletes United for Peace, in addition to receiving the Man of the Year Award from the noted organization, 100 Black Men of California. I interviewed Martin Wyatt at Café Dejéna, an Eritrean gathering hole located at Martin Luther King and 40th Street in Oakland.

Martin Wyatt: I met Ali in 1975 at "The Thrilla in Manila." It was before the fight. I flew over from Seattle. I was one of the black guys who covered the fight. Marcos put up all the money. I went over there two weeks before the fight.

Ishmael Reed: What was the atmosphere at the fight?

MW: Wow. For me it was my first big fight. I didn't know what to expect. But it was like the first news conference I attended where I saw Ali in person. There must have been three hundred guys from the media where the news conferences took place. They arrived from all over the world. They had a planeload of Japanese writers.

What happened was I had joined the NOI in 1972. I was treasurer of the mosque in Seattle. So I went to some of the guys from Chicago who were with Ali and I said, "Hey, I'm here. I'm covering for NBC."

They asked, "Are you a Muslim?"

"Yes."

So they ushered me in and introduced me to Ali and said, "Hey, this brother is a Muslim who lives in Seattle." He really made an effort to make sure I was included because otherwise a little guy from a local station in Seattle might not have an opportunity. So he made sure that whenever he did something, I was part of the group. That was the kind of guy he was.

Earl Abdullah was one of Ali's guys, and he said, "I heard about you," because the Nation was so small. He was from a black radio station in Chicago. He set up things for me.

IR: What about the claims made by Ali's biographers that the Nation and Herbert Muhammad ripped Ali off?

MW: I don't believe that. Here's the deal. The general white media were afraid at that particular point, because they didn't know how to deal with Ali. So when Herbert [Muhammad] comes in, all of a sudden he has game, if you want to put it that way. The Mafia had to respect him. They didn't know how it was going to play out.

Jeremiah Shabazz from Philadelphia and some of the other guys in New Jersey were crooks. Jeremiah Shabazz was a player because Philadelphia was a player's town. So when I say a crook—he was big, and he took a lot of money. Ali lived in Cherry Hill, which was close to Philly.

IR: Did Ali front some criminal operations in Cherry Hill, unwittingly?

MW: Not to my knowledge. But, Ali was open. After the Manila fight, some white guys up in Seattle wanted to promote fights and said, "Look, you did that thing with Ali in Manila. Do you know Ali?"

I said, "Yeah, I know him."

They said, "Look, we'll fly you to Chicago and maybe you can get Ali to come. Just to put on an exhibition in Tacoma."

These were gangsters. They said, "We'll pay you."

I said, "I'll take it to Ali and if he wants it, fine."

So I flew back. I told Ali about the proposal; he listened to the proposal but didn't buy it. He was that kind of person. If you were inside of the Nation, you would get access to present whatever proposal he would be open to.

IR: What about Ali's suspension by Elijah Muhammad?

MW: Well, Ali had a lot of problems. He had money problems; a lot of women problems. That was 24/7. He was training for the second [Leon] Spinks fight, and an old-timer from Detroit was there. There were people from all over the world who had come to this little camp. And I said to the old-timer, "Have you ever seen anything like this? Look, all of these women!"

The old timer said that Joe Louis was the biggest hound. What fighter hasn't had many women? Joe was notorious for being a womanizer. Joe Louis was the guy. Tallulah Bankhead, etc.

IR: What about Ali and Imelda Marcos?

MW: I didn't know about that one. But Ali had to fight them off. It is the aggression, the macho thing, the feeling of superiority. That's a part of it. In Manila—he was there with Veronica, his third wife. Khalilah flew in to Manila and stayed at the Hilton. I was staying at another hotel and my guy said, "Hey, Khalilah's in town," and all hell broke loose.

Then she flew out, after seeing Veronica's picture with Marcos and Ali in the palace. She got mad and got on the plane. Ali's there with four hundred guys. Dick Young, one of the most racist guys in the media, was there. Sportswriters were all around Ali after his workout. They're saying, "Ali, what are you going to do? Your wife came here and you got this fight in three days."

He said, "Wait a minute. This is not going to interrupt me. I am bigger than boxing." And that caught everyone. Have you heard that line before?

He said, "You can bring Frank Sinatra here and I can take him to downtown Manila and nobody would recognize him. I would have to introduce him." This was the next day, after Khalilah had flown out and they were really picking at him.

I tell you, they had stuff going on in other Philippine islands where the Muslims were fighting Marcos. I wasn't politically savvy, but I knew something was going on and he went to join the Muslims in Jum'ah prayer and I went with him. The fight was held during the

month of Ramadan, but he wasn't fasting because he had to fight.
There were about five of us who went with him. There were all these
poor people. I couldn't believe it. Here's the biggest name at that
time in the world, and he's out here participating in prayer with poor
people.

That's the kind of cat he was. He was inclusive. And there were
some white guys with him, like Dundee, and he'd roll with them.
Elijah Muhammad, and this is my understanding, said that "there
are some white people who aren't the devil, but they are few and are
ineffective with their work. You best consider them all that until they
are proven not." And Ali, he knew the deal.

IR: What about Ali's Italian girlfriend?
MW: I'm not surprised. He chased them all. He said that the
Malaysians were the prettiest ones in the world when we were in
Kuala Lumpur. I have been around four or five women who used to
go with Ali all over the world. I never met a white woman who said
that, but I wouldn't be surprised.

IR: You were with him at the Spinks fight?
MW: The second one in New Orleans? Yeah. I went to Deer Lake
where he was training with my kids; he was training for weight then.
It was for the look, to look good. He was living off of guile and skill;
he wasn't the fighter he was in Manila. That was his greatest fight,
more so than Liston and Foreman. When the fight was over, Ali
passed out in the ring.

IR: What about the Frazier camp's claim that Ali quit in the thirteenth round, but they didn't catch the signal from Ali's corner?
MW: I don't know about that. I'm ringside, but I didn't see that. We
go back to his dressing room and everyone wants to talk to him. I
was the only guy left after a while. He was sitting there and he said,
"It was like dying. Dying couldn't be more painful." That fight took
him to the max. That was his greatest fight.

IR: Should he have quit after that?

MW: I don't know. He fought Frazier again. "The Thrilla in Manila" was the second one.

IR: Do you think that he went over the line with his attacks on Frazier?

MW: Well, knowing Ali, no, but knowing Frazier, yeah. He was a big kid making a joke, but it did become racist. He called Joe an Uncle Tom. Joe was looking out for Ali at first. They made him the bad guy.

IR: What about Bundini Brown?

MW: Funny cat whom Ali carried for years. He stole stuff. Bundini was a bad guy. He was carrying drugs and Ali protected him all the time. I heard he had Ali doing drugs, but I don't know if that was true. He may have gotten Ali involved in some drugs. I never saw that. But I know that he was a bad man. Ali liked him. This is why Ali was the best touch that there was.

Present at the second Spinks fight were Herbert [Muhammad] and his group, and the Cuban guy [Luis Sarria] who was his masseur, and Youngblood, who was a scout for the Kansas City Chiefs. And Ferdie Pacheco.

IR: What about Veronica?

MW: Veronica was just there to look good and be good. Jayne Kennedy and Isaac Kennedy were there. Jane and Ali had something going on. Kennedy was a straight up pimp. She got really big and very religious. She was a beautiful woman. She got big and gained a lot of weight.

IR: What about his knocking out Khalilah in Zaïre?

MW: That might have happened because she was desperate at the time to stay with him. She loved Ali's dirty drawers. She got into drugs. Very bad.

IR: Whom did you join when Elijah Muhammad died?
MW: I left and went to join Wallace [Imam W. D. Mohammed], but I still support Farrakhan. I support them both.

IR: What about Ali's denouncing Farrakhan?
MW: I don't believe that.

IR: What about Yolanda (Lonnie) Ali?
MW: She is very protective of Ali, very protective of his image. She is good for him. She is Muslim.

IR: [I told him that they were serving liquor at the Ali Gala.]
MW: Is that right? I'm not surprised. I have been to Mecca and some of them take off the robes and start smoking cigarettes, and some of them have homosexual problems. They've got marijuana in Mecca. Nobody is perfect. But Ali is humble. When I brought him here for the sports image event in 1995, he wouldn't let me grab his bags when I picked him up at the airport.

IR: What about Foreman?
MW: Back in the day Foreman was a jerk, but he is pushing his projects.

IR: The Holmes fight in Las Vegas?
MW: That was very sad. He thought he was going to win. He didn't spar in Vegas. When I saw him there in the last two weeks, I never saw him spar. This is my recollection. It struck me. He was doing the bag work, the heavy bag and the conditioning. I think he was getting his weight down.

IR: Was Ali better than Joe Louis?
MW: Louis was really a light heavyweight, while Ali is a true heavyweight.

IR: What about criticism of Imam Wallace D. Mohammed that he is into assimilation and American patriotism? [Imam W. D. Mohammed died on September 9, 2008].
MW: Right, right, right.

IR: And that he's too timid?
MW: You know, I agree sometimes. Everybody has a role. Wallace's movement is splintered because he decentralized everything. Every Imam runs his own thing, like in Iran. So he's got fifty Imams in fifty mosques.

IR: What about Jesus Muhammad's claim that Wallace seized the Nation after the death of his father?
MW: Well, Wallace was put out of the Nation but came back before his father died.

IR: What about Sonny Liston taking a dive in the second fight because he was afraid of the NOI?
MW: I don't believe that. Crooks surrounded Liston. He should have been afraid of them.

IR: How did covering "The Thrilla in Manila" affect your career?
MW: When I went to "The Thrilla in Manila" and had access to Ali, my career took off. Then I did a documentary on Bill Russell's life. I won an Emmy and that got me the D.C. job. So Ali gave me an opportunity.

IR: Why did you join the Nation?
MW: It just rang right for me. I wanted black people to get together and do something. And that seemed like the right thing. I would finish my newscast at 6:00. And then I would go out and sell my *Muhammad Speaks* newspapers at 7:00, for an hour, with the brothers on the corner. I didn't reject him [Martin Luther King]. I just felt like we should do more, put our money together. We got shops, bakeries, farms, we got fish coming in. You know about Elijah's deal with Peru,

importing the whiting fish? Elijah would say, "You would be surprised at the big, white officials who love what I say." Who embraced his policies, but not openly.

Jeremiah Shabazz told me once at Deer Lake, "Elijah Muhammad sent me to Alabama to open up a Mosque. The KKK embraced me and they invited me to a Klan meeting and they said, 'See this Negro here? He's okay. He believes in what we believe in.'"

IR: What about lighting the Olympic torch? Because they enjoyed seeing him humbled?
MW: How can you bring Ali down? He's going to be the number one greatest fighter, even though the whole world stopped when Joe Louis fought Schmeling.

I'm from Memphis. I remember Joe Louis as a kid. Everything stopped in the barbershop when Joe Louis fought. But Ali is my generation. When I saw Joe Louis, he was a shadow, couldn't speak well, was viewed as an Uncle Tom. I didn't know Joe Louis as a young man. That's why I say I'm biased. I saw Ali's early fights. I thought that Doug Jones beat him and they didn't want Ali to lose. It was the money. I think his legacy is going to be that of a humanitarian. He cares about everyone, from where he started to where he is now. He cares about his religion, and if people are taking advantage of him, what can he do?

I took him up to Bob Johnson's house, the PG&E guy, to watch the Holyfield-Bowe fight. 1995, 1996, the second or third fight. When they were making their entrances to the arena, I asked, "Do you miss it?"

He said, "No, but I miss the excitement and the anticipation."

CHAPTER 36

Like Zeus Descending from Mount Olympus

"It was only a moment, sliding past the eyes like the sudden shifting of light and shadow, but long years from now it will remain a pure and moving glimpse of hard reality, and if Muhammad Ali could have turned his eyes upon himself, what first and final truth could he have seen? He had been led up the winding, red-carpeted staircase by Imelda Marcos, the first lady of the Philippines, as the guest of honor at the Malacaûang Palace. Soft music drifted in from the terrace as the beautiful Imelda guided the massive and still heavyweight champion of the world to the long buffet ornamented by huge candelabra. The two whispered..."

Mark Kram

Excitement and anticipation would certainly characterize the mood of the Philippines before the arrival of Muhammad Ali in Manila. Filipino-American journalist Emil Guillermo, a former NPR regular and editorial writer for *The Honolulu Advertiser*, said that it was like Zeus descending from Mount Olympus in a country where boxing was a popular sport. The first Ferdinand Marcos International Amateur Boxing Tournament was held on May 26, 1981. I interviewed Emil (author of *Emil Amok*), whom I met in 1989, during a phone call to Hawaii where he was still writing for *The Honolulu Advertiser*.

Emil Guillermo: In the 1960s, the Philippines was going through tumult. Marcos had declared Martial Law [September 1972], and his government was known for its iron hand and corruption. Back at that time, Marcos was known for jailing people who didn't agree with him. The rights of the Filipinos were compromised; it was still a dictatorship of the United States. He had thousands of people killed, and blamed it on a Communist rebellion. That's why the Martial Law was put in place. A lot of what was going on was believed to have been with the blessing of the United States because of the Cold War mentality.

This was a very critical moment for me as a Filipino-American because I was just coming into an understanding about what it meant to be a son of Filipino immigrants. I was going to Harvard and I was taking courses on Asian History, which coincided with this enormous activity in the Philippines—the 60s land reform and the Hucks revolution. The Hucks were groups that were about creating equity and land reform in the Philippines. And with this global spectacle, "The Rumble in the Jungle" was seen as having made a coup, because Marcos was competing with Cairo for the rights to the fight.

For the Filipinos to get the fight and have it focused right there was a source of pride to our humble nation. Not only was this feeling expressed by the elites but by the regular people who live in places like Pondo. Pondo is where my family is from. I'm sure that they knew about the fight and felt good; it wasn't the everyday cockfight that they were used to.

In 1975, the Ali-Frazier fight gave Marcos the opportunity to prop up his country with this major spectacle and lavish display, thereby belying the real problems of the Philippines, like poverty and the other issues that really counted. Back at that time, it was still a country of haves and have-nots, like this country.

Ishmael Reed: If Ali was seen as a god, how was Joe Frazier treated?
EG: Joe Frazier was not a bad fellow. "Smoking Joe Frazier." But it was Ali's charismatic style that Filipinos were suckers for, the whole glitz and all. This was the culture that produced Ferdinand Marcos, a dictator who liked to box. He was a fight fan. He made sure that everything was on time and organized and he insisted that people work hard to show off the Philippines. Everything—from the arrival of Ali's entourage, the press conferences, the receptions—had to be carried out

with professionalism. The handsomest, most telegenic referee was chosen for the fight. They chose this guy, Carlos Sonny Padilla, Jr., because,
everything was a show. Of course, there was scandal. Ali introduced
Veronica Porsche as his wife. Marcos met Veronica Porsche and he said,
"You have a pretty wife," and Ali looked at Imelda and said, "You didn't
do too badly yourself." They all had a laugh that day.

Ali was a god. This was [the] thing that the Filipinos were waiting for. These were the heavyweights. These were the gods showing
supremacy. This was Marcos' type of thing. He was a fight fan.

IR: How did the local Filipino community feel about the fight?
EG: If you were part of the earlier migration of immigrants, like my
father who came here in the 1920s, and you heard this negative stuff
about your country, you didn't feel good. Even if you were American,
like my father was, a naturalized citizen, you were a person of two
countries. My father was a very simple man. His name was Emiliano
Guillermo, but they called him Willie. He never complained. He was
happy in doing what he was doing. He never went to college. He had
experienced all of the kinds of discrimination you could experience. He
didn't have much opportunity. He worked in the kitchens, he worked
in the fields, and there weren't any opportunities because he didn't have
an education and he wasn't very skilled. So he was happy just coming to
America in the 20s. It was a big deal for him. And then to have a family.
He was content. He fought so hard to keep his head above water most of
the time. But it really bothered him when he heard this criticism about
his province and when he heard criticism about his country.

Of course when the fight came up, he was really beaming because
the fight was to be held in Manila. It was the point of pride for all of
these older Filipino immigrants. My father was from Ilocos Norte, the
same province as Marcos. Your province is everything to a Filipino.
This was just what Marcos needed. The fight was a much-needed
shot in the arm for the country. It showed that the Philippines were
alive and prospering.

The Bay Area has the biggest Filipino population in the United
States. You were either pro-Marcos or anti-Marcos. There were exiles

here that wanted to keep their money from Marcos. They came here in the 60s, the 70s. Benigno Aquino and his sisters were here. They lived in San Francisco. This was the second Philippines, right here. The anti-Marcos people loved the fight as fight fans but they were sickened by the fact that the fight was Story A. In Manila you had homeless kids on the streets and poverty. They wanted the world to see what was really going on, how Marcos was subjugating the people. And so there was a split between the communities of exiles. If you were an early immigrant, my father's group, then you were for the fight. But if you were against Marcos, you opposed it.

IR: Ali is known for his generosity. Were there any examples of it shown during his stay in the Philippines?
EG: Ali got his checkbook and wrote a check for twenty-five thousand dollars for one man. When he was asked why he gave him such a big sum of money, Ali said that it's all right because he was a religious man and a religious man wouldn't cheat him.

IR: How did the Filipinos react to Ali calling Frazier a monkey?
EG: I remember when my father came to the United States, he was called a monkey on the streets of San Francisco. He and men of his generation had worked in restaurants or out in Stockton picking avocados and tomatoes. There were anti-miscegenation laws that prevented them from marrying outside of the race. Yeah, the white man could date or marry anyone he wanted, but if Filipino men were seen with white women, they were beaten up. They went to dance halls and danced with white women. You know, when I took Cathy [Emil's wife is white and an author] to a Filipino organization in the eighties and introduced her to an older man, he said that if he had done that as a young man he would be killed.

IR: What has been the lasting effect of the "Thrilla in Manila"?
EG: Here were the Philippines, regarded for a century as a "little brown brother," the hosts for one of the great sports events of all time.

CHAPTER 37

I arrived in New York on February 22, 2006, my birthday. I checked in at the Affina, which is the name of the hotel under new ownership that I have known for years as the Southgate Towers. On the dresser of the suite we checked into lay a miniature King Kong doll with a card attached. It read, "Please leave me here for the next guest to enjoy. If you'd like to take home one of my relatives, they can be purchased for fifteen dollars at the front desk."

My first gig was at the Boy's Club, downtown on Avenue C. I decided to read a translation for which I received the heavy assistance from the masterful Yoruba teacher and poet, Adebisi Aromolaran. It appears in my book, *New and Collected Poems, 1964-2006*. Originally written in Yoruba, it's about some hunters who have to navigate their way through fantastic cities in order to get home. One of the cities is the City of Snakes, ruled over by Oloja Ibinu, the King of Snakes everywhere. The same can be said of Muhammad Ali. He navigated through his own City of Snakes. The entourage, the leeches, the scam artists, like Richard Hirschfield, Ali's former business manager, who tried to use Ali to swindle fifty million dollars from the government. At one point he even passed himself off as Ali, mimicking the voice of the champion in phone conversations. One could say that Ali had found his way home, to Louisville, to his spirit.

Afterwards, the boys, many of them from Africa and the Middle East, requested autographs. They all had copies of my books. This younger generation takes lots of hits, but I have found such a scene not to be rare. There must be some reason why the reading scores of black male kids are beginning to climb, a fact overlooked by the Tough Love industry, which holds the lack of personal responsibility among blacks to be the chief obstacle to their succeeding in American society rather than racism.

The staff invited me to an Italian restaurant because one of the staff members was having a birthday, I was told. I went along and explained that I could only stay for a minute. Turned out that they wished to celebrate my birthday, which falls on February 22, and at the end of the dinner the waiter brought out a cheesecake with two large chocolate candies on the side.

The whole restaurant sang "Happy Birthday" to me—incredible. I doggie-bagged a couple of lobsters for the hotel fridge.

Friday at the Schomburg Library, I appeared with the late great jazz violinist Billy Bang, with whom I had performed from time to time. That night I read from Daisaku Ikeda's book, a section called "The Path of Revolution," with Bang accompanying my reading. Afterwards, Quincy and Margaret Troupe, Earl Caldwell, Lena Sherrod, Maria Arias, Billy Bang's companion, Billy Bang, and I adjourned to Jumbo's Hamburger Palace, 535 Lenox Avenue at 137th Street. I ordered a lamb gyro sandwich and pulled out my tape recorder. Billy Bang was first.

Violinist Billy Bang was:

[B]orn William Vincent Walker in Mobile, Alabama, in 1947. His family moved to New York City's Harlem while he was still an infant. In junior high school he was nicknamed Billy Bang after a cartoon character, and over his initial protests, it stuck. Around the same time, his primary interest turned to music, and he took up the violin, switching to percussion in the early sixties when he became captivated by Afro-Cuban rhythms. While attending a Massachusetts prep school under full scholarship, he met and began playing with fellow student, folk-singer Arlo Guthrie.

Drafted into the army following graduation, Bang was sent to Vietnam, an experience that profoundly affected his life, often quite painfully. Returning home and radicalized, Billy became active in the anti-war movement, and by the late sixties had returned to music.

Heavily inspired by the exploratory fire of John Coltrane, Eric Dolphy, Ornette Coleman, and the liberating energy of the free-jazz movement, Bang returned to the violin as his principal means of expression. Attending New York's Queens College and studying privately with renowned violinist Leroy Jenkins, Bang became a key member of the dynamic New York avant-garde scene of the seventies." (Lunched Management and Booking, "Billy Bang," online.)

Ishmael Reed: When did you first hear of Muhammad Ali?
Billy Bang: When he was Cassius Clay. I don't know the year. I saw him fight against Joe Frazier and I remember "The Rumble in the Jungle." I respected his courage to defy the government and to still be successful. That directly reflected on me, because I wish I'd have had the same courage to tell the government where to go. But instead, I was drafted. My mother took Muhammad Ali's position. She sat me in front of the TV and had me watch people who refused to go to the army, including Ali. This was in 1966. It was either being drafted or spending five years in jail. I was more afraid to go to jail.

IR: Do you think that he really went to jail because of his religious convictions?
BB: I really don't know the answer to that. I honestly think that he didn't go because he felt it wasn't a place for a black man to go. But the fact that he was in the Nation of Islam helped to reinforce that.

IR: What was the effect of his stance on the morale of black soldiers, fighting in Vietnam?
BB: When we were in Vietnam, there was not information about what was going on with black people in America. I hadn't heard of the Black Panther Party until I came back. The only information I got about any kind of consciousness back home came from the Vietnamese. The women told me—like one time when I was on R&R in Hong Kong. I'd take ladies out for the evening. One Chinese lady asked me, "Why are you in the army?" She said, "I see white people on TV sic'ing dogs and using water hoses against your people. Why would you fight for these people?"

That's when a light bulb came on in my head. I said, "She's right. Damn. What am I really doing here?"

So I started questioning the war. This was in 1967, in Hong Kong. I was kind of closed off. It wasn't one of the issues that came up among black and Puerto Rican soldiers. We stuck together, trying to protect each other so that we could get home. We didn't have the consciousness. When I came home, I was most amazed at what was going on. We'd never heard of a Huey Newton; we hadn't heard of anything. I went to a party where a sister said her husband was in jail. I said, "Well, shit, if he didn't do something wrong, there's no need to lock him up." She said that he was a political prisoner. I had no idea what that meant. I really had to learn a lot.

I was in Vietnam from 1966 to 1967. So my consciousness was raised by the Asians.

IR: What was your assignment?

BB: Guys my size were tunnel rats, the smaller guys. I had my flashlight and I had a forty-five. I would come across a bunker to find whether a sniper was in there. When entered, I had to look for booby traps. The Viet Cong were very smart with booby traps.

IR: What about fragging [murdering members of officers belonging to one's military unit]?

BB: I didn't know that was a term. A few officers were shot.

IR: Your mother was a militant?

BB: My mother told me to follow Malcolm X. I wasn't into the Nation of Islam. I came from the Baptist church. The Nation didn't affect me. I know I'm different now.

IR: How will Ali be remembered?

BB: For blacks, he will be remembered for his stance against the government. If I talk to the cats in my band, the two white guys, they might know him as a boxer. But I remember his being a man, being a black man.

IR: Why do they [white people] love him now?

BB: Maybe the guilt from not treating us right.

IR: What about his lighting the Olympic torch?

BB: That was a little confusing for me. I loved him more when he was whipping Foreman's ass because I didn't like Foreman running around with the American flag. This was when the brothers were making the black power salute. I had turned completely opposite politically when I came out of the army. I made a 180-degree turn. I had consciousness. I was looking for the Black Panther Party.

Billy Bang died in 2011. He was haunted by the Vietnam experience until his death. He tried to express his hurt with the beautiful CD, "Vietnam: The Aftermath."

Earl Caldwell was next to speak. Caldwell is moderator of his own show, *The Caldwell Chronicles*, on WBAI in New York. A former reporter for *The New York Times*, he was a participant in a landmark Supreme Court decision. His court problems began when he refused to turn over his notes, accumulated during his reporting on the Black Panthers, to the FBI. Thirty-five years ago, while reporting from *The Times'* San Francisco bureau, Caldwell rebuffed FBI requests for his notes, twice refused to testify when subpoenaed before a federal grand jury, and took the fight for his rights as a working journalist to the Supreme Court. His stand against the government inspired the creation of the Reporters Committee for Freedom of the Press and led to expansion of state shield laws protecting journalists.

The Supreme Court ruled five to four against Caldwell in the 1972 case of The United States Vs. Caldwell. Caldwell refused to turn over information about The Black Panther Party to the F.B.I. and the Nixon Adminstration. The decision established, for the first time, a basis for some form of constitutional journalistic privilege. To Caldwell's dismay, William Rehnquist, newly confirmed as an associate justice, did not recuse himself, even though he had argued as a lawyer for the Justice Department that Caldwell must testify. Rehnquist cast the deciding vote against Caldwell. Caldwell called it the "stolen decision." (After his death, it was revealed that Rehnquist was addicted to the drug Placidyl. "Doctors interviewed by the FBI told agents that when Rehnquist stopped taking the drug, he suffered paranoid delusions, including imagining a CIA plot against him." The *Washington Post*, January 5, 2007.)

Caldwell said:

I grew up in Pennsylvania where the big thing was the heavyweight champion. We heard Joe Louis' fights on the radio. There were no black people where we lived. There were Italians. I remember him fighting an Italian [Primo Carnera, Tony Galento].

I met Ali in California. It was 1967 or 1968. I had come to California to cover the Black Panthers for *The New York Times*. Ali was visiting the late Carlton Goodlett's *Sun Reporter* newspaper. So I went over to see him. He was so intelligent and calm and making everyone laugh. Yet he was very strong on his draft position. It impacted the hell out of me, because little did I know at the time I would find myself in the same situation.

He was the one that told you what your conduct should [be] by the way he stood up. He stood up to the government with no fear. Like you don't have to be afraid, you can do it. He made it easy for me because I was riding on what he had already done. His case went to the Supreme Court, and he won. Mine went to the Supreme Court, but they stole the decision.

When *The Times* mentioned all of the important cases in which *Times* people confronted the government—this was when Judith Miller went to jail—they didn't mention mine. It was like it never happened. *The United States vs. Caldwell*. This was when the FBI tried to get me to inform on the Black Panthers. They hired a big San Francisco law firm, Pillsbury, Madison, and Sutro. John Bates, a partner, told me that there was a problem "out here with the Panthers" and he asked me to bring my notes about the Panthers and he said maybe some of it should be turned over to the FBI. The Nation came to my assistance because of the Ali connection.

And another thing about this period involving Ali, black people were coming together around the issue of race, black doctors, black lawyers, and black reporters.

Ishmael Reed: The NOI takes credit for the media hiring black reporters?

Earl Caldwell: They should. I was a reporter in Rochester. At the last minute, they requested that I go to the church where Malcolm X was speaking. He laid the media out. Oh, did he lay them out! He talked about how the media turned stuff around and made black victims the bad guys.

Later, they were calling me up to go to Harlem to cover the riots, because the crowd was shouting, "White reporters out!" So they had to get a black reporter. This created a demand for the blacks, because the white media were viewed as the enemy.

The Black Panthers had a great sense of how to manipulate the media. The Muslims had that too, but they also had their own newspaper, *Muhammad Speaks*. At *The Sun Reporter*, Ali was explaining why he wasn't going to fight. He said he was going to stand by his decision. He was just about my age—he inspired me. He had a lot of support from the young people.

IR: What about the Muslims threatening or assaulting black reporters who wrote negative news stories or books about them?

EC: Claude Lewis was a reporter for *The New York Herald Tribune*. He had a big career in Philadelphia, where he is retired. He teaches at Villanova. The Muslims told him that Ali was a Muslim, but not to say anything. He told a white reporter who printed it. Claude Lewis was terrified because he was afraid of reprisals from the Muslims. Ali intervened and got the threats removed. After that, for me, Ali could do no wrong. A writer who doesn't bite her tongue and has challenged institutions that are far more powerful than the NOI is Jill Nelson.

◆

I got an email from Jill Nelson, author of *Involuntary Slavery* and one of the writers who've taken black women's fiction into a new, hip direction, rescuing it from its high harlequin rut. She continues the direction that was begun by writers like Carlene Hatcher Polite,

Toni Cade Bambara, Ntozake Shange, Jayne Cortez, and Thulani Davis. She was coming to town to see her ninety-year-old father. In two thousand fourteen he was ninety-nine!

At about the same time, Sam Hamod sent me an email saying that he was coming up to visit his friend Ahmad Jamal, the famed pianist, who was performing at Yoshi's jazz club in San Francisco. I planned to hit Nelson and Jamal up for interviews.

I picked up Jill at her dad's house on Berkeley Way. He was living in a comfortable, sparsely-furnished apartment. He was a tall and lean figure, with an aristocratic bearing. His speakers, located on the floor, were sending out some sounds that, to my ear, sounded like the Basie band. On one wall was a poster which featured some African Americans enjoying themselves on Martha's Vineyard. Jill's grand-father on her mother's side was the accountant for Madame Walker, who became a millionaire by selling hair products. Her daughter A'lelia was the Harlem Renaissance's organizer, and Langston Hughes wrote that when she died, the Renaissance died.

Except for an operation that required the removal of his larynx, he was in good health at the time. I told Jill that I'd bring my mother out to meet him. She was looking for a boyfriend. (Incidentally, she died in 2012. Jill's daughter was astonished that an eighty-eight-year-old woman was looking for a boyfriend. I reminded her of a study which indicates that the elderly have more sexual fun than young people. After all, by that time you should have a good idea of where to put things.)

Jill and I adjourned to Café Dejéna, where we both ordered lox and cream cheese omelets.

Jill Nelson: I first heard of Muhammad Ali when he fought Sonny Liston for the first time. I remember my parents saying that he was beautiful, and exciting. My mother laughed at how he used to throw rhymes.

Ishmael Reed: [I asked whether Ali was considered beautiful because, in Joe Frazier's words, he was a "half breed."]

JN: They admired his dignity, his integrity, and his presence. He represented the authority to be funny without being a coon; funny in a dignified manner, not just shuckin' and jiving. It's easy to say with hindsight that by contrast to Sonny Liston that he was the white hope or the light-skinned hope, the middle-class hope, or the bourgeoisie hope, but the fact of the matter is that Liston didn't acquit himself well even if Ali and Liston were pitted against one another.

Now, despite our progressive talk, I'd still be for Ali because he was taller, funnier and better looking, a better speaker, brighter, younger, and with a better physique. He had a presence that radiated internally outward. At the minute he stood against the government, then you were just in love.

IR: Even though he was merely following Elijah Muhammad's orders?
JN: Who knew that then?

IR: [I asked about Jack Newfield's quoting Muhammad Ali, that he didn't start believing in Allah until the 1980s, because that's when miniskirts went out of style.]
JN: Sounds like him, doesn't it? The age was charged, I mean many people can say that we loved Martin Luther King, Jr. now, but at the time when he was assassinated people my age were through with him; his techniques weren't working. I wasn't going to turn the other cheek.

IR: [I asked about the Muslims selling woof tickets (all talk and no action) when Ronald Stokes was killed by the LAPD and the feeble answer from the spokesman for an organization that was supposed to be so tough and prepared to retaliate against "devils" was that Allah would attend to it. And when Kennedy was killed, the hatred for the leading "white devil" became, "We Mourn Our Leader," a reversal of attitudes toward whites that astonished some fans of the NOI. Meanwhile King, an object of ridicule from NOI machos, was going to jail, having his house bombed, and being blackmailed by the FBI.]

JN: It's easier to deal with that forty years later than then, whether one follows non-violence or resorts to mau-mauing [intimidation]. Whose legacy is greater? It's Martin Luther King, Jr., but young people were attracted to the Black Panther Party.

IR: But what about the women? The way Elijah Muhammad treated women? And his followers say that Malcolm was a hypocrite because while accusing Elijah Muhammad of adultery, he was committing adultery himself. One follower of Wallace Mohammed says that by the time Malcolm was assassinated, he had left Betty Shabazz.
JN: The way women were treated is disgusting and boring.

IR: Sonji said that when he [Ali] divorced her, he'd been ordered to do so by Elijah Muhammad.
JN: We know now that Elijah Muhammad was a hypocrite and in collaboration with the United States government.

IR: How do you know that he was in collusion with the United States government?
JN: The government told him how far he can [could] go, and warned him that he could go no further. Plus the NOI received money from the United States. I believe that the reason Jesse Jackson is still alive is that the government told him how far he could go and he said, "Okay."

IR: In most biographies of Ali written by white men, they go out of their way to impute misogyny to black men, but ignore that committed by members of their group. I've noticed that in academia, white male academics use the misogyny in the works of some black women to indict black men for misogyny.
JN: In order to be the preferred privileged Other, there has to be an evil.

IR: Why all the affection for Ali now?
JN: I find it heartbreaking. I still have a lot of affection for him but I feel that he has Parkinson's because they took his title and he stayed

in the ring too long. But no matter what he does, they're never going to forget all of that rhetoric. He ended up a broken man. Like an old black retainer. Like, I don't like to see him like this. It's insulting and heartbreaking. When he carried that torch at the Olympics, they saw a black man whose anger has dissipated at no cost to them. They're comfortable with him now because they kicked his ass and broke him. And now we can all be friends. It's all about maintaining white supremacy and white privilege. You're either brought down or killed, like King and Malcolm.

IR: What about the fascination that white, northeastern writers have for Ali?

JN: It's like embracing the animal in black men that is overpowering and over-endowed without being racist.

IR: What about Joyce Carol Oates? In her fiction, black men are rapists or they come on sexually to women, but she praises black boxers.

JN: It's because they are restrained. Their animalistic nature is restrained. It's like Mumia [Abu-Jamal, an activist and journalist sentenced to death]. Mumia has become a fetish for them. They call my house demanding that I support Mumia. The same thing, like the ring is a prison, the ropes of the ring is like the bars of a prison. If Mumia were twenty-five, anonymous, and was walking up their block, they'd cross to the other side or call the police.

IR: Ali's legacy?

JN: He'll be remembered as a man with trembling hands who lit the torch at the Olympics.

CHAPTER 38

I attended the Poets and Writers' award dinner. I'd been invited by Elliot Figman to be the guest writer at a table. The people for whom I was the host were from John Wiley & Sons, a global publishing company. My wife, Carla, has talked to them in the hallway where people were having drinks before dinner. Her book, *Rediscovering America*, was at Wiley before her editor, Chris Jackson, left for Random House and took it with him. We ran into poet Michael Weaver, biographer Hettie Jones, and novelist Russell Banks.

Banks and I have had a sometimes-contentious relationship, though we have been friends since the 1970s, when we met as board members belonging to the Coordinating Council of Literary Magazines, which at the time was headed by the late William Phillips of *The Partisan Review*. I challenged his quoting Sam Roberts of *The New York Times,* during a panel held at a literary conference at Aix-en-Provence, and criticized some of the television projects for which panel member Richard Price, George Pelecanos, and David Simon are writers including *The Wire* and *The Corner*. As a result, Russell as well as some of the other New York panel members, Price's friends, all got pushed out.

However, Banks, for attempting to promote an image of John Brown different from the one in popular culture (that of a stark raving mad lunatic who was attempting to upset this wonderful Southern Camelot), might be considered a traitor to the white race in some circles. Unlike Pelecanos, Simon and Price, Banks with his novel,

Book of Jamaica, shows how a white writer can give depth to black characters instead of relying on best selling clichés and stereotypes like those offered by Roth, Bellow, Wolfe, Price and Pelecanos. He was standing next to Daniel Halpern of Ecco Press, which published *The Muhammad Ali Reader*, edited by Gerald Early. Dan was responsible for my having a residency in the writing department at Columbia in 1983. In 2014, I felt support for my position when Professor Karl Alexander of John Hopkins examined the district that was depicted by David Simon in *The Corner*. Alexander found that it wasn't a drug mart as it's shown on Simon's *The Corner*, but one inhabited by working class blacks and whites.

Russell Banks is the author of a number of books, including *Book of Jamaica*, which received an American Book Award. I had the chance to interview him and Dan Halpern.

Ishmael Reed: [I asked Russell his assessment of Ali.]
Russell Banks: One of the four or five great men of the twentieth century, because he made it possible for us to listen to a black man. We, as white people, could listen to him even though he wasn't speaking our language. So he educated white people. You knew he was saying something you had to pay attention to, you had to listen to, and cut through the resistance. He was the greatest athlete and entertainer of the century.

IR: What about the NOI thing?
RB: That never bothered me. My mother is a Christian Fundamentalist, born again, and I've got it all over my family. He never tried to kill me. I'm no blue-eyed devil, but I know the history and so I could accommodate his belonging to that group.

IR: Why do people like him so much now?
RB: He's harmless now. Now it's easy to like him. You don't have to work hard. He's a nice, old man who is sick. He's peaceful. It's easy to honor him. He doesn't confront our time and our moment in any way that is threatening, so he's emblematic; he's iconic.

Dan Halpern: [He was standing nearby, and disagreed with Banks.] I don't think it's because he's harmless now. The guy represents something because he is the greatest boxer that ever lived. Then, he continued to do good throughout the world.

IR: Others say that Joe Louis was better.

DH: They're never gonna fight.

RB: You don't become an iconic figure in the culture because of boxing. Besides, Joe Louis ended up terrible. Ali is the greatest man in the world. I think what he represents to kids all over the world— for little kids in Africa, he's a god. He's great for what he did after boxing; went around and understood people and related to people and got them to understand who he was and what the world was all about. He became a bigger man when he got out of the ring. It's the young Cassius Clay who was so fast and so intelligent; verbally fast, intellectually fast. You realize that the kid was saying some stuff that normally whites don't listen to, but I felt that I had better fucking pay attention, or I'm going to miss something important. Ali made white people listen. He did this in a charming, seductive way.

DH: He was a poet.

RB: He was a poet and a seducer. He had a smile on his face when he was telling you shit.

IR: What about his lighting the Olympic torch?

RB: That depressed me because it was the late-twentieth-century version of being a greeter, like Joe Louis in Las Vegas, because he was being used by corporate America. It bugged me and saddened me. And when he's used that way, I get depressed. That's why I prefer to remember the early Ali, the kid who came out of Louisville, the kid who was on fire.

DH: It [the lighting of the Olympic torch] wasn't horrible, because that's not who he is and what he has accomplished. I had a party right after the book [*The Muhammad Ali Reader*] came out. He came in and sat down next to my wife; they had the most amazing conversation.

IR: [I asked Halpern what about.]
DH: She never told me.

I strolled over to talk to detective-fiction writer Walter Mosley. He said:

> I was scared of him in the very beginning because he was so loud and rash and outlandish and he scared me. I was only ten years old. Anybody who was brash and loud scared me. By the second fight with Liston, I loved him. It's an interesting transition. It was the confidence he exuded.
> Then I got to understand him. I loved boxing even when a kid. I liked the middleweight guys. Almost all of them. [Gene] Fullmer I never liked, only because of the way he fought Sugar Ray. I watched those fights the other night. I loved the way Robinson knocked out Fullmer, in their second fight. That left hook.

Ishmael Reed: What about when Ali joined the NOI?
Walter Mosley: When I was a kid I went to a Victory Baptist Day School, the only school in Los Angeles that was teaching black kids what they were. I wasn't a Christian, but I identified with them. The Nation of Islam was foreign to me, but Ali was wonderful and he was from that and Malcolm also, so they bridged the gap in my understanding of Islam.

It was announced that dinner was served. Author and journalist Anna Quindlen was the main speaker. In her speech, she compared the writer to a spider. I'm not an expert on spiders, but from what I have observed of spiders, they'd never make it in the world of non-fiction. They seem too laid back. Writing this book, I found myself on the road. Maybe she had fiction in mind. You can spin a fiction without having ever to leave the house.

◆

We returned to New York on March 30, 2006. I had been requested to appear on a panel held as part of the annual Black Writers Conference at Medgar Evers College. As we exited the terminal, I walked past the limo driver who had taken me to the Affina Hotel on the previous trip. Carla guessed that he looked Albanian, dark hair and dark features. He remembered my name as "Isaiah."

We checked in at the Beekman Hotel, an art deco hotel on 49th and First Avenue, a block or so from the East River. This seemed like a pleasant and quiet neighborhood. I priced the available apartments at a real estate office across from the Beekman and they were affordable, but I'd have to leave California, which always appeared on the brink of destruction. California was like a drug that elated your spirits but had bad side effects. The sun rules us here. It's impossible to remain indoors with such a sun inviting you to the outside. In New York, the arts flourish, especially in the winter, when it is cold outside and dark during the day. You remain in your home and get a lot of work done.

I couldn't get as much work done in New York as I have in Oakland because there were too many distractions. The main distraction in California is nature. The days are sometimes so beautiful in California that I feel guilty living here, having grown up in a town where the sky seemed always to be overcast and where the winters were very serious. While living here we've survived a major earthquake and a number of smaller ones and a catastrophic fire that was rapidly approaching our home before it was extinguished.

On Friday, I went up to the Zwirner & Wirth Gallery at 32 East 69th Street, to see David Hammon's Selected Works. There was an American flag, but the colors were green, black, and red, the colors of the black nationalist Marcus Garvey's Universal Negro Improvement Association. In 2013, with David's permission, I adopted the logo for my magazine, *Konch*.

This flag reminded me of the late Professor Charles Davis' remark, printed in his book *Black is the Color of the Cosmos*, that the black nationalist movements of the 1960s were in the American tradition.

Hammons had constructed a basketball hoop made of wood, wire and rubber balls. The backboard was decorated with beer-bottle caps, which I took to represent the numerous breweries that advertise their poisons during basketball games. The materials used in another construction consisted of a steel pole, upon which was a green metal hoop. A car windshield served as the backboard. Three vintage microphones were entitled "Which Mike Would You Like to Be Like," a play on Michael Jordan's name and based on a Nike commercial that promised a consumer could be like Michael Jordan.

Hammons has also done some work based on the career of his hero, Muhammad Ali. I would have to pursue this, because during my interview with him he didn't mention this.

Hammons' friend, Steve Cannon, is mentioned in the catalogue as a great poet. I stopped by Tribes, his gallery, on the way to the annual Black Writers' Conference at Medgar Evers College. We decided that we'd split the cab fare. He was preparing to travel to Paris for a reading of one of his plays at Cartier's.

An hour or so later, in the room set aside for the conference's panelists, I interviewed novelist Elizabeth Nunez and *Wall Street Journal* writer Chris Farley. After the panel, I finished the interview with Walter Mosley that was interrupted when we were called to dinner at the Poets and Writers' award ceremony that had been held the month before at the Ritz Carlton.

Dr. Nunez is a native of Trinidad and former chairperson of Medgar Evers' English Department. Her best-known novel is *Under the Limbo Silence*, winner of an American Book Award. In 2001, she was appointed Distinguished Professor of the City of University of the New York.

Elizabeth Nunez: In Trinidad, I heard about Muhammad Ali as a mythical character. Trinidad was an English colony and so we heard about England and the colonies, but nothing about America.

The American we heard about was Paul Robeson. Then we heard about this courageous and beautiful guy who had the audacity to say that he was the best. That he was pushy and that he was beating up people.

I didn't really know much about boxing. I hung out with a lot of girls, so I didn't know anything about boxing as a sport, and I couldn't really care less about boxing. But we heard about this person who said that he was better than anyone else, and the next thing I heard was that he was unbeatable. When I came here I learned more about him. You hear all about these stories, about the oppression of black people and black people getting beaten up. Here was a guy who made a profession of doing the beating. We heard a lot of stories about him. We didn't have a great view about America, both black or white.

Then I came to America and was struck by how handsome he was. He was a beautiful man. He made you feel good about yourself.

Ishmael Reed: What about his calling Joe Frazier a gorilla and calling other black boxers names?

EN: That didn't change my mind. I saw him as a winner and as a beautiful, black guy. He was the opposite of some of the stories I was hearing and he was a source of pride. The stories that we heard growing up in Trinidad were not the most complimentary stories about America. Black or white. The stories I heard about black people in America were similar to those I heard about the relationship between the Jews and the Nazis, which on the one hand your heart went out to the situation, but you were longing for a hero.

IR: What about the NOI?

EN: I don't have a problem with the Nation of Islam. Farrakhan has said some things that are offensive, but they pale in comparison to what some whites have said about black people. I also thought that Ali's position on the war was admirable. That upped the ante for me in terms of his being a hero.

IR: Why do you think they love him so much now?

EN: I think that is a very interesting question because there are so many other black people who have achieved in areas besides sports. When I told you I admired him, it was because he was the first popular figure surfacing, but I am not happy to see him relegated only to the area of sports.

IR: But why does the white public that once despised him admire him now?

EN: Because he is safe. He has almost become a minstrel figure in a way; the smiling, the waving of the hand. It's pathetic now and there's something obscene about putting him at the top of the pedestal. In his time he was a hero because he was bucking the system. It's hard for white people to acknowledge that blacks have reached the top in a variety of fields, not just sports. It doesn't matter what he supported. I don't agree with Condoleezza Rice, but I think she is brilliant.

IR: The Fruit of Islam?

EN: I like to see the good guys with the bow ties standing on the corner. It takes a lot of guts to stand on the corner and sell bean pies. **Walter Mosley**: Muhammad Ali's legacy is one of greatness. He has made a space for himself and all of these other people in the world who did not exist before him.

IR: What about his shift to the right, his support for Reagan, and his friendship with Orrin Hatch?

WM: I don't know enough about it to say anything about it. I never talked to him about [it]. When you talk to me, my biggest enemy is the Democrats.

CHAPTER 39

Bigger Than Boxing

In April 2006, a reporter on San Francisco KRON TV 4 News cited an international survey in which the respondents were asked who was the most famous person. Jesus of Nazareth was first, Muhammad Ali, second, and Adolph Hitler, third.

In New York, I attended a fundraiser for The Author's Guild of America held at the Metropolitan Club. Feminist Erica Jong was present. The week before, she'd said on Bill Maher's TV show that she supported immigration because she would not have been able to raise her child had there not been immigrant help. I'm wondering whether she ever took her immigrant nanny to a women's lib meeting. I noticed former Congresswoman Patricia Schroeder. When Gay Talese entered, there was a flurry of activity. Unlike some of the other swells, Literary Agent Timothy Seldes is down to earth. I was on a trip with him to Africa that included writer Susan Shreve. I joined him and his sister who were seated at a table. A woman came up and made a big fuss about Timothy's sister. She was dressed like a diva and was wearing a turban. Carla recognized her as Tony Award-winning actress Marian Seldes. I had some more hors d'oeuvres and then went back to work. I spotted Barry Beckham, the author of the novel *My Main Mother*, and asked him about Muhammad Ali.

Barry Beckham: I was in college at Brown from 1962 to '66 and one of my students bought me tickets to see the Joe Frazier fight on closed circuit TV. I always thought Muhammad Ali had the greatest style of anyone I had known since Sugar Ray Robinson, who a lot of people don't recognize anymore as having such a unique style. [This neglect would end in April 2006, when the United States Post Office honored Sugar Ray Robinson with a stamp with his image on it.]

I also thought the person who didn't get a lot of publicity was Kid Gavilan. Remember the bolo punch? You take Sugar Ray Robinson and Kid Gavilan, you have two of the most incredible stylists in boxing.

Ali's changing his name was a major political statement, which was unusual. I was a teenager, and black consciousness and standing up for who you are was his major impact on me. Before Ali, we were all quiet and accepting. And another example was Kareem Abdul-Jabbar's response to the '68 [Summer] Olympics. He was the only one who did not go, as a protest of the '68 Olympics.

Ishmael Reed: What about George Foreman's remark that by politicizing the Olympics, when John Carlos and Tommie Smith raised their fists—a gesture that became known as the black power salute—they set the stage for the massacre of the Israeli athletes at the Munich Olympics [September, 1972].
BB: Politics are in everything and that was an unfortunate remark from Foreman.

IR: What about Ali's affiliation with the Nation of Islam?
BB: He thought that there was a moment where one makes a stand. Malcolm X, a member of the Nation, and Marcus Garvey [a black nationalist leader of the 1920s] were major heroes to me. Garvey said that we were from kings and queens and we should be treated as such and should be acting like queens and kings. It's always easy to love the past when the past is explained in positive terms.

IR: Why is Ali loved so much?
BB: Part of it is because he is infirm and he gains sympathy for that. As for his lighting the Olympic torch—anything he could do or is allowed to do to reinterpret his position positively is fine.

Oscar Hijuelos, the author of the Pulitzer Prize-winning novel *The Mambo Kings Play Songs of Love*, was the keynote speaker for the evening. I interviewed him before he entered the dining room.

Oscar Hijuelos: I heard about [Ali] in 1965, or 1966. I saw him in the Garden fight with Jimmy Young. I was up in the rafters. Ali was really amazing. Twenty years ago, I was in an airport and Ali came sauntering through and the atmosphere changed. The only other person I felt this way about was Pope John Paul II. I was in the Vatican and I was waiting with some people and the same thing happened, something changed.

Ishmael Reed: The draft?
OH: I was with him. I was taught by Jesuit priests—the Berrigan brothers—and I grew up around Columbia, around City College, West Harlem basically, and a lot of my friends got killed in that war. Numero Uno. He was a great man, he is a great man. Why am I talking in the past tense?

IR: Why do they like him now?
OH: I think there is such little sincerity in the world that the real thing speaks to people. He may be different in some of his ideas, but he always stood by his principles. People respect that. He's not plastic.

I was friendly with George Plimpton, the guy from *The Paris Review*, and we used to talk about Ali. He went to Kinshasa to see the Ali-Foreman fight. He said that Ali was an accessible being, but at the same time transcendent and very beautiful. I think he will be remembered as a real icon.

CHAPTER 40

Tribes Gallery, New York, April 2006

I met Steve Cannon when I arrived in New York in 1962 and was living from place to place, working at different low-paying jobs, and writing poetry. Steve had a job in a sign-painting factory. Steve was someone who'd read everything. He'd lived in London and his main interests were German philosophy, Wagner, and Ralph Ellison. His wife was in a Southern jail, having been arrested for civil rights activity in the South. He belonged to some of the radical Lower East Side organizations at that time. When Black became the vogue once again in the 1960s, Steve was hired by colleges to teach African-American literature. He finally settled at Brooklyn's Medgar Evers College.

By the 1990s, Steve had lost his eyesight; he attended a conference in Paris organized by Michel Fabre of the Sorbonne. Participants were amazed when Steve, without notes, did a brilliant, forty-five minute response to three papers that had been read, the subject of which was the novels of author Chester Himes. When Steve returned to New York, he discovered that he had been fired.

He had invested in a three-story building of the Federal style, a home that was once occupied by the Hamilton Fish family, and which he bought for thirty-five thousand dollars, which he earned from his bestseller, *Groove, Bang, and Jive Around*. Here he began a magazine called *Tribe*s and an art gallery that became the scene of poetry readings, jazz, and exhibits. The gallery drew artists, writers, students, and interns from all over the world. Wynton Marsalis, Steve's friend from New Orleans, cut a record at Tribes Gallery. It became internationally famous with visitors from the world over, but in 2014 Steve lost the gallery after a lengthy, much-publicized dispute with the landlord. The gallery part has been ended, but in his new apartment, Steve continues to churn out *Tribes*.

Ishmael Reed: When did you first hear of Ali?
Steve Cannon: When he was on the cover of *Time* magazine. Then he came to New York and recited his poetry at the Bitter End. The first time I went to see him fight was when he fought Joe Frazier. I thought that shit was pretty funny at the time. The only problem I had with him and the Nation of Islam was his not understanding the religion properly. They mixed it up with Black Nationalism.

I thought that was jive, his renouncing Malcolm X and siding with that Chicago crowd. It was his naiveté. Expelling Ali from the Nation for returning to the ring was a dumb move on his [Elijah's] part, because that's the way Ali made his money. With his fists. The way he made his money was through that.

I agreed with his stand on the draft one hundred percent. I feel that they shouldn't have been over there messing with those people in the first place. When he told the Nation that "no Vietnamese ever had called him a nigger," he made a good point.

IR: What of his move to the right?
SC: Oh, God, I thought that was sad. By that time he was punch drunk, I guess like Joe Louis working as a bouncer in Las Vegas. They like him now because he moved to the right and he can't talk.

IR: At the Olympics?
SC: I thought it was a good move. I didn't see anything wrong with it politically. I think he should take a stand on the war [in Iraq].

On this day, *Tribes* was presenting a reading by Boadiba, a Haitian poet whose work, *Under Burning White Sky*, I published, and throwing a party to honor artist David Hammons and me.

David Hammons is one of the country's most provocative artists. His work inspires outrage and is sometimes attacked, physically:

> 29 November 1990: Ten black men armed with sledgehammers attacked a 14x16-foot portrait of Jesse Jackson, entitled "How Ya Like Me Now?" At the time of the attack, the portrait was being installed two blocks from the Washington Project for the Arts (WPA), Washington, D.C. The WPA commissioned the work as part of an exhibition at its space, entitled "The Blues Aesthetic: Black Culture and Modernism." The reason the men gave for their assault on the work was that they felt the work was racist because the artist, David Hammons, had represented Jackson as a white male, with blue eyes and blonde hair. While the three men who were installing the work during the attack were white, the artist, David Hammons, is black, and created the work to denounce racism. Philip Brookman, the show's curator, explained that the attackers [only saw] "that Jesse Jackson was painted white, they didn't stop to think about the complexity of the message."
>
> The demolished work was re-installed and on 2 December, Jesse Jackson, who claimed to "get a kick out of the painting," spoke at the site of the portrait about the work and its assault. During his speech, Jackson said, "Sometimes art provokes; sometimes it angers. That is a measure of its success. Sometimes it inspires creativity." Maybe the sledgehammers should have been on display too. ("A Partial Guide to the Tools of Art Vandalism, *Cabinet Magazine*, 2001)

Ishmael Reed: [I asked David the first time he'd heard of Ali.]
David Hammons: '60s maybe. Yeah. It was about someone who could predict a round that someone was going to get knocked out. I heard about him long before I saw him. Then when I heard him talk, I wasn't interested in someone who was that egotistical. I was a great fan of Gorgeous George, his being transsexual and his odd style. And then Ali picked up on that. It was no longer about boxing. It became a conduit for all kinds of other things.

I never saw him as a boxer. I saw him as Jesus Christ coming back in another form. Everyone was joining the Nation of Islam at that time in some form.

IR: What about when he abandoned Malcolm X?

DH: It's because Ali wasn't that deep. He was still a fighter.

IR: He defied the draft.

DH: He didn't do it for himself. He did it for the masses. A lot of us do that. We're not doing it for personal reasons. It has to be done. We're caught up in the time that we're in. A lot of the work that I'm making is not the kind of work that I would like to be making, but it's up to me to speak about something that might not get said.

IR: Why is there such affection for him now?

DH: He's a hero. Everyone wants to be a hero. They want to earn some money. It goes back to the living myth that Sun Ra used to talk about.

IR: What do you mean by that?

DH: [Hammons sings the Sun Ra piece, "The Living Myth, The Living Myth."]

Yes. That's how Sun Ra saw himself. It is very interesting to be a living myth. But we can never forget when The Living Myth goes to the toilet, his smells are like those of everyone else's.

Paul Spooky Miller

Paul D. Miller is a conceptual artist, writer, and musician working in New York. His written work has appeared in *The Village Voice, The Source, Art Forum, Raygun, Rap Pages, Paper Magazine*, and a host of other periodicals. Miller's first collection of essays, *Rhythm Science*, was published by MIT Press in 2004, and was included in several year-end lists of the best books of 2004, including *The Guardian* and *Publishers Weekly*. Other publications include *Sound Unbound* (2005), an anthology of writings on sound, art, and multi-media by contemporary cultural theorists, and *Book of Ice* (2011), his multidisciplinary study of Antarctica.

Paul Miller: I tend to think of Muhammad Ali as an operating system. You know, he's somebody who allows others to think and to kind of create outside the definition of the norm. Even by renaming himself, even by going against the Vietnam War at the height of that kind of nationalist fervor, he set the tone for other figures in black popular culture as a way of saying, "Look, we need to redefine the role that we give people." So he's, like, saying, "Take this identity and run with it."

Muhammad Ali is hip hop. That's what I'm saying. To me, hip hop is an operating system for redefinition of self. It allows not only African Americans, but anyone who engages in the rhythm patterns that the music evokes to say, "Look, this is about creativity and improvisation." The way that you use language to sustain and reinvigorate identity. And he was someone who combined this with physical prowess. But of course, with his example, he was looking back at someone like Jack Johnson, who also defied convention by associating with white women, and exhibiting flamboyancy when black men were expected to be low-keyed.

You could also look at Mike Tyson as an update of what Jack Johnson was doing. When you look at the twentieth century, to me at least, there was a conflict of identity values. And in twentieth-century American culture you had this insane amount of regimentation, like the company man. People felt like they would have lifelong employment; whites did. In black culture, on the other hand, you saw an unprecedented amount of transformation. Migration to the North, the veterans coming back from World War I and being lynched, because they were wearing uniforms, all these kinds of echoes and ripples of the Civil War were resurfacing. It was like black culture saying, "We need to update some of these identity issues."

But whites weren't willing to let go of historical roles. There was transformation in advertising, away from Aunt Jemima and stuff, but then you could see that mass culture, radio, and TV transformed the way people related to Blackness, but boxing somehow was still the mark of masculine identity, something that people still had a visceral response to. So Muhammad Ali, by choosing a Muslim name at the height of the Christian black bourgeois scene, was radical.

Ishmael Reed: What about Elijah Muhammad?

PM: I definitely tend to think we need different visions. What I am worried about—I also tend to think that when we look at Muslim culture—it has a lot of issues that we could either pick or choose from, or look at it and say, "This is a different operating system."

Well, the reason I keep using operating system is that it is like a structure, like Lego blocks, like where you take one block and put it here or take another block and put it there, but you build a structure. A lot of problems with these imported religions are that people tend to use them to consolidate power.

IR: When did you first hear of Ali?

PM: Probably he was one of the pop culture figures I heard about in the seventies when I was growing up. I was about four or five. He had legendary status. Brilliant. You know those kinds of things. I had no problems with his joining the Nation.

I grew up in Washington, D.C. My father was the dean of Howard Law School. My mom was a designer of African fashion, and we traveled to different parts of Africa to see how they made fabrics. I have never been that keen on boxing, because I'm not really into violence *per se*. I viewed it as economic violence. You can say people have internalized the fact that masculinity is about warrior culture and all of that. As an artist, I tend to feel like masculinity can be multiplex. It doesn't have to be, "I'm going to beat you down and take your women." [Laughter]

But you know Foreman was already a legend, and that legend became part of the basic fabric of everybody's imagination of how black culture operated. Foreman and Ali were Titans.

IR: Why does Ali transcend boxing?

PM: He is a choreographer and a poet. I look at his style of fighting, like, he controlled the dynamics of the engagement where he danced and his partner didn't know the dance. [Choreographer Garth Fagan, whose most famous work is "The Lion King," told me that, as a dancer, Ali was "nimble, wonderful, majestic, and lethal."]

IR: Why does everybody like him so much now?

PM: Everything is in the mirror of history, you know. But society has an idea of the emasculated black. Michael Jackson is moving to Dubai. [This interview was conducted in 2006.] That's so weird and deep that the media can't touch that; like he's gone beneath the radar. On the other end of the spectrum, you have to imagine that Blackness is viewed as a subtle mirror for Whiteness. You know Bert Williams who did Blackface? There are whole layers of how Blackness has been transformed. Recently, 50 Cent dissed Kanye West for dissing Bush. Kanye West said Bush didn't care about black people and 50 Cent called Bush a "gangsta."

In black culture, complexity and nuance has always been a tool for language, to kind of somehow get out different values. Muhammad Ali synthesized the idea of the rebel slave with the idea of somehow figuring out how that gave other people inspiration. The impact of television played a role. If he were around in the nineteenth century, he would have been a verbal legend, but he was telegenic the way that Kennedy was, and they both represented a transformation of certain values.

I had the chance to speak with Darius James, novelist and author of *Negrophobia*:

> I was a kid. I must have been like six, seven years old when he [Ali] was doing his first championship fight after the Olympics and there was this incredible sound bite: "I am the greatest!" That was unheard of at the time. You didn't see many black people on television speaking with such confidence. He was a person of character, which is unfortunately lacking in the culture. He was a precursor of black pride. I mean, you could say the same thing about Nelson Mandela. I mean, he actually represents something to the culture. He was the greatest.

IR: What about his belonging to the Nation of Islam?

Darius James: I made my views about the Nation of Islam pretty clear. There is a book you're in, where I wrote an essay on Elijah Muhammad." [*American Monsters* by Jack Newfield]

CHAPTER 41

June 2006, Louisville, Kentucky

On the day before I left for Louisville for the gala opening of the Ali Center on November 19, 2005, an eighty-million-dollar complex housing Ali memorabilia, Agieb Bilal calls to tell me that he has been renditioned, what in South America are called "disappearings" or government-sponsored abductions, by the people from Homeland Security, because of an Islamic school where he was principal.

He says that he is the only member of Wallace's community to attract such attention. The federals came early morning on Wednesday, and flew him to a place that he thinks was in the South. He says after hours of interrogation, they cleared him.

He tells me to look into Muhammad Ali's associates when exiled from boxing, when he lived in Cherry Hill, New Jersey. He was used as an unwitting front by some people who were involved in narcotics traffic. Some of them were in on the murder of the followers of Kareem Abdul-Jabbar, over letters written by Elijah Muhammad's rival, which were considered insulting to Elijah Muhammad.

Agieb Bilal says that the rival leader felt that his version of Islam was more authentic than the NOI's and was jealous because Libyan leader Muammar Gaddafi gave money to Elijah Muhammad's Nation, instead of to the leader, Hamaas Abdul Khaalis, who followed Orthodox Islam.

I arrived in Louisville near midnight the next evening; Louisville, a city that poet Ntozake Shange calls "a southern town with pretensions."

The original Galt House was established in 1834 on the northeast corner of Second and Main Streets and was Louisville's best-known hostelry during the nineteenth century. This Galt House played host to such notables as Charles Dickens and U.S. Generals Grant and Sherman.

Dickens wrote of his stay at the Galt House that he and his companions had been "as handsomely lodged as though we had been in Paris." And it was at the Galt House during the Civil War where Generals Sherman and Grant met to plan the invasion that eventually led to the "March to the Sea."

After being host to such historic figures, the first Galt House was destroyed by fire in 1865 and was replaced in 1869 by an even larger and grander Galt House, located at the northeast corner of First and Main. Due to financial difficulties, this hotel closed in 1919. The building was demolished in 1921. Finally the third Galt House, on Fourth Street and River Road, was built in 1973 as a part of the Riverfront Urban Renewal Project. The Galt House East opened in 1984.

This time, my daughter Tennessee accompanied me to Louisville: city of whiskey, horses, and Muhammad Ali. Across the street from the Galt house is a landmark dated 1783 for Evan Williams, Kentucky's first distiller. He held the post of Harbormaster for the city of Louisville. Louisville's success with whiskey has been traced to its limestone water. Besides whiskey, there are heavily mascaraed blondes, who favor attire dabbed with large amounts of the color sky blue.

The black women are conservatively dressed and have a 1950s style. They apparently spend a lot of money on their hair. Young black men are dressed like the old lawn jockeys; they wear caps and the lengthy jerseys. As evidence of symbolic victories that the blacks have achieved in the South, however, the old lawn jockeys on display in the hotel are white.

It was in the presidential suite of the Galt House that, according to David Kindred, Ali told the sports writers about his fear of the Fruit of Islam (the NOI's paramilitary unit). He was supposed to have expressed the same concerns to Sugar Ray Robinson.

This is the city where Cassius Marcellus Clay II was born to Odessa and Marcus Clay on January 17, 1942. The Clay family has a connection to Henry Clay, whom Ali's aunt says was Cassius's great-great-grandfather. Odessa Grady Clay's part-Irish father, according to Odessa, looked like a white man, the same comment I got from my mother and her late cousin when I interviewed them about their roots. My mother said that her grandfather on her mother's side "looked like a white man," and her cousin said that her grandparent's father was a "mean" Irishman. Apparently when Irishmen came in contact with African women they couldn't keep their hands off of them; but it's obvious from the comment made by Thomas Jefferson's sister that these Irish overseers were often blamed for the plantation's bi-racial children, when it was the old man himself who was helping himself to the merchandise.

Mary Chesnutt, in her *Civil War Diary*, claimed that every planter's wife was aware of the carrying-on with African women in every planter's wife's home except theirs. Clay's father was named for the slave master who liberated his father. William R.Townsend, described by Jack Olsen as a family historian, said that "The grandfather of Cassius Marcellus Clay was a slave who belonged to the old lion [Cassius Marcellus Clay] and was liberated by him and that in gratitude he named his son Cassius Marcellus Clay, who, in turn, so named his son," whose talent for loquaciousness was evident from the start. (Olsen, 1967)

Cassius Sr. said:

> He loved to talk, too. I'd come home and he'd have about fifty boys on the porch—this was when he's about eight years old—and he's talking to all of 'em, addressing them, and I'd say, "Why don't you go in the house and go to bed?" (Remnick, 1998)

The house was located at 3302 Grand Avenue. According to two of Cassius Sr.'s friends, whom I would later interview, the house is still there. After he won the Olympic Light Heavyweight championship in 1960, Ali returned to Louisville to receive a hero's reception. He has returned many times, and there is talk of his returning to Louisville to live the years that are remaining to him. He now lives in Berrien Spring, Michigan, on a farm once owned by mobster Al Capone.

During one 1979 visit to receive an award from the National Council of Christians and Jews, he met Janene Shakir, a beautiful, twenty-two-year-old woman. Janene Shakir came to the Galt Hotel to interview Muhammad Ali after requesting a meeting with him in September 1979, at a public ceremony where he was receiving an award from the Council of Christians and Jews. She was a Muslim. In exchange for her skipping a class to hear Ali, her journalism professor assigned her to obtain an interview from the champion. According to Shakir:

> I took myself up to the stage and asked for an interview. He [Ali] said to come to his hotel room in the Galt for the interview at 8 a.m. My caretakers, the brothers who were watching out for me, went with me. There were four people in the room with us.
>
> We were members of The World Community of Islam in the West. I took my daughter, who was five years old at the time. We sat and talked. My daughter fell asleep in his lap and he placed her on the bed. He said that he didn't know that there were Muslim women in Louisville. He asked me would I marry him if he divorced Veronica. I said no. Months later, he divorced Veronica.
>
> I saw him on several other occasions when the judge gave the Muslim community's money to Farrakhan. The estate of Elijah Muhammad sued the community in 1981 and gave the money to the family. I went to Chicago and Muhammad was there, too. Farrakhan ended up with the Stony Island mansion. In 1988 they raised the star and crescent atop it. There was always larceny in the NOI.

Janene Shakir was referring to a case in which nineteen children of Elijah Muhammad fought for 5.7 million dollars of Elijah Muhammad's estate. The defendant was the Dai-Ichi Kangyo Bank of Japan. Elijah Muhammad died without a will in 1975. On one side of the split family were Herbert Muhammad and his brother Wallace, who inherited from their father the leadership of the Nation of Islam, which was known as the Muslim Community of America. In a series of legal skirmishes dating from the late 1970s, nineteen legitimate and illegitimate children of Elijah Muhammad contended that Herbert and Wallace kept property that should have gone to all the heirs.

According to *The New York Times*, November 3, 1987:

> The two brothers have responded by contending that their father kept his personal property separate from that of the Nation of Islam. But the rival side of the family has won a number of judgments against them, and last March the Muslim Community of America filed for reorganization in Federal Bankruptcy Court here, hoping to save several pieces of the organization's property, including its South Side mosque, from creditors—primarily the 19 Muhammad children.
>
> Among the judgments that have favored the nineteen was one issued by the probate division of Cook County Circuit Court, which ordered that the $5.7 million bank account—$3.3 million in principal at the time of Elijah Muhammad's death, $2.4 million in interest since then—be turned over to the children. (Special to *The New York Times*, Print Headline: "19 Children of Muslim Leader Battle a Bank for $5.7 Million")

After assuming leadership of the movement his father helped to found, Wallace Muhammad did a house-cleaning that included consolidating the Nation's assets and satisfying its creditors. He also outed some of the criminals who'd infiltrated the Nation.

At one meeting, he denounced the Yacubism that his father embraced yet abandoned in the 1960s. He said that the real devils "are some of those ministers sitting behind me."

These are good people, Janene and her husband, Atar Shakir. I met them in November 2006 when I attended the opening of the Ali Center. The plane was an hour and a half late from Atlanta, which put us down in Louisville at 1:45 a.m. We phoned ahead to tell the Shakirs, who are Sunni Muslims, and followers of Wallace, that we'd take a cab, but they insisted that they pick us up. They drove us to the Galt House. They live in one of the apartments that the hotel is renting out. They had moved into the Galt House a week before and hadn't unloaded their boxes. The apartment was long and spacious and had a view of the Ohio River. Tennessee and I awoke the next morning to the sounds of construction work. She's not only essential in assisting me in the writing of this book, just as she was in the writing of *Blues City: A Walk in Oakland*; she arranges the interviews, she remembers everybody's names and their pets. She's a charmer and will probably end up in politics. (Tennessee ran for school board in 2008. And though we were outspent she got ten percent of the votes.)

The construction work nearly blasted us out of our beds. I called the front desk to complain and they apologized and offered us an upgrade with no extra charge. We got a suite. One of the entertainments suggested by the "Things to Do in Louisville" was a Stephen Foster musical.

When we took the elevator to the Shakirs' upstairs apartment to interview them, a meeting of young men with whom Janene works was breaking up. She said that her job is working with people "who are killing each other."

The young men have good manners and introduced themselves to me. She got a man who worked inside the Ali Center on the phone and invited him and his wife to dinner. They'd heard of my work and agreed to come. While I was awaiting the arrival of Janene, Atar told me about his background. He became interested in the NOI not while serving time, the usual representation of a NOI member, but while attending Amherst University in Massachusetts. The guest also has a PhD in science and, like Bobby Seale, co-founder of The Black Panther Party, has worked on missile projects for the government.

While The Ali Scribes characterize the members of the NOI as "thugs" and worse, both NOI and the Black Panther Party attracted black men who were high achievers. I was struck by the number of speakers at the funeral of the late Black Panther leader, Huey Newton, who were either PhDs or in graduate school in the process of earning one. Their emphasis on education has influenced their children. Bobby Seale's son is a doctor and his daughter is a college graduate. The daughter of another Panther luminary, Elaine Brown, is a Spellman graduate. Ozier Muhammad, Elijah's grandson, is the Pulitzer Prize-winning photographer for *The New York Times*. I haven't seen these legacies mentioned when The Ali Scribes ridicule and denigrate both the Panthers and the NOI. They concentrate on the thugs and criminals involved in both movements. Even Huey Newton, the co-founder of the Panthers, who ended his life as a drug addict and criminal, owned a PhD. After he received a PhD in the History of Consciousness from the University of California at Santa Cruz, he said, "From now on you'll have to call me Dr. Nigger."

In the early seventies, I wrote about some hoods and opportunists who'd infiltrated the Black Power movement in *The Last Days of Louisiana Red*. It was to be expected that there would be criminal activities among the NOI, since many of its members were former convicts, but many of those who were former convicts reformed and began to lead decent lives.

One could understand why some black prisoners would view whites as devils. Some of them were confined to California prisons, run by the powerful Corrections lobby and prison guards union, before whom even the He-Man Governor, Arnold Schwarzenegger, quaked. Governor Jerry Brown, the former progressive turned Neo-liberal depended upon them for campaign contributions and has tolerated prison conditions that are considered among the worst in the world. It was reported that while George Jackson was imprisoned at San Quentin prison, fiendish white guards served black prisoners meals mixed with feces and urine. Aryan gangs beset them, murdered some of their fellow prisoners, and accosted them with racist taunts, like threatening to kill them, and "cut off their wooly hair and use it like Brillo pads to scrub toilets."

When Muhammad Ali went to prisons like San Quentin, and treated even those prisoners regarded as incorrigible with respect, you could understand why once on the outside, they would join the NOI. It would be interesting to determine whether the recidivist rate among those who have joined the NOI is lower than the national average. I suspect that it is.

One of the reasons The Ali Scribes ignore the fact that among those who were attracted to the NOI were the black brightest and best is that their vision of different ethnic groups is framed by their education and the media: the average white journalist or academic knows as much about the full range of black possibilities as the average white person.

Yet they dominate the nation's opinion space about race. Men who've never suffered the indignity of racial profiling or mortgage discrimination, or the hostility from whites that blacks, especially black males, experience every day even in progressive zones like Berkeley. Nicholas Kristof of *The New York Times* has more power to define the black experience than any one hundred black intellectuals and academics. Maybe millions of ordinary whites know more because, unlike the members of the academic and media elites, which I've said are fifty years behind the south in terms of diversity, these whites work alongside blacks each day. Since Daniel Moynihan tried to impress Richard Nixon by explaining the black underclass's situation as a victim of its own personal failure, politicians, Op-Ed writers and academics have used his argument to explain everything from unemployment to the shooting of blacks by the police. Occasionally the argument blows up in their faces. When it was thought that five black and Hispanic kids had raped a white woman as she jogged through Central Park, a number of opinion makers used the Moynihan argument to explain the incident. Commentator Roger Rosenblatt went beyond that and said that the kids were evil. He invoked Lucifer. They were innocent. You can understand why thousands of blacks become so frustrated with communicating with whites, even the progressives among them, that they advocate separatism, even to the extent of refusing to even speak to whites.

CHAPTER 42

Though the Nation of Islam was accused of selling woof tickets and punking out when the LAPD murdered Ronald Stokes in 1962, when provoked by the white authorities they sometimes retaliate, especially when whites harass NOI women, or when the police invade spaces they consider sacred.

Muhammad Ali's example and that of the Nation of Islam appealed to black men who felt their emasculation in a society ruled by white men. The Nation of Islam was known to beat up police who disrespected their women and violated their sacred spaces.

Muslims were regarded as "crazy niggers," like those men and women who defied the Jim Crow laws, long before Rosa Parks and Martin Luther King, Jr. One of the reasons that the mob left Sugar Ray Robinson alone, his son told me, was that he was considered crazy, and when a commission investigating the second Ali-Liston fight asked Liston why he didn't get up when knocked down by the "phantom" punch, he said because he thought Ali was crazy.

Attorney Howard Moore, Jr. represented Atlanta members of the NOI who had a violent altercation with the police. Their arrest began when they assaulted someone who spoke disparagingly of Elijah Muhammad. At the station house, the police and the Muslims went at it. Six officers were beaten into unconsciousness. One officer said that all he remembered before blacking out was someone shouting "Allah Akbar!" The notorious NYPD, an outfit riddled with corruption and bad attitudes toward minorities, which, under Mayors Giuliani and Bloomberg, Police Commissioners Kelly, and Bernard

B. Kerik, who went to jail, has been exposed as having a policy of arrest quotas for blacks and Hispanics, implemented a policy of stop and frisk. (Bernard Kerik served jail time for tax evasion and lying to authorities yet was brought on to CNN by CNN president Jeff Zucker to call Ferguson protestors "savages" and "animals." Zucker also rewarded Mark O'Mara, who used the prospect of the Black Rapist to frighten white women on the Trayvon Martin jury to acquit his murderer George Zimmerman.)

In 2011, six hundred forty thousand New Yorkers, black and Hispanic men mostly, were stopped and frisked with very few stoppages resulting in an arrest. (In the old days, the NYPD went around beating up people because they looked "Jewish" (Marilynn S. Johnson, 2004)).

Therefore, one can understand the rejoicing that occurred among the black population when members of this force invaded a Harlem mosque and were beaten. The headlines of *The New York Amsterdam News* read as "Muslims Do Not Play."

Here again, as in books about Muhammad Ali, the NOI receives short shrift. It's hard for these authors to understand why not only black athletes but also black intellectuals were influenced by Elijah Muhammad and the NOI. Now that some of those intellectuals who were influenced by the Nation of Islam have become members of the establishment, they have been accused of distancing themselves from the Nation.

Askia Muhammad, editor of *The Final Call*, a publication that reflects the religious and political attitudes of Minister Louis Farrakhan, chided participants at a recent Howard University forum about the Black Arts Movement for neglecting the NOI's influence on 1960s black intellectuals:

> I am sick and tired of the shallow, prevailing, black, intellectual view of the Nation of Islam. It's not just the Neo-Cons and the White Evangelicals of the world who have problems with Muslims.
>
> Our own black intelligentsia has issues with the Islamic influence— particularly the Nation of Islam—on Black literature and culture in the United States and they refuse to admit it. Black literature and academia

lionizes Brother Malcolm X, highlighting only the fourteen months or so of his life after he broke with the Nation of Islam, while trying to wipe out his twelve years of steadfast service and leadership within the Nation, his platform for earning national attention in the first place. We've done the same with Muhammad Ali.

As we were sitting at the table, with a view of the Ohio River, I asked Atar Shakir, who once sold *Muhammad Speaks* newspapers, why The Ali Scribes viewed the Nation of Islam as mainly one made up of thugs. Atar responded:

> That reputation was partially due to the fact that we did have a few people who had become entrenched and became part of the Nation of Islam and were thugs. They brought that lifestyle into the Nation. Some of these people ended up working their way into Elijah Muhammad's inner circle. A lot of them were exposed, usually the small ones, not the really big, major ones. By major, I mean those who held positions as Imams or Captains, high up in the Nation's hierarchy. I really wouldn't know what percentage of them because I haven't ever really seen any statistics.

Ishmael Reed: Have they been weeded out?

Atar Shakir: No. No, because I look at Orthodox Islam and I see thugs. You will have that in all religious groups. You're going to have people with ulterior motives enter these groups.

The Nation of Islam came about on the heels of the Garvey Movement. For black people in America, they were an alternative. Black people faced the Klan, and the overall racist system. So it made no difference whether you went into business or into the army, you still faced the same type of racist behavior and problems. So first, the Garvey Movement was a haven and the Nation of Islam became a haven for people. It was also a push for people to do some introspection. It was time for them to clean out some internal demons, which had developed out of historical circumstances like our hatred of us, a distrust of each other. I mean it offered hope to people who thought they had no way out; people who had been addicted to drugs or who had been caught up in the whole penal system.

IR: How does Muhammad Ali fit into this?

AS: When I think of Muhammad Ali, I first think about him as being an athlete because that's what I saw. Later, when he was confronted with going to Vietnam, and he made his statements about that, I saw him as more than just an athlete.

IR: Even though he was guided by NOI policy that affected all of its members?

AS: Yes.

IR: The Ali Scribes say that the Nation took all of Ali's money, but members of the NOI whom I talk to say he gave no more than anybody else.

AS: What society does not utilize somebody who shows that they have some charisma and they have some magnetism or leadership qualities? In some cases they end up getting exploited and even assassinated.

IR: How did Imam Wallace Deen Mohammed change Muslim thinking?

AS: Wallace tried to make a transition. People had been brainwashed, where they couldn't think out of the box, and so if they had problems they'd talk to the Imam and then call Chicago. People were tightly controlled that way. Wallace tried to get people to think for themselves as well as take on the moral and spiritual responsibility for their religion because before that they looked to their Imam. Wallace made us more responsible as followers and believers in the Muslim religion.

IR: Critics accuse Wallace of teaching American patriotism and as evidence of this they point to the American flag appearing on the cover of his newspaper, *The Muslim Journal*, and ask why Ali hasn't taken a stand on the war in Iraq, even though Ali is a Sunni. They say that Wallace is asking African Americans to be Arabs, whom they accuse of holding racist attitudes toward blacks.

AS: Neither from his writings nor his speeches do I get that impression. In those, he deals with issues that we have to deal with here. I really think that theirs is not a fair judgment.

IR: What about liquor being served at the opening of the Ali Center? Liquor companies advertising in the Center's program? [Both Janene and Atar found the liquor connection to the Ali Center to be appalling and a contradiction.]
AS: You have to look behind the screen and what you see behind the screen is who is running that Center.
Janene Shakir: The board of directors' chair is Ina Bond, daughter of the owner of Brown-Forman Distillers [Old Forester, Early Times, *et al.*].

Ironically, some of the Louisville investors, whom Ali deserted when he came under the control of the NOI are contributors to the Ali Center. William Faversham, the vice-president of Brown-Forman Distillers, was "manager" of Ali on behalf of the Louisville Sponsoring Group.

AS: When the state of Kentucky pulled the money out, they went to Atlanta trying to solicit the rich black folks. They were rebuffed and then September 11 happened and everything went lockdown.

IR: Do African-American Muslims feel superior to overseas Muslims?
JS: [Janene said that she thought that this was true.]
AS: There is a schism. For example, immigrant Muslims believe that people who have converted here are not as good and vice versa.

IR: [I mentioned that there were instances of some immigrant Yemeni Muslims selling drugs in the African-American community of Oakland.]
JS: There was one around the corner from where we live who was selling dope to our boys and the police knew about it.

On August 5, 2006, *The New York Times* buried a story about members of the immigrant Muslim population selling accessories for illegal drugs.

> A federal judge has ruled that law enforcement agents did not single out South Asian convenience store owners during a sting operation, which began in 2003, designed to catch clerks who were illegally selling the household ingredients used to make methamphetamine.
>
> Twenty-three of the twenty-four stores named in the sting indictment were run by South Asians, and forty-four of the forty-nine people charged are Indian.
>
> Federal prosecutors say they did not single out Indian, Pakistani, or Bangladeshi store owners because of their race, but because the tightly-knit South Asian business community was catering to local methamphetamine dealers for hefty profits.

AS: Ali's condition is worse and their attention is being focused on him and not on the Center. So other people who are running the Center are the ones who are bringing in the alcohol.

JS: They had their first international event, which hosted the new ambassador from Saudi Arabia, one of the Faisals. Ali seemed to be holding his own. He had a walker but he was doing his sparring thing coming down the steps.

IR: What about Ali's womanizing?

JS: Ali is the kind of guy that women like. In Christianity, the men give the women away. Like when Abraham sent Sarah to the pharaohs, he said, "Don't tell him you're my wife, tell him you're my sister." So they use the women and place them in the way of the black athlete. Like [the ex-wife of O. J. Simpson,] Nicole. Her daddy gave her to O. J. when she was seventeen years old.

There's some professor who had clearly gone online where she read everything she could about Islam, and read everything she could about Muhammad Ali, and was talking from a feminist position about his wife, and his being a womanizer, which, as far as I'm concerned, as a Muslim, I can say he's a womanizer, but she's not a Muslim.

IR: Maybe she wanted him to hit on her.

JS: No, no. Wait a minute, wait a minute. It's deeper than that. She's the type that most men wouldn't hit on. I'm just telling the truth. I'm not mean. It's not about feminism. So when I as a black woman confronted her, I said that she spoke out of turn without consideration of how he sees himself in the light of being a Muslim man. A Muslim man, according to the religion, may have four wives at a time. He didn't have four wives at a time, according to what they say. He might have had some mistresses, but none of that was hidden. So that's the whole thing. Am I telling the truth?

Janene and Atar suggested that I interview a man who was familiar with the behind-the-scenes goings-on at the Ali Center. Janene invited him and his wife to dinner at six. It was four in the afternoon. We returned to our suite until the time for dinner. Janene prepared a wonderful and simple meal of chicken, rice, greens, salad, bread, and strawberries.

In 2006, I spoke with an Ali Center Administrator, whose name is withheld by request.

Ishmael Reed: Ina Brown?

ACA: She's the heiress to the Forman-Brown fortune.

IR: What about the large liquor influence on the Center and the Muslim notions about alcohol?

ACA: Basically, I'm the only Muslim on the staff. Does that explain it?

IR: What about the company, CKX, that bought eighty percent of Ali's image for fifty million? I wrote and asked whether there were Muslims or African Americans on that board, but never received an answer.

ACA: Do you really want to know? No. Until now there weren't. It's a company out of New York. They own the names, they buy names and basically what they are doing—they inherited the staff of the

GOAT [Greatest Of All Time]. One of the things that is really an issue is how the name is going to be used.

The Ali's only got pieces of this toward the end. Besides, what do you do when you have a person as sick as Ali? One of the things that really amazes me is that very few people seem to understand the neuropathy of his ailment.

He has a cerebral stimulant device implanted in his brain. It has various names, but it is basically implanted in the part of the brain where the disease affects him the most. And what that does is it stimulates the production—it pulses his brain at a rate to counter the tremors. You counter the tremors by stimulating other parts of the brain. What he's having is neuron firing, and so you put it in an agonist area of the brain that prevents that firing. That is the only thing that keeps him from shaking apart. When that stimulant device is turned down, it loads him with beta-endorphins, and when it's turned down, he falls asleep. To be honest with you, to turn him on, we time how long he's going to be on, and then we turn him off. He's gone beyond the stage where drugs can affect the blood brain barrier.

The problem is the neuropathy of this disease says that one day, what's going to happen is his baroreceptors in his lungs are going to fail. He's going to wind up on a ventilator. That's a sad thing to say, but it's going to kill him and they have spent a lot of money and a lot of effort to give him the quality of life.

These are the demands that are taking a toll on him and Lonnie is managing that. I don't know too many boxers who ever surrounded themselves with people who only care about their own interests. Not too many boxers are good judges of character in terms of other people. I don't know, but the point is that Mike is one of those. He's a carpetbagger. He's a smooth operator.

IR: And so he's also pushing Ali to make appearances and show up?
ACA: Yes. That's correct.

IR: What about Lonnie's carting him around?

ACA: That had nothing to do with the Center. But those are appearances that he wants to make. People look to him for inspiration. He has a bigger persona outside of this country than in this country. The Prophet Muhammad, his own people, his own clan, got ridiculed in the city of Mecca. Jesus, and all of the prophets—very few of them were popular in their hometowns. It is the same way here in Louisville, and the Center is making it worse, because it's distancing itself from the community.

IR: What is the participation of the Muslim community in the Center?

ACA: As I told Muhammad Ali recently, "The Muslim community here is divided." It is divided between the old Muslims who came here in the seventies that were economic refugees and the immigrants, mainly from Pakistan. But what happened was, when the Israelis took the Golan Heights, they displaced all of the Palestinians that were there, and most of the Palestinians that were on the Golan Heights, which was under Syrian control, a lot of them came to the United States. They are the major business owners here. And the Pakistanis came here as engineers and physicians. They are the professional class. They [Palestinians] are both Muslim and Christian. They are Maronites and Druzes and I explained that to Ali. I said, "They are divided. They are even turning each other over to the FBI." I tried to give him the flavor of the old community and new community divided. I said, "The communities aren't together and this Center should be a spot that becomes neutral ground, such that we can at least begin working with their children so that they will not commit the sins of their parents."

IR: [I asked why Lonnie is dragging him all over the world, and wouldn't fifty million dollars be enough? Both Janene and the guest agreed that Ali wants to go to these events.]

ACA: He has no depth perception. It's gotten worse.

IR: So Laila [Ali's daughter, a boxer] was right about his condition?

ACA: Well, they don't want people to really know how bad he was. There is tension among all the kids because they know how bad he is. When they turn that device down, he just is in uncontrollable tremors. I've seen it. The drugs won't work anymore. He was palming the drugs. You have to understand, he is totally aware in his body. His mental function has not decreased. He only responds to the things he wants to.

That's one of the reasons I told him about the *Fitnah* [an Arabic word meaning when Muslim fights Muslim]. That's the worst thing to see, is a Muslim fighting another Muslim. What I was going to explain—you know that one of the things that may or may not be well known is Ali and Lonnie maintain separate staffs. Ali's secretary and Ali's personal writer were separate from Lonnie's secretary and personal attendant. Now both of them, Kim and Deborah, do not get along at all. The first thing Lonnie did after they sold the Ali name was to fire Kim, Ali's secretary. David was Ali's personal writer. David is a very honorable man. He's a doctoral student in Middle Eastern Studies at the University of Arkansas. He has a personal relationship with the royal family. He has been studying tribal issues in the Emirates, which are really bad.

One of the things that the GOAT sale [to CKX owner Robert Sillerman] caused was that there was a major disruption between those who were very loyal to Ali, and David was one of those people that got really hurt, may Allah ease his pain. David is a really good person and he did not deserve what Lonnie did to get back at that staff, which was really headed by Kim. David was fired. He's getting his Doctorate at the University of Arkansas at Little Rock. Kim's probably back here. I haven't seen Kim, and Deborah, who is Lonnie's secretary, is still there. Many of these invitations and things that came for Ali came through Ali's staff. Lonnie didn't see them. I don't know. What I'm simply telling you is that one of the bones of contention is that information about all of these people who wanted to see him get honors went directly to his staff and were not filtered through Lonnie.

IR: How often are the Ali's here?

ACA: They bought a camper. That's how they travel. She doesn't fly. They got three guys that work for them, whom they raised, and they drive the camper down.

I saw when they turned off his stimulator and they had him in a restrained chair. He has no control over his mouth. He can't swallow. He's going to lose muscular expression. He's in the end stage. May Allah ease his pain.

CHAPTER 43

The next day, as a result of Janene Shakir's lead, Tennessee and I took a cab to 28th Street and Broadway in Louisville. Located there is a McDonald's, which serves as a morning gathering place for some of the Louisville old-timers. By contrast to the sparkling downtown with its glitzy mall, this side of town is run down. Here, we met Waajid Sabree and Omar Rose, two of Cash Clay's friends.

The portrait of Cash in books by The Ali Scribes is not complimentary. For them, he is a nascent Garveyite, whose harangues against the white establishment formed Ali's radical views, which left the eighteen-year-old susceptible to the lures of the NOI. However, Cash had objected to his sons' joining the NOI; he accused the organization of exploiting the champion.

When Rudolph Clay, Muhammad Ali's younger brother, became Rudolph X, Cash refused to accept his collect calls, as a protest against his son's name change. Ed Hughes, whom we met by chance, says that Cash took offense to his sons' dropping the family's name.

For The Ali Scribes, Cassius Marcellus Clay is a domestic abuser, an alcoholic, and a show-off. I wanted to hear from black men who actually knew the father of the former Heavyweight Champion. I ordered a fish sandwich with mayo and Tennessee ordered a Sprite. I wouldn't ordinarily eat at McDonald's, having picked up some of Berkeley's food snobbery, but I must admit that this sandwich was good.

Janene had arranged for me to interview Waajid Sabree and Omar Rose, who had personal knowledge of Ali and his family.

Waajid Sabree: In the early 1980s, late 1970s, Muhammad Ali's daddy worked on a library between 18th and 15th on Jefferson. It was a public library, but they turned it into a law office. He painted the sign that was over the door for the lawyers. It may be still there. The building is located on the site of a graveyard. If you look up over here you see the sign. I think he signed his name to it.

Ishmael Reed: What kind of a worker was he?

WS: He was a diligent worker. Cash liked to talk. Anything you wanted to talk about. [Laughter] Wasn't no subject that was off limits, but he would work, draw a little bit, lay out the letters, come over, talk, and then he would go back and lay a little bit more.

Omar Rose: Well, when I met Cash, he was as much of a womanizer as anybody else. He liked women, liked to mess around with them. He liked big women, women with big butts. My father had a barbershop and there was a woman barber that Cash liked. She's still around. It was the San-Ser-Re (Sanitation, Service and Relaxation) Barbershop. Cash was crazy about that woman. I think Cash painted the letters in there. He mainly stayed with one, his wife, most of the time. He was a man about town. He was everywhere. He was at all of the churches just about. You would go to any church and you would probably find a mural by him in there.

His wife was a nice lady, a very nice lady. She took care of the kids and stayed on top of him to keep him out of the joints, stuff like that. He had a beer joint. That was at Clay and Gray. Muhammad Ali was going in and out of it. There was a jukebox, no band. Other than that, he was basically an average type of man. He took care of his kids, did paintings, and hardly ever worked for anybody but himself. He had a lot of voice, a lot of mouth. He knew something about everything you wanted to talk about. Muhammad is just like him in conversation. I think that's where he got it from, his daddy. His daddy had the gift of gab. He got it good.

Other than that he was a good father, a very good father. He might have gotten arrested. I don't really remember any arrests. I never knew too much about him beating his wife. She always came after him. I worked at a club around the corner, called The Bronze Lantern. He came around there. He stayed there because he lived right around the corner. The club was at 32nd and Grand and he would come in there every day. She would come after him and bring him home, because he liked to go to the club and drink beer. But he worked in a lot of clubs. He worked for himself, all over, because he never worked for anyone else. He kept pretty good money. I thought he was a pretty nice fellow. He drank like everybody else. Mostly beer. I never saw him really drunk and falling out, but he would get high and act up. He would mess with ladies in the club and stuff like that. They wanted him off of them; they wanted him to be moved or put out or something.

He dressed well, like a painter would dress. A hat, average clothes with different colors. He dressed well. He dressed as good as anybody. He liked a lot of color. He never had a studio or anything like that, I know because he took care of his family first. He was around town every day and everybody would have him make signs and do letters and pictures. He just picked [the art] up. He was just a natural. I have never known him to do art other than murals in the churches. He never really did any particular art. He would do anything you wanted done, paint anything that you wanted done. He did it to raise his family. That's all he done. He raised them pretty well. This joint, The Bronze Lantern, is probably still there.

All of those churches are gone. There are new churches. It was a pretty good neighborhood. Ali's house is still there. It is on Grand between 32nd and 34th and it is basically about the same.

WS: Cash's son, Rahaman, I know him. Rahaman is trying to restore his old Cadillac for me, his old green convertible Cadillac that his daddy drove, and I kept it over at my place for him for a couple of years, so he finally came over and got it. I don't know if he ever finished restoring it.

OR: Yeah, you can get a lot of information from him. He's a live-in at the Galton House, on the North Side. Yeah, he's there, I guess he's still there.

WS: Yeah, Rahaman, he is still in town. There are two high-rise buildings. He's on the north side. He was pretty good the last time I saw him. I haven't seen him lately. Rahaman is also a painter first. He did a lot of portraits. His former name was Rudy Valentino. He did a lot of paintings. He probably still has them. Yeah, or he even sold them. He did a colored painting that was pretty good. He did a lot of paintings on Muhammad's fights. They are probably still up for sale. Somebody is going to buy them. He showed them to a few people. Fats Hughes is really tight with him. You would get more information from him than anybody. He has been in this neighborhood all his life. He was with Muhammad until the end of his career.

IR: How about the Center?

WS: The Center is something everybody should go see. It's phenomenal. I was highly impressed. They did a really good job. The exhibits and all that—it's amazing. I was there yesterday with my sister-in-law and she went to school with Muhammad Ali. I don't know, between eighth and twelfth grades. Fats and Jimmy Ellis would tell you more.

OR: Fats Hughes can tell you a lot about Muhammad. He went with him on trips and was around after the end of his career. Lately he hasn't been with him on account of Lonnie tightening things up. She didn't want people calling him all the time, harassing him all the time, asking money from him all the time, people asking him to do something for them all of the time. I think she was a blessing for Muhammad, myself. Well, if you looked at what she's done, she's a blessing for Muhammad. Lonnie wouldn't let Hughes get to him. He was a buddy of Ali's. He lives around here.

WS: He's got a business over there on Chestnut between 13th and 15th. They make pound cakes. Chestnut Street goes east and the building is on the north side. I don't know what's his first name. His nickname is Fats Hughes. Somebody will give you his name. I don't know about that. All I know is she cut off people from talking to Muhammad at will because she's worried. Hughes didn't like it.

OR: Hughes is doing well. He has a hair product.

IR: How has the city changed?

WS: I think people build new houses and cram everybody up like they are rats in a cage. There are too many people down here. All they are doing is creating a ghetto again. They tore down the projects and you have to put them somewhere. You've got a good mayor. Mayor Abramson. He knows how to bring money into the city from the federal government. But it's too crowded. All they're doing is creating a ghetto again. There were a lot of people that came in after they filled those empty lots with houses and apartments. The average neighborhood is crowded. They took the projects down to eliminate the crowding.

IR: What was the reaction in Louisville when Ali joined the Nation of Islam?

OR: There was no reaction. People didn't know about Islam. Ali made people learn what the Nation and Islam was all about. They didn't know anything about it. He was the one who put it on the map, him being who he was. It was in the papers. Before that nobody knew what it was.

IR: Were people angry?

OR: Elijah's group was raising all kinds of hell about the white man being a devil. [Laughter] Everybody was raising hell about that. Boys were joining the Nation and going to their jobs and telling the white man that he was the devil. They were down here losing jobs. The white man cut them off of jobs and they had kids and they couldn't take care of them and they were falling out with their mamma and their papa and everything. That took a toll on things around here because Elijah never gave them a Koran.

All they knew about Islam was what they read in the newspapers. Elijah told them that the white man was a devil because he was kicking their butts. He was kicking everybody's butt. The blacks that were educated didn't like them referring to the white man as the devil and all of that.

IR: Why do the whites like him now?

WS: The whites like Muhammad because he backed up off Farrakhan like Jesse Jackson backed up off of Farrakhan. Most of them backed up off of Farrakhan because they didn't want to be affiliated with that 'cause the white man kicked ass. That's happening every day.

Ali's famous. Everybody wants to be with somebody who is famous, you know. You got a lot of people who will gravitate toward somebody who's famous. That's the way it is.

OR: He made himself a positive black man. Most blacks don't ever do that. He could predict things and make them come true. He made a believer out of people all over the world. That's why he is still the way he is. If Lonnie hadn't got him and kept him like he is and kept the people away from him and kept him clean, he wouldn't be who he is. He probably wouldn't have that museum up there. He probably would have been boycotted. He left Farrakhan alone. He left the devil thing alone.

IR: Did Ali's success change him?

OR: He pretty much stayed the same. My older brother grew up with him. The way he is now is like the way he was in school. He had a lot of confidence in himself and he talked a lot; boasted a lot.

When Ali heard the Black Nationalism call—at the time, everybody was drifting toward Black Nationalism. That was the thing at the time. When time got on he was exposed to the real Islam. If he had just pushed Islam and left out "the white man is the devil," he would have been accepted more. They went into that devil thing and it kicked their butt when it came to getting a job. Farrakhan couldn't give them no job. They went to work telling their bosses, "You the devil." Told their mothers not to eat pork. Mama been eating pork all their lives. And feeding him pork, too.

Black Nationalism told the black man who he was. Before that he didn't know whether he was black, green, or grey. He would have accepted anything that came along that lifted him up. Most of the time he didn't know what he was. They didn't know anything. They didn't know there was a conflict between Christianity and Islam.

Any black man at that time would have accepted Islam. They were trying to find a place for themselves. They were trying to find out what was going on.

Your mother and father didn't tell you what was going on between black and white at the time. They raised you. They carried you to the back of the bus, but didn't tell you why. Nobody told you why you sat at the back of the bus or why the white man was kicking your ass. Anybody who came along with whatever they came along with, people would have accepted it. Now everything has changed. Everything is in shambles now. Ali was a black man and he wanted his race to be positive. I told him that once he announced that he was Muslim he would no longer be champion, they would cut him off. He didn't believe it.

Hughes could probably tell you more. He probably got some pictures at his house. THERE HE IS, RIGHT THERE!

And in one of the coincidences that happen so frequently in this writing life—coincidences that stopped surprising me years ago—Ed "Fats" Hughes drove into the parking lot at McDonald's as the two men were talking about him.

The late Edward Hughes was eighty-three years old when I interviewed him. He was a close friend of the champion and knew the Ali family. He said that he was Ali's oldest friend. He had accompanied Ali to Las Vegas, Manila, and Germany. They called him Fats because at one time he weighed 310 pounds. He owned a bakery shop called Armando's Cakes.

We all walked outside as Ed Hughes and his wife, Amanda, drove up in a 1999 Cadillac. The two others explained to him that I was writing a book about Muhammad Ali. They then teased Hughes about his relationship with Lonnie Ali and they managed to rile Hughes, who accosted them with some expletives. Tennessee and I got into the back seat of the car and I turned on my tape recorder.

Edward Hughes: Yeah, Rahaman paints pictures. He had Joe Frazier look like Muhammad and Muhammad look like Joe Frazier.

[Laughter] Rahaman is sick. Before his daddy died, he said, "Hughes, both of my boys are sick."

Lonnie don't like me. She won't let me talk to him, because I cussed his secretary Kim out up at Michigan. Man, listen. Muhammad is forgetful. He don't know nobody. I might die before Muhammad, but Muhammad is sick. She won't let him come around me. I said, "Lonnie, what's the matter? Why won't you let me see him? I'm his oldest friend."

Everybody said that he talked too much. He was fifteen years old then. I said, "Stop telling that boy he talks too much. You niggers work on jobs where you can't talk. The white man would fire your ass for talking."

Lonnie. You got to know something about the child in order to know the grown-up. I love Lonnie, and she loves Muhammad, but she don't love me. She called me about a month ago because her mother was sick. But I don't know, when she first married Muhammad, she asked my wife, Amanda, to tell Muhammad to take his medicine. [Mockingly] "Miss Amanda, make Muhammad take his medicine." That was a long time ago, but you know Muhammad. I took him places; she accused me of taking him. Shit, I took him where he wanted to go. That's the way he was.

You don't know Lonnie. She's forty-eight and he's sixty-three. She was really a little girl when she met him. If I were a young, fine girl, I would be in love with him, too, with all that money and fame. Listen, she loves him, but she keeps him from his old friends who love him, too.

OR: Lonnie is the best thing to happen to Muhammad.

EH: Financially yes.

OR: In every way. I don't think he'd still be living were it not for her.

EH: No, no, no, not every way. She takes care of him. Did you hear what I said? But when you take a poor-ass, black-ass nigger and they get rich, they forget where they come from, all of them. All of them do that but...

Omar disputes him; it is obvious that Omar enjoys needling Hughes about his relationship with Lonnie Ali.

EH: Wait a minute, man, money don't make a man. Money don't make man, man makes money. Money's not the most important thing.
OR: She loves Muhammad.
EH: Man, you got to know.
OR: Who else would put up with Muhammad's ass all this time if she didn't love him?
EH: She puts up with him all on account of the green. Let me tell you something. I got a close friend who is a heart specialist. He calls me "Pops." He saw Muhammad at the gala. He said, "Pops, you better go see your friend. He's on his last leg. He's really sick." Gene Gilroy called me from Las Vegas. We talked for a long time. Lonnie don't like him either.
OR: Do you think that Muhammad is sick; do you think he has his mind? Why don't you think he hasn't called you himself?
EH: [Agitated] He's out of sight, out of mind. I told you he's forgetful and he can't talk. I told you. He starts off talking and then he starts to mumble.
OR: [Enjoying Hughes' discomfort] Then that's good enough reason for you not to see him.

Hughes began to drive away from the McDonald's lot with Tennessee and me in the backseat, tape recorder still running. I asked him where he was taking Tennessee and me. Amanda told him about the errands she had to do. They were going to a dance and Amanda wanted to wear a fur coat; he objected, saying that you don't wear fur in June. They had this discussion on and off. He drove us to his bakery where he put in an order to one of his daughter's sons who worked there, and then he kept his appointment at the factory owned by a white chemist friend of his. The chemist had done well selling medicine for arthritis. Hughes helped him get his start and was taking over a cologne that Hughes invented. He wanted the chemist to test it at his plant. There was one of those airport-type limousines parked outside with an American flag on each side of the bumper. We took a tour of the plant and were given some samples.

I asked him about the mood in the Ali entourage, when Ali received a life-threatening beating from Larry Holmes. He said that Cash, Ali's father, told him to quit.

EH: I told him to listen to Cash when he told him to quit. I said, "Listen to your daddy, Muhammad." I knew Larry Holmes. He used to sell my hair products. I know. He's a good fighter.

After the Holmes fight, Ali said, "Hughes, I got a gift for you."

I said, "What kind of gift could you give me, Muhammad?" He said, "What's the matter, you don't like money anymore?"

He gave me five thousand dollars cash. Before the fight he had given me a five-hundred-dollar ticket and paid my hotel and airfare. He asked me whether I could go to Zaïre when he fought George Foreman. I said no. He gave me eight thousand dollars anyway.

Things are different now. Lonnie excluded me from everything. I invited her to dinner and she didn't show. She said, "I'm sorry. It slipped my mind."

Muhammad wanted to see me before I died. He's sicker than I am. It kind of hurt my feelings. I cried the first of May, thinking about how close we used be. Ali wouldn't go to sleep, unless I was there with him. He'd say, "Hughes, stay in the room until I go to sleep." He wouldn't go to sleep if I didn't stay in the room with him. The minute he'd go to sleep, I'd leave the room.

Someone says that Cory stays up with Muhammad late at night. He's Ali's companion for watching late-night movies on television.

IR: Who is Cory?

EH: That's Marilyn's son. Marilyn is Lonnie's sister. She used to be a beautiful girl but she's gotten fat. She the same way. She says, "Hughes, I'll call you back."

IR: Is the family stuck up?

EH: They used to not be. Now they are. They told Cory not to talk to me. Cory is scared to talk to me. You've seen that book that Bingham got out? He treated me fine when I was with Muhammad.

He gave me a two-hundred-fifty-dollar ticket to a fight and he said, "That ain't good enough for you." Then he gave me a five-hundred-dollar ticket. Now he don't call me. I wanted to volunteer to be an assistant curator at the museum. He told me I was too old.

We drove around for a while and then he spotted Omar, sitting in front of his house, playing an instrument that looked like a banjo. Omar came over to the car, removed his cell phone and dialed Rahaman Ali, Muhammad Ali's brother.

EH: I'm gonna call Rahaman. Rahaman ain't going to talk to you unless you got some money. Lonnie won't let him get to Ali either because he's always asking for money. His own brother.

[Hughes called Rahaman] Rahaman, what are you doing? Am I bringing you some money? There are some people here—I got plenty? You the one got the money. There's a fellow named Ishmael. He's here with his daughter. Have you had your lunch?

OR: [Interjecting mischievously] Call Lonnie and ask her for some money. [Hughes howls with laughter at Rahaman's response.]

IR: [In 2013, Rahaman complained publicly about Lonnie's management of the champion's life. I asked Hughes what Rahaman said.]
EH: I ain't going to tell you what he said. [Rahaman hung up.] You got to tell him that you have some money for him.

IR: [I asked Hughes would offering Rahaman fifty dollars be enough to get Rahaman for an interview.]
EH: Hughes said, "Man, I asked him Cash's opinion of Lonnie. Man, I can't tell you what he said."

We drove over to the housing projects where Rahaman lived. We asked a man named Snake, a tall, lean man who wore a necklace adorned with a snake amulet, the whereabouts of Rahaman. "He's sitting around the corner," he replied.

We turned the corner and Rahaman was sitting on a bench with some women. He said that he couldn't talk to me unless I gave him some money. I told him I'd give him one hundred dollars. He said that white writers had given him five hundred dollars for an hour's interview. We negotiated for a few minutes and I got him down to 150 dollars for one half-hour, during which he began a spiel he must have done a thousand times. People at the Ali Center said that he's always over there trying to hit them up for some bread.

Rahaman Ali: I was not shocked by his beating Liston. Muhammad is the greatest fighter of all time. He has a strong will and strong desire.

Ishmael Reed: How was your childhood?
RA: It was the greatest pleasure I've ever had. It was like Christmas every day. As a young boy, Muhammad was loquacious, he was cocky, he was brilliant. Muhammad Ali always had a fast mind, a quick mind. He would play marbles good; he would play all kind of sports good. He was a heavenly young man. He was a prophet at a young age. He made predictions.

He told the children in the neighborhood, "One day I'm going to be a great boxing champion," and they would make fun of him. "Aw, you can't do nothing. You ain't gonna do nothing." He would sort of shake them off and say, "One day I'm going to be great."

He always predicted that he would be the greatest boxer; when he was twelve years old he said he would be the greatest.

He did it. He accomplished this feat and today I'm proud of my brother. He's the world's most famous person. Everything he said he was going to do as a young boy, he did. He has the gift of gab. Got it from my daddy.

Not only could my daddy talk, he was a hell of an artist as well. He was the greatest artist that ever lived. He could paint signs and portraits; he could make furniture, anything that had to do with art, my father could do it. He was the best. He was a very smart man, educated, a genius in his right mind. That's why my brother Muhammad Ali was so great. He had my father's blood in his body.

Me, myself, I dedicated my life and my style to helping out my brother. I was a great amateur boxer. I had ninety-three amateur fights. I only lost six. I was the Kentucky Gold World Champion for seven years straight from 1953 to 1960. I won the Golden Gloves. I was a boxer, too, but I dedicated my life to my brother. That's why I wasn't as fast as him. When he won the Olympics, at that time in my life, that was the greatest thing I had ever experienced.

My brother had already predicted that he would win the Olympics. Before he won it, he said he was going to win it. We watched it on TV, when he beat the Pole; it was a very exciting time for my family, and my mother and father were very proud. He accomplished the gold medal. Up until that time it was the greatest experience we had ever achieved.

I was not shocked when he defeated Liston, because I believed my brother had the ability to do it. George Foreman? I was not surprised. Ali is the greatest, his feet and his hands are the fastest and quickest. Anything he has done in boxing, I am not surprised because I am his brother. I have total faith in my brother, and I know his ability. I'm not surprised. Even today, with everything he has accomplished today, even with Parkinson's.

My health is excellent. I only have short-term memory loss. I'm now sixty-four [interview in June 2006] years old and I had a slight stroke and Bell's palsy. My doctor says Bell's palsy caused me to have slight memory loss. Other than that, I am in excellent shape. Yes. I tell people that everything in my body works at sixty-four years old. I'm in good shape. I'm getting married to a very beautiful Louisville lady, marriage number six. She told me she loved me and she would be good to me. She said, "Darling, I got a good job and I will help you in any kind of way."

IR: What happened to Ali's second wife, Khalilah?
RA: She's somewhere in Las Vegas living her life. I don't see Veronica (Ali's third wife) that much. I don't keep in contact with them. If I see them, I hug and kiss them and they hug me. We're friends. People go different ways in life and they do their own thing.

IR: Some writers say that she didn't give Ali enough time to remove his things from the Los Angeles mansion.

RA: Damn the writers. They can kiss my… where the weather don't shine. To hell with them. I saw my brother about two weeks ago. He's doing good. He had surgery so he is not shaking anymore. He walks kind of funny. He has a dedicated, loving wife to take care of him; she takes care of my brother hand and foot. I love Lonnie.

Now I'm trying to find a wife like that. I have been married five times. All my wives gave me problems; I couldn't stay with them. I said when I meet wife number six, I want someone like Lonnie. I can tell you that. My fiancée is younger than me, and she's pretty, and she got money to help me.

IR: What are some of the things that you and your brother did as youngsters that haven't been written about?

RA: We would shoot marbles in the courtyard and we played basketball. He was a good basketball player. He was good at making three-point shots.

IR: You two like jazz?

RA: I was a jazz fanatic: John Coltrane, Thelonious Monk, Miles Davis, and Gene Ammons, the greatest tenor player of all time. Nicknamed "Jug."

IR: What kind of music did Muhammad like?

RA: He liked Duke Ellington and Count Basie. Muhammad always had class.

IR: What about your dad? What did he like?

RA: He liked Billie Holiday, Diana Washington, Dakota Staton, Gloria Lynne, and Louis Armstrong. We had a great childhood. Our parents didn't beat us or hurt us. They fed us and clothed us, and gave us confidence to be good boys. My dad was the greatest provider. I never went a day hungry. He was a commercial artist. He painted signs around Louisville for black people and white people. At that time in the 1950s, you didn't see many black people and white people working together. The white people had him paint signs for them. He was the best sign painter in town.

IR: How has the old neighborhood changed?
RA: Well, it's changed a lot. It's mixed now. People have integrated with each other. It is better. Black folks are more advanced now. We lived in the west-end part of Louisville called Parkland. My father and mother bought a home on a very beautiful street with tall trees, green grass, and nice people. It was really great. In those days nobody broke in. There wasn't all of this killing and murder. You could go to sleep and nobody would try to break in.

IR: Why do you think it changed?
RA: It was because of Satan. Satan is trying to take everybody to hell with him.

IR: Which do you follow, Wallace or Farrakhan?
RA: They're all my brothers. Muhammad and I don't follow anybody. We're Muslims. We are Sunni and Orthodox.

IR: How did your father react to your joining the NOI?
RA: My father was upset because we were raised to be Christian all of our lives and we converted to Islamic faith and he did not have any knowledge of it. In those days, when people did not have knowledge of something, they condemned it. He didn't participate in politics. He was independent; self-made man, self-taught. He didn't work for white people. He was into commercial art. A great man.

[He asked about Tennessee. I told him that she was my daughter. He said that I must be like him and Ali—I must like my women pretty. He said that Tennessee is pretty and so her mother must be pretty.]

RA: All of my wives were two colors. My mother was beautiful. Pretty, long hair.

IR: What about Don King?

RA: Don King would kill his mother. He is that cold and that nasty.

IR: What about [boxing promoter] Bob Arum?

RA: Same thing. No good. Muhammad is a good man. He gives money to the people of the Islamic faith, and the Christian faith.

IR: What of Malcolm X and Elijah Muhammad?

RA: Malcolm X and Elijah Muhammad were great teachers.

IR: What did the two of you read as children?

RA: We read comic books like Batman, Superman, Woody Woodpecker. Mickey Mouse. We liked cowboy movies like "The Cisco Kid," "The Lone Ranger," ones with Roy Rogers and movies like that.

IR: Did your father take Muhammad to see Gorgeous George?

RA: I think my brother went to see Gorgeous George on his own. In those days, Muhammad would do things on his own. He loved Gorgeous George. He said Gorgeous George was a good entertainer and good wrestler. He saw George fill a whole arena. He said that talking draws crowds.

IR: What about [trainer] Fred Stoner?

RA: Fred Stoner was the greatest boxing trainer ever lived. He taught him more techniques than Joe Martin. More accurate punching. Joe Martin was a good man, but Stoner was a better trainer.

IR: What do you think of the Ali Center?

RA: The Center should have been done a long time ago. The city is showing my brother's greatness. It is a wonderful center. The opening gala was wonderful. Many celebrities came from Hollywood. [Former president] Clinton came and shook my hand. He's a great man.

IR: Were you there for the torch-lighting?

RA: No, I was not. I saw it on TV. I cried when I saw my brother with the Parkinson's lift the torch while his hands shook. What strength and integrity. A proud man.

IR: What about the fifty-million-dollar image buyout?

RA: I think that's wonderful. But they could have gotten more. Muhammad Ali is a great man. Whatever Lonnie decides to do is best for them. I wish them well. I love Lonnie. She's my blood. She's great.

The next morning, before heading back to Oakland, Tennessee and I had breakfast with Ed Hughes and his wife, Amanda.

Ed Hughes: I've been knowing Rahaman since he was a teenager. Quiet, a good boy. Both boys were so nice. Their mother was full of love and she taught them that. Odessa was a beautiful woman. Let me tell you something. Cash was a good dancer, handsome when he was young, talented, you know, he was talented.

You know what? Let me tell you something about Cash. We went to Germany and that place was packed. They asked Cash to sing. Cash got up to the stage and started singing "My Way." Cash could dance, sing, was handsome, he had an artistic ability, and he was nice looking when he was young. I would see them out together, dances and different things.

Ishmael Reed: He was such a good provider and a hard working person—qualities that many white screenwriters and novelists claim are absent among black men. Why do you think that Ali's father is the subject of such ridicule in books about the champion? (Jack Olsen's *Black Is Best*, portrays Cash as an ogre.)

EH: Caucasians somehow respect a black man's mother, but not the father.

IR: They love Odessa.

EH: Let me tell you a story. In the Philippines, Bobby Goodman, a fight promoter, was at the mic talking about what was going on with Muhammad. He introduces everyone but Cash. So I wrote on a piece of paper, "Mr. Goodman, do you realize that Muhammad's daddy is here with him?"

He opened the note; he knew it was [from] me. He read it and threw it down, but he introduced Cash after that. In Germany, he told the people at the stadium not to let me go through to the seats. I had on an NBC badge, which entitled me to go anywhere. He hadn't gotten over the fact that I made him introduce Cash in the Philippines. Before the fight, they interviewed me and they put that tape on before the fight. Larry Bryant told him, "That's Muhammad's barber, remember him?"

Goodman saw my NBC badge so he backed off. That tickled the devil out of me.

Another thing that happened in Germany was that Bundini got hurt. The stage collapsed. Ali got on Bundini one time in Texas. Bundini was ribbing me. He said, "Bundini, leave Hughes alone. You just mad 'cause you ain't as good lookin' as Hughes." That's what he told Bundini.

But, some of these things I'm telling you, is going to be in my book. Bundini, any place we went, he'd walk up to any fair-complexioned man and say, "Boy, what's your name, boy? Don't you know who you're talkin' to? Answer me, boy. What's your name? Do you know your daddy when you see him?" You know what he meant by that, don't you?

Bundini was the type of guy who, when somebody got the better of Muhammad in the ring, he'd shout, "Champ! Champ! He called your mother a whore, Champ!" Ali would go out there and beat the hell out of him.

Bundini's got a son. Have you met him? Drew Bundini Brown. He's a producer. Yeah. He was a flyer in the Navy. His mother was Italian.

IR: What about Veronica? [Veronica Porsche was Ali's third wife.]

EH: I liked Veronica. I liked Veronica. She was a nice person. Veronica was a good-looking woman at the time. But Muhammad had those children and he would try his best to be with the children.

IR: Did you go to Odessa's funeral?

EH: Did I go to Odessa's funeral? Was I dead? Was I sick? Of course, I was there. It was held at Saint Stephen Baptist Church because Rahaman's wife, Phoebe, said it was the biggest church. Odessa had stopped working in the church. She traveled with Ali. She had church at home. You can have church in your living room. So anyway, she was very beautiful. Cash went on "Good Morning America" on Father's Day and I went with him. We got off the plane and they picked us up in a limo.

IR: How did Ali relate to his fans?

EH: One time at O'Hare Airport, two very religious women were holding the Bible. They would say, "Excuse me, Mr. Muhammad, could we please have your autograph?" So they gave him something to write on and he signed autographs while he was still talking to people. They said, "Thank you, Mr. Muhammad." So when he and I got off to ourselves, I said, "Muhammad, those were some shitty autographs." I said, "You're lazy."

He said, "Whatcha talkin' about?"

I said, "When they said, 'Thank you, Mister Muhammad, for your autograph,' you should have said, 'Thank you for asking me.'"

So the next time someone thanked him for his autograph, he looked at me and then looked back at them and said, "Thank you for asking me."

IR: What about the ninety-year-old aunt who wasn't invited to the opening of the Ali Center?

EH: That was so evil. That's his aunty, Cash's sister. Another thing— his first cousin, Jimmy, and he were very close. When Jimmy died, I called up to Michigan and I said to Kim, "Jimmy, Muhammad's first cousin passed and his body is at Williams' Funeral Home in Louisville, Kentucky, on Broadway." There's not but one Williams' Funeral Home. They didn't send no flowers. Later on Lonnie said, "Well you didn't leave us no address."

CHAPTER 44

July 2006

In 2006, we were back in New York, this time on the eastside at the Eastgate Towers. I'd lined up interviews with filmmaker and novelist Melvin Van Peebles, Ray Robinson, Jr., and got a surprise interview with musician/composer Fred Ho, a Chinese American who was once a member of the Nation of Islam.

While Ali was expressing his defiance with rhyme, the Panthers by monitoring the police, the NOI by challenging the integrationist techniques of Martin Luther King, Jr., and the SNCC by challenging the Jim Crow South, Sam Greenlee and Melvin Van Peebles were using film to protest the oppression of black Americans. *Sweet Sweetback's Baadasssss Song* defied the stereotypes of African Americans that had held since the early days of Hollywood. Their efforts recalled those of independent black filmmakers of the 1930s and 40s.

The streets to Van Peebles' house were blocked because a man had blown up a three-storey residence so that his wife wouldn't get a sum of money. I remember walking through Greenwich Village in 1970 and hearing an explosion. Members of the Weather Underground had blown up a building.

Melvin Van Peebles is a slight, dapper man who tries to remain contemporary and succeeds. When I returned from this trip, I saw him posing with some hip hoppers in a magazine.

Ishmael Reed: [I asked him his reaction to Ali's ring successes and his defiance of the draft.]

Melvin Van Peebles: I was living in France beginning in 1960. In Europe, news from the United States would be filtered by the time it reached you and so you had to read between the lines. I heard about Clay and Liston when Clay won the title. I was a reporter for the French newspaper *L'Observateur* [ancestor of *Le Nouvel Observateur*]. I wrote an article about his conversion to the NOI about three days after he'd won and wrote that he had to watch out because they were going to take his title, the way they did Jack Johnson.

IR: [When Muhammad Ali saw James Earl Jones in "The Great White Hope," he told the actor that "Johnson's was his story." I told Van Peebles about my introduction to his film to a French audience at Aix-en-Provence, that the hero in his film was based upon the fugitive slave narrative.]

MVP: I wanted to free us from stereotypes. While we fear dogs, he killed the dogs, etc.

IR: Were you influenced by the political climate of the time? I notice that the Black Panthers supported your film.

MVP: I didn't refer to the Panthers, even though I was highly sympathetic to them. There were those who were considered trouble-makers before the Panthers. A defiant man named Joe Jefferson was killed in Chicago; he was an early Panther. In 1953, I was chased by a mob because I was an officer and a white man saluted me.

IR: What was the reaction to Islam and Ali in Paris?

MVP: I didn't hear much about it until there was a march on the American Embassy to show solidarity with the March on Washington. I was not part of the expatriate community. I didn't want to be there as an American runaway. I lived as a French man, learned French, wrote novels in French and hung with French people. I conducted interviews. When I met [writer] Chester Himes, I didn't know who he was. He was writing detective stories. I knocked on the door and Himes came to the door and I asked him in French for Himes, and Himes said, "Go away, I'm expecting a reporter." [Laughter]

IR: You interviewed Malcolm X?

MVP: It was Malcolm's last interview. They didn't publish it because of Interpol, the CIA, and the French. I asked him what he thought was the most important event of that year. Malcolm said, "The Chinese getting the bomb."

I met with Ray Robinson, Jr. at Starbuck's on 41st Street and 2nd Avenue. He said that the incident in the bathroom where Muhammad Ali attacked his first wife, Sonji, did happen.

Ray Robinson, Jr.: Dad didn't like that type of incident to be going on with a major fighter, even though he used to beat on my mom. My mom had five miscarriages from ass-kicking. So the souls of those five kids are probably present in my kids.

Ishmael Reed: Sugar Ray said that boxing was a barbaric sport and that he didn't like it.

RR: The sport is a violent sport, but Dad enjoyed the game of boxing, but not the business. It was a crude, rough, and racist operation, especially in those days.

IR: What happened between Ali and your father when Ali became a Muslim?

RR: He didn't understand why Ali had to become a Muslim. Dad was steeped in God, Mother, and America.

IR: Why do they love Ali now?

RR: He's the lion that was tamed; his physical condition has led to his being peaceful, from a violent field nigger to a passive house nigger.

On Wednesday, I went to Harlem for a party given by Terry McMillan and Margaret Troupe. They were celebrating the publication of a book about textiles. There I encountered Fred Ho, Chinese-American jazz musician and composer. He said that he became familiar with Ali through television. His father, Franklin Houn, was Professor of Chinese and Political Science at the University of Massachusetts.

Fred Ho: Like people of color and oppressed nationalities, I identified with Ali because he stood up to the establishment. When Ali defeated Liston, I saw it as part of a larger social struggle and symbol of a new era, a dawn of the defiance of spirit of not being sycophantic to the status quo. The establishment was backing Liston.

I was recruited as the first non-black member of the Massachusetts NOI. There was a Filipino guy on the West Coast when I became Fred 3 X. I asked, "Why do I need an X instead of my last name, which is not a slave name?" They insisted that I had to have an X in order to be in the Nation.

"But I'm an Asiatic black man," I persisted. They accepted me.

I went to drill classes, sold *Muhammad Speaks*, but became disappointed when they were no longer anti-imperialist. This happened after Malcolm was killed. Muhammad Ali symbolized that major shift. With his outspokenness and eloquence, he captured for all of us the spirit of integrity and defiance, and when he refused to join the draft, all of us shouted hooray.

My father had to swallow the bitterness of racism. He was the most published member of his department and he was the least paid, and his grad students made fun of him because he spoke with an accent. He would take this anger home, but didn't want to speak out at his job, because he was fearful. He didn't want me to join the Nation, but he understood and he rooted for Ali and those who stood up against the establishment.

Ali defied the stereotype of the passive, obsequious black. He spurned Malcolm, because he was under the autocratic rule of the Nation of Islam. He was probably scared of the Nation. The Fruit of Islam were people who might have assassinated Malcolm.

They had a paramilitary component. I had a little fear when I left the Nation. They sent their person to the dorm to question me about why I wasn't coming to classes anymore. It wasn't a physical threat, but there was an ownership quality in the voice of the person who questioned me. I quit in the fall of '75.

IR: What of his cozying up to dictators like Marcos and Mobutu?
FH: He's complicated. Sometimes he doesn't know what he's doing. They love him now, because he's never been a radical and never been dangerous to them. At the time of the war, he was dangerous because he represented the country's own seams coming apart. Now, he's been sanitized like so many other people. The system will appropriate iconic figures and recontextualize them to serve its own interests. He will always be remembered as the people's champ, however.

Though he was extravagant in his lifestyle, he was always accessible and reveled in being in the company of the average person. He was not someone who was shut off or closed off or elitist, and during a period of social change and upheaval, he took stands that meant a loss for himself financially. A person's legacy [might be] subject to the predation of capitalism like everything else.

Fred Ho was wearing a two-piece outfit that had a quilt-like pattern. He'd designed it himself. I asked him how he would describe it. He said it was "an Asian-African motif. It's called a Mau Mao design."

Clipping from Jet Magazine, June 28, 1973

CHAPTER 45

Bad Company

On the way back to Lincolnshire, Illinois, where the MacArthur Fellows were in conference, my thoughts were about Major B. Coxson. I first heard of him from Reggie Barrett when I interviewed him in Louisville. Neither the authorized biography of Ali written by Thomas Hauser nor David Remnick's *King of the World* mention Coxson, nor is there mention of Coxson in the book meant to interrupt Ali's on-going victory lap, *Sucker Punch*, by Jack Cashill.

Other books make no mention of Ali's connection to the notorious Black Mafia of Philadelphia and its alliance with criminal elements within the Nation of Islam's Temple Number 12, called by some locals, "The Hoodlum Mosque," or "The Hit Mosque." While the champion's supporters, like Gene Kilroy, view Ali as the advocate for the "the poor, powerless, depressed, and deprived," his fronting for the nefarious activities of these organizations of narcotics peddlers, with connections to Italian-American criminals and murderers, tells a different story.

When I returned home, I called Agieb Bilal. He had mentioned Ali's fronting for some mobsters during the time when he and his family lived in Cherry Hill, New Jersey. From the Middle East, Bilal returned my call. He referred me to Sean Patrick Griffin, a former Philadelphia police officer who is a professor at Clemson University. Griffin is the author of *Philadelphia's Black Mafia* and *Black Brothers Inc.*, subtitled *The Rise and Fall of Philadelphia's Black Mafia*, books that disproved the myth that blacks were incapable of constructing a sophisticated crime organization.

Mafe (which is Coxson's nickname) was described by a black magazine, *Philly Talk*, as a "Hershey bar dipped in a vat of cyanide." He lived in luxurious home and owned a fleet of cars: "Rolls Royces, Lincoln Continentals, Jaguars, a Mercedes 350 and a Maserati."

Always one with a knack for slick public relations, after the Feds seized his Mark IV and his Cadillac Limo, for back taxes, a photo of him and his chauffeur appeared in *Jet* magazine. They were riding a tandem bicycle; the chauffeur was wearing a chauffeur's cap. Described by the Feds as a member of Philadelphia's Black Mafia, with access to an "extensive narcotics network," Coxson held forth at his bar called The Rolls Royce Supper Club, whose interior reflected his kitschy tastes. Griffin described the club, from its "fancy velvety walls with fleur-de-lis designs (gold and black at the bar, red and black in the dining area), the black chairs rimmed in bright red velvet, and the large chandelier inside, to the big neon and aluminum sign, white-trimmed blue canopy scripted with the letters RR, and carpeted sidewalk outdoors" (Griffin, 2005).

Muhammad Ali, his friend, was a frequent visitor and was present on opening night. As a result of a drug deal gone wrong, Coxson was executed by some of the Black Mafia's personnel. On June 12, 1973, *The Baltimore Afro-American* described the murders:

> Coxson, 43, who recently ran unsuccessfully for Mayor of Camden, N.J., was bound and gagged and then shot in the head while kneeling on the floor in his bedroom in this community across the Delaware River from Philadelphia.
>
> The other three victims, Lois Luby, 36, her daughter Lita, 14, and son, Toro, 15, were also bound and shot in the head. They were hospitalized in serious condition.
>
> Mrs. Luby's third child, Lex, 13, was tied up with neckties but managed to slip through a first-floor door and hop to the home of a neighbor who notified authorities about 4:30 a.m.
>
> Ali, reached at a training camp Friday at Deer Lake, Pa., was described as being "shocked and very reserved, very reflective."

He was quoted as saying, "I have clean hands. I am a Muslim. I believe in Allah, and Allah will always take care of me because I have always done the right thing."

Ali was a neighbor of Coxson and had put his $36,000 Silver Rolls Royce at his friend's disposal. He also campaigned for him in last month's election.

Mrs. Luby rallied after surgery to remove a bullet from her head. Surgeons at Cherry Hill Medical Center fear she may lose her sight because of damage done by the bullet.

Lita was in critical condition after surgery to remove a bullet from her head and her sight was also questionable.

Toro did not require surgery and was in fair condition.

One hospital spokesman said the assailants "knew where to shoot."

After the execution of Coxson and the maiming of his wife and children, Ali, who endorsed Coxson's campaign for Mayor of Camden, New Jersey, after his second fight against Jerry Quarry, June 27, 1972, and who constantly palled around with the gangster and was with him hours before his gangland-styled execution, claimed that he didn't know Coxson all that well. Yet Griffin writes:

Muhammad Ali's presence in Philadelphia was significant because it lent credibility to the Black Muslims and, by extension, the Black Mafia, as the two were becoming increasingly interlinked. His mere presence and his alliance with persons embedded in the Black Mafia social system also created public relations difficulties for the authorities, and fed the concern of victims and witnesses that law enforcement would not take their complaints seriously.

Moreover, Griffin quotes one observer as saying that, "To Ali, Major's a God. He can do no wrong" (Griffin, 2005).

In Griffin's account, Sam Christian, a man with an extensive police record and who was described as a two-hundred-fifteen-pound bully, founded The Black Mafia in September 1968. Their early activities included "holding up crap games and extorting drug dealers, numbers men, as well as illegitimate businessmen," people who obviously wouldn't report these crimes to the police (Griffin, 2005).

"At some point", Griffin continues, "the Philadelphia Black Mafia began competing with criminals within the Black Muslim community over the narcotics trade. Overwhelmed by the strength of the Muslims, the Black Mafia merged with this criminal element, becoming the Black Muslim's "extortion arm." Griffin is careful to say, "The 'Black Mafia' did not represent the totality of African-American organized crime in Philadelphia" and did not "represent all Philadelphia Black Muslims or all Muslims who were African-American" (Griffin, 2005).

Griffin adds:

> The Black Muslims had much to gain, as they would now receive portions of the Black Mafia's narcotics and extortion rackets, while maintaining the profits from their own illicit activities. One of the other benefits of the merger was the ability of the Black Muslims to hide "wanted" criminals throughout their national chain of mosques.

When Wallace D. Muhammad succeeded his father, Muhammad Ali followed him and became, like Wallace, a Sunni Muslim. The Sunni and Shia division was based upon what is probably history's most famous family feud: an argument between Muhammad's daughter, Fatima, and his last wife, Aisha, over who would succeed the prophet. The friction began in the year 632 upon Muhammad's death. Muhammad's son-in-law, Abi Talib, who was married to his daughter, Fatima (who didn't get along with his last wife, Aisha), was favored by Fatima as her father's successor. Her wish was overridden when Aisha's father, Abu Bakr, was appointed to be Muhammad's successor. Ali, however became the fourth caliph in the year 656. Shia and Sunni were living among each other and intermarrying before the invasion of Iraq. Murtaza Hussain writes:

> Indeed, the simple truth is that if such a war existed Sunnis and Shias would not have been intermarrying and living in the same neighbourhoods up to the 21st century. Furthermore, were they truly enemies, millions of people of both sects would have stopped peacefully converging on the annual Hajj pilgrimage many centuries ago. If Islam is to continue as a constructive social phenomenon it is important that these

traditional relationships and ways of life are not destroyed by modern ideologies masquerading as historical truths. ("The myth of the 1400 year Sunni-Shia war" *Al Jazeera*, July 9, 2013).

I asked Dr. Sam Hamod, an Islamic scholar, to tell me the difference between Hanafi and Sunni. He wrote:

Hanafi is a school of jurisprudence in Islam; it is also primarily Sunni (which means the orthodox, those who followed Abu Bakr after the death of the prophet Muhammad; as against the Shi'a who felt Ali should have succeeded Muhammad—but that real split occurred when the Mu'aweeya family ambushed the grandson of Ali, Husayn or Hussein, who was the grandson of the prophet's daughter, Ali's wife, when Hussein came for a truce meeting and was unarmed—he and his entire family were wiped out).

Thus, Hanafi is a school of law and very tolerant in Islam, and not as judgmental as some of the other schools of Islamic jurisprudence. Thus, some of the Hanafi judges have said that even blasphemy is not for them to decide, but should be left in God's hands for punishment.

The Sunni are the majority of Muslims in the world followed by the Shi'a (and in that group are the orthodox Shi'a and also such offspring groups as the Alawhite, i.e. Basher al Assad of Syria, and other groups like the Sufis, and even the Druze came from the Shi'a, as well as most of the literature of Islam and art in Persia etc.).

As a result of a feud between Philadelphia's Black Muslims and the Hanafi Muslims (Orthodox), the Black Mafia committed one of its most horrible crimes. On January 12, 1973, two carloads of Black Mafia members traveled to Washington, D.C., to kill Hamaas Abdul Khaalis, leader of the thousand-member Washington sect. Khaalis had offended the Black Muslims when, on January 5, 1973, he sent a letter to Black Muslim ministers denouncing Elijah Muhammad as a "false prophet" and "a lying deceiver."

Basketball star Kareem Abdul Jabbar, a Hanafi, had contributed seventy-eight thousand dollars to the purchase of the sect's home at 7700 16th Street NW in an "upper-class, largely African American, neighborhood called the Gold Coast" (Sean Patrick Griffin, *Philadelphia's Black Mafia: A Social and Political History*, 2003).

Details of the slaughter were described when two of those serving time for the murders had their appellant hearing conducted between February 21, 1978, and September 28, 1978, at the District of Columbia Court of Appeals:

On August 15, 1973, seven individuals were each indicted by a grand jury on twenty-three counts of murder, assault, robbery, burglary, and conspiracy to commit the substantive offenses. The charges arose out of events culminating in the deaths of seven persons at 7700 16th Street, N.W., on January 18, 1973. The ghastly crimes committed there came to be known collectively as the "Hanafi" case because all *8 of the victims were Orthodox Hanafi Muslims. Five of the seven defendants were jointly tried.

After a lengthy and rather complex trialthe jury found appellants William Christian, John Clark and Theodore Moody each guilty of seven counts of first-degree premeditated murder, seven counts of first-degree felony murder, two counts of assault with intent to kill while armed, one count of armed robbery, three counts of attempted robbery while armed, one count of first-degree burglary while armed and one count of conspiracy.Motions for a new trial were filed on behalf of appellants and denied. They were sentenced to life imprisonment on each of the premeditated murder counts, those sentences to run consecutively to one another, but concurrently with all other sentences; to life imprisonment on each of the felony murder counts, those sentences to run consecutively to each other, but concurrently with all other sentences; to life imprisonment on each of the remaining substantive counts; and to one to five years' imprisonment on the conspiracy count. (…)

On January 18, 1973, approximately eight armed men entered a house at 7700 16th Street, N.W., and proceeded to rob, shoot, or drown every person present. Seven persons, including five children, were brutally murdered; two others were seriously wounded.[6] The home was the residence of Calipha Hamaas Abdul Khaalis and the headquarters of the Orthodox Hanafi Muslims. The government's theory at trial was that the murders were the culmination of a conspiracy by members of the "Nation of Islam," the so-called "Black Muslims," to seek revenge against Hamaas Khaalis for his criticism of Elijah Muhammad, then leader of the Nation of Islam. Khaalis had voiced his disapproval of

Elijah Muhammad in two letters sent to Nation of Islam mosques throughout the United States. In support of this theory, the government produced Amina Khaalis, the only competent surviving victim of the massacre and daughter of Hamaas Khaalis. She testified at trial that during the melee, one of the intruders had questioned her as to why her father had written "those letters." Before being taken to the hospital on the day of the murders, she was able to tell police her assailants were some of "Elijah's people."

In the wake of the murders, several leads soon developed which prompted investigators to turn toward the city of Philadelphia in their search for the killers. Several pieces of evidence were abandoned by the intruders as they made their getaway: a large blue suitcase containing two sawed-off shotguns, ammunition, a copy of the Philadelphia Daily News (not sold in Washington during January 1973), credit cards belonging to a William Horton of Philadelphia, and a brown paper bag from which a fingerprint of Clark's was later identified. Also discarded were three pistols, one of which was registered to a Eugene White of Philadelphia, who had previously reported it stolen in an armed robbery. Moody was subsequently identified as one of the perpetrators of that robbery. An eyewitness saw the getaway cars and recalled their Pennsylvania license plates. Found later on the escape path was a piece of paper on which was written "Brother Lieutenant John 38X." The name is of the type received by one who has joined the Nation of Islam and was, in fact, used by Clark. Clark and Christian were identified as being associated with the Philadelphia mosque.

Records of Clark's home telephone number revealed that on January 17 and 18, 1973, several calls were made between his Philadelphia home and the Downtown Motel in Washington, D.C. The motel's records disclosed that a man purporting to be William Horton had registered a party of six on January 17, 1973. Two handwriting experts positively identified Clark as the person who had forged Horton's signature. A call from the motel also was made to Christian's home in Philadelphia. One of the motel's employees identified Christian *10 from a photograph and again in court as one of the persons she had seen at the motel on January 18, 1973.

Other evidence showed that Moody had purchased a used Chrysler in Philadelphia on January 16, 1973. Gasoline for this car was purchased at Exxon stations in Philadelphia, Washington, D.C., and between the two cities over the next few days. Used to buy the gasoline was a stolen credit card issued in the name of Lorrene Goode. A handwriting expert testified it was "probable" that Clark was the forger of Goode's signature. Further evidence indicated that Christian had used the Goode credit card in the Philadelphia area in January and February 1973. (Justia.com)

In the spring of 1973, the grand jury investigating the Hanafi case issued subpoenas for appellants to appear in a lineup. Moody and Clark were incarcerated in Philadelphia on unrelated charges and were transferred to the District pursuant to writs of *habeas corpus*. When Christian was served with the subpoena, he chose to ignore it by fleeing to Florida where he (along with codefendant Griffin) was apprehended in October 1973. At the lineup, Amina Khaalis identified Moody as one of the men she had seen in the house on the day of the murders. Two eyewitnesses identified Moody as one of the individuals seen fleeing from the scene. Clark was not identified at the lineup proceedings. At trial, Amina Khaalis made in-court identifications of both Moody and Clark. Two other witnesses identified Moody at the trial.[1]

Since Jeremiah Shabazz was the leader of the hit mosque, street knowledge, according to Griffin, pointed to Shabazz as having ordered the hit. However, Griffin found no evidence for this accusation and Shabazz denied involvement.

---

1. Christian v. United States **394 A.2d 1 (1978)** William CHRISTIAN, Appellant, v. UNITED STATES, Appellee. Theodore MOODY, Appellant, v. UNITED STATES, Appellee. John W. CLARK, Appellant, v. UNITED STATES, Appellee.Nos. 8809-8811 and 11042.

CHAPTER 46

Coxson, A Very Charming Rogue

In the most popular books about the champion, Jeremiah is cited only as someone who provides information about Ali's boxing career. Jeremiah Shabazz is the man who persuaded Muhammad Ali to settle a suit against Don King for $50,000 instead of the $1,750,000 to which he was entitled. According to Jack Newfield, "King always operated on the premise that any fighter would be more impressed with $10,000 in cash in his hands than with a bank check for $1 million." Newfield continues that Shabazz was given a suitcase containing $50,000. King told him not to give it to Ali until he signed a contract. Shabazz, accompanied by a notary public, visited Ali at the UCLA Medical Center, where he was being treated for his "failing health." Newfield concluded, "Ali had taken the beating of his life [from Larry Holmes] to earn this money. Now he had taken $50,000 from a friend and given up the right to collect $1.1 million." Newfield said that when "Ali told Michael Phenner, his lawyer in his suit against King, he had signed a release ending the lawsuit without telling him, the tough corporate litigator sat in his office and cried" (Newfield, 1995). Lonnie Ali's defenders would say that someone had to intervene before Ali was abused by people who weren't concerned about his health as much as how much money he could earn for them.

During the week beginning February 12, 2007, I talked to Kitty Caparella of *The Philadelphia Daily News*. She'd covered the Black Mafia in Philadelphia. I asked her about Ali's claim that, after Coxson's assassination, he didn't know Coxson all that well.

Kitty Caparella: The Black Mafia and the Black Muslims of Temple #12 were the same thing, which was under Jeremiah Shabazz. And the murderers of the Hanafi Muslims also came out of that Temple. Sean Patrick Griffin got Shabazz's FBI files under the Freedom of Information Act. Jeremiah was always covering up the Temple's criminal activities that were going on behind the scenes. When W. Deen took over he steered the religion away from black separatism, but some of the separatists continued under Shamsud-din Ali, Shabazz's succesor. The Philadelphia Mosque was one that had many criminals in positions of power. They split with Wallace and Shabazz's successor, Shamsud-din Ali, was convicted of racketeering, and the believers in that mosque have ended up taking him to court and they ended up taking back the mosque and now it's called Philadelphia Masjid.

Ishmael Reed: Why did Ali accept Shabazz into his entourage in 1976 after he'd been expelled from the Temple by Wallace and in view of his criminal past? Do you think that Ali was so naïve as to not understand what was going on with Shabazz?

KC: In that world there was this combination of con men and others and they appealed to Ali's blackness to embrace Islam through the NOI—there wasn't anybody telling him something else. When you have this group around you, who were only there to get the money—I don't know whether he was that naïve or not.

IR: What of Griffin's comment that law enforcement was reluctant to go after these criminals because they were using Ali as a front?

KC: I can't say because I wasn't talking to the government, but it's not outside the realm of possibility. But my experience in covering the Feds and local law enforcement was that if they saw there was criminal activity, they'd go after it. They finally figured out what Coxson was doing, but that was after his assassination. But when he was running for Mayor of Camden everybody took it as a sort of funny kind of thing. Coxson was a very charming rogue.

Sean Griffin returned my call on February 24, 2007. I wanted more information about Ali's connection to Major Coxson, called "The King of Heroin" on the East Coast, and Jeremiah Shabazz, leader of the notorious Temple #12 in Philadelphia.

Griffin said that Ali and Coxson were such close neighbors they could walk between their homes. Jeremiah Shabazz, who headed Temple #12, surrounded himself with hardcore criminals. Jeremiah knew who these guys were and what they were doing, he said.

Sean Griffin: The enforcement arm of the Temple, the Black Mafia, only numbered in the dozens, though the FBI had their numbers in the hundreds. For them, any African American who was associated with the members of the Black Mafia was considered part of the group. Jeremiah Shabazz was much feared. So feared was he and his followers that you could park a brand new car in Philadelphia's roughest neighborhood, roll down the windows, unlock and you could leave it as long as you had a copy of *Muhammad Speaks* on [the] dashboard. Ishmael Reed: [I asked whether there was proof that Shabazz was linked to heroin trafficking.]

SG: I don't own a single document that shows Shabazz as a drug dealer, but the FBI released a document in the 1980s which claims that he was a drug dealer and a heroin trafficker in the 1970s.

IR: Why didn't the FBI inform Philadelphia law enforcement about Shabazz's activities?

SG: The relationship between former Mayor Frank Rizzo and the Feds was strained because the Feds was on him about Civil Rights violations. I have been told that Shabazz had the ear of most white politicians in Philadelphia. Other criminals associated with the Temple got arrested but Shabazz always got off scot free.

(The night before Griffin called, Agieb Bilal called me from the Middle East. I asked him about Temple #12. He said that after W. Deen Muhammad succeeded his father, he sought to cleanse the Nation of its criminal elements. As a result he was the target of several assassination attempts by criminal elements that had infiltrated the Nation. Wallace was able to move Shabazz out of Philadelphia, but, as Griffin told me, there's always been an element remaining there.)

SG: All the hardcore Fruit of Islam guys never went away. They're still in the news. They have done their time in prison and are back on the streets presenting themselves as mainstream Muslims. I had a book event [in] downtown Philadelphia attended by about two hundred people. In the crowd, Nation of Islam and reformers were each using my book against each other. Reformers were using my book, telling the NOI people, see we told you, you guys were no good.

IR: [I also asked Griffin about his assertion that the criminals were using Muhammad Ali as a front for their illegal activities.]
SG: The criminals were socializing with Ali and Cecil Moore. [Ex-Marine, Councilman, president of the Philadelphia NAACP, who led the move to integrate Girard College.] This made it tough for the public, the media and law enforcement to say that these were hardcore criminals. Shamsud din-Ali, who succeeded Shabazz, was convicted of racketeering, but it's been hard to mobilize opinion against him because he presents himself as a peace-loving Muslim. I look at what happened to Ali like Sinatra's relationship to gangsters in Las Vegas. Frank knew whom he was hanging out with. He knew exactly who they were.

IR: Do you think that Ali knew what his criminal associates were up to?
SG: Absolutely. When he said that he didn't know Coxson, that was just a PR version of avoiding the reality that he was very close to him. The question you're asking should have been asked in 1973. If you're immersed in the Major's social network, what did you know? That's the reason that Ali received law enforcement protection, because if Ali knew what Coxson knew, Ali could be next.

IR: You say in your book that James "Bubbles" Price identified Shabazz as the person who ordered the hit on the D.C. Hanafi Muslims.
SG: The only document that includes this testimony is still under seal; I couldn't get the court to unseal the file. But this is what is said in the streets. That Shabazz ordered the murders. A London company is preparing a documentary about Ali. While they have a sanitized view of Ali as a Civil Rights activist and humanitarian, they're trying to be balanced. They came upon my book and wanted to know what he had to do with these criminals. Their questions were naïve—like did he really know he was associating with criminals? Hanafi leader, Hamaas Abdul Khaalis accused Muhammad Ali of sharing the blame for the killings because Ali was a Black Muslim and helped finance the Nation of Islam.

When asked whether members of Mosque # 12 had anything to do with the Hanafi murders, Shabazz denied it. Muhammad Ali also denied that the NOI was involved.

◆

At the end of January, I had called Ed Hughes and asked him about Ali's relationship with Coxson. Hughes said that Ali didn't know what was going on. You hear Ali defenders say the same thing about Ali's relationship with other crooks, relationships from which the champion benefited. They contend that Ali was unaware of what they were up to. No wonder Ali expressed a fondness for Ronald Reagan. One could say that both were Teflon coated.

Ali would find it difficult however, to distance himself from Jeremiah Shabazz, formerly Jeremiah Pugh. Suleiman Bey was Shabazz's enforcer. According to Griffin, Sam Christian changed his name to Suleiman Bey, and was immediately made captain of Philadelphia Mosque #12's Fruit of Islam (FOI), the mosque's paramilitary unit. Griffin said:

Bey was responsible for sanctioning murders and other criminal acts
and reported directly to Jeremiah Shabazz. Shabazz's 'right hand man',

according to Griffin was Lieutenant Gerald X, described as 'ruthless,' and 'a murderer'. One witness, James Price, said that the hit on the Hanafi was ordered by Shabazz. When Wallace Muhammad succeeded his father, part of his effort to cleanse the Nation of its hoodlum elements was to oust Jeremiah Shabazz.

How did Ali react to the ouster of Jeremiah Shabazz, who was connected to narcotics trafficking and possible murders? In 1976, he was accepted into Ali's entourage. If there's anything that might stain Ali's legacy, indelibly, it would be his still murky relationship with Philadelphia's Black Mafia. If it could be gleaned from these relationships that he knew about his friend Major Coxson's having the reputation as the "King" of the East Coast heroin trade, heroin and crack—which agencies of the government knew their anti-communist allies were peddling—debilitating the inner cities of the country, all of his victories in the ring, his philanthropy and goodwill would be overshadowed. If there is any truth that his associate, Jeremiah Shabazz, ordered the hit on the Hanafi Muslims in Washington, D.C. and Ali knew about it, Ali's entire glorious career would be disgraced.

CHAPTER 47

Ali and the largest embezzlement scheme in Wells Fargo history

Muhammad Ali's link to shady criminal operations didn't end with the assassination of his benefactor, Major Coxson. He benefited from a scheme organized by Harold Smith and Ben Lewis, who worked for Wells Fargo bank.

> Ben Lewis, who was the prosecution's key witness, testified that at Mr. Smith's direction he had manipulated an accounting system that monitored the flow of funds between Wells Fargo branches. He said the money was used to establish a monopoly on championship fight promotions in the United States. (*New York Times*, June 2, 1982)

Smith's defense argued differently. The defense argued that the Wells Fargo employee Ben Lewis was the mastermind. "There is a difference between actually managing and manipulating a criminal enterprise. Harold Smith knew nothing about the internal operations of the bank," as Howard Moore, Jr., Harold Smith's lawyer, argued.

Over lunch, Moore told me how he'd come to represent Smith.

Howard Moore: I represented Harold Smith's wife, in 1981. She was indicted for check laundering in Mobile, Alabama. The judge who had jurisdiction over the case was the same judge before whom I'd tried my last case before coming out to represent Angela Davis [Moore was Davis' attorney and successfully gained her acquittal from murder charges]. She'd passed 1.5 million dollars in bad checks. Her family was relatively well off and so they asked me to represent Harold.

Harold made a fool of himself before the grand jury and the grand jury had fifteen hundred pages of grand jury transcripts and thirty witnesses. He was accused of embezzlement and transporting stolen property across state lines, and at one point he had a one million dollar contract with Larry Holmes. He showed Larry all of this money in a suitcase. Larry broke out in a sweat, went to all of the windows and closed the blinds.

He said that Don King told him never to take cash, and after an hour or so they heard a knock at the door and it was Don King. Don King ran Harold off by gunpoint. Now in my opinion there are two honest men in the United States: Willie Brown (former mayor of San Francisco) and Don King. He got tried and sued every year. Willie Brown was investigated by the U.S. for fourteen years and was never charged with anything. Harold wanted to act as Holmes' promoter and Ali was in retirement. Harold and Ali were close. He'd organized Muhammad Ali Amateur Sports, and in many ways Harold helped the sport: the big purses, fighters receiving training regimen, nutrition, and conditioning. In the amateur and professional sports, they were winning everything. The scheme that got him busted was one in which he wanted to stage four championship fights. He was going to take the ticket sales and pay back the line of credit that had been extended to him by an insider at Wells Fargo. It was his friend who was an officer of the bank. He gave him a cashier's check for the amount needed to stage the fights. Wells Fargo instituted new procedures after this happened. [Considering the fact that Wells Fargo bank has shown discrimination against black borrowers, steering toxic loans into black and Hispanic neighborhoods, and has been fined for this attitude, would a white borrower have been granted a loan for Harold Smith's idea?]

Sometimes we'd go down to Ali's house in Los Angeles at 5 a.m. I felt sorry for the champ. People would call from all over the country. "Champ, send me some money," or "Champ, they're about to evict me, Champ." "Champ, I'm starving. Send me some money."

This would not be the last time that Ali and Moore's paths would cross. In November 1979, Harold Smith approached heavyweight champion Larry Holmes in his suite, while Don King was present. Smith, who had been a four-minute-ten-second miler at American University in Washington, D.C., was new as a boxing promoter. According to Holmes, Don King told Smith to "take his black ass and be on his way."

Holmes continued: "I was busy inside the suite and could hear, but couldn't see them arguing back and forth, in the language of the streets. It got loud and nasty and eventually Smith left" (Larry Holmes with Phil Berger, 1998).

Smith later told Holmes that he left the suite because King had waved a gun at him. Smith gained the reputation among boxers as a soft spoken, intrepid promoter who paid boxers handsome fees, sometimes in cash stuffed in pillowcases and shoeboxes.

Muhammad Ali, who gained a reputation for lending his name to dubious enterprises, permitted Smith to use his name for Smith's organization, Muhammad Ali Professional Sports (MAPS). In exchange, Smith paid Ali a percentage of the net profits of MAPS-sponsored events. MAPS promoted the 1979 Ken Norton-Scott Le Doux fight.

In March of 1980 Smith offered Holmes 1.3 million dollars to fight Scott LeDoux, with two hundred thousand dollars in cash to be paid up front. He offered Holmes two checks from Wells Fargo bank, and a million dollars in cash. Holmes refused to sign the contract, because he was suspicious of the origin of the cash. (Smith's rival, King, warned Holmes that it might have been drug money.) Smith had gotten the money through a scam that he and a Wells Fargo bank insider had concocted. By the time that the government caught up with him, he had spent 21.3 million dollars, in what The Times described as one of the nation's largest bank embezzlement schemes. Convicted of twenty-nine counts of fraud and embezzlement, he was sentenced to ten years in prison and fined thirty thousand dollars and ordered to perform three thousand hours of community service. According to The New York Times (June 2, 1982): "Mr. Smith was sentenced after delivering an emotional plea to the judge, requesting a short sentence: 'I've got a beautiful wife and a beautiful son,' he said. 'Please don't take them away from me. I'm a good person.'"

Working for Smith on the inside was Sammie Marshall, a former Wells Fargo employee and a friend of Mr. Smith. He was sentenced to three years in prison.

Throughout the court proceedings, he has maintained that he is innocent, saying that the money was extended to him through a valid line of credit. The bank denied the existence of a credit line (*The New York Times*, June 2, 1982).

CHAPTER 48

I wanted to get the views about Ali from two writers whose groups are not usually represented in books about the champion. Wajahat Ali is a Pakistani-American playwright whose play, *The Domestic Crusaders*, about a Pakistani-American family, was performed before sold-out audiences in Berkeley and San Jose, California. I also wanted to hear from novelist, playwright, and essayist Frank Chin, one of the founders of the Asian-American Renaissance in literature. My family and I met them at the Café Dejéna, an Eritrean restaurant that is about three or four blocks from my house and a place where I conduct business. I've taught Chin's novel, *Donald Duk*, about a young Chinese-American kid who thinks that he is Fred Astaire. Chin uses American popular culture, Chinese folk tales and opera to weave a tale about a Chinese-American kid who is uncomfortable with his culture. In the August 2004 issue of *Playboy*, I cited this book in an article about unions. Very few historians are aware of Chinese Americans' contribution to the building of the railroads in the West. I specifically mentioned a strike conducted by the Chinese in the 1800s.

Frank had suffered a stroke while in residency as a visiting writer at Boulder, Colorado, and the left side of his body is weaker than the right. The esteemed writer Victor Hernández Cruz also suffered a slight stroke when, like Frank, he was in residency at Naropa Institute, an accredited school of poetry located in Boulder, Colorado.

When I was a guest there, I experienced extreme headaches. We joked that some whites had finally discovered a place where, were we to visit, we'd get sick. But all kidding aside, Naropa has perhaps the most diverse list of visiting faculty that I'm aware of. All one has to do is examine *Poets and Writers* magazine to find that the NYPD is more integrated than the conference and residency scene of poets, novelists, and creative non-fiction writers.

Despite this medical setback, Frank has recovered his swift sharp intellect. When Carla, Tennessee, and I arrived at the Café Dejéna, Frank and Wajahat Ali were already there. After exchanging greetings and engaging in small talk, I asked them both about how the Chinese-American and South-Asian communities viewed Ali. Since this interview was conducted, Ali has become a regular on Al Jazeera's "The Stream."

Wajahat said that educated Muslims knew where the doctrines espoused by Elijah Muhammad deviated from Orthodox Islam, but the average Joe among South-Asian Muslims dismissed his group as "Black Muslims," something less than Islam.

He said that the South Asians he knows followed the fighter as he morphed from Cassius Clay to Muhammad Ali. They admired him for his stand against the government because what he believed in was more important than the roar of the crowd. In this sense, he was more than a champion. Boxing for him was less important than whether the war was right. He risked the resentment of people who couldn't understand why he gave up the perks that go with being a champion.

Some Chinese Americans, Frank said, saw his stand against the war as merely an attempt to gain publicity because there weren't that many boxing fans among this group.

They were also concerned about a boxer still boxing at the age of thirty. They saw Marciano retire at thirty-two. Though Bert Sugar says that Rocky Marciano wanted to come out of retirement to fight Ingemar Johannson. (Odd, '83) says that Ezzard Charles helped Marciano along to his retirement. Even though Marciano knocked him out in their return fight, he put such a whipping on Marciano that the beating became a factor in his decision to retire (Odd, '83).

Also, from the condition of Marciano's face, after he took a beating from Jersey Joe Walcott before knocking Walcott out, you'd think that Walcott won the fight. Marciano defended the title only six times and three of his major fights were fought against aging opponents like Jersey Joe Walcott and Archie Moore. He also had a hard time with Ezzard Charles, who was actually a blown-up Light Heavyweight. He knocked out Joe Louis, who was shot by the time they fought. Jersey Joe Walcott was in his late thirties when they fought. No wonder Larry Holmes, who was heavyweight champion from 1978 to 1985, got pissed when Marciano received a higher ranking than he did.

Wajahat said that Ali was acceptable to Muslims, both Shia and Sunni, because he was an icon. They ignored his adultery. But for both South Asians and Chinese Americans, Elijah Muhammad was an adulterer and a charlatan.

I asked Frank, who has done much work on the Japanese internment and is responsible for the Japanese American "Day of Remembrance," whether he knew about Elijah Muhammad's pro Japanese sentiments—sentiments that led to his being arrested for sedition. Frank hadn't heard.

So successful has been the portrayal of Elijah Muhammad in film and in the media that all that he comes down to is a buffoon who couldn't keep his zipper up. That his life began with Mike Wallace's "The Hate That Hate Produced" and ended with Malcolm's accusations about his infidelity.

Much of this stems from Malcolm X's accessibility to the media and their publicizing Malcolm X's denunciation of Muhammad's alleged illicit sexual activities. While according to Elijah Muhammad's supporters, Malcolm X was engaging in sexual impropriety, while criticizing Elijah Muhammad. Few have delved into the early history of a man whom both Chin and Ali said lacked Malcolm X's charisma and lived in Chicago and not the media's epicenter, New York. Writer Debra Dickerson even accused the NOI leader of incest, that dragon among taboos that is always dragged out for the smearing of black men. The other charge against black men that excites the consumers of infotainment is rape.

The facts however are more complicated. Given his humble origins, his lack of a formal education, which sometimes is an advantage, Elijah Muhammad, if he were white, would be considered a great man. If all of the great men who committed adultery or were given to palace intrigue by undermining their rivals were removed from public recognition, the textbook industry would collapse and hundreds of Washington D.C. statues would have to be removed. There would be little to teach. Were it not for Elijah Muhammad's refusing to fight against Asians, it's highly improbable that Muhammad Ali would have refused to fight against Asians, and he would have been considered just a champion of boxing; because of his stand against the war, he became more than a champion. And from Marvin X's testimony, Ali's stance against the war was not a matter of free will, but a policy imposed upon him by NOI discipline. In addition, Elijah Muhammad refused to fight in a popular war, while Ali took a stand against a war that among the American public at the time there existed doubt and uncertainty, especially when the grunt duties were no longer only assigned to the poor, and white middle-class males became eligible for draft. He had a point when he said that two senators, Wayne Morse and William Fulbright, had opposed the war as had Harlem Congressman Adam Clayton Powell, Jr. (*Washington Post*, March 29, 1966). And Budd Schulberg notes that by the time Ali fought Frazier for the first time, in 1971, seventy-five percent of the public was opposed to the war. But while Ali was spared a prison sentence for his defiance of the Selective Service laws and lived in relative comfort while forced from the boxing ring, Elijah Muhammad was persecuted and jailed for his refusal to fight "the Asiatic black man." In November 1942, in Washington D.C., Muhammad was indicted for sedition on the grounds that he was discouraging black men from cooperating with the Selective Service:

> Contrary to Section 33 of Title 50 in that the United States being then at war they willfully attempted and did cause insubordination and refusal of duty in the military and naval forces of the United States to the injury of the United States, and the United States, being at war, they willfully obstructed recruiting and enlistment services of the United States. (Karl Evanzz, 2002)

As evidence, they submitted excerpts from three of Elijah Muhammad's speeches. One was delivered at the Chicago temple on August 9, 1942:

> The devil will trick you into believing that you will have to fight for him, but don't pay attention to him. His time is up. You should pay no attention to what he says about registering for the draft, because he can't force you to do a thing. His laws don't mean a thing. You shouldn't fear the devil when he tells you that you must go and fight in this war. You should refuse to fight... The newspapers are lying when they say that the Japanese are losing. We are going to win. (Evanzz, 1999)

Another speech was made on August 16, 1942:

> The Japanese are the brothers of the black man and the time will soon come when from the clouds hundreds of Japanese planes with the most poisonous gas will let their bombs fall on the United States and nothing will be left of it.

And again on August 20, he said:

> The Asiatic race is made up of all dark-skinned people, including the Japanese and the Asiatic black man. Therefore, members of the Asiatic race must stick together. The Japanese will win the war because the white man cannot successfully oppose the Asiatics. (Evanzz, 1999)

If Muhammad Ali's example was troublesome to the government, Elijah Muhammad was double trouble. Not only did he say, in so many words, "no Japanese ever called me a nigger," he also called for the victory for an enemy of the United States in a time of war in speeches that were pro-Japanese. And unless one believes that Elijah Muhammad was the lone "fanatic" or "oddball," pro-Japanese feelings among African Americans were pronounced. Indeed, one could argue that the events that led to Muhammad Ali's refusing to step forward when his name was called began in 1905, with the Japanese defeat of the Russian Navy.

The conflict between the two powers began with Japan's defeat of China in the Sino-Japanese war. On the night of February 8, 1904, the Japanese fleet under the Admiral Tōgō Heihachirō attacked two Russian ships at Port Arthur. After a series of land and naval battles, Japan defeated Russia in the 1905 Battle of Tsushima. The defeat marked the first defeat of a European power by an Asian one in modern times and sent shock waves through Western capitals and cheering in some non-Western ones who had viewed them as being under the boots of white supremacy. Elijah Muhammad was not alone in his sympathy for the Japanese in the United States. Leaders of the African Methodist Episcopal Church "believed that the ability of the Japanese to compete with Europeans and Americans on their own terms dispelled the myth of white superiority. The AME leaders wholeheartedly supported the Japanese in the war again Russia" (Horne, 2004).

W.E.B DuBois said, "We regarded that Russian defeat by Japan as the defeat of the West by the East." He said that "the Asiatic race is made up of all dark-skinned people," and that "members of the Asiatic race must stick together." The novelist and columnist George Schuyler wrote a series of articles for the *Pittsburgh Courier* that were so pro-Japanese that they weren't printed. Writers James Weldon Johnson and Arthur Schomburg also expressed sympathies for the Japanese. There were more blacks belonging to Japanese front organizations than communist ones. One writer even suggested that African Americans learn Japanese.

Tom Brokaw refers to the World War II generation as "The Greatest Generation"—a generation that, as the line goes, fought against fascism and racism abroad. Overlooked in this feel-good version of history is the fact that members of the greatest generation operated a segregated army and practiced discrimination and even violence against blacks at home, even blacks in uniform.

Writing in *The New York Times* (June 10, 2006), Brent Staples describes the experience of the esteemed historian John Hope Franklin:

> Dr. Franklin was a newly minted Harvard Ph.D. at the start of the war. Like most black intellectuals at the time, he was well aware of the nightmare life that awaited educated black men who were drafted

into the Army. He hoped to escape that fate by "selling" himself to the Navy, which was desperate for men after the attack on Pearl Harbor. The recruiter seemed stunned as Dr. Franklin reeled off his qualifications, which included shorthand and typing (at 75 words per minute) as well as his doctorate. But the recruiter, he writes, "said simply that I was lacking in one important qualification, and that was color."

He next turned to the War Department, which was hiring dropouts from Harvard to write the official history of the war. He submitted his qualifications, which included a book already in press, and even solicited support from the First Lady, Eleanor Roosevelt, all to no avail. "I decided that they did not want to win the war," he told me in an interview, "they wanted to win the status of white people in this country."

Dr. Franklin is not the only African American who felt this way. My day on Saturday, July 22, 2006, began with a 7:30 a.m. interview with the great novelist John A. Williams, veteran of World War II. In the late afternoon, I attended a fifty-dollar-ticket "Evening with Harry Belafonte." My day ended with a late evening sit-down dinner among hundreds of Pakistani Americans, at a reception for Syed Moynul Islam and his bride, Sadiya Shaikh, who performed in a play I produced at the Berkeley Repertory Theater called "The Domestic Crusaders," written by then-twenty-five-year-old theater wunderkind, Wajahat Ali (who was introduced in Chapter 48). The Pakistani crowd was not only entertained by musicians performing Pakistani music, but by Bob Marley and Sonny Rollins' "Tenor Madness," played by the bride's two brothers.

John A. Williams, in my opinion, is one of the country's best craftspersons. He hasn't received the recognition that he deserves because his content, like that of John Oliver Killens, is hard to take. Both of their writings about American history, especially World War II, don't mimic the current Brokaw line about "The Greatest Generation."

John A. Williams is one of those who believes that present day boxing is a "big joke." Since this interview was conducted, Williams has become an Alzheimer's patient at a New Jersey veterans' hospital, with little notice from the American literary establishment, which favors black male bashing over art. He said:

I did follow boxing but after a while it became a big joke. I'd look at guys like Henry Armstrong and Joe Louis and three or four other guys and then they'd start showing these turkeys and they'd be pissing around the ring. It became boring. It wasn't the same old thing. My old man was not a real boxer; he was a street boxer and he showed me all kinds of stuff, so I wasn't ignorant when it came to that stuff.

On The Nation of Islam, John said:

When Ali joined the Nation of Islam—let me put it this way—I walked into my closet, took my coat and left. It doesn't work out to be this great Muslim and be out there punching out people. He should have been like Joe Louis, who didn't have much to say, who went in there and did his job, took his fine old lady and went on about his business.

I liked Malcolm; he was a likeable guy but there was something in his eyes that told me—watch him. His importance was that he could draw so many people and get so much press and he could stand up there and talk to those TV people and do his thing on the radio—he was just magnificent.

Ali turned his back on him [Malcolm]. It was like a property struggle about who was going to get what.

Ishmael Reed: What about Elijah Muhammad refusing to fight the Asiatic black man?

John A. Williams: I was out there in those Islands. I ran into some Japanese prisoners, and I got along well with them 'cause I was pissed off with the Navy Seabees, a branch of the Navy that did a lot of different work, built trenches, put ships together, and put this together, that together, and moved materials.

IR: Was the Navy the most racist branch of the armed forces?

JAW: Oh yeah, and the Seabees were part of the Navy. The Navy was horseshit. It was a struggle and battle for position and getting those crackers off our backs all the time, and it didn't matter whether we were in the States, or overseas, or the Islands. I ran into it because I was a corpsman, and I'd run into these crackers with bullets up their asses, and they didn't want you to touch them and so I said, "Well fuck you then, jack." That was it.

IR: In your works you talk about out-and-out battles between white and black troops.

JAW: That stuff was going on in the States, before we even shipped out of Chicago at the two Great Lakes' naval stations and there were two or three other stations. A lot of the guys who came from my area of the country, New York and Massachusetts, got along okay. It was those stupid fucking Southerners, and then some of these Northerners thought they were hip to behave like Southerners. There were fistfights, etc.

IR: What about out-and-out combat?

JAW: There were stories about the Army guys going through the same thing. It was pretty much a mess, and a number of guys ended up in the brig for fighting. I did some brig time myself. On Guam, I told an officer, "I'm not your nigger, you cracker motherfucker." But it happened other places like Guadalcanal, Bougainville. They'd say, "Hey nigger, what you doing with that cross on your arm?" I was a corpsman and they're not used to seeing black medics and so that always got me into trouble. So I hit [the guy] and he looked at me in surprise, then I ran around behind him and kicked him in his ass. Then he turned around again and I laid it on him. Bam! I saw Joe Louis. He was a big strong cat, but he was a very quiet man.

IR: Why do they call the World War II generation the Greatest Generation, and call the war, the good war?

JAW: Just copy. Just bullshit.

IR: Why do they love Ali now?

JAW: He survived the hatred and he survived it with everything intact. Joe Louis was a quiet guy, but Ali said, "If you don't like me, fuck you."

IR: Elijah Muhammad was right to resist the draft?

JAW: He was right.

John A. Williams isn't the only black GI who said that he got along with Japanese prisoners better than with some of his white comrades. Later at Geoffery's, a black club in downtown Oakland, eighty-year-old Harry Belafonte submitted to two-and-a-half hours of questioning by a local activist. In the background was a huge flag with the red, black, and green colors of Marcus Garvey's Universal Improvement Association. Belafonte's talk ranged over a number of issues. Most of it was devoted to his friendships with Nelson Mandela and Martin Luther King, Jr. He also talked about his efforts to build a coalition of Latinos, whites, African Americans, Native Americans, and others for the purpose of ending the high prison incarceration rates and youth violence. He was very critical of Condoleezza Rice and Colin Powell, who, at that time, were members of the Bush administration, and said that he'd been barred from speaking at the funeral ceremonies for Coretta Scott King because President Bush's security wanted "a clean environment."

I figured I'd ask Belafonte some questions rather than get his contact and, like some of the other celebrities of whom I'd requested interviews, call their numbers and get the run around. He'd begun his talk by describing his experience in the armed forces, which, like that of John A. Williams and other black GI's, was one marred by racial incidents. He mentioned the Port Chicago tragedy.[1]

Given this, I asked him, during the question and answer period, whether Elijah Muhammad had been correct in refusing to fight during World War II. He didn't answer the question, but when I

---

1. "July 17, 1944: At 10:20 p.m. two devastating explosions killed and injured more than 700 U.S. Navy personnel as munitions were loaded on Liberty Ships at the Port Chicago Naval Weapons Station, near San Francisco. Of the 320 fatalities, 202 were African-American seamen, 15 percent of all black servicemen killed during all of World War II. Weeks after the tragedy, 258 black sailors were ordered to return to the dangerous duty, though white servicemen were given leaves after the tragedy. The black sailors refused to load munitions under unsafe conditions and were arrested and charged with mutiny. Threatened with the death penalty, 208 sailors returned to the high-risk duty—reserved for "blacks only"—and the remaining 50 were court-martialed and sentenced to 17 years in prison." Black Hollywood, Education and Resource Committee.

asked him about Muhammad Ali's legacy, he was very generous in his response. I followed him to his limousine and asked whether he would be available for some follow-up questions. He gave me a number to call, was helped into the limousine, and drove off. I gave him a slip with my number on it. Tuesday morning, Harry Belafonte called and said he'd make arrangements for an interview. He said that he didn't want me to think of him as a negligent celebrity.

Jack Olsen, author of one of the best books on Ali, said that Ali's joining the Nation was an escape from reality. He obviously preferred his blacks to be Christian, yet what could be more of an escape from reality than the belief that Jesus of Nazareth, a man who has been dead for two thousand years, is going to suddenly appear in the sky and vacuum up all of his followers. This belief has become part of United States foreign policy. Uncannily, the same pejorative was used to dismiss Muhammad's predecessor, Noble Ali Drew. Also, the claim by The Ali Scribes that the Nation of Islam fleeced Ali of his ring earnings has also been disputed by the members of the Nation, who have been dismissed as "thugs" by members of The Ali Scribes. The ones who got to appear in movies like *When We Were Kings.* Unlike Ali, whose opposition to the Vietnam War would eventually reflect the attitudes of the majority of Americans, Elijah Muhammad opposed a war that is called "the good war," even though its goodness is based upon a lie. This war was not fought to liberate the European Jews, which is the popular mythology. Americans were indifferent to the plight of the Jews. *The New York Times* even apologized for not paying sufficient attention to Jews who were persecuted by the Nazi Party. (Black Americans, Africans, and others were also placed in concentration camps—a fact which make those charismatic leaders who praise or praised the Nazi regime sound silly. Those black intellectuals who are prone to idol worship find it difficult to believe that W.E.B. DuBois, who some of them have deified, was such a person.) England, under Prime Minister Anthony Eden, refused to admit Jewish males fleeing Nazi persecution. Many of the French and Dutch were collaborators. And citizens of some Asian countries claimed that they received better treatment under the Japanese than they received under the British.

The "good war" amounted to Europeans fighting each other over the world's resources and resisting Japan's attempt to get in on the piracy. In Nazi Germany, blacks were also thrown into concentration camps and captured African-American soldiers were executed, which was also the policy of the much-vaunted Confederacy when dealing with captured black soldiers. The Nazi regime, one of the evilest in history, is rightly condemned, but at home, the Confederacy, which was also built upon cruelty and slave labor, is praised and celebrated in *Gone With The Wind*, *Birth of a Nation*, and most recently films like *Gods and Generals*.

CHAPTER 49

"Lonnie is a stabilizing force."—Harry Belafonte; October 29, 2006

When I read that Belafonte was returning to Oakland, I sent a request to Belafonte Enterprises for an interview. They told me to call Belafonte after 5 p.m. the following day, October 29. I reached him at the downtown Oakland Marriott hotel. He told me to come over within ten minutes. Carla and I piled into the car and sped to the hotel. I took Carla to take some photos, but the battery had died. His suite was located on the twelfth floor. He answered the door after about seven minutes and greeted us in his famous gravelly voice. At eighty he looked like a much-lacquered grand piece of mahogany. It was the day after a nephew hacked up Trevor Berbick, Ali's last opponent. He was shocked. I asked him to recall the first time he'd met Ali.

Harry Belafonte: I met him when he was still Cassius Clay. Right after the Olympics. He came to New York for a hot minute. Then he came to Chicago and I saw him there as well, and then in the Louisville, Kentucky, airport. There's a picture of us chest-to-chest and face-to-face with the caption: "Tell the truth, who is the greatest?" He and I didn't have any synergy until he had denounced the war. For a long time, he was quite insulated in the Nation of Islam from those of us who came from a different political stripe or had another point of view about how this struggle might be engaged. This kept him somewhat distant from us.

Then we met in Vegas. I was working at Caesar's Palace at the time. Joe Louis was the host and I was performing there and Ali was fighting Jerry Quarry. It was at that time he became famous. I admired him greatly when I saw him. He and I started to talk about the politics of our time. I saw in him the embodiment of what we said we wanted our young men of color to be: he was courageous, gifted, and deeply moral. He had a commitment to the liberation of people that was unflinching. When I had talked to him about Dr. King—what we were doing, he challenged King's idea that non-violence was the only way.

Then there came a time when he nearly ended his career as a boxer. He began to evidence the desire to become more socially engaged than he had ever been up to that point. This was after Mecca, and he began to speak in much broader terms. It was always interesting to me because almost the same thing happened to Malcolm. After Malcolm had come back from Mecca, he said he had been to the Holy Place. He had seen that the God of Islam is Allah. He did not recognize color at Mecca; he'd seen every hue and shade and stripe and he then began—not to retreat [from] his positions about the cruelties of America—but [he] began to retreat from his positions on race. He became much more inclusive. To a great extent Muhammad Ali began to express the same broader outlook, and in Las Vegas he had more humor and wit than he had in his early years.

Ishmael Reed: Did you meet Sonny Liston?
HB: Yeah. He just walked around in a constant state of brooding, nurtured by nothing but perpetual anger. He couldn't seem to find social balance.

IR: At Madison Square Garden they're trying to determine whether Ali's fighting there or the Pope's visit was the most important ever held there in fifty years. What do you say?
HB: Ali, of course.

IR: Was Joe Louis greater than Ali? He's accused of avoiding all of best black boxers in his prime, while Ali faced the best black boxers during his.

HB: I have no way of mentioning who was the greatest. There is no measurement.

IR: Lonnie Ali's role in his life is controversial.

HB: She is a stabilizing force. Of course, Ali is older and as one ages, one gains "stability." [Laughter] He has maturity. Ali and I were never intimates in the sense that we called each other and talked to each other's world.

IR: What about the draft?

HB: When I officially began to deal with him he'd already taken a stand on the draft. I thought that his position on the draft was the most stunning evidence of someone who did what I liked. He began to think outside the box. As I am going to say at this meeting tonight, America does not encourage radical thought. It doesn't encourage thinking that goes outside the norm. You must play inside the box, by their game and their rules, exclusively. If you're a radical, they mark you almost instantly.

IR: You were in the Navy, the most racist branch of the armed forces, during World War II.

HB: Unlike the infantry where you're on land, when you're at sea, you're on the ship, and you're confined to those rules.

IR: Like hell?

HB: Yeah, it was tough.

IR: John A. Williams said that he got into a fistfight.

HB: Just one? [Laughter] There were a lot of those. A lot.

IR: John A. Williams says that Elijah Muhammad was right to oppose World War II against the Japanese.

HB: Color does not exempt those from different tribes and races from moral and humane behavior. I think the Japanese were fascist, and they served and honored the principal of anti-humanity, and I think they were very cruel on balance. I make no case for anyone who goes to war because war in itself is inhumane and cruel and immoral.

IR: What did Dr. King think of Muhammad Ali?
HB: He admired him. We talked all the time about Ali. He had a lot of differences with Elijah Muhammad, and Muhammad didn't think highly of Martin Luther King either. But I think it was Malcolm, who in the context of the Nation, began to engage in non-violence and certainly engaged people from the other side, so to speak.

IR: Who assassinated him?
HB: The Nation was infiltrated, but that didn't exempt the assassins from culpability.

IR: Do you think that the blows from Holmes and Berbick con-tributed to Ali's Parkinson's disease?
HB: He took some rather cruel blows. In using the rope-a-dope he was constantly pounded, and I am sure somewhere in archives of medical practice those blows dislodged something. He paid the price for those injuries. If I had an opportunity to vote against the sport of boxing, I would vote against. But, I cannot wait to turn on the TV set to watch the next match. I am somehow conditioned, by culture, or somewhere in my DNA, that overrides my philosophical reservations about the sport.

IR: Is this because of Joe Louis?
HB: First of all, Joe Louis meant a lot to Black America. He gave a sense of revenge when he struck a blow against someone, especially someone of another race. You saw the blow as a blow for our cause. It was the dignity he had, even as a greeter, he never changed.

IR: What will be Ali's legacy?

HB: I think that because boxing gave him the international platform and universal recognition, but he will be remembered for his remarkable courage and having stood up to a vicious society, and he spoke out against a war that was immoral, unethical, illegal, and racist. He will be remembered as the courage he evidenced as a young man.

A cancer survivor, Belafonte went on to talk about his prostatectomy. He had become an advocate of regular check-ups, especially for black men, a high-risk group. He tells black women to follow the lead of the women in "Lysistrata," only instead of withholding sexual favors for men engaged in war, he advises women to withhold sex from black men who refuse to get prostate exams. He tells the men that no doctor who ever gave him a digital exam ever asked him for a date. As we left, he asked Carla whether I was keeping out of trouble. I didn't have the slightest idea of what he was referring to and didn't ask.

The next night Carla and I watched Belafonte's appearance on the Bill Maher Show. He was on a panel that included Andrew Sullivan, who gained media prominence by dissing black Americans and black American culture in *The New York Times Magazine* section, and who said that one of his proudest moments was to publish excerpts of *The Bell Curve* in *The New Republic*, the publication of which led to the resignation of some of its staff. The other guest was former Governor Christine Todd Whitman of New Jersey, who came under fire for patting down a black man while accompanying the New Jersey police on a patrol.

While both the Democrat and Republican leadership have directed their appeals at the middle class, Belafonte, on this program, spoke about the needs of the poor. This was unusual in today's political climate in which, after years of propaganda against them from segments of the white and black punditry, intellectual elite and think tanks, all of whom have discounted the influence of racism on the status of the poor, most of the poor work in either the above-ground or underground economy and yet many must subsist on food stamps. What I find ironic is that these blame-the-victim pronouncements occur regularly in publications that print reports and studies that show racism still influences who succeeds and who doesn't. Recently, books by Professors Martin Kilson and Houston Baker, Jr. challenge this position held by the Talented Tenth elite that the personal behavior of the poor is responsible for their plight.

At the end of the show, Sullivan approached Belafonte, grinning and gushing and pouring himself all over him, even though, in one of a number of his take-downs of black celebrities, he called Belafonte "a bigot" for referring to Colin Powell as a "house negro." This was on the October 25, 2002 Salon website, a "progressive" publication that defended the Albany jury's acquittal of the police who murdered Amadou Diallo in 1999.

CHAPTER 50

Abdul Rahman

During that week in late 2006, Abdul Rahman, formerly Sam X, returned my call. He was in Phoenix. Though some authors of Ali books give Jeremiah Shabazz or Malcolm X credit for introducing Ali to the teachings of Elijah Muhammad, the consensus among both Wallace and Farrakhan's followers was that it was Abdul Rahman.

Abdul Rahman: I knew Ali way before Jeremiah knew him. 1961 was when I first met Ali.

Ishmael Reed: So why do people say that Shabazz or Malcolm introduced him to the NOI?

AR: I don't know why people say those things. Some say that Malcolm X brought him into the Nation. I had him in the Nation three years before Malcolm ever met him. He was nineteen years old. Soon as he returned from the Olympics. I met him in Miami when he first turned pro. He was on the street and he saw me selling copies of *Muhammad Speaks*. He was wondering why we [were] called "negroes," and he started quoting Minister Farrakhan's song, "The White Man's Heaven is a Black Man's Hell." He said, "My name is Cassius Clay, and I'm the next heavyweight champion of the world." I took it from there.

I started taking him to meetings at Mosque #29 on Second Avenue. He was going to be who he was going to be, and he was very serious about the teachings. In the beginning we kept it quiet because being a Muslim at that time wasn't popular. We gave Malcolm a trip to come to Miami, November or December, 1963. Elijah Muhammad hated all sports play, but you're not going to prevent a man from making a living at what he does. After suspending Ali, Elijah Muhammad brought him back in and permitted him to use the name again. Around '72, I was right with him when he didn't take the step. I'm the one who told him to tell the press, "No Vietnamese ever called me nigger." It happened in Miami. How the hell can anybody else take credit for it when it happened in Miami? I was in his house where the Muslim cooks cooked for the brother. He told me that there were reporters outside who wanted to know why I didn't want to go to the army. "Tell them you ain't got no quarrel with the Vietnam, and they ain't never called you a nigger." I told him to say, "They ain't never lynched you, they ain't never raped you." Then he went out there and said it and you know the rest.

IR: Was he influenced by Elijah Muhammad's example? His refusing to fight the Japanese, who to him, were colored people.
AR: Yes. Yes, it had a lot to do with it, by what the Messenger did. He asked me what I would do and I told him that the Messenger went to jail. That's what I would do. They discount all of that. They don't want to credit the Nation with having any kind of influence on him. That's why I'm not in these movies about Ali. There's too much Islam in them.

This remark seemed to separate Rahman, a Nation of Islam stalwart, from the Orthodox Islam advocated by others. Rahman seemed to agree with Gene Kilroy, who said that "if it hadn't been for Elijah Muhammad, nobody would ever have heard of Ali."

An outpouring of media affection occurred on the occasion of Muhammad Ali's sixty-fifth birthday. ESPN ran two programs, "Ali 65" and "Ali's Dozen." Again there were the extravagant claims. One writer received a lot of attention for his claim that Ali had invented rap, a form that dates to at least the 1880s and prior to that, hundreds of years in West Africa.

Youthful versions of Gene Kilroy and Ed Hughes were shown commenting about Ali's greatness. During my research I found an interview that Gene Kilroy gave to a Las Vegas sports broadcaster. On this broadcast, January 2, 2004, unlike Rahman's claim that Ali's stance on the draft was inspired by Elijah Muhammad's World War II example, Kilroy suggested that Ali's decision to refuse the draft was based upon the class inequities that he saw in the draft. That poor people had to go to war while the rich got out of the country. By "going to Paris." Ali refused the draft because, according to Kilroy, "Ali said that it was an unjust and unholy war."

In this interview with Ali's former business manager, Gene Kilroy, as with the previous ones that I conducted, he expressed his awe of the athlete. He told the sportscaster that the entourage was not a "traveling circus," the judgment of some critics, but one that included "apostles" and "disciples." Apostles were of the inner circle; the disciples, the outer circle. "All of us around Muhammad considered our lives small and his large. All of us loved him. He was fun to be around."

Kilroy said he had a lot of respect for Ali and a lot of respect for the people around him. "There wasn't one man around him who wouldn't have taken a bullet for him," he stated, an assessment that contrasts with Khalilah Ali's claim that those surrounding Ali were out for themselves. When he talks to Ali, he asks, "You ever think about the old times and all the fun we had?" And Ali answers, "Yeah, Gene, I sure do."

On this 2004 program, he repeated his estimate of Elijah Muhammad, calling him "one of the greatest men on planet Earth. He wanted freedom and justice for his people ... He had the ability to have his son Herbert Muhammad manage Ali." In the 2004 interview, Kilroy said that Ali was a prisoner in his own body. "The doctors told him that he must rest eighteen hours in order to function for six. Movement is dangerous for anyone with Parkinson's disease." He was concerned about Ali's travel schedule, which had him, in 2003, two hundred and twenty days in the air, flying. Gene Kilroy said:

This is suicidal… Karl Malone, Jim Brown, all of us say, "I'd like to see our brother rest instead of traveling all over." You pick up the paper, you see him going here, going there. The people who really love Muhammad would like to see him just rest.

He then made an extraordinary appeal to Ali as though Ali were listening to the program: "And so Muhammad, if you're listening to this program, realize what we're talking about." He likened Ali's health to an auto tune-up. "It's pay me now or pay me later; if you don't change the oil you'll pay later. You've been good to all of us; you've been good to planet earth."

He then went on to cast the years 1964-74 as a golden age for heavyweight boxers and maintained that heavyweights Frazier, Bonavena, Quarry, and Terrell would beat any of today's heavyweights. He attributed this to their discipline and devotion to the sport. They would train to be champions by preparing to go for fifteen rounds. He described Ali's intense training session:

In the early morning, he'd run four miles with heavy combat boots on. Then, the great trainer Luis Sierra would take Ali through calisthenics. After breakfast, I set up films of whom he was fighting. He would study them all. I'd wake him up at twelve, go to gym to work on the speed bag and heavy bag then he'd spar for fourteen, fifteen rounds. He would prepare himself; he didn't take short cuts. He'd work with sixteen-ounce gloves. I see kids nowadays with twelve-ounce gloves, which are lighter because they don't want to look bad.

Another thing: the camps were open in those days. Everybody could come to watch the fighters train. Money isolates people because of television. Promoters made one hundred and twenty million from Mike Tyson's fights, and he got seventeen million, and he thought that it was a big payday.

Nowadays, the networks are reluctant to pay out the big bucks as they did some years ago. Four percent of the fighters are making money while the rest are starving. And the ones who are making the money—they don't help anybody. When I was with Ali I told him that he had to pay everybody right—the cook, etc.—because if you don't pay them, you have to pay the government. That's why Bundini, the cheerleader, was getting one hundred thousand per fight. We took care of the people. Trainers nowadays are cheerleaders, they don't tell the fighters what to do. Larry Merchant is a joke. Ferdie Pacheco is another joke. Pacheco got arrested in Miami for Medicare fraud. George Foreman got tired of describing the fights for HBO. He said he didn't want to sit down with co-moderators. He said they didn't know what they were talking about, and Bobby Czyz got arrested for drunk driving and HBO dropped him.

They denied Ali the right to fight because of his stance on the Vietnam War. This was wrong, and so I hooked him up with a man named Richard Fulton. Then there would be sparring sessions. I met with the governor of Mississippi to get a boxing license but somebody let the cat out of the bag, but then he got his license. I told him, you're paying eighty thousand to a hundred thousand for hotels, food. Have your own camp and use it as a write-off, and so took him to an accounting firm and he got his own camp, Deer Lake. I was working on a deal that the state would buy it [for a] shrine, but Ali's wife sold it to some guy who was in the karate business, and now he claims that he was Ali's trainer. He bought it for a hundred thousand and tried to sell it for five million a couple of months ago.

Kilroy gave his version of the famous encounter between Ali and his idol, Sugar Ray Robinson:

Ali ran all the way up Fifth Avenue to Sugar Ray's and waited five hours until Sugar arrived. He told Sugar that he was going to the Olympics and when he came back he wanted Sugar to be his trainer. Sugar said, "sure kid" and gave him the brush-off. Ali went back to the hotel with tears in his eyes and vowed he'd never do that to anybody. Sure enough he never turned anybody down. One time Sugar Ray's mother came to camp. Her electricity was turned off and Ali gave her ten thousand dollars and gave another check for her lights to be turned on.

Ishmael Reed: What was his opinion of the film "Ali"?
Gene Kilroy: It was terrible. They lost ten million dollars. You can't sell people hot water and call it vegetable soup. There were so many things wrong with that movie. It could have been so great. I met with Michael Mann, who is a great director, but he surrounded himself with the wrong people. He started listening to Bingham about [Ali]

and Bingham wasn't around us that much. The problem with the people who are around Ali today is that they make themselves the big shot instead of Ali. When we were around Ali there was one wheel. All the rest of us were spokes. I'm not bad-mouthing Bingham, I'm just telling it the way it is. They talk about Babe Ruth visiting a sick kid and saying that he was going to hit a home run for him. There was a kid with cancer. His father brought him to the camp. Ali asked why he was wearing a skull-cap. His father said that he had cancer. Ali told him, "I'm going to beat George Foreman, and you're going to beat cancer," and I took a photo of the kid with Ali with that inscription on it. Later, I got a call from the father and he was at hospital, and [his son] wasn't going to make it, and so after training and breakfast we went down to the University of Pennsylvania Hospital.

Ali and I went into his hospital room, and he had blonde hair and was as white as a sheet and Ali said again, "I'm going to beat Foreman, and you're going to beat cancer." And he said, "No, I'm going to see God, and I'm going to tell him I know you." And both me and Ali and the kid had tears in our eyes, and it was like, I would say, if you go to Las Vegas look up so and so. And he died, and I went to the funeral, and they had the boy in the casket with the inscription.

He continued with a story about Ali's response to a rumor that Joe Frazier had died after their first fight.

GK: When we were in Philadelphia, Budd Schulberg called and said that Joe Frazier had died in St. Luke's hospital and Ali said that "if Joe Frazier dies, I will never fight again." I called the hospital and the doctor said that Joe had passed the crisis. Joe said he took the taunting too far and that "my kids had to go to school and hear what Ali said about him."

A few years ago a man said that if Ali and Joe toured together, he'd pay both a million dollars. Frazier had already spent the money in his head, and the guy went to Ali, and his wife said they wanted more money, and then the guy backed out of the deal, and that made

Joe more angrier with Ali. Joe doesn't hold any animosity. They went to a basketball game together. Joe now has diabetes, and he's a good compassionate man.

He commented on the state of boxing today:

GK: The judges don't know about boxing. You got someone who became a judge because he gave money to the governor. You got people on boxing commissions who don't know about boxing. It's scary. It's killing the sport. People are listening to non-athletes announce the fights.

He said that Howard Cosell and Ali were never close and that Cosell had dissed Ali as having no class in a book about Sugar Ray Leonard. He also discussed the atmosphere in Zaïre during the Ali-Foreman fight and Ali's comments about his current condition.

GK: But Cosell was not our friend. We were never in his house, he was never in ours. He just used Muhammad. Muhammad was good to a lot of people. You never heard of Zaïre until that Ali fight. They did this for publicity. We went to Caracas, Venezuela. Ali told the press that when they got to Africa all of the writers who had written badly about him would be put in a pot and cooked. Everybody laughed.

When we got back to the training camp we got a call from Mobutu's top man. "You tell Ali we're are not cannibals here. We're putting on this fight to promote Zaïre, Africa, not to ruin it; we don't put people in pots and cook them." I said, "Here, you tell him." Ali told him that he was just kidding.

I made contact with the American ambassador in Zaïre. We had all of the privileges, we had movies and food. All we had to do was rest. He has good recall. He looks at things in a positive way. He said, "I could have had cancer." He says, "This is nothing. Allah is punishing me for some of the wrong I did. I can't walk fast, I slur my words, but this is nothing."

He's a blessed man. I am a blessed man on planet Earth to be calling Ali my friend. This was in the day when the white man was the devil; I was a white man in that entourage, and I was accepted by black people. I see all the struggles the black man had to go through. When I was growing up we had a black Saint Martin de Porres that we revered.

Ali said that the reason that he converted to Islam was his father was a painter who painted all in the churches [where] all the saints were white, all of the angels were white. The blacks were in the kitchen serving the dinner. Elijah said we don't have our own name on our country, our own culture. We got [to] unite, be something, make the world proud of us, be good to each other, proud of each other.

Kilroy told me, during a follow-up interview, that Hauser's official biography of Ali was not informed. He said that the film "Ali" was a failure because Howard Bingham had been one of the consultants. In contrast to the cooperative Kilroy whom I'd interviewed previously, the Kilroy, called by some "Mr. Vegas," I encountered in the follow-up interview was guarded and cross. He said that he'd talked to Muhammad Ali on his birthday. Ali, he said, "was doing pretty good, has good recall, talked pretty good."

I asked him about the movie Ali and his claim about Bingham. He was evasive. Bingham, he said was assistant producer or something. "I spoke to you before," he bristled.

He repeated his admiration for Elijah Muhammad:

GK: Elijah Muhammad gave him dedication, determination and discipline.

IR: Was Cosell at Odessa and Cash's funeral? Cosell wrote that unlike Sugar Ray Leonard, Ali lacked class.
GK: [Kilroy repeated his claim that Hauser, the biographer, "was never around us. Ask Butch Lewis. He misquoted every one of us."]

IR: *The New Yorker's* David Remnick? *(Author of King of the World.)*
GK: Never even met the guy.

I ended my conversation with Kilroy. It was clear that he was unhappy with me. I figured that the Ali camp knew, by now, that I'd been asking questions about Ali. I told Agieb Bilal about this attitude and he said, "They know that you can't be controlled."

In July 2006, Miguel Algarín, founder of the legendary Nuyorican Poets Café, called and said that he had been invited to the Naropa Institute in Boulder, Colorado, and would be stopping off in Northern California before returning to New York. He wanted me to line up a poetry reading for him. I got him booked at Anna's Jazz Island in Berkeley on July 14. After the reading, we adjourned to the Dejéna Café where, of course, I interviewed Miguel about Muhammad Ali.

Miguel Algarín: I heard about him as the best fighter we sent over to the Olympics. He was a classy presence in the ring and showed power without being bloody.

Ishmael Reed: What about his conversion to Islam?
MA: A lot of African Americans dealt with a crisis by going Muslim; we have to wait them out till they return to Jesus.

Both Wallace and Farrakhan, unlike Elijah Muhammad, have made overtures to Christians, and the Millions More March saw a number of Christian ministers sharing the spotlight with Minister Farrakhan. Elijah Muhammad referred to the Bible as "the poisoned book."

MA: We needed a first class boxer, not all of this extra baggage, this religious stuff. We have a hard enough time with Christianity; why do we take an Arab religion on? It's like Allen Ginsberg with Buddhism. Religion clouds the atmosphere. When Ali refused to join the army—that was brave, to reject the military. People whom I loved in the projects ended up in Vietnam because they were jobless. They were not part of the American Dream. Ali will be remembered as a boxer, not as a diplomat or a Muslim.

CHAPTER 51

My wife Jean and I and Jesse Jackson were over at Joe Louis' house. Jean, Jesse and I were sitting with Mrs. Louis in the dining room. Joe was in the bedroom, laying in bed, looking at television. Then he came to the door, and said, "Cassius is on TV; Cassius is on TV." So we all got up to see Ali on TV. He was being interviewed, and he was saying, "I'm not an Uncle Tom like Joe Louis." He kept on ranting and calling Joe Louis an Uncle Tom, and I'm standing there with Joe Louis. I don't know how on earth it happened that I got into a position. The Lord just put me there, I guess. Joe didn't say anything. He just went back on to bed. But the next time I saw Ali, I made a point of telling him, "I can't stand to have the hero of my adulthood talking like that about the hero of my childhood. Joe Louis meant so much to us. No matter what you think, you have no right to say those things about him. You don't know what you're talking about. You don't know what conditions Joe Louis came up under. If it hadn't been for Joe Louis, you wouldn't be here." —Oscar Brown, Jr.

In the 1960s, Malcolm X, Muhammad Ali, and others gave expression to the rage that millions of African Americans harbored in their hearts. For them the generation before were Uncle Toms: people who were afraid to speak up. Muhammad Ali symbolized the new generation, black, proud: the Had Enough generation. To him and his contemporaries, Joe Louis was just a Negro boxer whom they brought on to make up for Jack Johnson.

Really? Were the young Black Nationalist Turks of the 1960s correct about Louis? That he lacked consciousness? During remarks made at the Southern Conference for Human Welfare in late 1946, Louis indicated that he knew what was what. He said:

> Lots of people think that I'm doing all right as a fighter and that I should stick to my business. But they don't understand that fighting prejudice, disease, and second-class citizenship is my business, too. I hate Jim Crow. I hate disease. I hate the poll tax. I hate seeing people kept down because they are colored. I am not going to let this hate stay in my system, but I am going to help people fight Jim Crow and try to make this a better America. I am going to try to keep my punch in the ring as well as out of the ring.

While Elijah Muhammad paid for his defiance by serving time, a penalty that Ali avoided, Joe Louis, Sugar Ray Robinson, and Jackie Robinson showed the basic suicidal impulse of white supremacy. During World War II, both the British and American racists extended racist treatment to their colored subjects even though these subjects were assisting in the fight against the supremacists' enemies!

While Jackie Robinson is sometimes dismissed as a moderate, or even worse an Uncle Tom, he defied the taboos of the segregated army by beating up white officers who insulted him. White officers who called him a "nigger" were likely to turn up with missing teeth.

> A white officer yelled at a black soldier, calling him "a stupid nigger son-of-a-bitch." Jackie stepped in. He stood right in the officer's face. "'Sir,' he bristled, "You shouldn't address a soldier in the U.S. Army in those terms."
>
> "'Fuck you,' the officer screamed at Jackie. "That [nigger] goes for you too!" He broke almost every tooth in the white man's head before they pulled him off. It took all of [Truman] Gibson's diplomacy, and some lavish gifts from Joe [Louis], to persuade the commanding officer not to instigate a court-martial. (McRae, 2002)

Joe Louis and Sugar Ray Robinson also made violent retaliations against armed, racist Military Policemen, who didn't recognize them, and Louis' complaints about the segregated conditions in the army led to the elimination of those conditions. After he complained about segregated conditions at Fort Bragg, "the U.S. army passed a resolution banning all forms of segregation in every camp, station and military posting across America."

When reminded by a white MP that he was standing in a white bus station, Louis said, "I'm wearing an American Army uniform, just like you." The MP stuck a wooden club into the champion's ribs. Louis warned the MP not to touch him. "I'll do more than touch you, nigger." Before the champion could deck the MP, Sugar Ray had wrestled him to the ground. Joe fought two other armed military policemen. The fight ended when somebody called out, "That's Joe Louis." The two MPs were reprimanded after Joe Louis threatened to call the White House. Henry Armstrong beat up two cops who were trying to bait him. The judge was a fan. She dismissed the charges.

So while Muhammad Ali is saluted for his defiance of an unpopular war, he never had to face the danger faced by Elijah Muhammad, Ray Robinson, Joe Louis, Jackie Robinson, Henry Armstrong, or even Sonny Liston (who, after being targeted by the Philadelphia police, was the subject of a vendetta by police in every town in which he found himself, except for Las Vegas). These men made their bold and life threatening challenges of white supremacy in situations where there were no cameras to record it. Yet the 1960s generation cast them as lacking militancy.

I wasn't aware of the bold stands made by Joe Louis and Ray Robinson until writing this book, or that they were more than playboys who flitted from the boxing ring to the bedroom. Maybe the reason that black men of different generations find themselves at odds is the same reason that communications between Americans and the rest of the world are cluttered. A small class of men who own the media and opinion-men of the same background belonging sometimes to the same classes in school, the same country clubs, who party with each other—monopolize the avenues of expression. They're the ones whose opinions are sought on issues affecting world civilization when their attitude toward the religions and cultures of others is often influenced by European ethnocentrism.

When they want to know about China, they go to the same white American "expert" whom Chinese intellectuals consider to be out of touch. The military stumbles from blunder to blunder because they are the victims of false intelligence. The same could be said of the American public. Their education and the information they receive from the media are based upon false intelligence. All one has to do is listen to the talk shows, the ignorant comments, the flat world viewpoint, to discover the damage. The people they thought would greet them as liberators are doing their damnedest to drive them from their country.

This is the same kind of stacked, all-white sports and political jury that the young champion from Louisville faced when he announced that he'd become a member of a religion that was alien to them. The Jim Crow sports writers' industry was used to their black people being Baptists. They accused Ali of belonging to a separatist cult when some of them grew up in neighborhoods where if a black person were to wander in, he or she would be accosted. Charles Robinson, who contributed photos for this book, said that when he walked through an Italian neighborhood in Baltimore, he knew he'd have to fight. Melvin Van Peebles talked of being chased home by a mob.

Ali's critics worked for newspapers that had segregated newsrooms and segregated coverage where stories about blacks were consigned to the crime, entertainment, and sports pages. With the possible exception of ESPN, sports departments continue to be segregated.

"I guess I hope that any sports columnist who has chided a professional sports league for its lack of diversity will look at these results and decide whether they should be challenging their bosses to do better," said John Cherwa, then an editor at the *Orlando Sentinel and Tribune Co.* and now at *The Los Angeles Times*, when he released the "2006 Racial and Gender Report Card of the Associated Press Sports Editors" at the Editors' Convention in Las Vegas.

The primary author of the report, Richard Lapchick, said, in the summary:

> When 94.7 percent of the sports editors, 86.7 percent of the assistant sports editors, 89.9 percent of our columnists, 87.4 percent of our reporters and 89.7 percent of our copy editors/designers are white, and those same positions are 95, 87, 93, 90 and 87 percent male, we clearly do not have a group that reflects America's workforce.

And in the world of sports, they are covering a disproportionate number of athletes in basketball, football and baseball who are African-American or Latino. On the high school and college levels, more than 40 percent of the student-athletes are girls and women.

Others might even have compared the black athlete to an animal. Gone are the days when an announcer at a fight would introduce a black fighter as "Al Jolson's Mammy Boy," as an announcer introduced Henry Armstrong when he fought Mike Belloise. Today, a writer might claim that the black athlete has a genetic edge. Jon Entine has written a book, *Taboo: Why Black Athletes Dominate Sports And Why We're Afraid to Talk About It*, asserting that those with a West-African ancestry have a genetic advantage over whites and concluded that "white men can't jump." Hitler said that about Jesse Owens. That the United States' victories at the Nazi Olympics were attributable to their "black auxiliary," and Joe Louis was considered a natural with animal-like abilities so much so that he didn't have to train. Entine might be concerned to know that Nazi citizens during the Third Reich period agreed with him that blacks are natural born athletes.

In his remarkable book, *Destined To Witness*, about growing up black in Nazi Germany, Hans J. Massaquoi writes about the attitudes of German citizens about black athletes, as the Olympic games were approaching:

> The man-in-the-street type of "knowledge" was not too far out of line from that of the better-educated Germans. Herr Dutke [one of his teachers] preempted any possibility of a black Olympic triumph by telling us that blacks weren't athletes "in the true sense of the word" since they were "born runners and jumpers—like horses and animals."

The only difference between Entine and the opinion of the Germans is that, according to Massaquoi, many of the Germans changed their minds when meeting the black athletes, whom they learned were well mannered and college educated. Entine cited an article in *Scientific American* that supported his views. He left out one important dissenter, and CNN, which promotes the "racial divide" for ratings, neglected to offer the views of the late Stephen Jay Gould, the Harvard University professor, who said that, "There are too many potent social factors for there to be any truth in the belief that blacks have a genetic advantage in sports." He appeared on a panel with Olympian Kipchoge Keino at the New School of Social Research.

Olympian Kipchoge Keino's observations were also neglected. The Kenyan is quoted in the *New York Daily News* (April 5, 2001) saying, "75 percent is physical training and 25 percent is mental. It's the mental process—thinking ahead and planning your moves—that comes to the fore, and proves the most valuable."

At this writing, the Klitschko brothers have dominated the heavyweight championship division. So just as black male body parts have been marketed over the years (Cheney, 2006), maybe someone has found a way to market their genes. Maybe one of the recipients is Canadian Steve Nash, who was the NBA most valuable player for two years. He said that if he hadn't won, he would have nominated Dirk Nowitzki of Dallas, another white player. Maybe that's why the 2006 first draft NBA choice was a foreigner. All over the world, white athletes are causing a stampede. To hell with steroids, give me some of them black genes, they're pleading.

Another writer, John Hoberman, who has found a consumer demand for books that assure readers that the stereotypes about blacks are true, writes about how blacks are obsessed with sports. So obsessed that African-American athletes are leaving baseball, perhaps the result of a successful twelve-step program, which led to their kicking the sports' jones.

The website *Baseball Think Factory* posted a link to an article in the *Seattle Times* about there being fewer African-American baseball players in recent years. Maury Brown, a site contributor, writes:

> Five teams—the Boston Red Sox, Baltimore Orioles, Houston Astros, Atlanta Braves and Colorado Rockies—had no African-American players on their active rosters... while several other teams had just one or two.
>
> The stark fact is that fifty-eight years after Jackie Robinson integrated baseball, considered by many to be the single most significant event in the history of professional sports, the American-born black baseball player is slowly disappearing from the game.

"Jackie would be sick," said Grover "Deacon" Jones, an Orioles scout who played for the Chicago White Sox in the 1960s and is black. "This is my forty-ninth year in professional baseball, and man, this is incredible. It's insulting to me, personally."

The numbers tell the story. Since 1975, when twenty-seven percent of major-league players were African American, the number has steadily declined. A *Seattle Times* analysis of active rosters, including players on disabled lists, showed that 8.9 percent (79 of 888 players) were African American.

White and black panel members of a younger generation of a sports panel appearing on an ESPN show attributed Hoberman's kind of thinking to the "old school" (white) sports writers, some of whom are charter members of The Ali Scribes; those who refuse to see blacks as cerebral beings. With the possible exception of ESPN, sports commentary continues to be loaded with white supremacist notions and the use of a double standard when evaluating black and white athletes. Floyd Mayweather believes that this is true for boxing commentary.

Floyd Mayweather once complained that boxing commentators, except for the boxers among them, are biased toward black fighters. The disrespect shown Mayweather by some sports writers when he finally met Manny Pacquiao on May 2, 2015 is proof of his assertion. Fight moderator, James Brown, who hosted the fight for Showtime/ HBO, was right when he condemned the description of the fight as one between good and evil, a description proposed by Freddie Roach, Pacquiao's trainer. Mayweather was cast as evil because of charges of domestic violence, for which he served time, but Brown pointed out that Pacquiao was not the Saint portrayed by the media; the *Huffington Post* has also charged him with reactionary politics while serving as a congressman, that is when he showed up for work.

The Post reported on Pacquiao's anti-feminist anti-gay views the day before the fight, views that weren't covered by Melissa Harris-Perry during her and David Zirin's fight-day rant against Mayweather. Zirin is one of these guys who has become a volunteer black feminist, joining in on the bashing of black men, but ignoring the abuse of women who belong to his ethnic group, in this case the abuse of many Jewish women in American households and Israel.

This abuse has been documented by Jewish feminists. Even Gloria Steinem, whose accusations against black men are often vitriolic, has covered up this kind of misogyny. She told *The New York Times* that she's embarrassed when a person of her background is caught in a scandal, yet she rages, bitterly, against the living black ones and the dead ones like Jean Toomer and Langston Hughes. She and Henry Louis Gates, Jr., who has been disgraced, are responsible for black male writers becoming pariahs in the market place. But even if Zirin decided to discuss misogyny in the Jewish community, Mrs. Harris-Perry's white feminist producers who feed her the lines wouldn't go for it, nor would their boss, Brian Roberts, who supports Stand Your Ground and Voter Suppression. The two, Zirin and Melissa Harris-Perry, concentrated on Mayweather, even though public figures who, like Pacquiao, hold such views about birth control and gays are called out each week by Mrs. Harris-Perry. He opposed a bill that would increase the government funding for contraception and family planning services, according to *USA Today* in 2011. The boxer is also adamantly against abortion, which is illegal in the Philippine Constitution. "God said, 'Go out and multiply.' He did not say, just have two or three kids," Pacquiao said. He also believes that, "It's sinful to use condoms and commit abortion." During a 2013 interview with the National Conservative Examiner, Pacquiao discussed President Obama's support of marriage equality. Pacquiao was quoted as saying, "God's words first... obey God's law first before considering the laws of man. God only expects man and woman to be together and to be legally married, only if they so are in love with each other. It should not be of the same sex so as to adulterate the altar of matrimony, like in the days of Sodom and Gomorrah..."

David Zirin called Mayweather a coward on the same show. He has every right to criticize Mayweather and ignore the offenses committed against women by men belonging to his background, but as far as I know Michael Jordan and Pele aren't abusers. He has an itch in his groin about them too.

The campaign to demonize Mayweather worked. Before the fight, a public poll revealed that over sixty percent of the public was for a Pacquiao win while only a little over thirty percent supported a Mayweather victory. On the same day, CNN commentator Sam Cornish brought on Larry Merchant whom he called "The greatest TV boxing analyst of all times." He referred to the love that Merchant received when he told Mayweather that if he were "fifty years younger he would kick Mayweather's ass." This was after Merchant goaded Mayweather with a nasty remark about his being as "exciting in the ring as outside the ring," referring to his alleged domestic abuse, as outside of the ring. He said this after he had knocked out Victor Cruz, which those sports writers, who don't know anything about boxing, dismissed as an illegitimate knockout. Mayweather said that Merchant wasn't "shit" and that he didn't know anything about boxing, a sentiment with which George Foreman and Gene Kilroy, Ali's former business manager, would agree. Maybe, because he was seeking a lucrative contract from HBO, Mayweather apologized to Merchant; but in my mind no apology was necessary.

Larry Merchant, however, this nasty bigot, wasn't required to apologize after he insulted Mexican culture. This insult was reported by Roberto Rodriguez and Patrisia Gonzales on their site *Latino Spectrum*, on April 25, 1997. "This sucks!" They quoted him as saying.

> As the mariachis began to play a song, Larry Merchant, one of the announcers for the televised Oscar De La Hoya-Pernell Whitaker boxing match, couldn't have expressed his disgust more vehemently. You'd think cockroaches had just crawled onto his feast.
>
> While another announcer reminded the audience that De La Hoya was indeed an American, Merchant bitterly complained that having mariachis play before the fight was a marketing ploy to get "Mexican fans—not Mexican Americans—but Mexican fans to support De La Hoya."
>
> "This sucks!," Merchant exclaimed, with an unadulterated hatred rarely heard on a nationally broadcast sporting event.
>
> We wondered what gave Merchant, TVKO boxing analyst, the right to insult millions of fans in public?

During the interview conducted on the day of the Mayweather-Pacquiao fight, Merchant said that Mayweather was "the best pure boxer of his time," but added a dig. He said that Mayweather would "rather watch a dramatic fight than be in it." This is one of the strange comments about a black boxer from one of those sports writers who, like those in the past, lost their minds over Jack Johnson's "Golden Smile." Rather watch a dramatic fight than to be in one? His opponents have hit Mayweather with power shots that would have knocked out boxers with lesser skills. That was the case in this fight, when one sports writer said that the hardest punch in the fight was thrown by Pacquiao.

Michelle Beadle was brought on Jim Lampley's show "The Fight Game" to criticize the fight. All she did was parrot her patriarchal bosses. She called the fight a lot of hype. She, like the Bloomberg feminist Kavitha Davidson, who was critical of Mayweather, didn't attend the fight.

Well, the late Emmanuel Steward would call Mayweather the winner because he threw more punches. Mayweather landed 67 of 267 jabs, to Pacquiao's 18 of 193; he landed 81 of 168 power punches to Pacquiao's 65 of 236; he landed 148 punches of 435 thrown, to Pacquiao's 81 of 429.

Mayweather survived Pacquiao's 81 blows to exhibit an artistry that is rare in these days when boxers are encouraged by TV commentators to fight in wild flurries hoping that one lucky shot would defeat an opponent. He escaped the less-skilled boxer's attempts to trap him on the ropes and kept him at bay by drilling him with jabs. That kind of fight might not make good television but, for boxing aficionados like me, the boxing that television producers and their commentators seem to desire is covered by cage fighting. In fact, Dana White of UFC came on to castigate both Mayweather and Pac-Man for a dull fight. Maybe it wasn't homicidal enough using the standards of UFC? One of the most disappointing comments came from Teddy Atlas, who, except for the boxers, is the best of the fight commentators. He said that the fans deserved more because they paid one hundred dollars per ticket. More of what? Of course,

Atlas had picked Pacquiao to win, just as he predicted that Canelo Alvarez would defeat Mayweather. He lost.

So after Mayweather beat Pacquiao, they criticized the way he won. One sports writer called Mayweather a coward for the way he fought. The most hypocritical comment about the fight came from feminist sports writer Kavitha Davidson of Bloomberg. She's brought on by the wealthy white men who own NBC to diss the brothers. Even though she didn't watch the fight, she was there to criticize Floyd Mayweather's domestic violence record. She works for Michael Bloomberg, who, when mayor supported Stop and Frisk. Black and Hispanic women complained that the police used Stop and Frisk as an excuse to molest them sexually. If she addressed former Mayor Bloomberg's allowing his police to assault black and Hispanic women, sexually, she'd be fired.

The *Times* account of the fight written by Michael Powell was vicious, hateful and bizarre. It was titled "Mayweather Wins, Preens and is Booed." Like the Bloomberg feminist, he couldn't help dragging other black athletes into his copy. They were Ray Rice a domestic violence perp, and Adrian Peterson, who was accused of harsh punishment of his child. (When a black mother punched out her child before live television during the Baltimore riots, the same accusers of Peterson hailed her as the mother of the year.) I can't wait to see an article about Tom Brady's cheating with deflated footballs in which Lance Armstrong is cited.

Powell even called in Darth Vader. He ended his rant with a crazy, bizarre paragraph. As if to wish harm upon the boxer he wrote, "Our culture, thankfully, is a swift-flowing river, and this champion boxer and abuser is in danger of getting swept over its rapids."

Unlike the sports writers who were disappointed that Pac-Man didn't knock out this "preening" braggart, those who had spent some time in the ring, ex-champions Bernard Hopkins, Lennox Lewis and Paul Maglignaggi gave Mayweather his props. Hopkins called him one of the "top fifteen fighters of all time." Maglignaggi said that Mayweather won because he controlled the range. As for Pacquiao's claim that he won the fight, Maglignaggi called him "a poor loser." Their opinion was overruled by Lampley's guest, Max Kellerman, a boxing commentator who said that the fight was "a minus." Yet, the following Saturday, former champion Roy Jones, Jr. agreed with the boxers and gave a point-by-point analysis of Mayweather's skills.

Hopkins and many other fighters believe that the goal of boxing is to hit and not be hit. As Lennox Lewis said, speaking in admiration of Mayweather's strategy, "If you can't catch it, you can't hit it." Is Mayweather the first fighter to be accused of "running," a charge made against him by a sore loser, Pacquiao? Experiencing burning eyes at the end of the fourth round in his first fight with Liston, Ali wanted Angelo Dundee to stop the fight. Was Angelo Dundee wrong when he told Ali "to get out there and run." Sonny Liston claimed that Ali ran in their first fight. Marvin Hagler accused Sugar Ray Leonard of running during their fight. And Henry Armstrong accused Sugar Ray Robinson of running. The sports writers who criticize Mayweather's tactics admire most of these fighters, and so there must be another reason for their venomous comments about Mayweather. Because of television and sports commentators, who know as much about boxing as many jazz critics have a knowledge of jazz, boxing is at its crossroads. Will it continue to have room for those boxers like Mayweather, who practice "the sweet science," or will it become a kind of human cock fight?

◆

In the beginning of 2006, they brought back the old, discredited Marciano-Ali computer fight and charged people seventy-five dollars to see it and guess the outcome. This computer fight might have soothed the feelings of American fans who wanted to see Ali "knocked out," but British fans didn't go for it. In England, the producer, Murray Woroner, had to change the ending of the film to show Marciano losing on cuts.

If these attitudes persist to this day, you can imagine what Muhammad Ali had to face when he announced that he was a

Muslim and then topped that by refusing to go to war. Some of the most virulent comments came from Southern congressmen. One said:

> Listen to this. If that great theologian of Black Muslim power… is deferred, you watch what happens in Washington… what has happened to the leadership of our nation when a man, any man regardless of color, can… advise his listeners to tell the President when he is called to serve in the armed forces,… "I'm not going."
>
> I cannot understand how patriotic Americans promote, or pay for, pugilistic [boxing] exhibitions by an individual who has become the symbol of draft evasion. While thousands of our finest young men are fighting and dying in the jungles of Vietnam, this healthy specimen is profiteering from a series of shabby bouts. Apparently he [Ali] will fight anyone but the Vietcong.

Another said:

> One Cassius Clay, alias Muhammad Ali, who several years ago defied the U.S. Government, thumbed his nose at the flag, and is still walking the streets making millions of dollars fighting for pay, not for his country… Where on earth is the Justice Department in this country? Why on earth is not that man Cassius Clay in the penitentiary where he should be?

At one time, when ethnic groups were struggling to go mainstream, when everybody below 14th Street was hyphenated, boxers were symbols of ethnic pride. When these groups moved uptown and became professionals, scientists, and the sons and daughters of the immigrants married into the mainstream, as Ali Scribe Gay Talese described about his marriage, it was no longer necessary to achieve racial and ethnic pride in the boxing ring.

Elizabeth Nunez complained about how the coverage of black life has been restricted to athletics, even though blacks have excelled in other fields. There are black scientists, astronauts, Fortune Five Hundred CEOs, and probably more black millionaires than ever before. The former head of NASA was black. The heads of planetariums in Philadelphia and New York are black. I even witnessed a circus in which one of the acts had a black woman lion trainer direct some big cats through their hoops.

Absent from the commentary of those black intellectuals, neo-con critics of black Americans and pundits is the statistic that black business has increased by forty-five percent during the last decade. It is possible that blacks are entering a post-sports period, having excelled since the 1960s in a number of fields. But in the sixties, black athletes like Muhammad Ali, Jim Brown, Kareem Abdul-Jabbar, John Carlos, and Tommy Smith, being the most visible ambassadors to the mainstream, made political points that drew the attention of the public. They were the trendsetters.

During this period, Ali also took heat for his mentor Elijah Muhammad's racist attitudes towards whites, yet those around the prophet said that his entertaining whites and Jews at his dinner table "blew" their minds. The Chicago newspaper columnist Irving Kupcinet, known by his nickname "Kup," was one of his close friends.

I think I know the reason for this contradiction. Blacks are new at racism, while their enemies have been at it since ancient times, according to *The Invention Of Racism In Classical Antiquity* by Benjamin Isaac. They're like some of the Native American tribes who owned slaves. Visitors to these territories found the slaves living better than their masters. Most of the black nationalists I knew in the old days grew up as integrationists. It was a few heinous acts by some dim-witted racists who turned their heads around, especially the bombing of a Birmingham church in 1963, which took the lives of four little girls. They were open to Elijah Muhammad's rhetorical red meat or, rather, bean pie. But unlike other preacher politicians, he didn't have the power of some of the white ones. Jerry Falwell, who said that God does not hear the prayers of Jews, is courted by powerful politicians like John McCain.

CHAPTER 52

"It's out there. Go get it!"
—Elijah Muhammad on the opportunities
in a capitalist society, appearing on *The Black Journal.*

So what is it about Muhammad Ali that causes him to be one of the most recognized persons on Earth? Is it because his ring antics were viewed by hundreds of millions of people—TV numbers that during one fight alone amounted to more than the audiences for all of the fights in history combined? Was it the entertainer who wowed half of the planet with his adroit moves? Was it because he was pretty and charming at the same time? (Writer Clark Blaise said that when he heard the heavyweight champion refer to himself as "pretty," he figured that we were entering a new era.) Was it because he stood up for his beliefs? He was obviously following orders of Elijah Muhammad, whom he saw as the prophet from God. The majority of Americans viewed that war as a disaster and Ali had the support of millions of young people, unlike Elijah Muhammad and his associates, who refused to be drawn into the patriotic fervor incited by the good war. Was it because of his literary efforts, his hyperbole, his rhymes?

I asked the thirty-year-old driver, who got me to the hotel on my birthday, how he remembered Ali. He said, "As an entertainer."

Henry Armstrong was a more sophisticated poet, and Gene Tunney lectured on Shakespeare. Was it because of his predicting the round in which an opponent would fall? Both Joe Louis and Jack Johnson had done that before. Was it because of his dancing in the ring? Sugar Ray Robinson was such a good dancer that he went into show business for a while and boxer Battling Siki did the Charleston in his corner. What distinguishes Ali from the rest is that he did all of these things and more.

And so when the Nation of Islam ordered Muhammad Ali to resist the draft, he became more than a boxer; he was an inspiration to black men needing uplift.

I was struck by the number of black men whom I interviewed who were inspired by his example, who became more assertive, more confident, as a result of his rebellion. In comparison to their fathers, who were not celebrities and who could not publicize their discontent, the younger generation wrote poems, made films, and had access to public forums. They didn't have to take racist abuse in silence, day after day, year after year.

Some of them, like Emil Guillermo's Dad, were stoical and kept their complaints to themselves. Others, like my stepfather, Cash Clay, and Fred Ho's father, were silent about the abuses and humiliation they suffered on the job but released their rage in dinner conversations. James Baldwin said that his father punished his family for the humiliations he suffered downtown. Fred Ho saw his father receiving a lower status on his job when his achievement was superior to that of his colleagues.

Ali made mistakes. After all, we forget how young he was. There were the women, the neglected children, the bad influences, the con artists, the schemes. There were the bad deals, the criminal associates, the vindictiveness, the hypocrisy. The man who ridiculed his friend Malcolm, cruelly, for being a holy man became a holy man himself. Here was a player on the geo-political stage, who was so gratified by the treatment he received in England that he doubted whether England ever participated in the war.

In an interview with Thomas Hauser, Ali said:

> As far as my outlook is concerned, I'd say that ninety percent of the American public feels just the way I do as far as racial issues are concerned; as far as intermarriage is concerned; forced integration and total integration such as many Negro civil rights groups are trying

to accomplish today... But as a whole, the whites believe like we do. (Hauser, 1991).

Is Ali, however, like "a minor Hindu deity," as Terry Berg said on March 16, 2006? Or "Zeus coming down from the mountain," as Emil Guillermo described his reception in the Philippines? Or, "Jesus Christ returned," as David Hammons said?

I don't think so.

Isn't it enough that Ali was an inspiration to young minority men, whether they were black, Asian, or Hispanic? These were men who found themselves under the boot of a society that did not respect them, who saw their fathers vent their anger in the privacy of their homes rather than risk losing their jobs where they had to wear the mask of accommodation. They were fathers who suffered thousands of insults until they walked with shoulders stooped.

When Muhammad Ali spoke up, he liberated a generation, regardless of whether he was ordered to resist the draft. Because of his example, they exhaled.

Rather than succumbing to the marketing hype, isn't it enough to view Ali as someone who redefined himself after many starts and stops? As a youngster who could barely read or write but who recently co-authored a book that included his favorite quotations?

Ali is a flawed human with heroic attributes. The people's champ and one-time supporter of radical causes also showed the power of capitalism, which not only thrives by gobbling up the world's resources but regurgitates those forces that are opposed to it.

Communism produced the intellectual—when's the last time you took *Das Capital* to the beach to read or tried to decipher what on earth Hegel was driving at? Be honest. While Communism had the intellectuals, Capitalism had the geniuses.

Of all of those I interviewed, Paul "Spooky" Miller, perhaps the youngest, demonstrated the ultimate end of the "black is beautiful" movement and the commercial savvy of the post-race generation. When I returned home from the New York trip during which I interviewed him, I opened a copy of *Vibe* magazine and there was a two-page slick ad, with Paul bent over his computer instruments. It was an Infiniti automobile ad. In the 1960s, Ali was black and beautiful; in 2006, a black, fifty-thousand-dollar car was beautiful. Featured in the ad was a parody for the generic "black is beautiful" poem of the 1960s. In 2005, John Carlos and Tommy Smith were honored with a statue at San Jose State University, with their heads bent and their arms and fists forming the black power salute.

Walking back to the Affinia Hotel from Patsy's, where I had lunch with my former editor, Shaye Areheart, passing through Times Square, I couldn't miss a gigantic, building-sized sign looming over 42nd Street and Broadway. It was hip hopper P. Diddy, with his head bowed and raising his arms and fists in the Black Power salute, the gesture that got Carlos and Smith in trouble. Only he was modeling clothes. Apple purchased two billboards that recently appeared on the way to the San Francisco airport. It showed a figure dressed in a black jumpsuit, holding an iPod in a clenched fist. Then in the fashion section of *The New York Times*, March 12, 2006, fashion designer Ramdane Touhami, a French Moroccan, announced his "Resistance" line: "It featured distressed jackets inspired by those worn by black-power sympathizers."

A year after I interviewed him, there was Bobby Seale at the YMCA telling me that *Essence* magazine had just completed a photo shoot of him and Kathleen Cleaver to celebrate the fortieth anniversary of the founding of the Black Panthers. You couldn't get any more corporate than that. *Essence* is owned by Time Warner.

Then, while sitting in the audience at Lowe's 34th Street theater on September 1, 2006, I got the shock of shocks. The first two lines of Allen Ginsberg's "Howl" were used to advertise popcorn. Perhaps I shouldn't have been surprised, though. Passages of Jack Kerouac's *On The Road* were used to advertise Chrysler. Recently, a fifty-thousand-dollar car was advertised with the pitch: "Sting like a butterfly, float like a bee, like Muhammad Ali."

On Friday night, February 22, 2008, heavyweight champion Wladimir Klitschko told an ESPN audience that by working for UNESCO, he was improving the lives of children all over the world.

His model, he said, was Muhammad Ali, who resisted the draft and led the black movement.

The same capitalism was able to make Muhammad Ali, who once said he despised his "white blood," acceptable to millions of whites. Like Malcolm X, Ali has become one that some liked or some disliked, as one would prefer a Toyota over a Chevrolet.

About his "white blood," Ali was wrong. His white ancestor was Irish. He wasn't a slave master. He arrived in the country broke. The *Columbia News Service*, March 13, 2002, carried the headline: "New York Irish Embrace Ali as a Native Son." The article, written by Kerry Burke, reported:

> Irish and Irish-American New Yorkers [were] celebrating the discovery of boxing legend Muhammad Ali's Irish heritage.
>
> The Clare Heritage Centre in Corofin, Ireland, says a man named Abe Grady from Ennis, County Clare, who emigrated to America in the 1860s, is the three-time heavyweight champion's great-grandfather.
>
> "We knew it all along," said Brian McCabe, forty-six, a proud Brooklyn Irish-American and former fight trainer. "Anyone that could fight and speak that well has to have some Irish in him..."

The Irish ancestry was not, however, news to Ali.

When Ali visited Ireland in 1972, "he mentioned his Irish forefather Grady twice to the press, but nobody picked up on it,' said O'Brien, the genealogist. 'A researcher discovered the interview while preparing a documentary for the Irish language TV channel TG4,' she said. "Some Irish Americans said that Grady's marriage to a black woman was not very far-fetched, despite the racism of the time. After all, Grady's social and economic position was not far removed from that of Reconstruction-era black farmers and sharecroppers. "Ali's Irish great-grandfather was as good as a slave in the 1860s," said John Murray, 36, a sound engineer from Woodside, Queens, by way of Dublin. "So, it's no wonder an Irish immigrant laborer found companionship with an American black woman."

When Ali visited Ireland, in 2009, he was greeted by thousands of fans.

Of Ali's 2009 visit to Ireland Gareth A. Davies of the Telegraph Co. UK wrote:

> Muhammad Ali's farewell to these shores will draw to a close when he is united for the first time with hundreds of extended family members in Ennis, Co. Clare.
>
> Over 50,000 people are expected to line the streets to give the former boxing champion a welcome to his Irish roots...
>
> [Ennis Town Mayor Frankie Neylon said] "Old and young are united in this. The older people are educating the young children about the great man, and the town's abuzz with activity. There are musical bands preparing, memorabilia is coming out, it is thrilling for everyone."
>
> Ali's great-grandfather Abe Grady was born and raised in Ennis before he emigrated to America in 1860, where he married an African-American woman. Ali's mother, Odessa Lee Grady, was his granddaughter. Abe Grady's father, John, rented a house and garden in Ennis for 15 shillings a year in 1855...
>
> The chief of the Grady clan is coming in from London, and three ladies related to Ali, Mary O'Dunovan, Imelda Grady, and Mary Grady Gormley, who all live in Ennis, will meet him. One of the three lives in a Grady family house in the same road his great great grandfather came from. This Ali had come a long way from the earlier version. "My white blood came from the slavemasters, from raping," he explained to a racially mixed audience. "The white blood harms us, it hurts us. When we were darker, we were stronger. We were purer" (Olsen, 1967).

CHAPTER 53

The late Ed Hughes told Tennessee and me about an incident that occurred in Manila:

A lady walks up to me and says, "I see you with Mr. Muhammad."
I said, "Yes."
"I've been trying to get up to that top floor ever since you've been here. I haven't been able to get up to the top floor. They won't let me come up there; I guess because I'm too old. But, anyway, listen."
"Well, what do you want to get up there for?"
"This is one of my grandchildren and I got seven and I've got to feed all of them and I don't have the money to do so."
"Now look, if I take you upstairs and when I say it's time to go, will you leave?"
There are two little boys who are running around and are dirty. So I took them up there by Security. Muhammad told me to stay on the side of the room, because he was talking to somebody. Let me tell you something: I knew him since he was a boy, so it was important for me to say, "Excuse me Mr. Muhammad, please, I got something very important." I said, "Do you see the boys over there? She told me she got several grandchildren and she doesn't have enough money to feed them."
So Muhammad beckoned them over to him. The little boy sat in his lap and he kissed him on the cheek even though his nose was running. Muhammad told the waiter and waitress to set up a table to feed him. It was at the new Hilton. Muhammad didn't carry much money on him. Nobody else had money. He looked at me and said, "I know you got some money."

So I went downstairs to the stand where I was in charge of the souvenirs and got the money from there. Muhammad asked somebody, "How much money would it take to feed a family for ninety days?" He took that amount of money from the souvenir pile and gave it to that woman.

So I took them back downstairs and when I went upstairs again, some of the entourage said, "You country boys got taken again. That's a game over here."

I said, "Well, if we got taken, we did it from my heart. I know Muhammad did it from his heart."

You hear this from a number of speakers and writers and witnesses to the Ali phenomenon, that he identified with the children, the defenseless, and the poor, and the most vulnerable. Dartmouth emeritus professor and poet Bill Cook says that he took some youngsters to see Muhammad Ali backstage during a performance of the late Oscar Brown, Jr.'s "Big Time Buck White," and Ali singled out one of the young ones for attention. She thought of herself as an ugly duckling, because she was overweight and teased by her classmates. I would hear this many times, that Ali would pay attention to those in his audience who were the most vulnerable. Like Joe Louis, his generosity could qualify him for sainthood. He still cares for the old, the infirm, and the poor. He gave away hundreds of thousands of dollars out of the goodness of his heart, but those with good hearts are often taken for patsies.

◆

How Will Ali Be Remembered? New York, January 8, 2005

After Reverend Jesse Jackson and Quincy Troupe finished their conference, I was summoned into Troupe's study for my interview with Jackson. It's too bad that Fox News, George Will, and even Spike Lee have made Jesse Jackson the butt of jokes. He is perhaps our best ambassador to the Middle East, and the respect with which he is given there was shown in his trip to Syria in 2006. Of his reception by the Syrians in August 2006, Don Terry of *The Chicago Tribune* wrote:

The Syrians have treated Jackson like a foreign dignitary. His delegation was met Saturday night by an eight-car fleet of black Honda Legends, idling on the tarmac of the Damascus airport. A motorcycle escort led the way, sirens wailing. The next morning, the delegation was whisked into the brown hills surrounding the city to the People's Palace, a sprawling white building of marble floors and towering ceilings.

Jackson led the way across a red carpet stretching from the front gate to a huge doorway where Assad stood waiting, a slight smile on his face. He and Jackson warmly shook hands. The men have met several times, including at the state funeral in 2000 for the president's father. ("Jackson: Syria to ask about Israeli soldiers," August 28, 2006)

I asked Jesse Jackson some questions about Muhammad Ali.

Jesse Jackson: I think the first time I met Ali was when he first began to fight. I was with Dr. King at the Hilton Hotel in Atlanta.

The worst nightmare for us Southerners was the sense of owning blacks. With Ali, the Louisville group had somebody they could own. They invested in him and they were his face. But there was also a fear that if somebody like Malcolm got into the minds of some our youth, they would pull away and he did.

There was a lot of trauma about his leaving the organization—they had a good thing and they didn't accept his mind changing. That was a big spiritual break. Breaking away from that group took a lot of guts. He grew up in Louisville, in that environment. He chose to hear Malcolm's voice over their voice. He and I became quite close. He was forced out of the ring and I was arguing publicly for him that this should not happen to him.

Remember when he was pushed out of the Nation of Islam, too? I'm not sure what it was about. I remember one incident where we spent a lot of private time together during that period. He was in search of his dignity and a place outside of the ring. It was all in search of his own development.

We used to have our weekly breadbasket meetings; he would attend. As a matter of fact, when he first got back in the ring (that deal was negotiated in Atlanta), I was with him. Before he went out to the fight that night, I prayed with him in the dressing room, and of course Herbert and some of the guys didn't like the relationship that we had. Then I think later on that he saw a sense of world

citizenship—being a Muslim and having worldwide following—and
he just kept rising.

Ishmael Reed: Why did Ali follow Imam Wallace D. Muhammad
instead of Minister Farrakhan after the break-up?
JJ: I think he trusted Wallace to handle the money, and Wallace
was really close to his father. While Ali was infinitely creative in the
ring, it was his mind that drove that creativity. So his quest to be
important, to be of value, to use celebrity as a change agent, searching
for himself, looking for his inner self.

The fact that he has this disease that has slowed him down, physically, has made him have more time to focus on the spiritual self.
He was born in the slum, but the slum wasn't born in him. We have
this infinite capacity to rise if given the opportunity. We don't have a
talent deficit, we have an opportunity deficit. Some flowers blossom
slower and later, but with more fragrance. Ali continues to grow and
his quest for spiritual maturity is infinite.

At the Oakland meeting, which featured Harry Belafonte, I asked
Belafonte about Ali's legacy. His praise was also glowing. He said,
"He was the poster boy for what the struggle was all about."

Had Cash gone to art school, had his talents not been frustrated
like so many other black Southern men, this would have been Cash's
greatest mural: his son as poster boy for what the struggle was all
about. All Cash dreamed of was to have the biggest chicken farm in
the country. His son wanted the globe. However, maybe Ali's most
important victory would be missing, because it occurred after his
retirement from boxing and Cash's death. During this period, Ali
had shown the path that his spiritual and intellectual journey had
reached. He, like Casanova and St. Augustine, had abandoned the
carnal days of his youth and was now devoting himself to matters of
the spirit: from the brash, young fighter who, after humiliating Floyd
Patterson in the ring, urged Patterson to read Elijah Muhammad's
Message To The Black Man, to the ex-fighter who met with the Dalai
Lama.

On August 25, 2005, eight Buddhist monks in Louisville, Kentucky, created a sacred artwork to commemorate the friendship of Louisville native Muhammad Ali and the Dalai Lama. Traditionally, the artworks are destroyed upon completion to symbolize the impermanence of beautiful things, a central tenet of Buddhist philosophy. This one, however, was secured with sprayed-on glue and dedicated at the grand opening, November 19, 2005, of the Muhammad Ali Center.

CHAPTER 54

The criminal elements linked to Ali are still in need of an explanation. He and his wife lived in a lavish home in Cherry Hill that was lent to him by Major Benjamin Coxson, reportedly the King of Philadelphia heroin. Yet when Coxson was murdered, Ali maintained that he hardly knew the man. His association with Harold Smith, a con man, garnered Ali twenty-five percent of the profits from Smith's Muhammad Ali Amateur Boxing Team, and its successor, Muhammad Ali Professional Sports. Furthermore, Muhammad Ali allowed himself to be manipulated by the notorious lawyer, Richard Hirschfeld, who tried to finagle fifty million dollars from the government on his behalf with the cooperation of the boxer. After Hirschfeld committed suicide on January 11, 2005, in a federal prison, the *Washington Post* mentioned his ties to Ali:

> Hirschfeld spent much of his life in the headlines and in trouble for his high-profile schemes, his veiled suggestions that he performed espionage for U.S. intelligence agencies and his close association with Ali, whom he represented for more than 15 years.
>
> But as with so many of Mr. Hirschfeld's endeavors, the relationship with Ali ended in dispute. In August 1999, the former boxing champion sued Mr. Hirschfeld, alleging that the lawyer had duped him into signing away the lucrative rights to his life story. Two months later, Ali withdrew the suit, and the terms of the settlement were not disclosed...
>
> In 1987 and 1988, someone purporting to be Ali made hundreds of telephone calls to senators, press secretaries, journalists and even Attorney General Edwin Meese III. The calls urged action on legal

or legislative matters that would have benefited Mr. Hirschfeld or his friends.

Some people who received the calls were suspicious because the "Ali" they heard had a grasp of foreign policy and American political history and spoke in the boxer's quick-witted manner of the 1960s, not in the slurred whisper of Ali's post-boxing years. Mr. Hirschfeld, who was known to do a convincing impersonation of Ali, denied making the calls. (Matt Schudel, "Flashy Fugitive Richard Hirschfeld Dies," *Washington Post*, January 13, 2005)

Regardless of how their relationship ended, Ali benefited from his association with Hirschfeld, who told Thomas Hauser:

He [Ali] didn't have to do anything to be paid, except to on occasion be there. I negotiated a deal with a gentleman from Switzerland [Wilhelm Wolfinger] that paid Ali twenty thousand dollars a month for a year. He got a salary of seventy-six thousand dollars from a company called Champion Sports that I founded. I put together a deal in connection with a refinery in the Sudan which paid a million dollars split three ways between Ali, Herbert, and myself. (Hauser, 1991)

Why would a "brilliant man" include people like Jeremiah Shabazz, Bundini, Harold Smith, and Richard Hirschfeld in his entourage? Hirschfeld was his lawyer for fifteen years and he was unaware that this man was a crook? And what of the rumors that the ex-champion is being used by his wife, Lonnie, and his agent? Thomas Hauser, whom I interviewed for this book, believes that the rumors are true. Hauser's essay about Ali, questioning his drift to the right, was excised from the book, *The GOAT*, on Mrs. Ali's orders.

Edward Hughes told me that on Muhammad Ali's birthday, his son, Muhammad Ali, Jr., was unable to reach his father by phone, further evidence that Lonnie has cut ties to Ali's former allies, friends, and even some of his children.

Also, if Malcolm X knew about Elijah Muhammad and his "wives" from the beginning, why was it such a shock to him after he was suspended from the movement? Was Malcolm X acquainted with "white" Muslims before leaving for Mecca and finding "white"

Muslims there? When Ali and Malcolm X returned from Mecca, they said that they had found a religion of brotherhood, and if whites in America could behave like the whites they found there, everything would be fine (or, as Ali said, a religion in which "color don't matter"). Yet, Malcolm X must have been acquainted with "white-skinned" Muslims, having attended United Nations sessions frequently. Nobel Laureate Wole Soyinka, the late Senegalese filmmaker Ousmane Sembène (in his film, *Ceddo*), and Somalian novelist Nuruddin Farah are also critical of Islam's effect on African civilization.

Is overseas Islam free of racial prejudice? For *The Complete Muhammad Ali*, I asked three of Africa's greatest writers that question. I had read Nobel Laureate Wole Soyinka's comment that he had more in common with a Cuban follower of Santeria, a commingling of Catholic and Yoruba beliefs, than he had with a North African Muslim. He replied to me on June 22, 2007:

> Regarding my sense of affinity with followers of the Santeria—absolutely. Their spirituality and metaphysical world-view, which are retentions of Yoruba beliefs, are mine. Both Islam and Christianity are alien religions on African soil. In varying degrees, they have brought nothing but grief.

Novelist Nuruddin Farah, whose reputation on the African continent is of such stature that he was enlisted to negotiate a peace between Ethiopia and Somalia, also answered my query. He wrote:

> Ishmael, Islam does not condone or tolerate racism—and all Muslims are supposed to transcend race. But in reality that is not how things work out between Arabs and Africans, and between lighter-complected Africans—from North Africa, the Sudan or Somalia—and the other African Muslims from South of the Sahara.
>
> Yes, there is colour caste in African Islam, although it is not as pronounced as it is elsewhere. Within specific countries, a good rule of thumb exists, in which one places the lighter-skinned person above the dark-skinned. Arab Muslims look down upon their black fellow Muslims, for whom they have denigrating terms. In the streets and in unrefined company, Arabs tend to use a term, which translates as

slave—or negro. But you are not likely to hear these terms in polite society; they are whispered.

In the North of Sudan, prospective husbands prefer wives with fairer complexion, parents likewise, especially because girls with darker skin colour are described as "unfortunate."

The same is true in Egypt and in much of North Africa. In my part of the world, in Somalia and Ethiopia, we harbour racist attitudes towards our darker-complected African brothers, from Kenya, Uganda, etc. and we employ terms that are similar to the ones the Arabs use with regard to the generic African.

Please do not hesitate to come back to me if this does not answer your question.

Chinweizu is one of Nigeria's leading intellectuals. This great poet, critic, and non-fiction writer answered my queries with questions and answers. His reply about a planned United States of Africa was the most scathing of the three:

Now, we need to examine our long history of living with Arabs on our continent, since they invaded Egypt in 640 AD. From that initial incursion, they have conquered and expropriated and settled on some 1/3 of the African continent.

How have they treated the blacks they overran? Have they not enslaved and Arabized the countless millions who came under their power?

What is the attitude of Arabs to Blacks in general and to black Africans in particular? Is it true that Arabs are given to colorism [color discrimination] against blacks and hold blacks in automatic contempt and view blacks as subhuman?

Is it true that Arabs for many centuries raided and enslaved black Africans?

Is it true that Blacks are still being enslaved in Arab ruled countries like Mauritania and Sudan? Why would black Africans want to integrate with states that still enslave blacks?

Is it true that Arab leaders have vowed to Islamize and Arabize Black Africa?

What would Arabization do to Black Africans? Are there examples to learn from? How would non-Muslim blacks, Christians and polytheists, fare in this USAfrica?

Is it true that Arabs are ethnic cleansing and grabbing land from Black Africans wherever both populations live together under one state, as in Sudan, Mauritania and Egypt?

If you are a black African, would your being Muslim protect you from Arab enslavers and ethnic cleansers? — i.e. protect you from the treatment inflicted on your Christian and polytheist fellows?

Marvin X's comments about Arab racism are mild in comparison to those of Chinweizu, the Nigerian critic. I was among those who received an email from him on August 14, 2006:

And they [Arabs] are still our enemies today, as in Darfur where they are still raping, looting, massacring and taking lands from Blacks. Why then should I, or any sensible Pan Afrikanist, spare a thought for what anybody, and especially their fellow whites, are doing to them, whether in Palestine, Lebanon or Iraq? We must get our priorities right. All too often, Afrikans are more concerned about the welfare of their white enemies than about their own. It's like a fool who is anguished about the agonies of an injured snake even while he is not taking action to cure himself from a bite inflicted on him by the same snake.

I asked Ade Aromolaran, a writer, poet, and my Yoruba teacher, his view of Arab impact upon African civilizations. He wrote:

Africa is the original home of humankind and the home of great civilizations: Kemet (renamed "Egypt" by the Arab conquerors). Others were Meroe, Nubia, and Axum. They were thriving centers of art, learning, religion, architecture, music, etc. The Arab conquest of Africa abrogated that civilization. In West Africa, the Arabs renamed Kuumbi to "Ghana." How did all this happen to the native peoples of Africa? History provides some answers. Remember Muhammad's conquest of North Africa in the 7th century? All of North Africa, and some parts of Northwest Africa, accepted Islam. Sudan, the largest African state, also accepted Islam. This is how the Arab-ruling states introduced a system of "apartheid" between Arabs and non-Arabs in Africa and how the Arab-ruling states ran the social, economic and political landscape to their own advantage, and to the disadvantage of the native African. As a result millions of native Africans have fled their homes, and have become refugees in other lands. A system of apartheid has always existed

THE COMPLETE MUHAMMAD ALI

where you have colonialism, in the case of the Arab-ruling states, it's internal colonialism. How has the African in diaspora reacted to a progressive erosion of the rights of native Africans? Do they look the other way when they realize what's going on? Of course, some of them accepted Islam, and take on Islamic names, and become a part of the problem. Many of them are not aware of what is happening in the south of Sudan on a daily basis where a genocide is being perpetrated against native Africans. It's a gradual decimation of native Africans!

The late Osama bin Laden, founder of the militant group al-Qaeda, who was being secretly applauded by those who wish the United States ill, said that African women were prostitutes and that Africans were sub-human. He showed his contempt for them by bombing Kenyans. Were Malcolm X and Muhammad Ali naïve or were they attempting to gain crossover appeal by using the Mecca trip to back off from some of the Nation's Yacubism? These and other questions deserve an answer. Despite the racist attitudes of many Muslims dating back hundreds of years, when blacks were viewed as ugly, evil-smelling, subs-human "bogeyman," the religion has often united its members when faced with hostile outsiders.

Though the image of the Middle Passage promoted in popular culture and even by some museum curators and black artists is that of emaciated, naked blacks huddled together in tattered chains, with only an occasional revolt or maybe one, Amistad, Greg Grandin, author of *The Empire of Necessity* (2014), writes:

> According to one study, 493 slave ship revolts took place between 1508 and 1869. The actual number is at least twice that, since many obscure uprisings, like those attempted on the *Neptune* and *Santa Eulalia,* aren't included in the tally. The vast majority were unsuccessful. As many as six thousand Africans might have died in these 493 cases, either killed in the revolts or executed following their suppression. Others committed suicide after their bid failed, as some of the slaves on the *Neptune* tried to do. Revolts that did lead to freedom tended to take place close to the shores of either Africa or America, where rebels could run the ship aground and escape.

A slave revolt led by Muslims, which captured the Spanish slave ship San Juan Nepomuceno and sailed back to Senegal, so alarmed slave traders in Peru that the viceroy urged the Crown to prohibit the importation of West African Muslims to the Americas. Muslims in Brazil were a constant threat to those who believed that people could be purchased and owned.

"There had been a Hausa rising in Brazil in 1807, a more general Islamic one in 1809, and less easily identifiable rebellions in 1814, 1816, 1822, and 1826; thereafter an upheaval almost every year. Many whites were killed before the rebellions were at last crushed," reports historian Nina Rodrigues. The most outstanding slave revolutionary movements in Brazil were the series of Islamic rebellions in Bahia from 1808-1835. There was a slave conspiracy in the city of Bahia, which was repressed in 1807, and a massive attack of three hundred *quilombolas* against the interior town of Nazareth das Farinhas in 1809 that was repressed with much bloodshed.

In 1810 came another such plantation uprising of Muslim slaves, followed by an uprising of coastal fisherman in 1814. Some fifty slave fishermen were killed by troops sent from Salvador, but not before many local white masters were slaughtered.

Five other uprisings took place between 1816 and 1835, in both the countryside and the city. In 1830, for example, twenty armed slaves attacked an urban slave market and freed one hundred newly-arrived African captives. However, the most organized by mostly Muslim slaves in both the city and on the plantations, it was eventually uncovered before it could be fully developed. Nonetheless, enough slaves obtained arms that deaths were numerous and destruction to property with quite extensive. More than a hundred of the Muslim slaves were executed, and the city and government were thrown into a panic, which was quickly spread to other regions (*Slavery in Brazil* by Herbert S. Klein, Francisco Vidal Luna).

These Muslims could read and write in Arab script and in one of the more dramatic of ship seizures—the Muslim takeover of the slave ship *Traval* on February 20, 1805—the captain was forced to sign a contract assuring that the ship would be returned to Africa.

This slave mutiny was the basis for Herman Melville's story, "Benito Cereno."

After the near-extermination of Islam in Brazil, elements found refuge in African Religion that some of the captives transplanted to this hemisphere. A big tent religion, African Religion was also capable of absorbing features of Native American faiths that had become extinct. It also offered refuge to elements of the Muslim faith. Ned Sublette, author of *Cuba and Its Music: From the First Drums to the Mambo*, writes: "The Orisha [Or "Saint"], who is the father of the most of the other Orishas and creator of mankind… this appears to be a syncretization." Obatala becomes the Orisha Allah.

CONCLUSION

The late, great boxing trainer and HBO boxing commentator Emanuel Steward, whom I interviewed, spoke about Ali's pitiful exit from the sport. I asked about his having to fight the last two fights suffering the symptoms of Parkinson's. He replied:

It was horrible. Angelo Dundee was one the few who cared, who didn't want to see him fight. I saw his last fight with Trevor Berbick in the Bahamas. I was there also because Tommy Hearns (a Kronk Gym alumnus) fought also. This was December '81. We were training together. Ali was beating on the bag one day and you could see that he had no coordination. Something was wrong.

"Good Morning America" wanted to have Ali and Tommy move around. Tommy idolized Ali, he was his hero from childhood and Tommy realized that he could hit Ali anytime he wanted to and Ali was helpless. And Tommy weighed 155 pounds. After one round, Tommy said he didn't want to fight him anymore and we told them not to show the film.

Ali had two people, his chef and Walter Youngblood. They pulled me aside and they asked, "Emanuel, what are you thinking?"

I told them, "You realize by asking that question and the expression on your faces, you've answered the question yourself. You realize that he shouldn't be fighting anymore. That's why you're worried."

They agreed. They were very concerned. He still had that entourage, all of those people to support. Bundini didn't care anything about him; he wanted him to fight. Angelo wasn't there. He arrived a couple of days later. He had compassion and was there to prevent Ali from getting hurt. He had to fight with Bundini and the rest to stop the fight with Holmes. He had to get up there and beg them to stop it.

I can imagine what Ali had to put up with from an entourage of a couple of dozen: a Bundini who once pawned his championship belt; a Jeremiah Shabazz who maneuvered the champion into a cash settlement with Don King that left him fifty thousand dollars short.

As an example of his will, Ali has survived longer than people expected and still manages to travel. The Muhammad Ali website presents his activities, the globetrotting, philanthropic and charitable efforts, and his coming to the aid of individuals: standing with a mother who is pleading for the release of her son held prisoner by Iran; talking a man out of a suicide attempt.

Muhammad Ali has traveled a long way from the hubris and hypocrisy noticed early by a couple of old-timers. Cus D'Amato warned that he was taking too many punches in the gym on the way to the fights. The late boxing writer, Budd Schulberg, recognized his tendency to indulge in activities for which he criticized others: "He criticizes Floyd Patterson for buying a house in a white neighborhood instead of living among his own, then buys his own mansion in a prosperous white suburb."

Ali said: "Take those big Negroes—Lena Horne, Eartha Kitt, Diahann Carroll, Chubby Checker, Sammy Davis. Take those big niggers Floyd Patterson, Sonny Liston. The whites make 'em rich, and in return they brainwash the little Negroes walking around. Liston lives in a white neighborhood. Patterson lives in a white neighborhood." (Olsen, 1967)

Writing about Ali in his 1972 book, *Loser and Still Champion*, Budd Shulberg stated: "He attacks boxing as a degrading spectacle held chiefly for the entertainment of the white man, but is ready to sign for a freak match against basketball star Wilt Chamberlain."

How does one explain that a man with so many flaws can become so adored and almost an object of worship? A man who, during a *Playboy* interview, threatened interracial couples with death, yet had a white girlfriend? A man who justified the assault by members of the Nation of Islam on fellow Muslims and entertained dictators—Mobutu and Marcos—who were guilty of inflicting heinous crimes upon citizens of their nations? And a man who was a pimp wannabe and a bad father to some of the children whom he sired with unmarried women?

Serious flaws in Ali's personality—so serious that at one point the late Betty Shabazz said she was glad that her husband, Malcolm X, did not live to see the kind of lifestyle that Ali had adopted—have been mentioned, but for the most part dismissed. Moreover many will never forgive Ali for turning his back on his friend, Malcolm X. And one writer went as far as to comment that if Ali were not such a folk hero, he would have been indicted as a result of his association with mobsters.

I saw a movie in which Samuel Jackson's job was to arrive and clean crime scenes of incriminating evidence. This was the job of the wives of icons like JFK and Muhammad Ali, whose legends were carved in the 1960s. The mess that was JFK's personal life—who assigned members of his entourage to solicit prostitutes and pimped a young intern, who had been servicing him, out to his friends—was transformed into a romantic Camelot where JFK was Arthur. Ali once boasted about having addressed a rally of the Ku Klux Klan, the hated group responsible for the defeat of Reconstruction through murder and lynching, of driving blacks off their lands and expelling them from political office with force. As a result of Yolanda's cleaning up (in more ways than one, according to civil rights activist Dick Gregory), Ali had become a "shining knight," the name given to the late Malcolm X by the late actor Ossie Davis.

How do icons like JFK and Muhammad Ali maintain their saintly status by overcoming flaws that would ruin an ordinary person? Like those lofty ones, King David, for example, an adulterer and murderer? They get a pass and are mythologized.

It's a discussion that is as early as the Puritan fathers, whose view of mankind was made by old theologian Jonathan Edwards himself. Edwards was one of the original fearmongers in those days when the terrorist threats came from the Indians, but there was an even worse fate that was in store for those whom he deemed beyond salvation. Edwards' view of humanity was not a very pleasant one. Following is a passage from a typical sermon:

The God that holds you over the pit of hell, much as one holds a spider, or some loathsome insect over the fire, abhors you, and is dreadfully provoked: his wrath towards you burns like fire; he looks upon you as worthy of nothing else, but to be cast into the fire; he is of purer eyes than to bear to have you in his sight; you are ten thousand times more abominable in his eyes, than the most hateful venomous serpent is in ours. (Jonathan Edwards, "Sinners in the Hands of an Angry God," July 8, 1741)

There was also, however, a Puritan mother, Anne Hutchinson, who outraged the Puritan patriarchs by preaching to a mixed congregation of men and women. The patriarchs tried her and she was eventually murdered by Indians on Long Island. The Fathers said that she got what was coming to her. Her offense? She said that mankind wasn't wretched and that within us all there is a divine spark, or as one commentator said, a bit of Zeus. Obviously, though, in the case of Malcolm X, Muhammad Ali, JFK, MLK, and others among the American elect, and those who seem to be born with a congenital halo, some have more Zeus than others.

END

AFTERWORD

Boxers' Rights?

The Muhammad Ali Boxing Reform Act was signed by the President on May 26, 2000. Among the findings:

(1) Professional boxing differs from other major, interstate professional sports industries in the United States in that it operates without any private sector association, league, or centralized industry organization to establish uniform and appropriate business practices and ethical standards. This has led to repeated occurrences of disreputable and coercive business practices in the boxing industry, to the detriment of professional boxers nationwide. (…) (3) Promoters who engage in illegal, coercive, or unethical business practices can take advantage of the lack of equitable business standards in the sport by holding boxing events in States with weaker regulatory oversight.

Let's say that the reform act had been passed when Ali took a pounding from Earnie Shavers in 1977 and was told by Teddy Brenner that he wouldn't allow him to fight again in Madison Square Garden. He would have been spared taking additional punishment on behalf of promoters, and a parasitical entourage, which didn't have his best interest in mind. Or when Gerald McClellan was nearly killed in the ring when he fought Nigel Benn on February 25, 1995. Benn defended his WBC super middleweight title against Gerald McClellan in London, England. The bout left both fighters with injuries, but McClellan's were life threatening. While Benn's kidneys were damaged, McClellan was left with brain damage. He is now eighty percent blind and nearly deaf. In 2007, Benn raised two hundred fifty thousand dollars for McClellan. Benn commented: "I always felt the American people (boxing fraternity) should have looked after him better than they did. If he'd been British, his house would have been paid for and he'd be getting the best of care." The people of Freeport, Illinois, have assisted McClellan and his family, and so has Roy Jones, Jr., but since boxers don't have the union that boxers like Eddie Mustafa Muhammad are trying to form, with the aide of the Teamster's Union, boxers don't receive the kind of compensation that union members receive.

In an interview with Jason Rhodes, printed in *Seconds Out*, March 15, 2015, Mustafa complained about the opposition to such a Union.

> I don't see a change, because they are still neglecting the fighter. There's no change. They are still neglecting the main people involved, who are the fighters. It's business as usual. You know, one fighter dies, and they're mourned for a week, and then it's back to business as usual. And what about their family? They don't care anything about that. You know, we're a struggling union, but we've helped a few fighters. We're not billionaires, but we've been able to help guys like Sugar Ray Seales, Greg Page and a few other guys we've helped out because they needed some support, and the boxing shows that we've been able to do have allowed us to help guys who are having financial difficulty. But as I've said, I don't take anything away from other organizations trying to help fighters. I applaud that. I applaud what they're trying to do to help these guys. But it has to start with the promoters. And if the TV networks see that the promoters are trying to do the right thing, there will be more opportunities on television that will open up for the fighters. And we could start a farm team, so to speak, to develop the talent. But until that happens—you know, they say boxing is starting to pick up. Give me a break. I don't even want to hear that.

Perhaps if the Muhammad Ali Boxing Reform Act had been enforced, Oscar Diaz, who died from injuries when he took a beating from Delvin Rodriguez, would still be alive.

Now that boxing has returned to network television, after thirty years, a debut that occurred shortly after the death of Oscar Diaz, the public might become sick of bouts in which the promoter's fighter is given the decision, or put in against soft opposition, sometimes against a fighter whose losses exceed his wins, or against a last minute substitute, who hasn't been in the gym. ESPN commentator Teddy Atlas complains about house decisions regularly and observes that after a fighter gets an unfair crooked decision, the fighter has to take a lot of punches in order to gain a ranking again.

The late Jack Newfield went beyond complaining. He proposed a boxing bill of rights. He suggested the creation a national commission to regulate the sport; end all recognition of international sanctioning organizations—the WBA, WBC, WBO, and IBF; generate impartial ratings; establish a pension system for boxers that includes a health plan and death benefits; organize a labor union, or guild, of all boxers; and finally end the practice of judges receiving expenses, including airfare and hotel arrangements, from promoters. Whether such a bill of rights will clean up the sport remains to be seen.

BIBLIOGRAPHY

MUHAMMAD ALI

Ali, Muhammad with Hana Yasmeen Ali. *The Soul of a Butterfly: Reflections on Life's Journal*. New York, NY: Simon & Schuster, 2004.

Ali, Muhammad with Richard Durham. *The Greatest: My Own Story*. New York, NY: Random House, 1975.

Brunt, Stephen. Facing Ali, *15 Writers, 15 Stories: The Opposition Weighs In*. Guilford, Connecticut: The Lyons Press, An Imprint of the Globe Peqout Press, 2002.

Cashill, Jack. *Sucker Punch: The Hard Left Hook That Dazed Ali and Killed King's Dream*. Nashville, Tennessee: Nelson Current, 2006.

Dennis, Felix and Don Atyeo, with additional material by Mark Collings. *Muhammad Ali: The Glory Years*. New York, NY: Hyperion, Miramax Books imprint, 2003.

Early, Gerald, Editor. *The Muhammad Ali Reader*. Hopewell, NJ: The Ecco Press, 1998.

Edmonds, Anthony O. *Muhammad Ali: A Biography*. Westport, Connecticut and London, England: Greenwood Press, 2006.

Evanzz, Karl. *I Am the Greatest: The Best Quotations from Muhammad Ali*. Kansas City, MO: Andrews McMeel Publishing, an Andrews McMeel Universal Company, 2002.

Ezra, Michael. *Muhammad Ali: The Making of an Icon*. Philadelphia, PA: Temple University Press, 2009.

Freedman, Suzanne. *Clay v. United States: Muhammad Ali Objects to War*. Springfield, NJ: Enslow Publishers, Inc., (Landmark Supreme Court Cases series), 1997.

Gamble, R.L. *The Last Bell: The Rise and Fall of Muhammad Ali*. Self-Published.

Hauser, Thomas. *Muhammad Ali: His Life and Times*. New York, NY: A Touchstone Book Published by Simon & Schuster, 1991.

Hauser, Thomas. *The Lost Legacy of Muhammad Ali*. Toronto, Canada: Sport Media Publishing, Inc., 2005.

Kindred, David. *Sound and Fury: Two Powerful Lives, One Fateful Friendship*. New York, NY; London, England; Toronto, Canada and Sydney, Australia: Free Press, A Division of Simon & Schuster, Inc., 2006.

Kram, Mark: *Ghosts of Manila: The Fateful Blood Feud Between Muhammad Ali and Joe Frazier*. New York, NY: Perennial, an Imprint of HarperCollins Publishers, 2001.

Lipsyte, Robert. *Free to Be Muhammad Ali*. New York, NY: An Ursula Nordstrom Book, Harper & Row, Publishers, Inc., 1977, 1978.

Marqusee, Mike. *Redemption Song: Muhammad Ali and the Spirit of the Sixties*. London, England and New York: Verso, an imprint of New Left Books, 1999.

Oliver, Ann and Paul Simpson, editors. *The Rough Guide to Muhammad Ali: The Man, The Fights, the Mouth*. London, England: Haymarket Customer Publishing for Rough Guides, LTD. Distributed by Penguin Group, 2004.

Olsen, Jack. *Black is Best: The Riddle of Cassius Clay. Stark, No-Punches-Pulled—The Inside Story of the Famous Heavyweight Champion Who Refuses to Be a White Man's Hero*. New York, NY: Dell Publishing Co., Inc., 1967.

Pacheco, Ferdie. *Muhammad Ali: A View from the Corner*. New York, NY: A Birch Lane Press Book from Carol Publishing Group, 1992.

Remnick, David. *King of the World*. New York, NY: Vintage Books, 1998.

Schulberg, Budd. *Loser and Still Champion: Muhammad Ali,* Doubleday, 1972.

Strathmore, William. *Muhammad Ali: The Unseen Archives*. Bath, BA1 1HE, UK: Paragon Publishing, 2001.

Stravinsky, John. *Muhammad Ai Biography*. New York, NY: Park Lane Press, 1997.

Torres, José and Bert Randolph Sugar. *Sting Like a Bee: The Muhammad Ali Story*. Chicago, IL; New York, NY; San Francisco, CA; et all: Contemporary Books, A Division of McGraw-Hill Companies, 1971, 2002.

Zirin, Dave. *Muhammad Ali Handbook*. London, England: MQ Publications Limited, 2007.

ISLAM AND NATION OF ISLAM

Barboza, Steven. *American Jihad: Islam After Malcolm X*. New York, New York; London, England; Toronto, Canada; Sydney, Australia; Auckland, New Zealand: an Image Book published by Doubleday, 1994.

Clegg III, Claude Andrew. *An Original Man: The Life and Times of Elijah Muhammad*. New York, NY: St. Martin's Press, 1997.

Diouf, Sylviane A. *Servants of Allah: African Muslims Enslaved in the Americas.* New York, NY and London, England: New York University Press, 1998; and 15th Anniversary Edition Paperback – Deluxe Edition, 2013.

Evanzz, Karl. *The Messenger: The Rise and Fall of Elijah Muhammad.* New York, NY: Pantheon Books, 1999.

Gomez, Michael A. *Black Crescent: The Experience and Legacy of African Muslims in the Americas.* Cambridge, New York; Melbourne, Australia; Madrid, Spain; Cape Town, South Africa; Singapore and Sao Paulo, Brazil: Cambridge University Press, 2005.

Hakim, Nasir Makr. *Is Elijah Muhammad The Offspring of Noble Drew Ali & Marcus Garvey?* Phoenix, AZ: Secretarius Publications, 2006.

Marsh, Clifton E. *The Lost-Found Nation of Islam in America.* Lanham, MD and London, England: The Scarecrow Press, Inc., 2000.

Muhammad, Elijah. *Message to the Blackman in America.* Phoenix, AZ: Secretarius MEMPS Ministries, 1965.

Muhammad, Jesus. *The Evolution of the Nation of Islam.* JMA Pub, 2002.

Muhammad, Elijah: *Message to the Blackman in America.* Phoenix, AZ: Secretarius MEMPS Ministries, 1965.

Perry, Bruce. *Malcolm: The Life of a Man Who Changed Black America.* Barrytown, NY: Station Hill Press, Inc., 1991.

Rodinson, Maxime, Translated by Rogers Veinus. *Europe and the Mystique of Islam.* Seattle, WA and London, England: University of Washington Press, 1987.

Walker, Dennis. *Islam and the Search for African-American Nationhood; Elijah Muhammad, Louis Farrakhan and the Nation of Islam.* Atlanta, GA: Clarity Press, Inc., 2005.

BOXING

Boyd, Herb with Ray Robinson II. *Pound for Pound: A Biography of Sugar Ray Robinson.* New York, NY: Amistad, an imprint of HarperCollins Publishers, Inc., 2005.

Cashmore, Ellis. *Tyson: Nurture of the Beast.* Cambridge, England and Malden, MA: Polity Press, 2005.

Dahlberg, Tim. *Fight Town: Las Vegas—-The Boxing Capital of the World.* Las Vegas, NV: Stephens Press, 2004.

Fitzgerald, Mike. *The Ageless Warrior: The Life of Boxing Legend Archie Moore.* New York, NY: Sports Publishing L.L.C., 2004.

Frazier, Joe with Phil Berger. *Smokin' Joe: The Autobiography.* New York, NY: A Simon & Schuster MacMillan Company, 1996.

Frazier, Smokin' Joe with William Dettloff. *Box Like the Pros: One of Boxing's Greatest Fighters Presents a Complete Training Course—From Getting in Shape to Landing the Perfect Knockout Blow*. New York, NY: Collins, An Imprint HarperCollins Publishers, 2005.

Hauser, Thomas, *Winks and Daggers, An Inside Look at Another Year in Boxing*, University of Arkansas Press, *2011*.

Heller, Peter. *"In This Corner...!" 42 World Champions Tell Their Stories*. New York, NY: Da Capo Press, Inc., 1973.

Hietala, Thomas R. *The Fight of the Century: Jack Johnson, Joe Louis, and the Struggle for Racial Equality*. Armonk, New York and London, England: M.E. Sharpe, 2002.

Holmes, Larry and Phil Berger. *Against the Odds*. New York, NY: Thomas Dunne Books. An Imprint of St. Martin's Press, 1998.

Louis, Joe. *My Life: An Autobiography*. Hopewell, NJ: The Ecco Press, 1978.

Margolick, David. *Beyond Glory: Joe Louis vs. Max Schmeling, and a World on the Brink*. New York, NY: Alfred A. Knoff, 2005.

Mead, Chris. *Champion Joe Louis: Black Hero in White America*. New York, NY: Charles Scribner's Sons, 1985.

McRae, Donald. *Heroes Without A Country: America's Betrayal of Joe Louis and Jesse Owens*. New York, NY: ECC, An Imprint of HarperCollins Publishers, Inc., 2002.

Newfield, Jack. *The Life and Crimes of Don King: The Shame of Boxing in America*. New York, NY and Sag Harbor, NY: Harbor Electronic Publishing, 1995, 2003.

Odd, Gilbert. *The Encyclopedia of Boxing*. Crescent Books, 1983.

Pacheco, Ferdie. *Blood in my Coffee: The Life of the Fight Doctor*. Champaign, IL: Sports Publishing, L.L.C., 2005.

Pacheco, Freddie, M.D. *Fight Doctor*. New York, NY: Simon and Schuster, 1976, 1977.

Patterson, Floyd with Milton Gross. *Victory Over Myself*. New York, NY: Published by Bernard Geis Associates. Distributed by Random House, Inc., 1962.

Sammons, Jeffrey T. *Beyond the Ring: The Role of Boxing in American Society*. Urbana, and Chicago IL: University of Illinois Press, 1990.

Silverman, Jeff. *The Greatest Boxing Stories Ever Told: Thirty-Six Incredible Tales from the Ring*. Guilford, Connecticut: The Lyons Press, 2002.

Sugden, John. *Boxing and Society: An International Analysis*. Manchester, England and New York, NY: Manchester University Press. Distributed by St. Martin's Press, 1996.

Sullivan, Russell. *Rocky Marciano: The Rock of His Times*. Urbana and Chicago, IL: University of Illinois Press, 2002.

Tosches, Nick. *The Devil and Sonny Liston*. Boston, MA; New York, NY and London, England: Back Bay Books. Little, Brown and Company, 2000.

RELATED SUBJECTS

Abdul-Jabbar, Kareem and Raymond Obstfeld. *On the Shoulders of Giants: My Journey Through the Harlem Renaissance*. New York, NY: Simon & Schuster, 2007.

Araton, Harvey. *Crashing the Borders: How Basketball Won the World and Lost Its Soul at Home*. New York, NY: Free Press, A Division of Simon & Schuster, 2005.

Brown, Jim with Steve Delsohn. 1989. *Out of Bounds*. New York: Kensington Publishing Corp.

Cullen, Countee. 1931. *Color*, New York. Harper & Brothers.

Entine, Jon. Taboo: *Why Black Athletes Dominate Sports and Why We Are Afraid to Talk About It*. New York, NY: PublicAffairs, a member of the Perseus Book Group, 2000.

Griffin, Sean Patrick. *Philadelphia's 'Black Mafia,' A Social and Political History*. AA Dordrecht, The Netherlands: Kluwer Academic Publishers, 2003.

Black Brothers Inc.: The Violent Rise and Fall of Philadelphia's Black Mafia. Wrea Green, United Kingdom: Milo Books Ltd., 2005.

Johnson, Marilynn S., *Street Justice: A History of Police Violence in New York City*, Beacon Press 2004.

MacCambridge, Michael. *The Franchise: A History of Sports Illustrated Magazine*. New York, NY: Hyperion, 1997.

Rhoden, William C. *Forty Million Dollar Slaves: The Rise, Fall and Redemption of the Black Athlete*. New York, NY: Crown Publishing Group, a Division of Random House Inc., 2006.

Southern, R.W. *Western Views of Islam in the Middle Ages*, Harvard University Press, 1978.

ALSO AVAILABLE FROM BARAKA BOOKS

Storming the Old Boys' Citadel
Two Pioneer Women Architects in Nineteenth Century North America
Carla Blank and Tania Martin

Barack Obama and the Jim Crow Media
The Return of the Nigger Breakers
Ishmael Reed

Going too Far
Essays on America's Nervous Breakdown
Ishmael Reed

Challenging the Mississippi Firebombers
Memories of Mississippi 1964-65
Jim Dann

Justice Belied
The Unbalanced Scales of International Criminal Justice
John Philpot & Sébastien Chartrand, Editors

Slouching Towards Sirte
NATO's War on Libya and Africa
Maximilian C. Forte

Rwanda and the New Scramble for Africa
From Tragedy to Useful Imperial Fiction
Robin Philpot

America's Gift
What the World Owes to the Americas and Their First Inhabitants
Käthe Roth & Denis Vaugeois

Journey to the Heart of the First Peoples Collections
Musées de la civilisation
Marie-Paul Robitaille, Director

The Question of Separatism
Quebec and the Struggle over Sovereignty
Jane Jacobs